THE JOY OF ART

THE JOY OF ART

HOW TO LOOK AT, APPRECIATE, AND TALK ABOUT ART

Carolyn Schlam

ALLWORTH PRESS
NEW YORK

Allworth Press books may be purchased in bulk at special discounts for sales promotion, corporate gifts, fund-raising, or educational purposes. Special editions can also be created to specifications. For details, contact the Special Sales Department, Allworth Press, 307 West 36th Street, 11th Floor, New York, NY 10018 or info@skyhorsepublishing.com.

25 24 23 5 4 3

Published by Allworth Press, an imprint of Skyhorse Publishing, Inc. 307 West 36th Street, 11th Floor, New York, NY 10018. Allworth Press® is a registered trademark of Skyhorse Publishing, Inc.®, a Delaware corporation.

www.allworth.com

Cover design by Mary Ann Smith
Cover illustrations: *Girl with a Pearl Earring* by Johannes Vermeer,
Still Life with a Guitar by Juan Gris

Author photograph by John Hudetz

Library of Congress Cataloging-in-Publication Data

Names: Schlam, Carolyn Dobkin, 1947—author.
Title: The joy of art : how to look at, appreciate, and talk about art / Carolyn Schlam.
Description: New York, New York : Allworth Press, An imprint of Skyhorse Publishing, Inc., [2020] | Includes index.
Identifiers: LCCN 2019009798 (print) | LCCN 2019010318 (ebook) | ISBN 9781621537045 (hardcover: alk. paper)
Subjects: LCSH: Art appreciation.
Classification: LCC N7477 .S29 2020 (print) | LCC N7477 (ebook) | DDC 701/.18—dc23
LC record available at https://lccn.loc.gov/2019009798
LC ebook record available at https://lccn.loc.gov/2019010318

Print ISBN: 978-1-62153-791-5

Printed in China

To:
My fellow artists who carry on and the art lovers who appreciate them.

"It has been said that art is a tryst, for in the joy of it maker and beholder meet."
—Kojiro Tomita

Contents

Chapter 1

Introduction: How the Book Originated

The idea for this book came to me while I was visiting a show of Picasso sculpture at New York's Museum of Modern Art. Being a Picasso lover, I was really excited about the show and was anticipating a long visit and the chance to really study the many works I was viewing for the first time.

The latter proved impossible, as crowds were deep, and just getting close to the work was a struggle. In addition, most everyone seemed to have their cell phones poised and snapping away at every piece. I wound up waiting for the seas to part and just managing a quick glimpse before moving on to the next work.

I wondered what, if anything, these avid photographers were getting out of the experience and frankly whether they would ever look at these photos again.

The interest was definitely there, and museum entrance stats do seem to bear that out. Wherever people travel, art museums are high on sightseeing must-go lists, and first-rate architects are competing to create new museums and museum additions that are ever more spectacular.

With demand clearly high, I thought, was there a way to make the experience of viewing art even more gratifying and elucidating?

As an artist, I have a particular method to view an exhibition. I am there to enjoy the work, of course, just like any viewer. But I am also on a hunt. I am looking for resonance, something in the work that speaks to me personally, suggests perhaps something I would like to explore further in my own practice. It might be a color, or a particular palette. A texture, treatment, composition, shape, material, anything really. Identifying why that particularity makes me take notice is a clue to what matters to me, and where I might want to take my own work.

My hunt makes going to the museum not just a viewing experience, or something to do on a rainy afternoon. It makes it an important part of my life, not an idle time-filling activity. It makes it personal. Making an experience personal means that I will remember it, relate it to the rest of my life, and actually get something out of it. I will learn something this day about art, and about myself simultaneously.

This is my method: I enter a room of the exhibition and do a general scan of the works. I may read the introductory writings, but probably not. More on this subject later. Though curators often do an excellent job in describing their curatorial bent, I often prefer to draw my own conclusions about the exhibit and don't want my thinking scripted. Though I glance at each of the works in the room, I will certainly be drawn to one or two that particularly pique my interest. I don't know why, but I follow my instinct and spend most of my time studying these pieces. I may look at the card identifying the title and date of the work, but not necessarily, not at this point. I then move on to the next room, performing the same routine, glancing and then focusing in on the works that attract me.

You may wonder why I concentrate in this way on only a few of the works in the exhibition. I do so because I know it is quite impossible to truly study them all. I would rather concentrate deeply on a few than take a parting glance at many. After all, we are only able to absorb so much information in one experience. When you try to see all, you go horizontal. With my method, I go deep.

After I've visited the whole exhibit in this way, I retrace my steps and review my favorites once again. On this revisit, I am making sense of what I've seen, noting the attributes of these particular works that interest me, and arriving at some tentative conclusions: I like this work because ____________. The artist has accomplished ____________. It is meaningful to me in this way ____________. Et cetera.

I have had a positive learning experience and I leave the museum happily. The process has taken an hour or two. I haven't tried to see every work, read every word written about it, and cram every possible tidbit of information into my brain. I've seen many works that I admire, I've noted why they appealed to me, and most importantly, I *remember* what I've seen. I've had a real experience.

Now, a caveat. I have studied art and practiced art-making my entire life. It is my profession. So I have many tools at my disposal that the average viewer does not possess. But I have also taken nonartists with me to the museum and exposed them to this method and talked to them about art. And I believe their experience has been enhanced.

And so, this book. I am taking you to the museum with me. We are going to learn the vocabulary of visual art. We are going to look at a selection of works of art, many of which may already be familiar to you. But we are going to look at them with the eyes of an artist.

This is a book about art appreciation and that is our goal, appreciation. You may enjoy what you do not understand, but my theory is that your enjoyment will be greatly improved and deepened with understanding.

We will talk about taste and style, and why these are so personal and so variable. Fashions come and go, and this is very much applicable to art. There are reasons why certain works are popular and why they have survived generations. We'll be examining this.

I'll be giving you an art vocabulary that will help you to understand and to discuss visual art. I'll also give you the tools to decode what you see and make sense of it.

We'll be looking at examples of Western visual art throughout history. There have been many thousands of artists who lived and made their contribution to art, but in this book we'll be choosing a sample, perhaps a little more than a hundred, to focus on. I've selected them for various reasons, not necessarily because they are the best or the most famous, but because they illustrate a concept that will help you to comprehend the overall scope and sweep of our subject.

They may be highlighted for their versatility, or the fact that they were forerunners of a new direction in art-making. Perhaps they were masters of a certain facet of art or exemplars of a technique, or created a work that became iconic. They are important for one reason or another, and I will point out what that reason is.

Some of the greats in the world of art are mentioned and even discussed, but images of their work do not appear in this book. I have been limited to photographs that are in the public domain, and the works of these greats, practicing in recent times, remain under copyright. I thank some of the artist foundations who have given me the right to use works under fair use, as this book has an educational purpose.

My hope is that this very broad overview will encourage you to delve further into subjects or artists that are of particular interest to you. I strongly suggest that you look up the artists under copyright and study their works. I also hope you will seek out other points of view, as mine is only one, and this is a big subject.

Though the masterworks of art have been much discussed and applauded, there are many unsung artists who are also wonderful and their works worthy of praise. A few of these are included here. My hope is that you will use the understanding you gain from this book to discover some of these lesser-known lights and even to collect some of their works.

Appreciation of art is quite subjective and opinions diverge. You may disagree with my assessments, and this is fine. If I've done my job, though you may not share my preferences, you will have learned more about yours. I won't tell you what to like, but I'll help you understand why you like it. You'll learn about art, and you will also learn about yourself. It will be fun, I promise.

So let's go. Come along with me as we look at art. There won't be any crowds. No one will be snapping photos with their smartphones. No one will be standing in front of you. It will just be us, and the joy of art.

Chapter 2
What Is Visual Art?: Some Basic Definitions

That's a big question, isn't it? And a good place to start.

In my book for children, *Art Smarts: A Primer for the Young Artist*, I define visual art in this very simple way:

> Visual art is something created by an artist that people look at and enjoy with their eyes and feelings. When an artist makes music, he turns his feelings into sounds. A writer uses words to express herself and a dancer uses her body moving through space. A visual artist makes pictures and objects that are meant to be seen.
>
> Visual art can be flat or solid. It can be a drawing, a painting, a sculpture, collage, assemblage, bas-relief, a video, or even a performance. It can be made of mud or steel or bronze or paper or canvas or clay or even things found in the trash.
>
> Art is a message from the artist to the world. Whether it tells a story or illustrates an idea or a feeling, the purpose of the artwork is to express and to share.

Now the adult version:

> Generally speaking, art is a heightened form of communication. It arises out of the consciousness of an artist who has an intention to express something felt or thought or both. The manner in which he or she chooses to express is determined by many factors. These may include but are not limited to ability, personality, interest, preferences, culture, age, gender, and experience, so many aspects that conspire to produce a unique means of expression.
>
> Just like the DNA of a person determines their appearance, characteristics, temperament, strengths, and weaknesses, so does the artistic DNA forecast the

art they will create. As a life unfolds, so does a body of an artist's work, as much a revelation to the artist as to those fortunate enough to view it.

Visual artists like to make things. The things they make may be delicate and ethereal or tough and powerful or any gradation and variation between the poles. But visual artists are charged to make their feelings concrete and available to be seen, and perhaps touched. They want their creations to be touched with your eyes certainly, and if these works engage all your senses, that is even better.

Not every visual artist, contrary to public opinion, is interested in making pictures. Many do "pictorialize," but not all the pictures are representational or even suggestive of anything. But regardless of how confusing or difficult to understand they may be, artworks are never random. They are made by a process I call "deliberate evolution."

What I mean by this phrase is that visual art is created with intention, but the eventual result is not known by the artist. It "evolves." One stroke leads to another and the journey to completion is just that . . . a journey. Something about the final work is likely recognizable by the artist as something that is "his" or "hers," that has arisen out of that artistic DNA.

Artists like to think and talk about their body of work. That is because each work is only a fragment of the whole picture, a sentence in a book. We recognize that we cannot say it all in one piece. We can only utter a single thought and, as I discussed in my book *The Creative Path: A View from the Studio on the Making of Art*, the more clearly that thought is expressed, the better will be that individual work.

You can't judge a book by its cover, or a life by a day, or an artist's work by one piece. You have to look at the whole to really make sense of it all. Looking at an individual work without knowing anything about the artist's output may give you an incorrect or insufficient conclusion about his effort. We have our good days and bad, dark and joyous moods, the full gamut. As a viewer, your appreciation of that individual work will be enhanced by your familiarity with the artist's body of work as you are able to see it in context. We will be delving into this as we go on with this course.

Think of this book as a "sampler," like a whirlwind holiday where you spend a bit of time in many ports and stops. Perhaps there are a select few artists or art movements or genres that will linger in your memory and whet your appetite for more. You can then make a decision to study them in depth, either as an appreciator or even as a practitioner yourself. My aim is to open doors and hopefully spark a new interest, passion or pathway as a result.

In the introduction I talked about going on a "hunt" when I visit the museum. An artist is always and completely on a daily hunt, a quest, to find his pot of gold. What is the gold, the prize, he or she is seeking?

A quest is defined as a difficult journey toward a goal. In folklore, a hero must overcome many obstacles and hardships to achieve it, and many quests involve arduous travel. The quester is often seeking something supernatural, and this something may be new, something that was taken from him, or that he believes will fulfill him in some way. The object of his search may be something he wishes to return home with but in fact, he may not be able to do so. It is highly likely that he will be transformed by the journey he undertakes.

The writer Joseph Campbell discussed the quest, suggesting that the hero sets forth from the world of the commonplace to a land of adventures, tests, and magical rewards. It is said that the object of a quest may be just a convenient incentive for the hero to undertake the journey. In this case, the journey itself is the purpose, the meaning, and the glory of the undertaking.

If this sounds like the process of undertaking creative work, I am on board with you. An artist is on a journey to find something unknown. He sets out forsaking the quotidian, on a march toward magic. On the way, he strives to find clues to what he is seeking. A shape here, a line there, a quality that he knows is his or hers. He keeps hunting and experimenting, climbing and falling back. Periodically, he receives reinforcement. Something looks right, looks good. He likes it.

As the viewer and student admiring or disparaging works of art, I beseech you to remember what I have said here about the artist's quest. It will help you to look at and understand what the artist is doing in any individual work, and in his entire body of work. Perhaps you will not judge him so harshly on any particular effort when you understand the personal historical context out of which it arises.

It takes time and many tries to develop the artist's craft, style, and approach. Artists take many twists and turns in their careers as they try out what might work, and how and what to best express their thoughts and feelings. Dealers and others who wish to market the artist's work are not usually on the same page as the artist. They would like to put a name on what the artist does, as it is easier to merchandise something that is a defined product. They would often prefer that the artist work on a certain track, and produce works that are very similar in design and focus.

The latter runs counter to the artist's quest, which exhorts him to try every road and byway that might bring him to the object of his quest, his Holy Grail, if you will. The artist wants to take the long way, not the short, and visit every little village where clues to his quest will be found.

Remember this when you walk through the museum and see works that look different and even unlike the artist's familiar works. Give him kudos that he diverted from his artistic comfort zone, and look to see how these excursions fit with what you know about him.

As you come to know the artist, you may have an interest in checking out the dates on the little cards identifying the works. Knowing when the piece was made will give you clues as to how this particular work fits into the whole. Did it set the artist on a new direction, or return him to a former period? We often turn back before we go forward.

You are already thinking from the artist's point of view. You are not an art historian per se. You are using aesthetic criteria to see the artist's body of work as a personal journey, and participating in his process. This already makes each and every work more interesting.

I am writing these words from the point of view of someone who has stood long hours in front of the easel, has struggled to make friends with the paint, and endeavored to express what is in my heart and mind. I know the artist's struggle from the inside.

I know how discoveries often happen after taking a wrong turn, how accidents can turn into victories and how sometimes what you thought was good just looked like a lie in the light of a new day. I am looking at the art of others with this experience in mind.

My thoughts and judgments taken from this standpoint may contradict the authority of students of art history. I am not a historian. I am an artist with a pair of trained eyes and I'm just telling you how I see art. There are many terrific books on art history that venture into the details of the artists' lives, and if you are interested, I encourage you to seek them out. What I am focusing on in this book, the thoughts that are in my wheelhouse, are the works themselves, and their particularities and peculiarities as they stand before you to be absorbed and studied. I hope that reading about them in this way will help you to enjoy them more.

Let's now talk about the different media visual artists use and why they might choose one above the other.

Drawing, Painting, Sculpture. This is the triad of static visual art. Recently, artists have invented new artforms, some with motile features. These include video, performance, kinetic sculpture, installations, as well as art created with a computer, digital art. We will get to these but, first, the basics.

Drawing and painting are art forms created on a flat surface, which have two dimensions only—height and width. No depth. An exception would be collage and assemblage, art forms in which different materials are adhered to a flat surface and cause it to therefore have some depth, though usually fairly shallow. The latter may still be considered two-dimensional or simply called **reliefs.** In the case of **assemblage**, where there are significant protrusions on the surface, these artworks may be classified as sculptures.

So we have the flat surface. The surface itself can be made of many materials—paper, canvas, wood, etc. The surface is also referred to as the "ground," and it is as important as the materials used to cover it. Different surfaces accept materials in a different way and participate in creating texture. A pastel artist might prefer a sanded paper, for instance, that accepts the chalky pastel in a most pleasing fashion, almost gripping it. Helen Frankenthaler, who was known for her "color field" paintings, used a raw, unprimed canvas that made the oil of the paint sink into the material, leaving the raw pigment to resonate on the surface.

Every artist makes myriad decisions in the creation of a work of art, and each one contributes to the ultimate content and appearance of the finished work. Noticing the surface is a first step in studying a work and will add to your understanding of what makes it look and feel the way it does. What is the surface the artist selected, and why? What effect does it have on the image and treatment?

You may have heard the phrase "the medium is the message," coined by Marshall McLuhan. In a greatly abbreviated translation, the meaning of this phrase as applied to our discussion is that the medium chosen determines what is being said. In fact, it is an inseparable aspect of the message itself. Any other medium would convey a different message.

So these choices are neither accidental nor insignificant. A full appreciation of visual art will take the medium and surface into consideration, in addition to other factors like the artist's gender, country, era, culture, etc.

Now on to the materials used to cover the ground or surface. The list is long as to what kind of materials we can utilize to create a work of two-dimensional art. These include ink, crayon, pastel (both soft and oil-based), watercolor, gouache, poster paint, oil paint, acrylic paint, hot wax (encaustic), pencil, marker, charcoal, graphite, fabric, and many others. Some of these materials are considered drawing materials and others painting materials, but in actuality, artists draw and paint with both.

There are multiple tools available for applying materials on a surface. Brushes are most common, but artists use a whole host of other tools to apply paint and other substances to a surface: rags, sponges, fingers, stencils, airbrushes, etc. Artists are also known to dribble, spill, smear, spray, scratch, pour, and literally throw paint onto a surface.

Some of us are neat and deliberate and tend to like mediums that make clean marks, like pens and pencils. Others of us find our meaning in a more playful mode, and prefer, shall we say, a more immediate (and messy) way to cover that surface. How we do it is our choice, and as we've said, that choice is intrinsic to our message. Truly, anything goes in art. There is no one way to get it done.

Let's turn now to the acts of drawing and painting, and the distinctions between the two. Drawing is often defined as "a picture made with a pencil, pen, or crayon (rather than paint) especially one drawn in monochrome." Painting is often defined as "the process or art of using paint in a picture as a coating or as decoration." (Both definitions by Dictionary.com.)

These definitions are a layman's concept of the two art forms. In actuality, artists draw and paint alternately and in a single work. They make marks, lines, and filled shapes in the making of a drawing and/or a painting.

We think of a drawing as a simpler statement, analogous to a poem, in writing; and a painting a more complex and complete one, like a story or novel. But none of this differentiation is accurate. Drawings can be quite complex and paintings can be quite simple. Drawings can be colored and paintings monochrome. They can both have lines and shapes. You can draw with paint and paint with crayons and other drawing materials.

Perhaps this is a distinction without a difference. Artists who make two-dimensional works of art have many tools in their toolboxes. They can draw, paint, glue, print, cut, sew, photograph, or use any combination of these methods. Sometimes these combinations are deliberate; others are chanced upon by accident or experimentation.

Some of these two-dimensional artworks appear flat. Others use perspective to create an illusion of depth. Some are created to suggest a shallow depth, like the works of the Cubists that are composed of flat planes illustrating spatial relations. See this Juan Gris work as an example (Fig. 1).

Objects have a somewhat flattened appearance, as if they are playing cards laid one on top of the other, each slightly askew. Sometimes we see only a fragment of an object. Take note that Gris's point of view here, looking down on the still life, is a feature of many Cubist works.

Other artists seek to create the suggestion of deep space, like landscapes that seem to retreat for miles. An example is this work by Corot (Fig. 2) on the next page. Our eyes move from more defined features close to us into the distance where color and linearity become ever less distinct.

These illusions are created by laws of perspective that artists study or use instinctively. One synonym for perspective is the phrase "point of view." In order to properly depict on a flat surface the relative height, width, depth, and position of objects when observed from a given point of view, artists employ what we call perspective. Some of these principles include the fact that objects appear smaller as they recede into space. Warm colors like red and yellow come forward, and cold colors like blues and greens appear farther away.

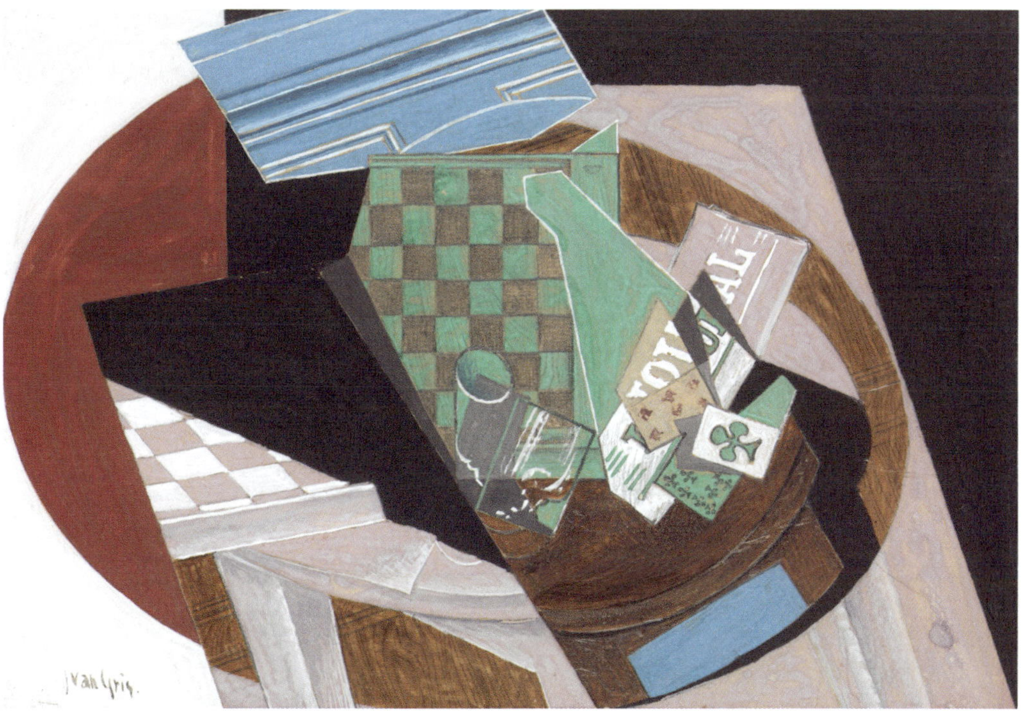

Fig. 1. Juan Gris, CHECKERBOARD AND PLAYING CARDS.

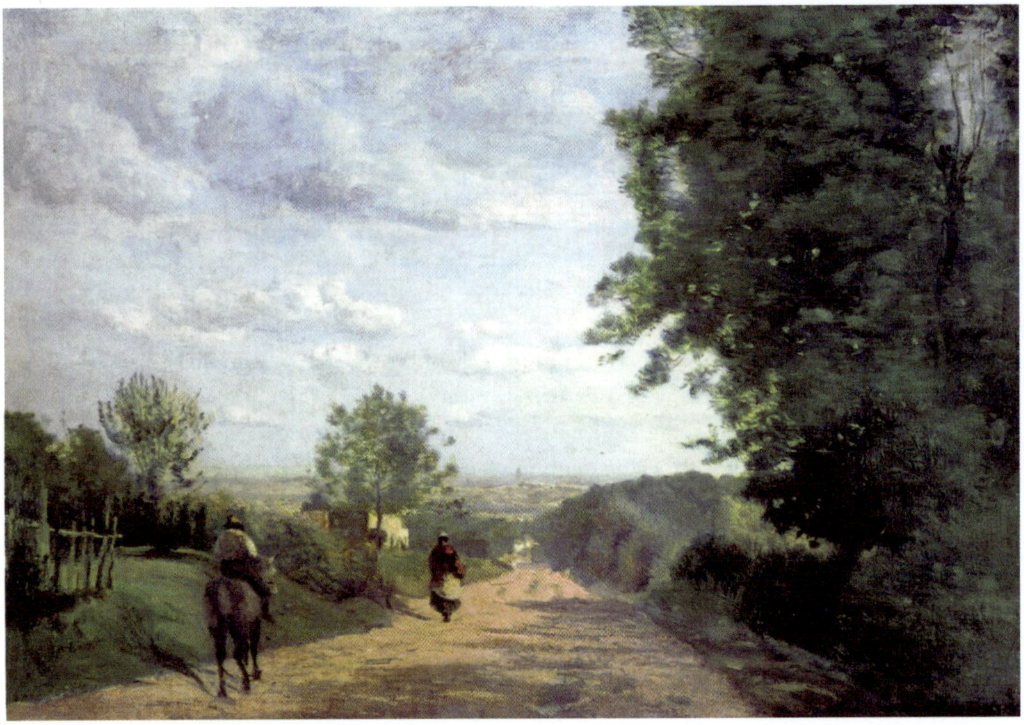

Fig. 2. Jean-Baptiste-Camille Corot, LE CHEMIN DE SÈVRES.

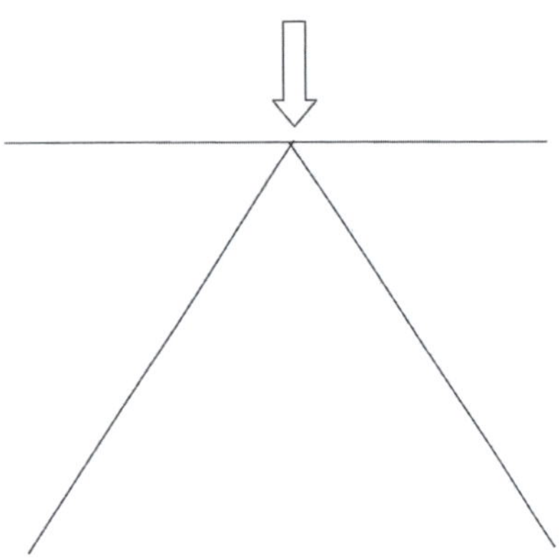

Fig. 3. Vanishing point (illustration).

In understanding perspective, two qualifiers will help to make it clear. **Linear perspective** is a way of explaining the illusion of distance on a flat surface. Objects are drawn in such a way that they convey an imaginary distance.

Imagine two diagonal lines describing the path to a house or railway tracks. The lines are far apart when they are close to your eye and then get closer as they recede into the distance to reach an imaginary point on the horizon when they converge. This point is referred to as **the vanishing point** because we are unable to see past it.

Or think of the drawing of a box you probably made as a child. See how the diagonal lines and the flat shapes one in front of the other give you the illusion of the third dimension.

In addition to linear perspective in drawing to create the illusion of the third dimension, artists use another kind of perspective in painting that we refer to as **aerial perspective**. By representing objects close to your eye with more intense color, and objects faraway as paler and less distinct, the artist is able to fool your eye into believing you are looking at a three-dimensional world.

With these simple rules of perspective now in your grasp, as you look at pictures note how the artist used lines and colors to give a two-dimensional work the illusion of the third dimension: depth. Even in the study of an abstract work, the lines and colors contribute to the illusion that certain shapes are forward and others are behind. Noticing how this is accomplished will add to your enjoyment of the work of art.

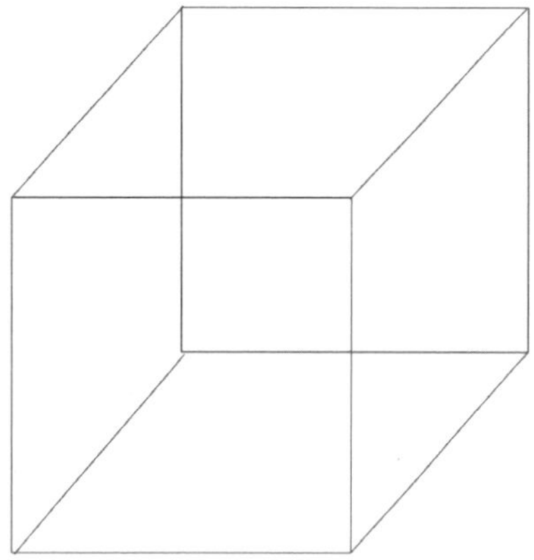

Fig. 4. Box (illustration).

Just as artists use perspective to create the illusion of depth, they have other ways to suggest that objects have weight and volume, what we refer to as form. Form is one of the elements of art, and in our next chapter we will get into some of the practices artists have employed to convince you that you are not looking at a flat surface.

When examining a picture take note of the manner in which the artist has composed the picture. Even artists working from identical subject manner will arrange the image in a totally different fashion. Here are some things to look for and questions to answer to guide the way.

What is front and center? The choice of what to focus on suggests what is most important to the artist. So too with the objects that are the largest and most vivid.

Is all of the picture detailed to the same extent? Artists often leave part of their work unfinished or in a state of becoming. The sculptor Michelangelo was famous for leaving part of his figures in this state (see Fig. 5 on the next page).

Michelangelo worked by a process of subtraction, creating a work from a solid block of marble and removing pieces to reveal the form. He is quoted as saying, "Every block of stone has a statue inside it, and it is the task of the sculptor to discover it."

By leaving some of the block in a raw state, deliberately unfinished, the artist is actually animating the figure. It appears to be climbing out or emerging out of the rock itself. The sculpture is in a state of becoming! Genius!

In a two-dimensional work, part of a scene or image is always cut off because it remains outside the artist's line of vision. But no matter. Notice how your eye and

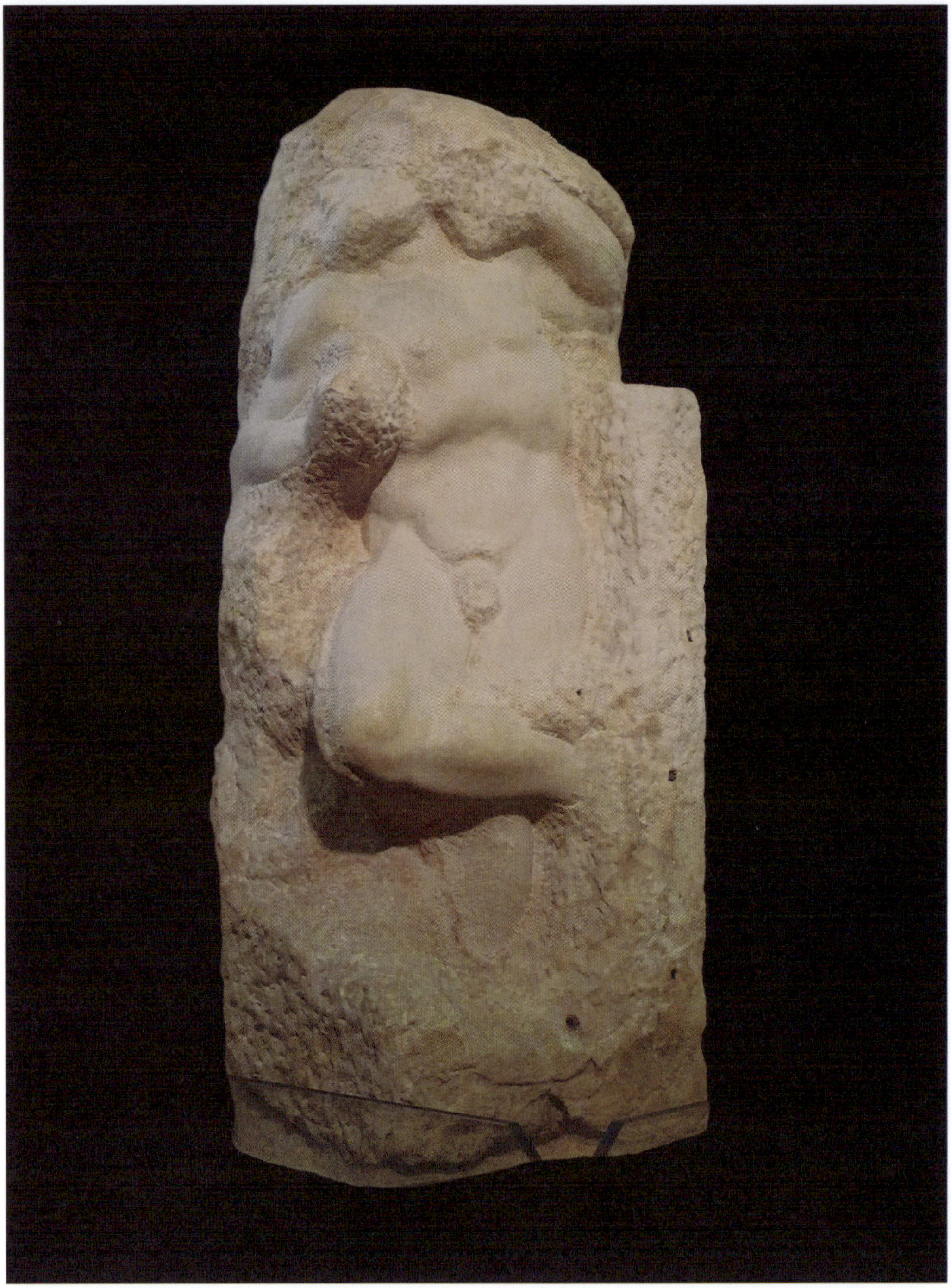

Fig. 5. Michelangelo, AWAKENING SLAVE.

imagination complete the picture for the artist. The viewer is a participant in the artwork, accepting the image as part of a larger world and in a sense, finishing it for the artist. The viewer cooperates in assuming that the feet of a figure are just out of the picture frame, not that the figure has no feet.

Take note of the intensities of color. Highly saturated color suggests nearness and objects in the distance are less distinct, foggier. This is especially relevant and noticeable in pictures that depict landscape. We live on a planet with an atmosphere, and the air, though it may seem invisible, actually informs the color and intensity of everything we see. Color that has been softened by the consciousness of atmosphere has a reality that overly bright color would not convey.

The Impressionists discovered atmosphere when they went outside to paint. And it was a revelation. It was such a mind-bending realization that Monet painted the haystacks at every time of the day, to study the effect the light and atmosphere played on them. Each represents an entirely different palette of color, as determined by the light conditions at that moment. The Impressionists remind us that there is no color without light.

Any painter who has gone outdoors to paint (*en plein air)* is cognizant of the fact that as the light changes, so does the color. It is a game of "beat the clock" to arrive at a consistent palette, and at best, the resulting work involves some guesswork. Think about this: How can you paint what you see, when what you see is constantly changing?

On the following page, see two examples of the haystacks, one painted in winter, the other in summer (Figs. 6a and 6b).

Monet is a bit of a scientist as he concocts the color formulas that say winter light and summer light. Why did he bother? He is fascinated with making the mixtures that will deliver an "authenticity" to his pictures, that will make them expressive and "speak." This is what the artist strives to accomplish; it is his message and his purpose.

Have you ever considered and attempted to describe the color of water? It is not something of concern unless you are a painter and have to make a color mixture to express water. Think of all the bodies of water you have seen. Some appear brown or green or gray or all combinations of blue and green. In truth, water is a no-color; it is the light, ground, and surrounding atmosphere that give the sensation of color.

Monet came to understand that the true subject of his work was not the haystacks but the light that made the haystacks visible. He became a painter of light and atmosphere and the water lilies he painted on his estate became a blur of color and light on the canvas. Monet became so obsessed with painting the light that he became an abstract painter in that realization. (You'll find a photo of *Water Lilies* in Chapter 7.)

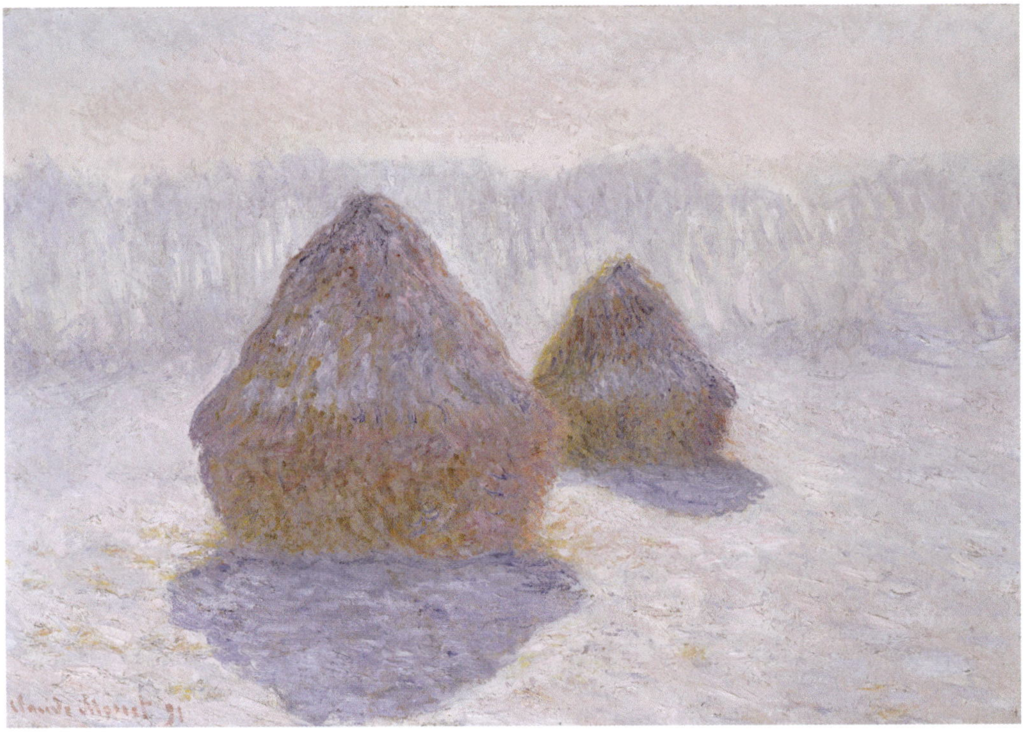

Fig. 6a. Monet, HAYSTACKS (EFFECT OF SNOW AND SUN).

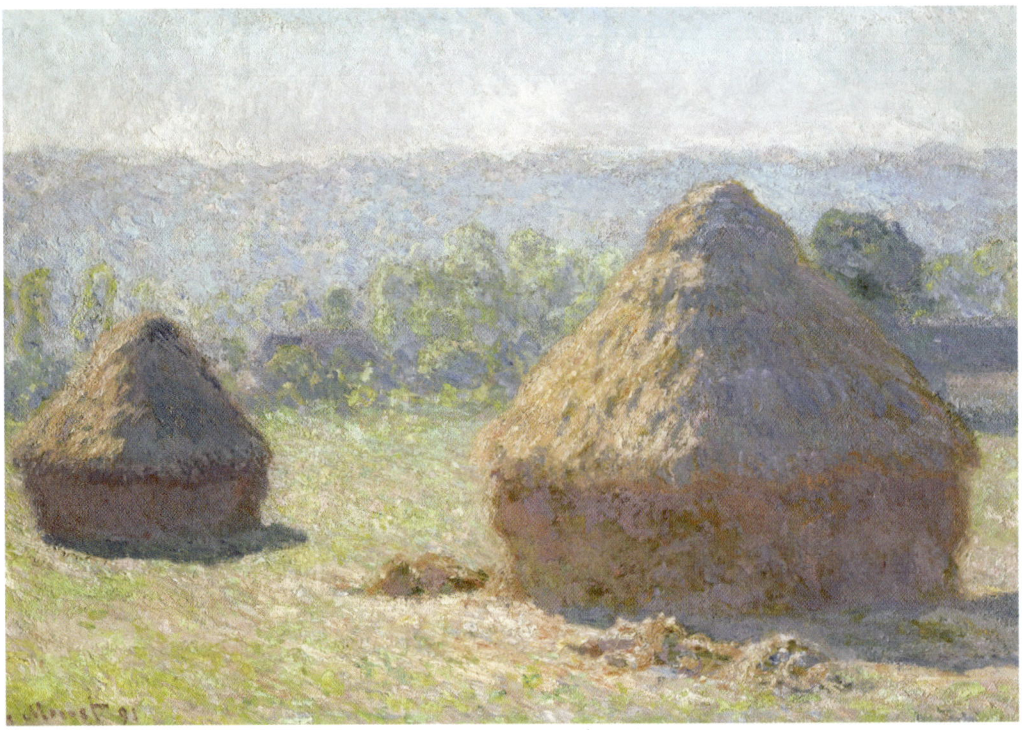

Fig. 6b. Monet, HAYSTACKS (END OF SUMMER).

By the way, the light that infused those water lilies was the fulfillment of Monet's quest as an artist. When I had the extreme pleasure of painting that famous water lily pond in 2008, I was moved to tears. That's how powerful and meaningful it felt to stand in the shoes of this seminal artist and see what he saw and know what he felt. Of course I painted them in an utterly different way, but that's the way it must be. Every artist's quest is totally different, and though there are commonalities of vision, each can never be repeated.

Leaving two-dimensional art for the moment, let's digress to define sculpture. The term sculpture encompasses art that is created in all three dimensions: length, width, and depth. It can be a relief, a piece basically flat on the back, with details protruding from the surface. These protrusions can be shallow, and we call those works **bas-relief** (French for low relief) or deep, as in high relief (or, in the French, **haut-relief**).

Most commonly, we think of sculpture as an object in the round, that we can actually circle as it stands freely and we can see it from all sides. But this is not a requirement; it is a sculpture if it has depth whether it is freestanding or not. It might be suspended from a ceiling like a **mobile**, or lying on the ground or in a body of water. If an artist can imagine and conceive it, as long as it has depth, we call it sculpture.

Sculpture, like painting, can be made of a whole host of materials. Stone, wood, metal, glass, ceramic—these are the familiar ones. But a sculpture can be made of uncommon materials too. It can be a collection of found objects, reassembled or deconstructed. It can be created from living plants as an **eco sculpture**. Even an entire landscape can be a sculpture—this would come under the category of environmental or **earth sculpture**.

These are some of the terms you will become familiar with as we discuss all the myriad ways artists have devised to express themselves. As we move on to discuss particular works of art in this book, we're going to need a language to discuss them. There are specific terms that pertain to visual art that are very useful to know, and we will review many of them in the next chapter.

The making of art is an essential activity of many cultures and groups throughout human history. But art did not always have the same meaning and purpose. Knowing why art was made in a given period is an important clue in understanding and appreciating it. Why did cavemen draw objects on the walls of their caves? Why did the Greeks make idealized sculptures? Why did the Dutch make portraits? Why are all the old paintings so dark?

We're going to get to many of those questions, I promise, but at this point just keep in mind the idea that making art was not always just a pastime or recreational activity. It had a purpose, whether it was keeping the gods mollified, or aggrandizing royals, or praying for rain. It was done for a reason, and this shaped the way it was done and the way it appeared. There were rules and standards of the time and place that informed art-making.

There was also a limit to what the people of the day knew and understood about the world. Let's remember that artists of yesteryear employed the tools and media available in their day. Painters could not call up Jerry's Artarama and order a full palette of premixed paints and fine bristle brushes. They had to make do with natural substances, inadequate illumination, and a host of other seeming detriments to creative expression.

Primitive artists endeavored to represent the objects in their world—animals, people, plants. They were realists representing real things. Their art training was limited, and so they represented them in a simplified way, like a child might. But do not be confused. Though the child's ability may be crude, his intention is clear. The child is a realist without doubt. He thinks he is drawing his mother even though we see something resembling a stick figure on the paper. So too with the individuals who created the cave drawings; in all likelihood, they did not consider themselves artists at all.

Many modern artists have been inspired by these simplified images. Picasso, for one—he was astounded when he discovered the freshness and spontaneity of African art. He liked it so much he wanted to imitate it. But he was a schooled, professional, modern artist schooled in the tricks of representational imagery. When Picasso simplified his work so it had a similarity to the work of primitive artists, he did it willfully, and with awareness and conviction. Was he being a realist? Not at all. He was creating semi-abstract work.

Let's now review the three approaches to visual art: **realism**, **semi-abstraction**, and **abstraction**. I want you to think of these three as stops on a train. You are going for a ride in the world of art and you can get off at any of these stops. You'll be able to change trains from each of these main stations to go to smaller genres—substations, if you will. But understanding these three will help make sense of all the others.

Realism is an attempt to depict people, animals, landscape, and objects as one sees them, without altering their form. As we shall discuss more fully later in this book, the artist-realist is not a magician, and he uses various techniques to transfer what he sees into paint on a flat surface—this requires an adjustment or a translation. But the intention is clear—to render the real.

A subsection of Realism is **Photo-Realism**, a technique whereby the artist renders such highly detailed and exact forms that they appear as believable as a photograph. Take note when you see a photo-realist work. In some cases, the hyper-reality of the image morphs into something so perfectly crafted that it, in fact, seems unreal.

A more painterly, less detailed work can have such emotional resonance that it "feels" more real than the photo-realistic one. Some photo realists, by the way, in an attempt to capture every nook and cranny of a photograph, project the latter onto a surface and then paint it. This technique is kind of a cheat—and the intention may be to fool the viewer, or impress him with hyper accuracy. Not exactly a laudable aesthetic choice.

When an artist wants to alter the appearance of his subject, rather than imitate it, he is moving into the realm of semi-abstraction. **Semi-abstraction** is a genre that deliberately takes aspects of the real and transforms them. The resulting work is not a copy but an interpretation of something that can be named. Why would an artist want to change what he sees?

The answer is that he wants to see it and wants you to see it in a new way. Maybe he wants to elongate the neck of his subject, as in this example by Modigliani (see Fig. 7 on the next page). Maybe he wants to show you several sides of the face at the same time, like Picasso did. Maybe he wants to flatten, distort, exaggerate, simplify, just to change it up. That is the privilege a modern artist entertains that was not available to his predecessors, either because the culture of their day might forbid it, or such transformation had not even been contemplated.

Maybe he wants to do away with any semblance of the real. This would have been inconceivable just little more than a couple of centuries ago. If he wants to chuck all the references, he can, and he has now gone to the next train stop, abstraction.

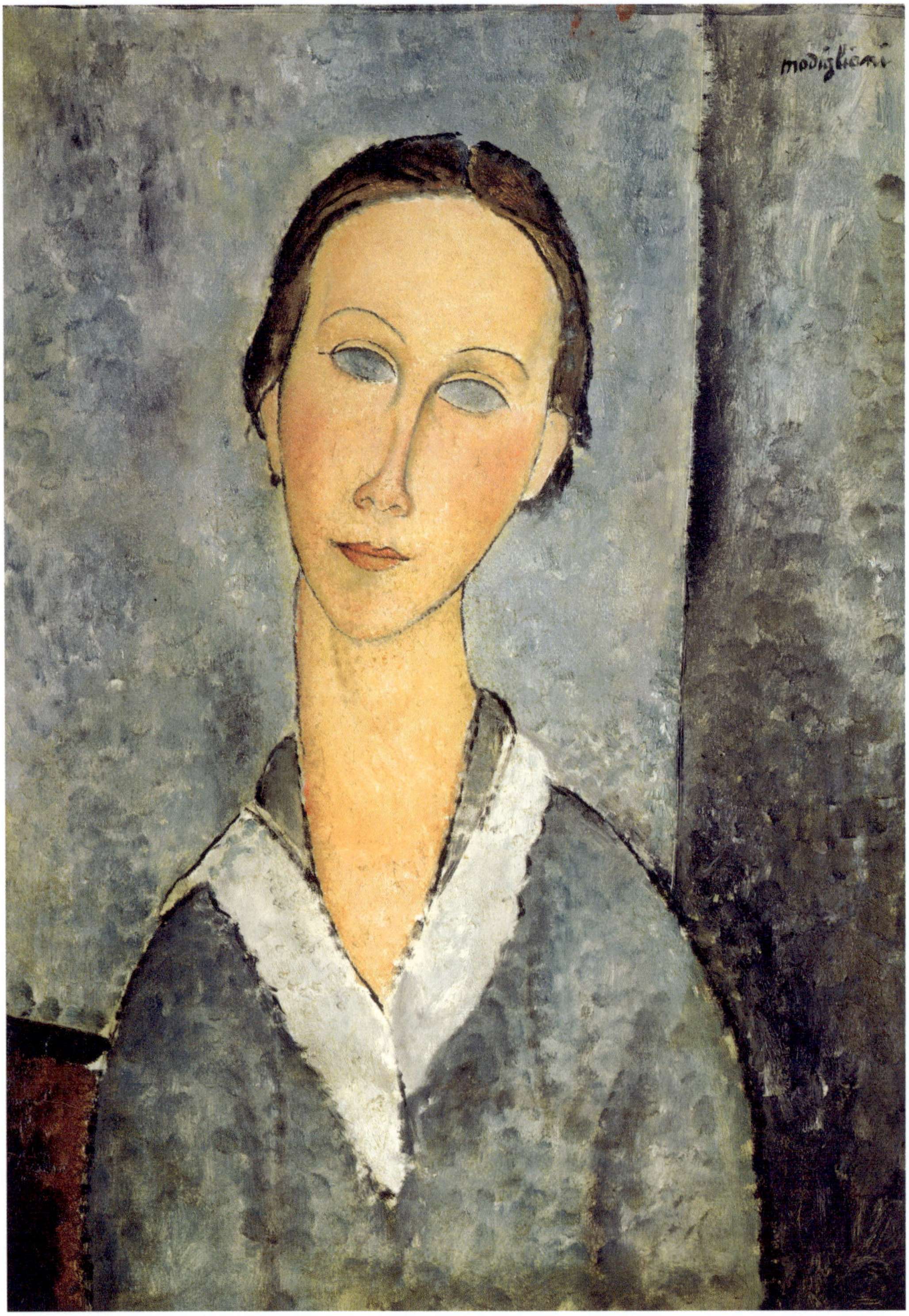

Fig. 7. Amedeo Modigliani, GIRL IN A SAILOR'S BLOUSE.

Abstraction is something very familiar to contemporary people, but it is very new in the world of visual art. What is it, exactly?

Abstraction is a process of eliminating references to real objects, even nonsolid ones, like the sky. If a painting suggests a landscape but does not describe one, it is considered semi-abstract. Even though you may not see a sky per se, the abstract painter may suggest the concept of distance, or atmosphere, solids and lines that seem to convey an impression of something, but you can't necessarily put a name on it. The artist may name the piece *Rainy Day*, but this is more metaphoric than descriptive.

Remember my statement about Monet and his water lilies. I said he set out to paint the water lilies but was truly painting the light. Light is abstract. Monet tells you he is painting water lilies with the name he puts on the work, but what do you see? The water lilies, the objects, disappear in the light. You see color, saturations, intensities, texture. All abstract things.

Keep in mind that every work of art starts out as abstract. The first lines and colors introduced do not yet add up to anything that resembles the real. We are all abstract artists in our beginnings. The only difference is that the semi-abstract artist or realist endeavors to travel on to the next stop, and the abstract artist chooses to linger in the first, refusing to make identifications, and just elaborating her marks more elegantly or purposefully.

The abstract elements live on in the work whether it resolves as pure abstraction, semi-abstraction, or realism. Look for these elements regardless of the end form the work takes. Find the abstract in the real and the real in the abstract! Perhaps you will discover that the individual result is less important than the universal elements.

Pure abstraction is a liberated and liberating art form. It takes us from the specific to the essential, from the literal to the metaphoric. When artists realized they could paint abstractly, that stop #1 could indeed be a destination, this was incredibly exhilarating. Painting the abstract, that which cannot be seen, requires tremendous imagination and courage. We now accept abstraction as a totally legitimate art form, even prefer it, but it was absolute blasphemy when it was first undertaken.

Today artists may freely choose to be realists, semi-abstract artists, or abstract artists. They have total free will, as least in the Western countries, to create their artworks in the manner and form they prefer. We will talk about all the substations of the three main genres in succeeding chapters. You've heard the names—Futurism, Surrealism, Pop Art, Minimalism etc.—and now you will understand them in the context of the big three.

Just a final word here. In this book, we are explaining and giving names to movements in the history of art and to individual works of art. But I do this with full cognizance that every fingerprint is unique, every signature is one of a kind, and every artist's hand produces his own fingerprint and signature. This goes beyond and overrides all efforts to categorize and name what is truly ineffable, ART!

Chapter 3

Art Vocabulary: Art Terms and How to Use Them

The *Oxford English Dictionary* contains 171,476 English words. Other languages, or at least their dictionaries, contain many more, like Japanese, which purportedly contains about half a million words. How many words are in the average adult English speaker's vocabulary? The answer I found was about 20,000 active words (those the speaker could actually use) and 40,000 if you count passive words (those the speaker could recognize but not necessarily use). When you do the math, you find that the average person uses only 11 percent of the words in his own language.

There are many specialized words not in common parlance and used by professionals in their fields. There are also new words that are being invented and borrowed from other languages. I read that Shakespeare invented about 1,700 new words.

For our purposes here, we're going to discuss some words and terms used in describing visual art. You may already be familiar with many, but your definitions may be very general. We're going to talk the talk like artists mostly do, and at the end of this course, you will have an enriched vocabulary you can use when you look at art.

In thinking about how to organize this chapter, I've decided against giving you the terms in alphabetical order. Though it would be neat, I can't imagine it would be easy for you to apply them unless you learn about them in context.

Let's talk about the **elements of art**. These are the basic concepts every artist must deal with whether she does so consciously or not. They are **light** (sometimes referred to as **value**); **color**, **line**, **shape**, **form**, **space**, and **texture.**

Artists use all of these elements, but often excel in one or more, and are known for their expertise or exceptionalism with it. After each section, I'll give one example of one of these stellar practitioners. You will undoubtedly find many more, and others you find even more outstanding. Suffice it to say that these elements are present in all visual artworks, and I give you these examples only to assist you in identifying and analyzing them.

LIGHT

Nothing would be visible without light. So light is the number one reality the artist deals with. There is **light**, the natural agent which makes all visible, and there is **lighting**, which refers to an artificial source of illumination. Painters deal with both and often choose or set up the conditions they most prefer. Artists who work outdoors and paint the light are called **en plein air** painters; this was a specialty of the Impressionists.

When you look at a painting, try to imagine what and where was the artist's source of light. In a realistic painting, you can find the source by studying the **shadows**. **Shadow** is a dark area or shape created when something is in the path of the source of light. If the shadow is on the right of an object, you know the light has come from the left.

Utilizing black-and-white film, a camera copies the areas of dark and light. This is all a camera does; in fact is the only thing the camera **can** do. And what does the camera achieve when it accurately copies the darks and the lights? It creates the appearance of objects, of **three-dimensional form**.

I often give my students an exercise in which they take a black-and-white photograph and turn it upside down. Then I ask them to reproduce the shapes and intensities of the darks and lights. They are imitating the photograph's spectrum of lights and darks, from the lightest light, white, to the darkest dark, black. This range of lights and darks is called a **gamut**.

A painting may have a long or a short gamut. **A long gamut** (from a very light light to a very dark dark) will produce a more dramatic effect, while a short one, for instance, a collection of very close middle tones, will produce a more subtle effect. Notice this when you look at art. Now don't be confused. We are not talking about colors here, only variations in light.

Painters can reproduce many shades of a color by adding white to a hue. A **hue** is the color—blue, red, violet, etc. The lightness of a hue is called its **value**. Remember that a painter is giving you a value manually, unlike the camera, which gives you the value automatically. The painter does consciously what the camera does involuntarily, and this gives the painter more leeway in changing things up.

Okay, so back to light. When my students paint the darks and lights copying their upside-down image, they are amazed when they turn their paper around and see that the shapes of dark and light have miraculously created an object. This is an important lesson. You see, artists don't create anything. They don't make trees, or faces, or anything. They just make hues (color) and values (darks and lights), shapes, lines, and textures. It is the values, shapes, textures, and lines that create the **illusion** of objects. An illusion is defined as a deceptive appearance—it's not really there!

When you look at the history of art and go through the museum looking at the work of centuries past, you will notice that painting, as we often like to say, has gone **from the shadows up**. It starts dark and gets lighter and lighter as we come into the present. Now you might attribute this to the fact that electric light was not available in bygone days, and this might account for some of the studio paintings created indoors. But why didn't it occur to artists to go outside and paint the light? The sun was out all day and artists could see the same sun we see today. And yet the paintings are decidedly darker. Why?

In a sense, one can look at the history of art as a march from the darkness into the light, an evolution of consciousness. The darkness is not only visual; it represents a lack of awareness. As scientific discoveries brought human beings to a greater understanding of the world they inhabited, eyes literally became more open and able to "see the light."

When the Impressionists realized they could paint not the objects illuminated by light, but light itself, we truly entered the modern age. Of course, there were many steps along the way and precursors to the visionaries of Impressionism—Monet, Manet, Renoir, Cézanne . . . There was Caravaggio, who discovered the magic of candlelight, and Turner, who found atmosphere.

Now that we've had this brief discussion about light, looking at how artists of the past painted lit objects and light itself will figure into your analysis of all painting. The light, the light, it is everything!

You should also take note of the many ways artists have developed to describe shadows in their work. An overall term is **shading.** There are many ways artist can express shade—with solid masses of darker values, and with various applications of what we call **linear texture**—a type of mark-making.

Some of the methods include the popular **crosshatching**—making a pattern of marks that cross to depict a shaded area; **stippling**—shading with dots that are very close or dense to those that are airier. Also **graffito**—a technique using little scratch marks.

Great Master of Light: Claude Monet

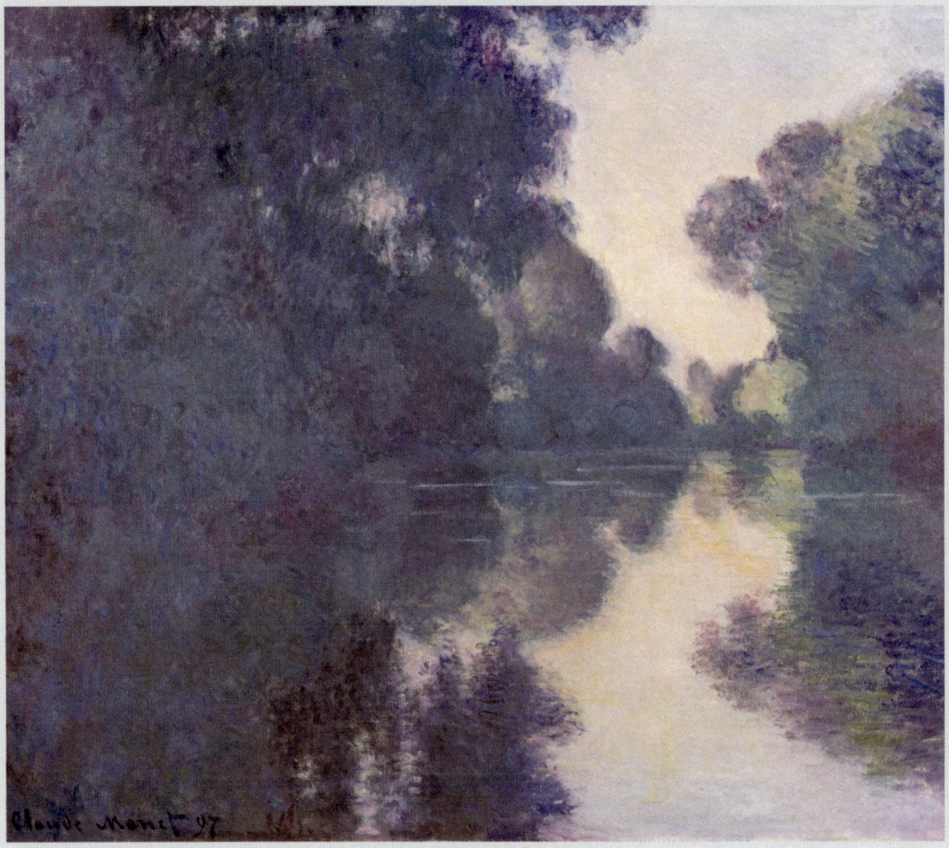

Fig. 8. Claude Monet, MORNING ON THE SEINE NEAR GIVERNY.

Why? All artists address light in their work, but for Monet, light was his very subject, and the objects he described only an excuse to paint the light.

OTHER MASTERS OF LIGHT: Turner, Caravaggio, Velázquez, and all of the Impressionists.

This is something interesting to note when you look at art. How are the shadows expressed? How has the artist achieved contrast between the lights and darks? Are the lights and darks treated differently in terms of texture?

COLOR

When light strikes something, it reflects back to the eye as color. We learn the names of colors when we are toddlers, but this is just one property of color—its hue. A painter also considers the intensity of color, i.e. how vivid it is, and also its value, how light it is. A painter works with all the aspects of color, adding white to create a **tint** and black to create a **shade**.

As my painting teacher used to say there are **colors** and there is **color**. The latter, singular color, is more than a collection or assortment of colors. It is the sensation of color itself, actually the feeling of the light. What is a color? It is only a particular wavelength of light.

If you've been to a paint store lately, you know that there are practically an infinite number of shades and tints of different colors. The tints and shades represent the range of lightness or darkness of every hue. You will recall from our discussion of light that the lightness or darkness of a color is called its **VALUE**. For the painter's purpose, a lighter tint or value is created by adding white, and a darker shade or value is created by eliminating white. The primary, secondary, and tertiary color (hues) in a myriad of values (light) create a seemingly endless array of colors.

Mixing colors is a main part of the painter's bag of tricks, but you don't need a lot of colors to achieve **color**. A painter achieves a pleasing or resonant feeling of color by the juxtaposition of harmonious, interesting, or expressive mixtures. It is incorrect to assume that a large variety of colors will achieve the *sensation* of color. In actuality, it is more likely that fewer colors, more carefully chosen, will succeed.

To create these specific mixtures, all you really need are the primaries and white—then you can make every color. Black, for instance, though not technically a color itself, can be made in many ways by mixing a variety of pigments in different combinations.

Another word for a selection of colors is **PALETTE**. Artists mix colors on a palette, a board usually, but the **palette** is also defined as the color scheme an artist may choose. There is a **limited palette**, where the artist chooses just a few colors in a schema to execute his work, or a **full palette**, the use of a whole array of colors from which the artist makes his choices. Take note of this when you look at paintings.

Is the range of colors wide or has the artist just selected a few with which to execute his composition? Are the colors bright and primary or muted and of a minor key? What words could you use to describe the color? Muted, minor, primary, sweet, neon, soft, and cold are a few. Think of others.

In our decoding chapter, you will see examples of color palettes and an analysis of how a few artists depicted color. Developing a palette that is personal and exemplifies the artist's prerogatives is a major preoccupation of many painters.

You may have heard somewhere about the **COLOR WHEEL**. The wheel is a representation of the hues in a circle—you probably memorized it in elementary school—ROYGBIV (red orange yellow green blue indigo violet). The **complementary colors** are opposite one another on the wheel and are said to, as the name suggests, enhance one another. The **analogous colors** lie next to one another and work together in more subtle relationships.

The **primary** colors are red, yellow, and blue and are called primary because no other colors can be combined to form a primary. When we mix the primaries with one another, we get the **secondary** colors of orange, green, and purple. Mixing a primary with a secondary will give you a **tertiary** color, blue-green, yellow-green, red-orange, red-purple, blue-purple, and yellow-orange.

I don't suggest to my students that they follow the color wheel in choosing colors and instead feel their way into a color scheme that works for them and expresses best what they wish to express. But as a viewer, you can take note of the colors the artist has chosen and see for yourself whether they work best. Would you have chosen another hue or value?

One more thing on color. The feeling of the color in a work of art depends upon a number of factors. It will vary with the texture of the surface used, and a number of other qualities of the paint itself. These include what is called the **chroma** (how pure the hue is); the **saturation** (the transparency or opaqueness); the **intensity** (how bright); and of course, the **value** (how light or dark).

All of these factors contribute to what I called the **feeling** of the paint, which is due to a host of factors. These include the hue, value, application, surface, and the palette or color scheme.

When it comes to application of paint, consider this. Paint can be applied to a surface in many ways. It can be mixed with oils and other thinners to appear transparent. One color can be layered over another to produce a **glaze** or it can be thickly applied to lay on top, and this is called an **impasto**. Artist who like thick impasto paint often use a knife rather than a brush to lay the paint on.

How an artist applies paint is part of his signature and gives his work the singular look and feel you recognize as his. It may appear dry or oily, shiny or dull, transparent or dense. These are broad categorizations, but each artist's touch is different. Take note of these textural signatures when you look at art.

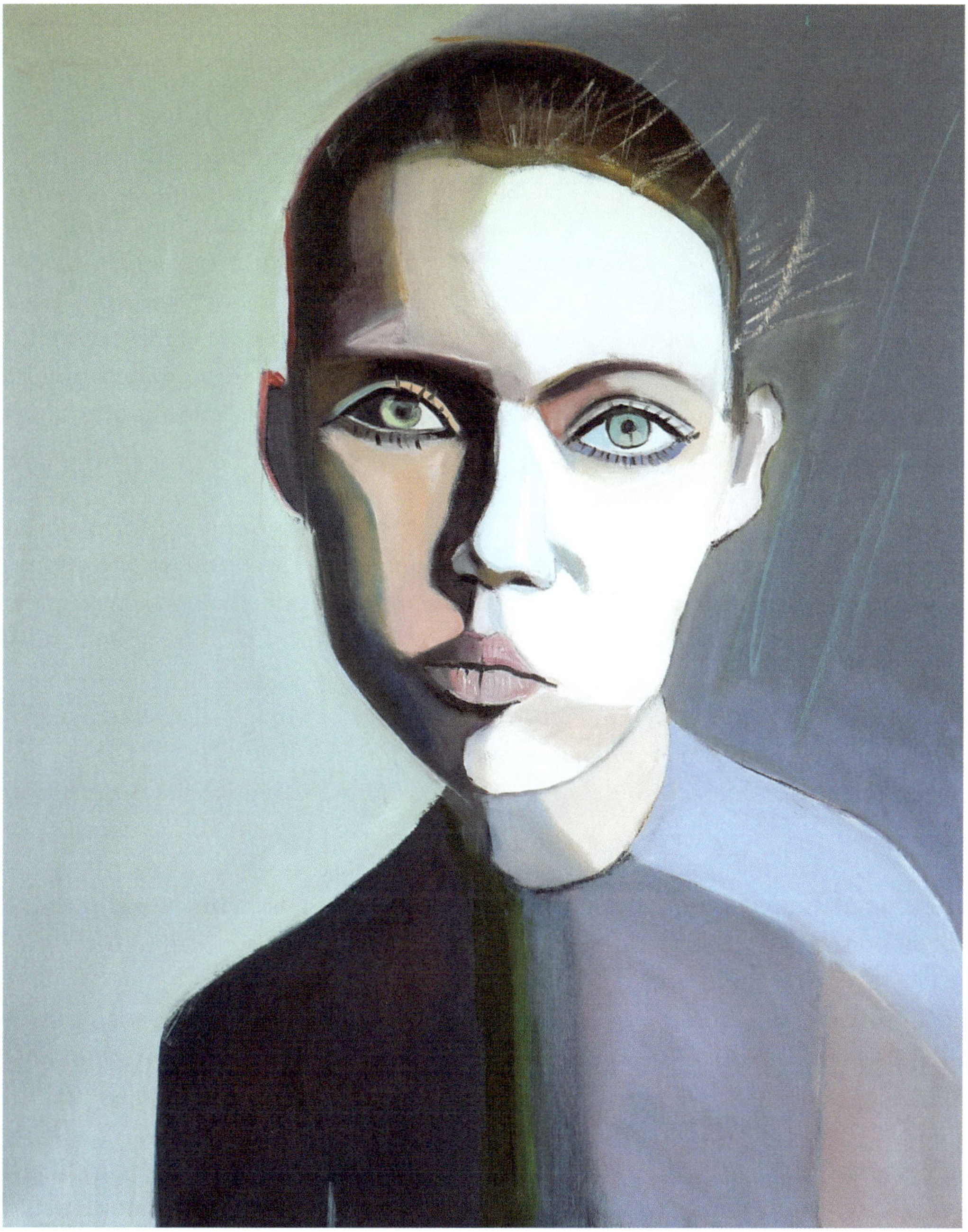

Fig. 9. Carolyn Schlam, GIRL WITH GREEN EYES.

So now when you look at a painting, you will notice the surface, how the paint is applied, and the variety of hues and values incorporated into the design. You can evaluate how clever the artist was in choosing color to present a design or image. If it is very closely imitates the colors we perceive, we call it **local** color; if it presents colors we usually do not associate with an object, it is called **imaginative** color.

See how your eye is the great equalizer and accepts the image the artist presents. Green leaves (local), yes; purple or orange leaves (imaginative), okay too. Remember, art is, above all, personal expression. And rules were made to be broken.

On page 29, you will see a portrait of mine in which I've used many hues that are nonlocal to create a face (Fig. 9). There's a blue nose, green cheek, brown forehead; and yet somehow you still accept it as a bona fide face. As you look at art, take note of the artist's color choices. You may not realize that you have accepted very unconventional colors that make sense in the context of the artwork.

Be cognizant that you may be more open-minded than you think, accepting notes as "real" or "accurate" that may veer quite a bit from the naturalistic. Remember, this is paint, not a living being. This realization changes the way we look at art. Realist or abstract, art is a work of the imagination.

LINE

What is it? A line is a dot that moves. Imagine it in your mind's eye. The dot moving in a direction creates the line, which can be thick or thin, and stop wherever it wishes. If the artist is drawing well, he feels the line moving through an imaginary space, and in doing so, creates the illusion of that space on the flat surface.

Lines can be made with many materials and can function in an artwork in many ways. A line with paint might be called a **stroke** or a **brushstroke**. A line can be thick or thin or variegated.

A line may have different qualities—it can be tender or bold. Elegant or clumsy. To a great extent the feeling of an artwork is dependent on the quality of its line.

There are a number of ways to use line in drawing. A **contour drawing** basically captures the outline of a figure or form. A **continuous line drawing** is a variant of the contour drawing wherein the artist's line follows the outline without stopping, his eyes set on the subject and not looking down at the drawing while his eye travels.

A **gesture drawing** uses quick expressive lines to nail the character or attitude of a subject without much detail. It is an exercise in spontaneity, a kind of automatic response without thought. Many artists use the gesture drawing to warm up in a drawing session and in many cases these quick sketches can be the best of the lot in a session's production, just for their authenticity and lack of self-consciousness.

Great Master of Color: Bonnard

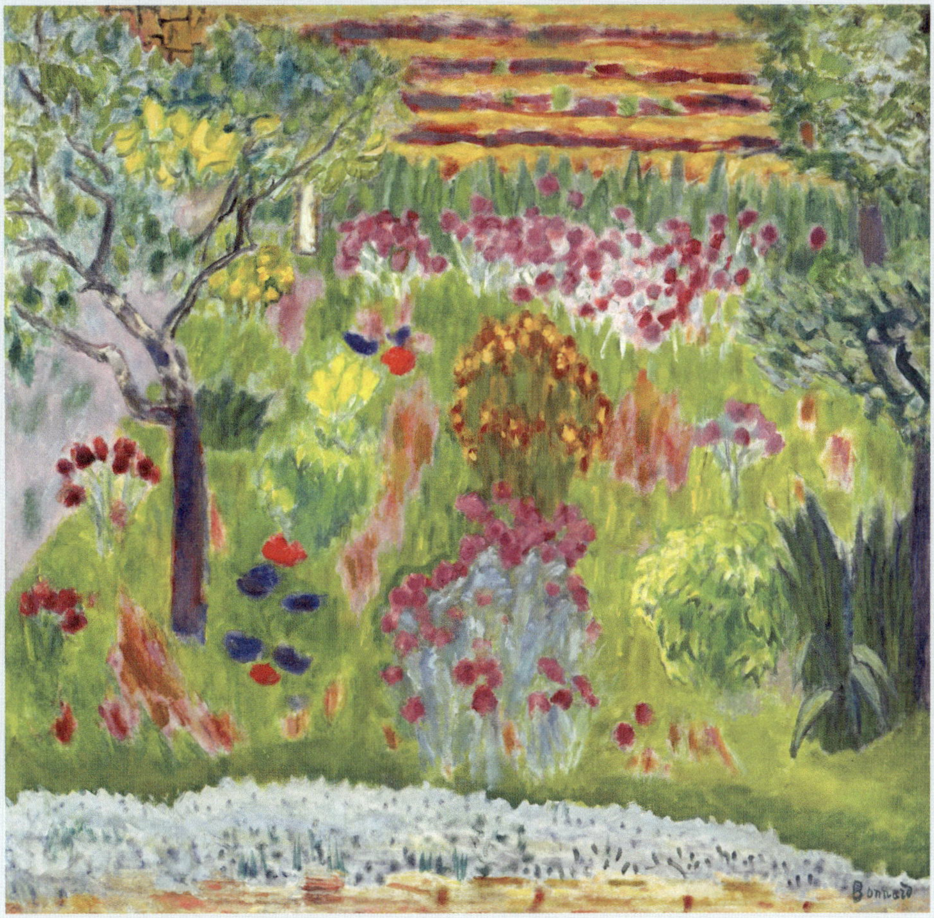

Fig. 10. Pierre Bonnard, GARDEN.

Why? The painter Bonnard had a joyous palette and adored color. His color has an unmatched vivacity and beauty. He was a liberal and imaginative colorist. Study Bonnard's bath picture in the decoding section of this book.

I encourage you to look at the work of other joyous colorists like the superb Matisse. Throughout his career, including his Fauve period into the latter-day cutouts, color was always an important element in Matisse's work. See Chapter 7 for a look of one of his glorious oils and get a book on Matisse to study his work. Many famous colorists—especially the lyrical abstract artists—are indebted to Matisse.

OTHER NOTABLE COLORISTS: Fra Angelico, Titian, Tinteretto, Rothko.

Great Master of Line: Toulouse-Lautrec

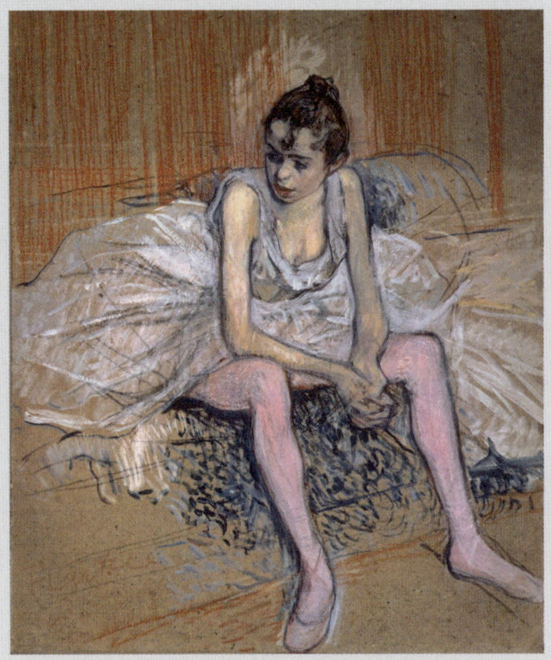

Fig. 11. Henri de Toulouse-Lautrec, DANSEUSE ASSISE AUX BAS DE ROSES.

Why? Toulouse-Lautrec painted the barmaids and dancers of Paris with great abandon. He had a strong, confident line and drew expressively. In fact, many of his pieces feel like colored drawings, where color enhances but the line tells the story. He was a highly graphic artist.

Here's an amazing fact. Henri de Toulouse-Lautrec loved drawing so much that in a twenty-year career he purportedly created 737 paintings, 275 watercolors, 363 prints and posters, over 5,000 drawings, and many other works including some in glass and ceramic.

OTHER NOTABLE LINEAR ARTISTS: Leonardo da Vinci, Botticelli, Schiele, Picasso, Rouault, Ingres.

This work by the French artist Henri de Toulouse-Lautrec is what I would call a painted drawing (Fig. 11). Notice that only certain areas are filled in with color. The slouch of the dancer is accomplished through the length, direction, and quality of the line. The coloring is decorative, and it is applied with what we call "linear texture"—straight and curved lines and marks that suggest floor, wall, fabric. Remember that what an artist leaves out is just as relevant as what he includes. Notice this when you look at art, as you consider what works may be "overdone," "underdone," or "just right."

Great Master of Shape: Juan Gris

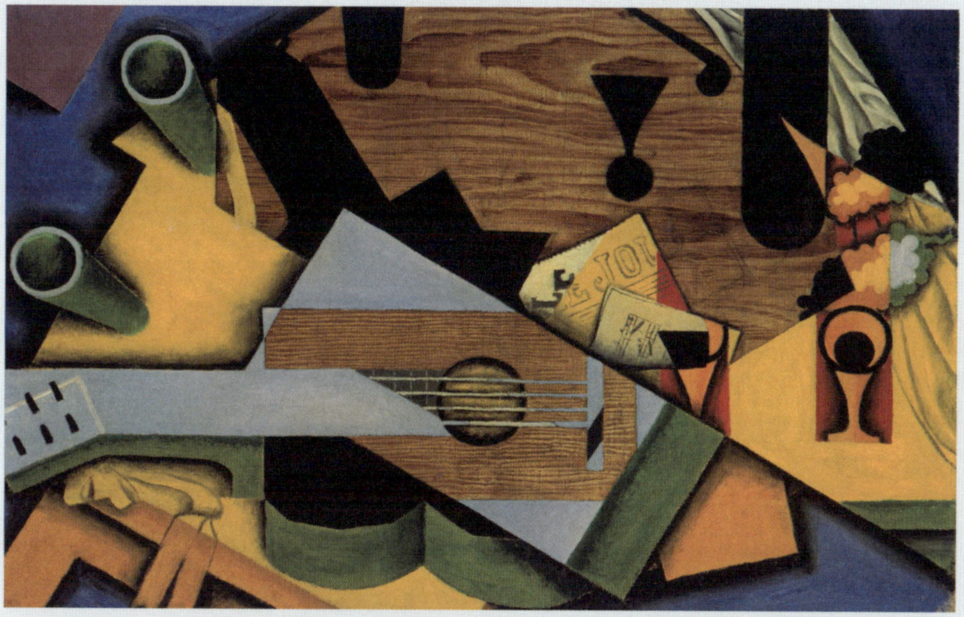

Fig. 12. Juan Gris, STILL LIFE WITH A GUITAR.

Why? Juan Gris and his fellow Cubists simplified form into interlocking shapes. They were more interested in design and composition than copying objects in an imitative manner. Gris's shapes are really pronounced and interesting. Gris's fellow Cubists, like Picasso and Braque, were important precursors to abstract painting and sculpture.

OTHER NOTABLE SHAPE-SHIFTERS: Klee, Picasso, Braque, Gorky, Kandinsky.

SHAPE

If the line returns to its starting point, it will create an enclosed area. A flat enclosed area is a shape. A shape can be **geometric**, like a square or circle, or it can be **organic**, free-form. Remember that a shape is flat. If it contains the third dimension, we call it a **form**.

A shape is imaginary. There are no shapes in nature. Of course, artists can simplify forms in nature and reduce them to shapes. We extract a shape from a more complex form.

A shape is a basic building block for an artist. Shapes can be arranged in myriad ways and filled in myriad ways. Shapes play a lead part in abstract paintings and sculpture.

Artists often begin a composition by breaking down what they see into shapes, and then proceed to add shading and modify the shapes into more complex forms. In this regard, you may want to consider the work of the Cubists who broke complex images into simple shapes and left these simplified shapes to better explain the anatomy or architecture of space.

FORM

A form is a three-dimensional object. It occupies space and has volume. It can be geometric, like a ball or box, or it can be organic, like a sculpture.

The illusion of form can be created by an artist in multiple ways. By utilizing perspective, artists create imaginary space. By using shading and modeling, artists create imaginary form.

When light comes in contact with an object, the light illuminates the form. What the artist does is to portray how the light interacts with the object, where it is strongest and where it cannot reach. In delineating the light, the artist creates the illusion of the object. Where the light hits directly, the artist creates a **highlight**, the lightest value. Where the light illuminates but indirectly, the artist makes use of a mid tone, and where the object obscures the light, we have a shadow.

When the object casts a shadow, and the artist delineates the shape of that shadow, he further defines the illusion of the shape of the object itself. If there are other objects in the vicinity, they may reflect back on the object of interest. That would be called a **reflected light**.

When the artist defines all of these, he imparts the illusion of form to his picture. Pay special note to this when looking at still life. How were the three dimensions of a pot or an apple created? See how the artist has broken up the apple or pot into shards of value to make it appear round.

SPACE

The illusion of depth on a flat surface is referred to as space. Some elements of the picture appear to come forward. We call that the **foreground**. Others seem to live in the middle; we call that the **middle ground**. Still others go back. We call the latter the **background**. Remember, these are just appearances; the surface is flat.

Artists use various techniques to create the illusion of space. They use variations of color and texture to identify parts of the picture they want to appear to come

Great Master of Form: Paul Cézanne

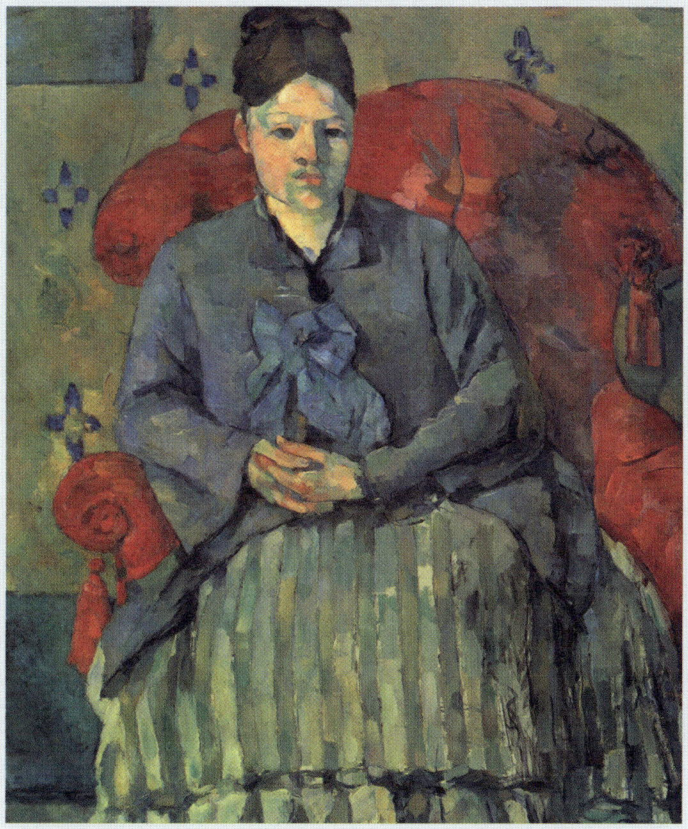

Fig. 13. Paul Cézanne, MADAME CÉZANNE IN A RED ARMCHAIR.

Cézanne's modeling of fruit is well known. He broke his apples and pears into patches of colored values that in their direction and shape created the illusion of three-dimensional forms. Here we see this expert modeling in a beautiful painting of his wife in a red armchair.

Note that not only is the paint applied in different colors, the pieces of paint working together create the roundness and weight of the form itself. Study the complexity of this modeling of paint, so subtle and yet so powerful in this beautiful work.

Why? Cézanne is worthy of study for many reasons, not least his treatment of paint to create solid forms. He is a much beloved master painter in this regard.

OTHER MASTERS OF FORM: Eakins, Henry Moore, Rodin, Botero, Maillol, Picasso.

forward or go back. Warm colors like red and yellow come forward while cool colors seem to recede.

As we mentioned in the previous chapter, artists utilize the principles of **PERSPECTIVE, both linear and aerial** to create the illusion of space. Perspective is a manner of representing space by establishing that things get smaller and less distinct as they go away from you, and recede to what we call the **vanishing point**, beyond which nothing can be seen.

The artist who gets the distinction of naming the factor of perspective in art was Masaccio, who lived a short life, from 1401 to 1428. He is credited with incorporating linear perspective in his painting and defining the vanishing point. Dubbed **Masaccio Perspective** for the artists that were to follow him, this new understanding explained the illusion of depth artists achieved in their two-dimensional work.

Remember that objects appear smaller as they recede into space. Imagine two sailboats, one close to shore and one in the distance. As you stand on the shore and look out, the nearby boat looks large and the faraway boat small. Size and placement are essential elements in creating the illusion of space.

Two more definitions here. **Positive space**, for an artist, is the space occupied by the object. **Negative space** is the space of the air around it or within it. Imagine a person with his hands on his hips. The triangles formed between the body and arms would be considered **negative space**.

The artist, though he may understand and acknowledge the meaning of negative space, knows that this is a misnomer. In fact there is nothing negative in his picture. The air, the atmosphere, the space between shapes and forms, is not a nothing. It is just as much a something as the dense object.

Artists have an awareness of the "negative space" and they pay as much attention to it as the positive. Drawing the specificity of the negative defines the positive. In truth, objects do not exist in a vacuum and for the painter everything is connected. The scene before him is a tapestry of substances of different weights, sizes, and characteristics.

Appreciating the connectivity of the visual field is a manifestation of a more engaged perception. Students of painting make a huge leap in their mastery of the art form when they no longer view objects as separate. More on this in subsequent chapters.

Great Master of Aerial Perspective: Albert Bierstadt

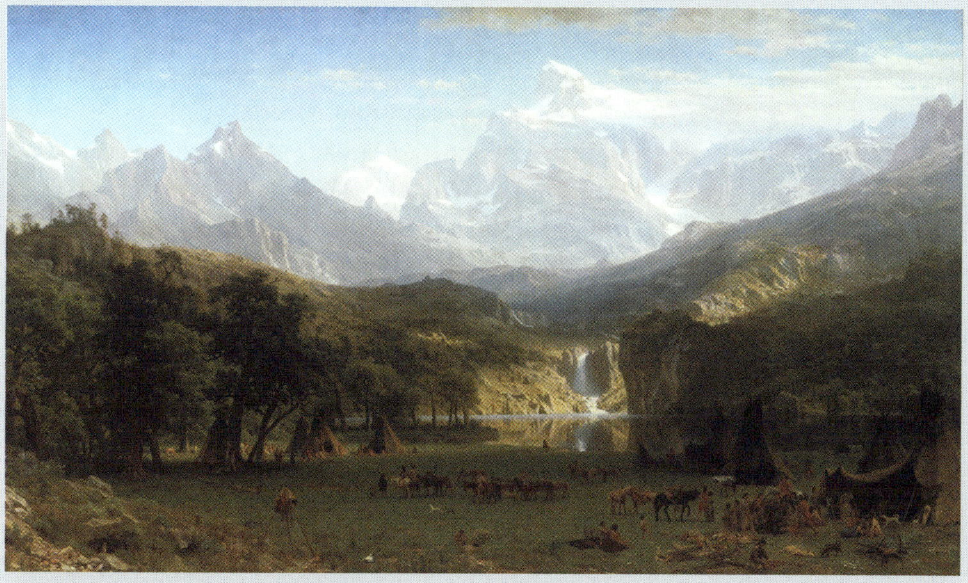

Fig. 14. Albert Bierstadt, THE ROCKY MOUNTAINS, LANDERS PEAK.

Why? Bierstadt was a dramatist of the American landscape, but his aerial perspective is spot-on. Notice how the colors fade as they describe the deep space.

OTHER NOTABLE ILLUSIONISTS AND MASTERS OF SPACE: Homer, Turner, Corot, Kandinsky, Motherwell.

When looking at an abstract painting, notice how the artist has created an imaginary space without the use of objects. Though the lines and shapes he has drawn and painted do not coalesce into recognizable objects, they do connote a sense of space based on their size, position, value, and color. In a way, it is easier to get a feeling of the space without the distraction of the objects. Abstraction brings space into art as the primary element, along with color and line.

TEXTURE

Texture is the feel of the surface. It can be real or actual, as a rough or smooth surface. But it can also be a feeling of a substance suggested by the way the paint or other surface coverings are applied and relate to one another.

Every artist has a personal preferred sensitivity when it comes to texture. Some prefer a smooth, even surface, others a pebbled, rough one. Some artists use the paint in a thin wash, others in a pasty glob. Notice and name the texture or qualities of the surface when you look at art. Don't be afraid to use descriptive adjectives. Is the feel slimy or dry, liquid or scratchy? The more you use descriptive language, the more sophisticated your appreciation of the art will be.

There are basically two main ways texture is employed in 2-D works. It is either **virtual, optical, or implied texture**, where the paint imitates an actual texture, or an **actual or physical texture**, which the artist accomplishes by virtue of his application of paint, adding substances into the paint, like salt or sand, or actually attaching differently textured materials to the surface.

Great Master of Texture: Van Gogh

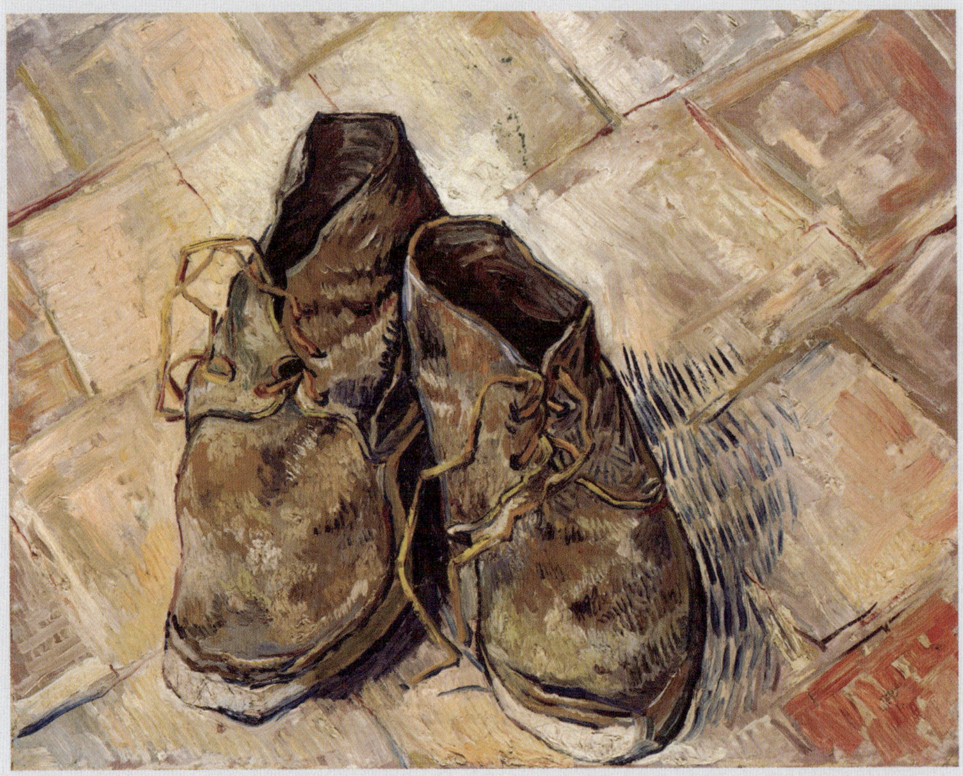

Fig. 15. Vincent van Gogh, SHOES.

Why? Need you ask? Everyone knows van Gogh. He is one of the most beloved and highly recognized artists in the world, which is very poignant as he felt so unloved and unrecognized during his lifetime. Van Gogh saw everything as vibrantly alive. He told us this with the vivid swirling texture with which he imbued his canvases. There was nothing flat and dull in his worldview.

OTHER GREAT TEXTURISTS: Soutine, Ingres, Rembrandt, Rauschenberg.

Artists drawing from life may use the paint to imitate the texture of the object; imitation is also called **verisimilitude**. The texture is implied or visual, and only appears textured. The surface is still flat. There are many examples in art of imitated texture—a silk robe, the glassiness of an object, a metal saber. Many of the masters of old created a tapestry of these imitated textures. Take note of them and how they were achieved. Notice whether the paint is thin or thick, the specific color mixtures that achieve the likeness, the folds that suggest fabric, and the drawing that illustrates soft substances as opposed to hard ones.

Artists may also create actual textures on the surface for their own sake. This is especially obvious in abstract work where the manner in which the paint is applied is sometimes the whole story. Many modern and contemporary artists actually add fabrics and other collaged elements right into their pictures.

When an artist uses different media in the same work, we define that work as **mixed media**. Examples of media that can be mixed include oil- and water-based paints, collaged elements with paint, crayons and pastels with paint media, as well as combinations of sculptural media like glass and ceramic, wood and metal, etc.

Look at this painting of shoes by van Gogh, in which the artist has employed both virtual and actual texture. The artist's attention to the shape and texture of these shoes makes them come alive—why you can almost imagine the feet that went into them!

Van Gogh was famous for his brushstroke technique, which made all of the objects in his works—the cypress trees, wheat fields, skies, flowers, and people—seem to vibrate. This is due to his amazing capacity for observation, coupled with a powerful emotive connection. The only way to explain this kind of mastery is that van Gogh put his heart into everything he painted, from the most glorious landscape to a pair of old shoes on the floor.

FEELING AND CONCEPTION IN ART

Every human activity incorporates elements of both thought and feeling, conception and intuition, in the process. Painters and sculptors express their feelings and thoughts in the choices they make—the subjects they choose, the color, line, shape, texture, etc. of every stroke. Some of this is deliberate and derived from thought, and some is an impulse derived from feeling.

An artist might express it this way: "The painting needed that red." "I used the big brush to say *power*." "I decided on the limited palette to express the somberness of the narrative."

Artists can tell whether they are "on," that is, intently engaged with what they are doing, or "phoning it in," just working from rote memory. When they are working well, they will say that they can feel their line moving through space, feel the light in their mixtures of paint, feel the paint itself.

What do I mean when I say the artist "feels" the paint? This may be confusing. When I use the word **feeling,** it has a complex meaning, and one that deserves greater clarification.

FEELING for a visual artist means the use of all of his senses—sight, hearing, taste, touch, and smell—to express himself. He uses them all together to aid in the development of the meaning of his work, its concept. My painting teacher's word for the complement of the senses was the **percept.**

The percept is the totality of what the artist's senses and emotion bring to his work. The concept is the mental contribution that identifies and names what the artist is trying to communicate. It takes both **percept** and **concept** to make art.

There is a distinction between "perceptual" art, derived from the senses, and "conceptual" art, derived from an idea. Artists tend to lean toward one camp or the other in their intention, though the distinctions are not absolute. Later in this book, we will discuss conceptual art, mainly in the context of modern art, and clarify those distinctions a bit.

The artist takes all the elements of art we have discussed and then places or arranges them to create his work. This arrangement is called **composition**. The way an artwork is arranged is intrinsic to its success. It might perhaps be clearer if you think of a piece of music and the function served by the arranger, who organizes how the piece is played. An artist does much the same thing when he "arranges" the notes of color, texture, line, etc. onto the surface and creates a composition.

There are many attributes the artist might strive for in composing his work. You know these words, but I'm going to give some quick descriptions here so you can utilize the language when you go to the museum to look at art. Whether a work of art contains any of these attributes or not is not a fact; it is up to the viewer to judge for himself or herself. Know the terms, and understand that you are using them subjectively.

BALANCE: Equilibrium or stability of a design. A composition can seem to be balanced when its two halves are identical (**symmetrical balance**); when they are not identical but seem to work anyway (**asymmetrical balance**); or as the parts relate to a central point (**radial balance**). For the latter, think of a mandala or flower.

Balance alone does not guarantee the success of a composition. An artist may deliberately negate balance to achieve emphasis. He may leave part of a canvas unpainted, for instance, or, to the contrary, highly detailed, while the rest is simple or flat. Perhaps he is making a point as to what he values by doing this.

If the work seems unbalanced or discordant, ask why. Is there a purpose you may not have entertained for this unbalance? Always use these criteria in an open-minded manner. There are many ways they can be applied.

EMPHASIS: Elements are not equal. Emphasizing some and minimizing others delivers the message of the work and tells you what is important to the artist. You may ask, what is the center of interest of the work? What is front and center is usually most important. This is a key element of the composition. Another consideration is **contrast**. Placing different elements against one another or in opposition to one another, like one dark and one light, creates emphasis and interest.

Remember, the way the elements are organized is a key to the work. A very noisy or busy part of a work may need to be offset by a quiet or subdued area, so the noisy part can be seen. The same goes for light and dark patches. A dark shape makes a light shape even more noticeable.

Take notice of the way in which the artist made something in his picture stand out. How did he compose it to achieve this emphasis? When you read the picture this way you are getting into the psyche of the artist.

MOVEMENT: Works of art, though they may be still, can suggest movement. The elements are composed in such a way that your eye moves around the surface. The surface is enlivened by the placement of the shapes, the colors, textures, and lines.

The artist may be offering you a way to enter the work as well as places where your eyes may rest—we refer to the latter as "quiet"—and also a way your eye may exit the work. See if you can visualize this road map for viewing a particular work. It is another way to actively engage with a work. Though it is a still image, you may navigate a trip to view it.

A subcategory of movement is **rhythm**—the artist may succeed in creating a rhythm to the work with his design. Rhythm can be created in a number of ways—via repetition of lines and shapes and intensities of color and line.

Many artists have named their visual compositions as musical forms, i.e. nocturnes, symphonies, etc. When you look at an artwork, see if you can identify and name a musical form that it may suggest.

PATTERN: When linear or color features are repeated, a pattern may be created. The patterning can add to the **rhythm**, **balance** and **harmony** of the piece.

Many artists incorporate decorative patterning into their works, either with line or shades of color repeated in specific shapes. This may also be called "linear texture" when marks or lines are used to create a certain kind of fabric or touch.

Certain cultures and periods have a particular interest in patterning, which shows up in the decoration of their architecture, clothing, and artwork. Some that come to mind are the Moorish patterns and arabesques, Art Nouveau and Art Deco periods, certain folk culture designs from Eastern Europe and others. Gustav Klimt was a specialist in patterning. Can you think of other artists for whom patterns and decorative designs are a significant element in their work?

PROPORTION; The relative size of elements in relation to one another. Artists may and do alter and exaggerate proportional relationships deliberately. The distortion may be a preference or carry a specific meaning.

Certain artists elongate parts of a figure for effect. There are many examples throughout art history of such deliberate distortions—El Greco and the Mannerists, and many painters (think Modigliani) and sculptors (think Giacometti).

Artists throughout history show a preference that often reflects the trends and fashions of their day. This is especially noticeable in figurative works where the fashion may be for plump, rosy-cheeked models or emaciated, frail ones. Sometimes an artist's preference for particular proportions can become a signature. For the voluptuous, think of Rubens, Botero, Maillol, or Henry Moore.

Notice the proportions when you view a work. Do you see irregularities or distortions in the relative sizes of objects? Can you guess the prevailing preferences of the artist's era? Do the exaggerations create a certain meaning or suggest an emotion?

HARMONY, **UNITY**, and **VARIETY:** When the elements of an artwork are working together, harmony and/or unity is achieved. But by no means does a variety of elements necessarily cause disharmony. It may just increase the interest or complexity of the work. Unity does not mean sameness. The artist struggles to achieve both harmony and interest in his work and, as this is a balancing act, may go back and forth, adding and deleting and changing elements until a resolution is achieved.

All of these attributes and principles may be interpreted by the artist in myriad ways. They are not even necessarily thought to be requisites for many artists. I list them here only because the terms are used to describe and evaluate art and, as a student of art appreciation, you should know them. Use them to explain to yourself and others what you perceive, feel, and think when you look at a work of art.

All of these criteria would fall under the purview of the field of Aesthetics. **Aesthetics** is defined as a branch of philosophy that deals with the principles of beauty and artistic taste. When we make judgments about an artwork, we have entered this realm, and the purpose of this book is to delve into aesthetics, and take a look at the underlying foundation of our judgments.

You may associate the word "aesthetics" with a different context. When an artist says, for instance, "This is my aesthetic," he is saying, "This is my sensibility, my approach, my personal vision." He is saying, "This is what art means to me."

We all have an "aesthetic" whether we are artists or not. It expresses in everything we do, in the clothes we choose to wear, in the furnishings we select for our homes. It is also reflected in our impressions of the art we see and the way we determine its value.

The word "aesthetics" literally means "pertaining to the senses." We use our senses, all of them, to determine our conclusive "sense" of what is beautiful, or not. We then apply our mental capacity to formulate a justification, or codify a standard that we apply to create aesthetic judgments.

"Beauty is the eye of the beholder" is a common aphorism, one which most people subscribe to. What it means is that there are no definitive standards that determine whether something is beautiful or ugly, and these determinations are subjective in nature. What is beautiful to me may be ugly to you. I may find beauty where others find nothing at all.

If everything is subjective, can we come to any agreement as to what is beautiful? Is beauty, in fact, relevant in our discussion of an artwork?

We have no way of knowing whether the taste I have of a peach is identical to your taste. When I say the peach is delicious, and you agree, does that mean we've experienced the same taste? This, unfortunately, is unknowable.

What we can do is to break things down, to more definitively pinpoint what we see and feel and identify why we like or dislike it. We define our criteria, like, for instance, proportion, and clarify why the proportions of a given piece of art are pleasing or displeasing to us. We may disagree, but the more we define our terms, the more we can come to understanding, and perhaps can reach some kind of consensus or aesthetic judgment.

You may like the work of Matisse, or dislike it, but whether you do or not, we can probably agree that Matisse used color in a particularly expressive manner. You may like or dislike Picasso's drawing, yet we may all agree that it is exceptional in character and expressiveness.

Reaching the conclusion that the Matisse work is beautiful, though, takes a further leap. Since our criteria for what is beautiful differ, we will never be able to agree on the conclusion.

We cannot definitely assert that an artwork is beautiful, only that it is pleasing to us based on our assumptions, preferences, cultural norms, and the like. Beauty or ugliness is a conditional judgment and can never be verified or conclusive. There is no absolute truth to be determined.

What is important is that we attempt to relate to and understand the artist's vision, to commune with it, to decipher what it has to offer, and to share this with others.

We are all aestheticians when we look at art.

Asking the questions and getting into the finer distinctions is not a frivolous exercise. Let us dig into those aesthetic questions and delve a little further into this whole matter in our next chapter.

Chapter 4

Twenty Questions . . . and One More for Good Measure

1. Does a work of art have to be beautiful?
2. If beauty is not a criterion, what makes something "art"?
3. What is a masterpiece?
4. Can a utilitarian object be art?
5. Is there a difference between craft and art?
6. Why do we like different things?
7. Commercial art vs. fine art: What's the difference?
8. How does art communicate emotion? What place does emotion play in art?
9. Can a child or an animal be an artist?
10. What's the difference between copying, interpreting, and expressing?
11. Is everything in a museum *art*?
12. Do we have to understand culture to judge a work of a given time or place?
13. Is there one criteria or aesthetic standard that transcends culture?
14. Why do some people take an interest in art and others don't?
15. Does thinking and analyzing art ruin the experience of it?
16. What is bad art?
17. Are there any gender differences in art-making?
18. Why do I feel more comfortable with representational art?
19. Is there low art and high art? Can there be a *little* art in something?
20. Can there be too much of a good thing?

And one more for good measure: Why does art matter in my life?

There are surely many more, but these are good questions, and we'll tackle them one by one. Before I do, let me clarify my position.

I'm a practicing artist, not a philosopher or a historian. I have an interest in aesthetic questions, yes, but my answers are all from the artist's point of view. They may not accord with those who approach from a different vantage point. So please take them in the manner in which they are given, as one person's opinions based on her experience. Yours are just as valid, and I hope my thoughts encourage you to delve into your own and express them. Okay?

So, here we go:

1. Does a work of art have to be beautiful?

We've touched on this subject in the last chapter, but it's an essential aesthetic question, so let's go deeper. Let's first define our terms:

Beauty is defined as: "a combination of qualities, such as shape, color, or form, that pleases the aesthetic senses, especially the sight." This is a very general, almost meaningless definition. Surely what pleases one may not please another. Accordingly, there is no general agreement on what is beautiful.

Yet we cannot discard the notion completely, because the word **art** has been inextricably connected to the word **beauty** for centuries. Perhaps what would be more useful is an opening up of the concept of beauty.

Surely, no artist strives to create something ugly in itself, though the particular message he wishes to impart may require something that is certainly not pleasing to the eye. What if we start from our premise that art is communication and judge the "beauty" of an artwork by its success to communicate the artist's message, whatever that might be? Beauty may be redefined not by its appearance, but its expressiveness.

If beauty in art were defined as expressiveness, it would apply to images or creations that might be bright or dark, attractive or utterly unflattering, as each in turn might equally express an emotion, a thought, a perception, a message that the artist intended.

Of course, even if we open up the concept of beauty to be more than attractiveness, and call it expressiveness, this too is equally subjective. We may disagree as to the expressiveness of the work just as we disagree about its beauty. But nonetheless, the former will probably produce more agreement than not.

There is usually common agreement that certain things are beautiful—a flower, a sunset, the smile of a baby—and agreement as well about things that are not beautiful, or are even ugly—a rat, a gnarled tree, a corpse. So too with abstract things; symmetry, light colors, and graceful lines are associated with beauty, while asymmetry, dark colors, and heavy lines are less so.

These associations and conclusions arise from our human incarnation and our particular experience in the world. Sunsets and flowers are nonthreatening and non-offensive; they bring humans simple pleasure. Darkness and death make us afraid; they connote pain and make us look away.

It is wise to remember our prejudices when we look at art and judge its beauty. As humans we are accustomed to a human face looking a certain way; surely an extra-terrestrial who was accustomed to a different universe and life-form would have an entirely different standard of beauty. Even on our own planet, artists from different times and cultures have standards totally different from what we now think of as beautiful.

Think of the nudes of Rubens or the elongated figures of El Greco. They are anomalous to our current "model" standards. I encourage you to keep this in mind when you view art. Throw away the normal, the familiar, the regular conceptions of beauty if you can.

Approach the artwork as a world unto itself. Rather than asking, "Is this beautiful?" ask "What is the artist saying in this work?" What does that treatment of the nude say? Does it have a sensuality a thinner figure could not impart? Why did the artist choose to express in the way he did? In looking at the El Greco, does the elongated figure deliver a feeling of ominousness a more portly figure could not have expressed?

When we see the artist's approach as purposeful, not accidental, as an intentional act to impart a specific message, we are investigating another approach that may lead us to change our opinion of what is beautiful.

This is how art plays a part in advancing consciousness. The artist, less tied to convention than many in his society, often leads a path into new territory and advances the thinking of his time.

Works of art thought ugly or blasphemous in their time are, in later centuries, hailed as hallmarks of beauty. They are accepted as the regular and the normal, only to be displaced by something entirely different that the artists of the time introduce.

Artists are forerunners, and as innovators, they point to a time beyond their experience. Our instinct as viewers may be to initially reject the new, but let's be patient and open-minded. Only "time" will tell us, and there is no other way to assess with certainty the value of a work of art. Certainly not its beauty, as that determination is sure to change with the winds.

2. If beauty is not a criterion, what makes something "art"?

Let's start with intention. If art is communication, which I take as a premise, there has to be an intention on the part of the artist to say something. If a baboon scribbles with a crayon on a paper, even if the result is pleasing, this is not art under this definition. The baboon had no intention to say anything, and any interpretation of the resulting work is accidental. The baboon is not an artist; he is a scribbler.

You might challenge me with the act of an artist who starts a work with no thought in mind. He just throws paint on the canvas willy-nilly, seeing what may turn up. Yes, there may not be an initial intention. However, as he progresses with the work and makes choices, a yellow here, a line there, he does so with intention. Not perhaps with a definitive object in mind, trying to fashion it into a "something," but rather in a kind of instinctive manner. The work needs a red here, a black there, a circular movement, etc. Why is this the case?

The artist is expressing something that does not yet have a name, may in fact never have a name, even if in the end he names it something like *Opus No. 1*, or uses an abstract term like *Serendipity*. The artist has an overriding intelligence that is directing every choice. This is intention, whether it is conscious or unconscious.

We don't often know where we are going with something. But we are continually taking action even without this knowledge. There is a connection between our brain and our hand that is engaged when we make art. It tells us when to go on and when to stop, and ultimately, when we have arrived at the end of the road and have nothing more to say on the subject.

We may even be surprised at what we have wrought, as most artists recognize that what they ultimately come up with is not exactly what they wanted at any given moment. But it is, nonetheless, where all the minute-by-minute choices we made led us. And we claim it as our own.

So, intention and intelligence are criteria. But what about skill? How does skill or ability figure in to whether something is art?

It goes without saying that the more skill an artist possesses, the easier it may be for him to communicate. If you cannot speak or have a limited vocabulary, communicating a message may be exceedingly difficult.

Art-making has been associated with skill for centuries, and artists have been classified as those who have developed the ability to draw and paint well and to make objects that are exceptional in design and craftsmanship. Expertise has been considered a hallmark of the artist's trade, just as it is in every other profession.

But is skill a prerequisite for making art? Can one be clumsy and unskilled and still create a work of art?

I'd love to be able to give you a simple answer, but like all complex questions, the answer is conditional. Firstly, yes, a clumsy, unskilled person can create art, and a work does not have to be expert, neat, and professional to be art. Sometimes, in fact, the clumsiness itself is fundamental to the artfulness.

Think of primitive art or what we call outsider art, where an untrained artist manages to express deep emotion in a childlike manner. Think of a simplified work like Munch's *The Scream* (see Fig. 16 on the next page). As unartful as this picture is, it captivates us with its directness.

Painting it in 1893, Munch took a big chance with this painting, deviating from the reliance on extreme skill of the artists that preceded him. Rather than paint an expertly rendered portrait, he used his brush to create a portrait of inner turbulence. This was a radical departure at this time, and his bravery led to way to Expressionism and the art movements of the twentieth century that followed.

And what propelled Munch to make such a radical departure? The words spill forth: bravery, passion, emotion, the desire to express. We return to expressiveness.

Communication. The painting is expressive and jars us. Its extreme expressiveness is what has made it one of the most recognized works of art as it has truly transcended its time.

We love some works of art and hail their skill, which is some cases is truly astounding. The precision of a Vermeer, the composition of Velázquez, the complexity of Braque, the line of Ingres . . . I could go on. I believe that underlying the skill, though, is something more important.

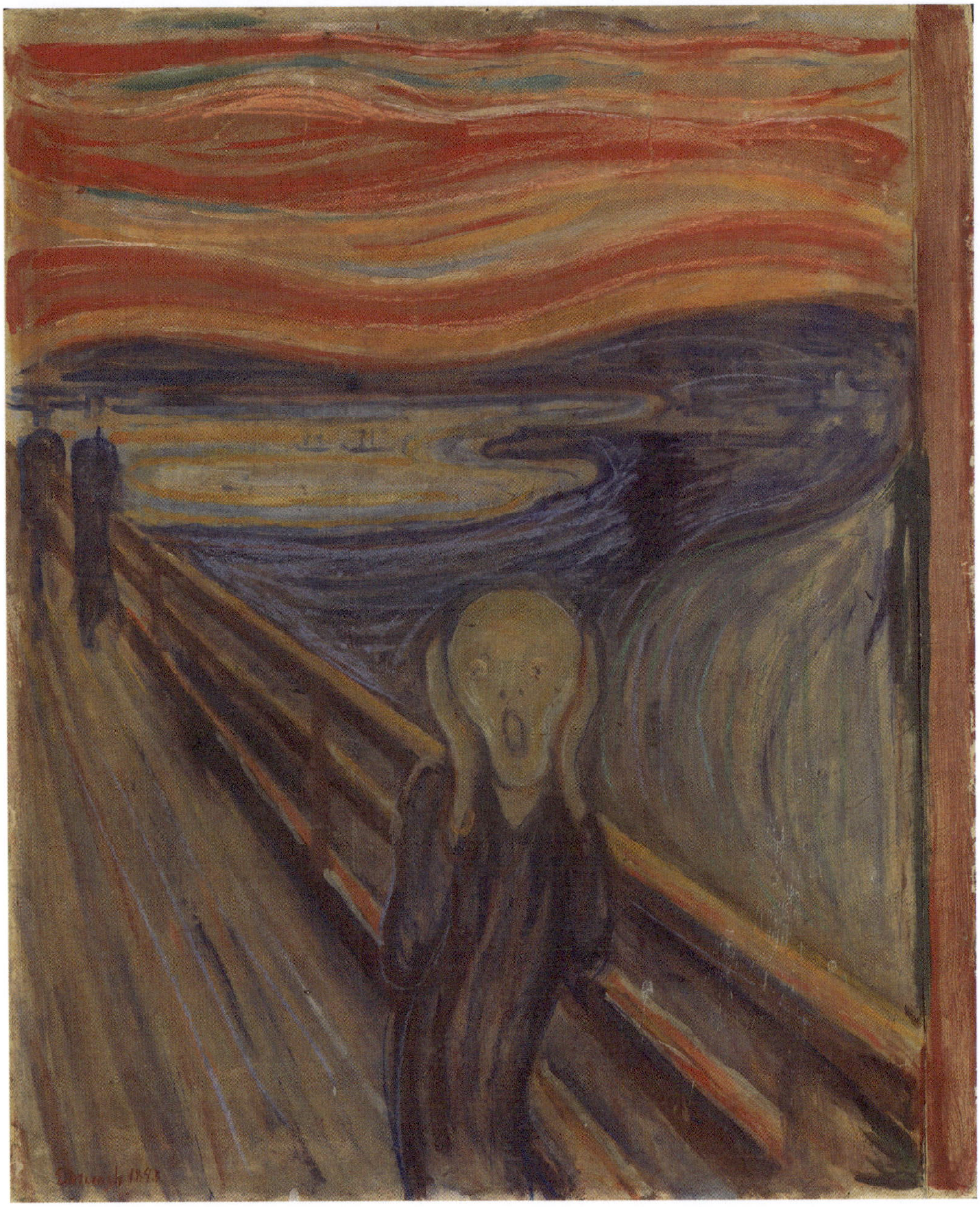

Fig. 16. Edvard Munch, THE SCREAM.

Underlying the skill is the love, the desire to keep studying, experimenting, drawing, until a level of expertise is reached. And why? The reason: to express and to express well.

Artists keep trying to express as fully as their ability allows, and this involves bringing their skill level up. Sometimes, though, the skill will get in the way and overshadow the content. Sometimes we go too far, get too complicated, too carried away, too self-conscious. Then we have to untangle, so as to get back to the essence.

A work of visual art is a unique expression of an idea or emotion. Visual art transcends language. You may try to describe its message, but words are insufficient. Its message lives in the pattern of lines, colors, darks and lights, and shapes that comprise it. Art involves craft, but it not craft alone. Art reflects its time, but goes beyond it.

Art is an expression that cannot be translated, defined, simplified, or changed. It says what could otherwise not be said. It is itself only, and cannot be otherwise. It arises in a crystallized moment in time, and lives forever. It surpasses its creator and is a gift to the universe.

Some works of art speak so effectively and are so pertinent to the human condition that we consider them masterpieces. This we explore in our next question.

3. What is a masterpiece?

An exceptional work? A work of exceptional skill? Yes, surely. But much more.

A masterpiece is a work that achieves with aplomb the delicate balance of skill and passion that so perfectly realizes its subject that we gasp in awe. It somehow stands out among the works created in that time, by that artist, and in that manner, as a work that transcends its time, the artist who created it, and the style in which it was created.

It becomes an emblem of a new time, a new style, and stands with all the masterpieces of all the times and all the styles by all the artists who reached that zenith of creative accomplishment.

A masterpiece often leads a path to something new or magnifies an element that makes us see in a new way. It is a visionary experience. Some examples:

The candlelit world of Caravaggio, a kind of magical illumination
The incredible pathos of a Rembrandt portrait
The exquisite construction of Michelangelo's *Pietà*
The feverish ferocity of a van Gogh sky
The joyous color of a Matisse collage
The gorgeous intimacy of a room by Vuillard
The voluptuousness of a Henry Moore sculpture
The fascinating composition of a Velázquez court painting
The dream of Monet's water lilies

Masterpieces of art are thought to be the best examples of any time or art movement, and there is always disagreement as to this. All of the artists mentioned above pursued their singular obsessions with such fervor that they moved into something they either became known for throughout the history of art, or that moved art into new territory.

See our game in Appendix A, where you can match qualities with artists. As you continue to explore art and become familiar with movements and styles, be on the lookout for the very best examples of the genre, finding in your favorite artworks or artists the very things that interest you or move you.

What makes these works exceptional? Is it the design, the quality of the paint, the drawing, the color balances? What elevates this work from others that are similar? As you ask these questions, your sensitivity to art and your enjoyment is going to the next level. You are becoming not just a lover of art, but a **connoisseur**, someone who, "by study and interest, possesses a heightened appreciation of art."

4. Can a utilitarian object be art?

Every human society makes things that are needed to sustain life. Tools. Utensils. Containers. Some are essentially utilitarian, made to perform a specific task. Invariably, though, the maker opines on the design of his project, making variations that better serve the task, or are more attractive.

He may decide to embellish his useful object, but even just changing the size or the shape of it has an impact on the way it looks. And the maker cannot help but notice that and be pleased, and then continue to make modifications. He is making choices based certainly on usefulness, but also on other elements that have nothing to do with usefulness, like color, decorative patterns, references to animals or faces or trees or whatever.

In so doing, the craftsperson is becoming an artist. Every craftsperson is not an artist and every object is not a work of art. But it can be; it is a matter of emphasis, and, as we discussed previously, intention.

It is also a matter of individuality. You surely don't think of the dishes in your cabinet as works of art. They are primarily utilitarian, though they may be embellished with designs. But you may have one dish that you selected for its design that was made by someone whose intention was to make a beautiful object or a work of art. The fact that it can be used as a receptacle does not diminish the fact that it was created as a work of art.

It may even have a primary purpose as a container, yet still be a bona fide work of art.

There are great examples of this in the museums of the world: elaborate canes with carved heads, fetish objects created for worship, sarcophagi adorned to contain the dead, and all manner of plates, bowls, hair ornaments, tools, chairs, etc. made as works of art.

But stop for a moment. Is a well-designed chair a work of art? Not necessarily; it is just a well-designed chair. Its design does not make it a work of art. It must cross a line to become art.

The line it must cross is the line that makes the work transcend its function. Its quality must be such that the design and treatment surpasses the function to become something other, more than, what the function demands. This is a difficult and ever-moving standard and certainly highly debatable.

We discuss this further in the next related question, but to answer this one: a utilitarian object can be art, but it must be more than well made to rise to this designation.

5. Is there a difference between craft and art?

What is craft? The utilization of skill to create something, usually associated with the making of objects. Though paintings and sculptures are objects too, these are usually excepted from craft. But there are many points at which craft and art intersect, and the differences are much debated.

Think of the crafts, or what activities are commonly thought of as crafts: carpentry and furniture-making, glassmaking, pottery and ceramics, metalsmithing, fabric and textiles, sewing and quilting, etc. All may result in the creation of useful objects, some of which may rise to the level of art, but not all.

Let's look at what is required in both activities. Skill, yes. Design, yes. Intelligence, planning, yes too. An artist must utilize craft. But does a craftsman necessarily make art?

There are some inherent differences. Making art arises from the intention to make a statement, be it emotional, narrative, or political. Making craft does not usually or necessarily arise from a similar intention. The craftsman may simply wish to construct a sturdy bench or a deeply grooved pot.

Can this be true of a painting or sculpture? It can certainly be mundane or merely decorative, lacking content. Every painting and sculpture is not, by its nature, a work of art.

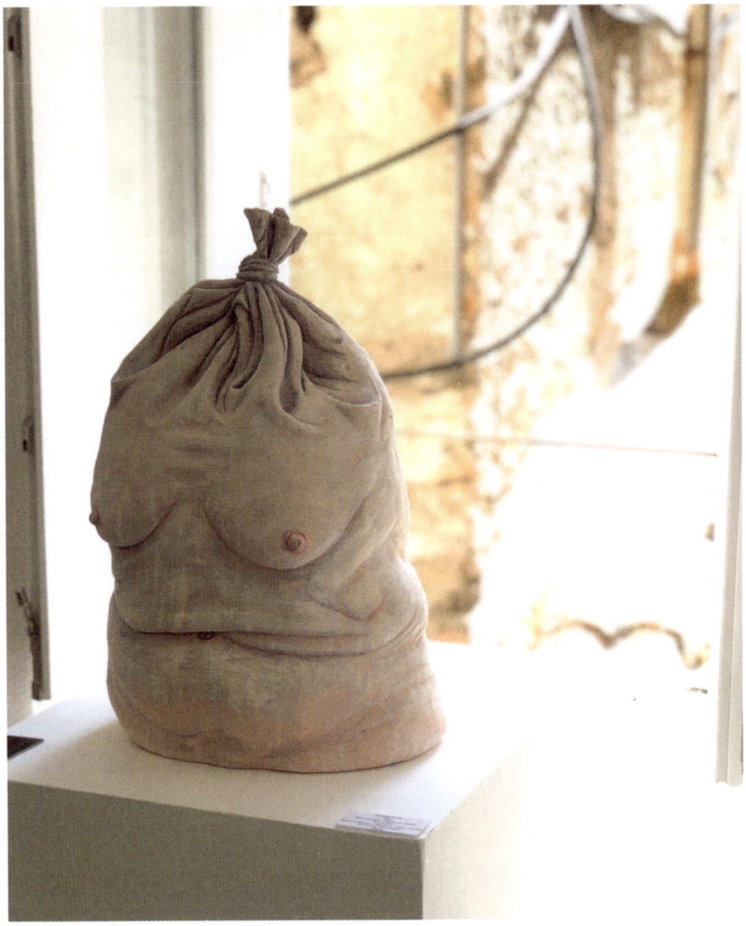

Fig. 17. Phoebe Scott, TORSO, PRESSED.

So it is not the medium that determines whether the object, be it a work of wood or textile or a painting, is art. Nor is it the process or the activities that are used to make it.

Again, we return to familiar ground. What makes it art is that it expresses something that arises out of the human experience, that transcends functionality, utility, and the like. It is not that art has to be a useless object. It is, instead, that its artfulness resides in something other than its utility.

Let me give you an example of a wonderful work of art created in clay by the contemporary artist Phoebe Scott (Fig. 17).

The work depicts a female torso tied by a string. Strikingly evocative, my first impression of seeing this work was to see it as a visual pun, that of the characterization of an older women as an "old bag." Phoebe tells me that much of her work is concerned with the lack of regard society pays to the aging woman.

This work is clearly a work of art, created with intention, artfully made and most important, truly expressive. The medium chosen is crucial to the message the work conveys; it could not have been expressed more effectively in another medium.

Art or craft? Neither the medium, nor the process, nor the material is determinative. There is craft (skill) required in craft and in art. And the line between craft and art can be very small and tenuous. And debatable. Art may incorporate craft, but transcends it. Art may lack craft and yet still be art; the crudeness of the message may in fact **be** the message.

Great craft can rise to the status of art when the object created possesses a unique beauty or character that speaks to us. Or it can just be great craft, something beautifully made.

6. Why do we like different things?

Ah, a great question.

We like different things because we are different. We have different experiences, come from different cultures, have different environments, live in different times.

Just as our taste in food differs, so does our taste generally. Can we infer that because many people like pizza and french fried potatoes and whipped cream that there is something to a popular or universal taste?

We do know that people in Russia like borscht, a cold pink soup, that is distasteful to people in the United States, that people in Japan like raw fish, which many people do not like, very few people like anchovies, and so on. But again, we don't know why, except that these foods are familiar and native to these communities and people may have "developed" a taste for them.

Aha.

Taste can be developed.

Just like food, certain familiar environments may please residents familiar with them, and fail to charm others from far away. We are comfortable with the familiar. The sight of haystacks to a rural person may seem comforting, but make little impression on an urban person. And likewise, the urbanite might adore that new skyscraper while the farmer sees an abomination.

Since most of us in modern life are now exposed to many environments and places, if not physically then through the Internet, our tastes may be widening and developing.

It is surely true that the more we are exposed to, the more our eyes are opened, and our tastes likewise may expand.

Nonetheless, we will always have propensities to like certain things, certain characteristics, over others. Most people, for instance, prefer symmetry over more random designs. Many like repetitive patterns, but may dislike ones that have a dizzying effect.

When it comes to color, people have strong preferences and likes and dislikes. Because we all enjoy the sky and are enchanted by water, blue may always be a favorite color.

Yellow, the sun color, buoys our spirits; red excites us, green is our favorite resting color. We like white for its simplicity and universality. When it comes to black, we like it in our clothes (partly because it makes us look slim) but not on our walls. These are the general preferences, though there are always exceptions.

And the exceptions are caused by our personalities, the unique combinations of DNA and experience that each human represents. Some things suit us, resemble us, and others seem foreign. Our tastes follow those patterns.

Every year the paint companies come up with a palette of colors that are the prevailing likes of that particular year. Some of these choices are a reflection of what's going on in society or in the world at the time. Neutrals are popular in stressful times; bright colors sometimes rise to popularity during exceptional occurrences. Sometimes we prefer to be understated; at other times bold.

In other words, taste is a function of many factors, some known and some not. Familiarity is basic and determinative. Mood is a major factor. Culture often influences our likes and dislikes as we are encouraged to conform.

Art is so varied that there are pieces that appeal to many people for many different reasons. That is a good thing—we can't all like the same art just as we can't all like the same hat. Some of it suits us, some not.

The interesting thing and what we're looking into here is not that you prefer one work of art over another—that is a given—but why?

Just like the popular color blue, many people find they can relate to the lovely hues of Impressionist works, with their recognizable forms and places, and the tender treatment with which the artist has rendered them. Impressionism is very accessible to many and is probably the most popular of all the art movements for these reasons.

But lovers of Impressionism can also enjoy the ingenuity of Picasso, the simplicity of Rothko, the genius of Rembrandt, all for different reasons. We love ice cream, but we don't want it at every meal.

Let's enjoy many art forms for what they have to offer us, while still honoring our particular set of tastes. As we move through this volume, we'll be exploring taste in discussion, exercises, and games, and I daresay that the result will be that while we are pinpointing what you like, your set of likes will tend to increase.

The more you know about art, the more you will be able to discern why you like something and the more open you will be to other forms of expression.

7. Commercial art vs. fine art: What's the difference?

The word *commercial* contains the answer. Commercial art has a purpose and that is to advance through imagery something that is for sale. It is usually associated with advertising and may have a mass appeal and exposure. But commercial art may also include illustration for entertainment, like cartoon or animation. It may and often does enhance text, as in illustration, and may be descriptive or fanciful. It is often created for a client who may be a seller, or other enterprise like a theater, film studio, or any other commercial venture.

Many commercial art pieces can rise to the level of being considered works of art. They can and often are highly expressive and potent. I can think of a few of these that were made for a sales purpose but went on to transcend that purpose. Consider, for instance the posters for the Barnum & Bailey Circus. They are marvelous and yes, art.

The difference between commercial and fine art is that fine art is created by the artist as purely an expression, with no intention of promoting anything other than itself. It may be subsequently sold but it is not created as a commercial venture. When a work is commissioned for a special purpose, it may cross the line into commercial art, but not necessarily. The distinction arises out of intention, not style or execution.

I think of some of the illustrations by Toulouse-Lautrec that were created as commercial art, but because of their beauty and universality, rise to the level of fine art (see Fig. 18 on the next page). Norman Rockwell would be another prime example. There are some exceptionally talented artists who create posters

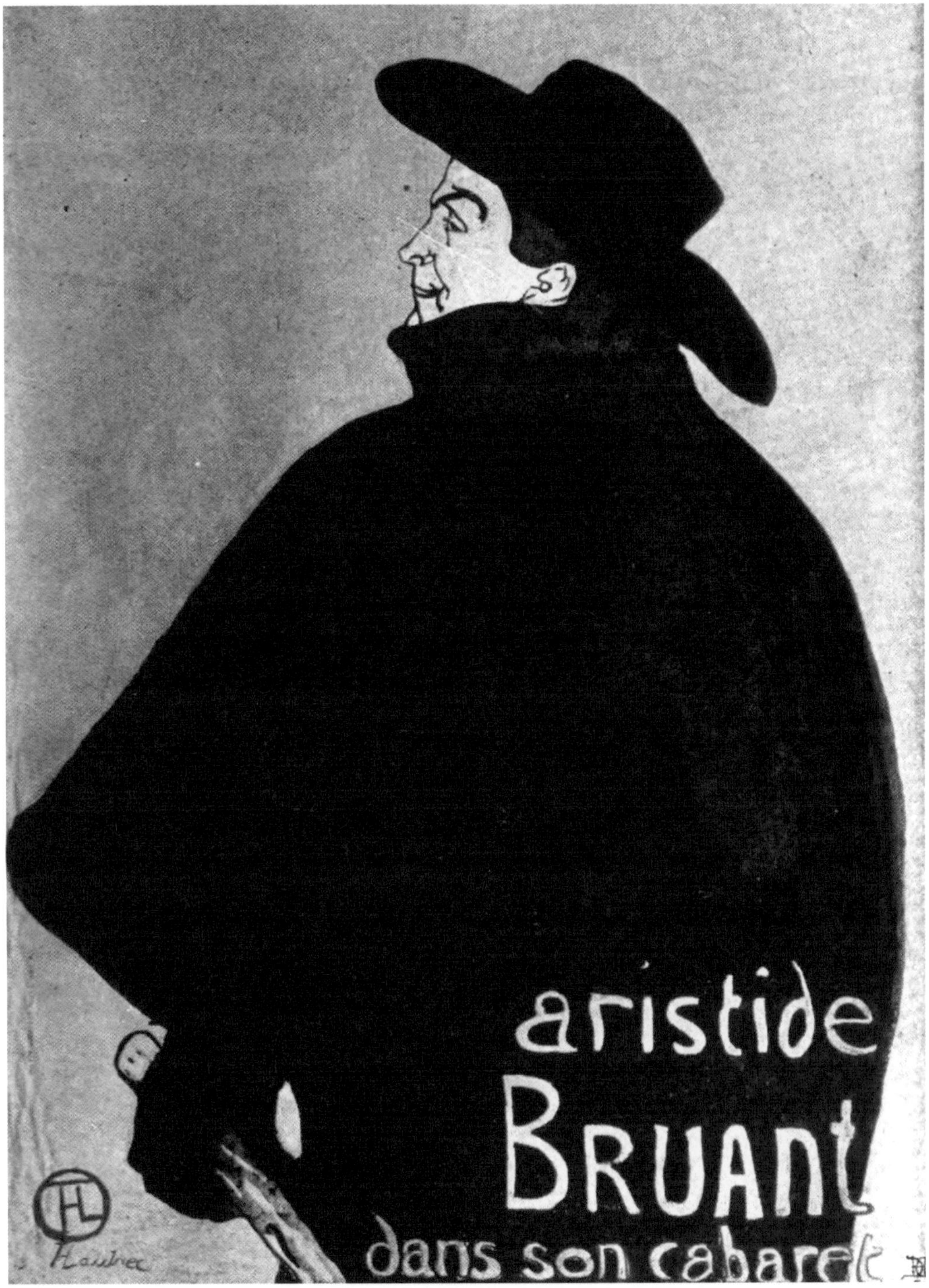

Fig. 18. Henri de Toulouse-Lautrec, POSTER FOR ARISTIDE BRUANT.

for theater productions and movies, and some of these are especially expressive, rivaling Toulouse-Lautrec in modernity. Look at the poster for the musical *Wicked* as an example. Someday in the future, these may leave their commercial purpose in the dust and be considered artworks in their own right.

8. How does art communicate emotion? What place does emotion play in art?

We are moved by many things. All the tools in the visual artist's toolbox have the ability to stir us. We react emotionally to color, shape, size, line, texture, and to the narrative or characterization an image may convey.

The unique ways an artist expresses his or her own preferences, likes, and visual obsessions are interpreted by the viewer and carry a mood and emotional temperature. You may interpret a set of somber colors as sad, and likewise be buoyed by a lively pattern of bright colors. You may be touched by the tender water lilies of Monet, amused by a whimsical sculpture by Picasso. You may enjoy the serenity of a Frankenthaler color field or the drama of a Motherwell black-and-white. The sensuality of a Moore sculpture may captivate you while the Giacometti thin man disturbs your equilibrium.

Artworks are made by human beings with a whole bag of emotions, and that comes through into their work. As a fellow human viewer you are able to read those emotions, and this plays a big part in determining how you feel about them and consequently whether you like them or not.

As we've said over and over, art is communication, and since emotion is a major component of our lives, it plays an essential part in art. Remember the word *art* lives in the word *heart*, and in fact heart is at the center of art-making and art-viewing. The work can be expert, but if it does not convey emotion, it may only be wallpaper. Wallpaper is decorative, but it is not art; art has to do more than cover a wall to be art. It has to express human emotion or cause us to have an emotion.

9. Can a child or an animal be an artist?

Only a human can be an artist because only a human has a developed consciousness.

When it comes to a child, the answer is more complicated. A child may do something that is artful, even beautiful, but he or she does not know why. The knowledge and awareness are just not developed enough.

Some children are very precocious and do have a sense of artfulness and make art choices more deliberately. Some people may consider them artists.

Though art effects can often be created by accident, the artist has awareness that those effects are valuable and important. Children often cannot tell the difference. It is my opinion, and I am sure many people would disagree, that being an artist requires a more engaged and aware consciousness that most children have not yet achieved. I, therefore, would not call them artists. They are talented children who may become artists as they evolve.

10. What's the difference between copying, interpreting, and expressing?

Artists use source material and prompts all the time—photographs, other artists' works, their own prior works, drawings—in addition to working directly from life or exclusively from their imaginations. Whether they copy, interpret, or express is a function of how they deal with those source materials, including their work from life.

It is a misnomer to use the word *copy*, as there is no way to make an exact copy. The word could be replaced by *translate*, as every copy is actually a translation into a two- or three-dimensional medium. The artist may believe he is copying, but this is nigh on impossible. He is actually attempting to imitate or reproduce the look of what he sees but is doing it in a different language, the language of his medium.

The intention when a realist artist draws from life may be to make a very close facsimile of what he sees. He is trying to imitate the relative size, shape, color, proportion, texture, and lightness of his source and reproduce it on his surface.

If, instead of a direct reproduction, his intention is to interpret, the approach is entirely different. The artist is permitting himself to take license with all of these elements and to alter their appearance to suit himself. He can alter just some of the elements or most of them, make certain things more prominent and others diminished.

To interpret and to express are close in meaning, with slightly different shadings. An interpretation is a way to see something and to explain it, and an expression is more involved with emotion. It is a way to make one's feelings known.

In art, an expression may possibly be more personal or exaggerated than an interpretation of the same source, yet both are specific to the artist and represent the intention to change the source in a particular way.

These words—copy, translation, interpretation, expression—are now part of your vocabulary in discussing art.

11. Is everything in a museum *art*?

What you see in an art gallery or art museum has been selected by a curator or curatorial board. The art accepted for exhibition fulfills the mission of these individuals and also their personal taste.

Art curators are often art history majors and not artists themselves and may have a historical bent rather than an artistic one. Their choices are a reflection of their education and orientation to art.

Art curators, like literature critics, often read into works of art connections that I, as a practicing artist, see as problematic and something, frankly, that the artist never considered when making the work. I know how art evolves and often find the little explanations of the artworks in the museum to be pure poppycock. Of course, it is entirely possible that they may elucidate something the artist never considered yet was nonetheless true.

The artworks in the museums of the world, though vast, represent only a small sampling of the art that has been and is being produced by many wonderful yet unsung artists.

Collectors, including museum collectors, often have a bias toward the most recognizable names in art, and fail to show many of the exceptional works by lesser-known artists.

Though museums are often not-for-profit cultural institutions, they have to remain open, and to do so they must attract the public. The big names in art accomplish that for them, and this influences the curatorial selections.

So, everything in the museum may technically be art, but it is not necessarily the best art nor the best examples of any particular artist. The explanations for the work may be true, partially true, or unsubstantiated.

Keep this in mind when you visit the museum. When you complete this book, you will have the tools to draw your own thoughtful conclusions about works of art.

12. Do we have to understand culture to judge a work of a given time or place?

Undeniably, it helps to have a context for evaluating a work of art. Understanding the forces at work in the societies and times in which the artists lived provides helpful clues.

Art movements are a reflection of the state of knowledge and prevailing culture of the artists' milieu. One leads to another. As new work enters the public consciousness, it becomes acceptable. Then usually artists will move to push the envelope even further, and new ways of making art enter the scene.

Artists by nature always seek new ways to individuate themselves and personalize their expressions. Once art genres become commonplace, the boundaries will begin to expand. This is true throughout art history.

It is also true that though culture influences art and is a reflection of prevailing mores and standards, art plays a large part in advancing culture. Artists are usually the most forward-looking individuals of their times, and their desire to express often encourages them to try new techniques and approaches, which in term have the effect of opening the minds of viewers and in turn advancing the culture.

Some notable examples include:

> **Leonardo da Vinci**, born 1452, defined as the epitome of the Renaissance, the "Renaissance man." Not only one of the greatest painters of all time, he is thought to be one of the most talented individuals in history. Creator, inventor, architect, genius.
>
> **Michelangelo Merisi da Caravaggio,** born 1571, who incorporated such a dramatic use of chiaroscuro in his work that he influenced many great painters to follow him. A true revolutionary of light.
>
> **Rembrandt van Rijn**, born 1606, considered one of the greatest painters of his day and of every age, his skill in portraiture unsurpassed. Beyond his enormous painting prowess, however, there is an intimacy and empathy to his creations that is amazing. So much so that another painter of great feeling, the magnificent Vincent van Gogh, said of Rembrandt, "Rembrandt goes so deep into the mysterious that he says things for which there are no words in any language."

Francisco Goya, born 1746, a court painter, who is one of the forerunners of modern art. He worked in a traditional style of his times in the making of his portraits, yet expanded the medium with his emotional, romantic diversions.

J. M. W. Turner, born 1775, a landscape painter whose airy washes presaged Impressionism.

Paul Cézanne, born 1839, is considered a Postimpressionist painter and a bridge to Cubism, with his color divisions defining planes of light.

Claude Monet, born 1840, whose revelations of light set the stage for Impressionism. He is considered by many to be its founder.

Pablo Picasso, born 1881, the great experimenter, who is almost synonymous with modern art. He kept pushing the envelope as his creativity knew no bounds.

Jackson Pollock, born 1912, whose decision to pour the paint and drip it, made us look at painting in a whole new way.

And many, many others . . . .

The more we know, the better. So yes, understanding history can give a framework to understanding art. It helps us to recognize the artists whose work contributed to advancing the culture from which their work arose, gave us new eyes, so to speak, and in their way, advanced civilization.

13. Is there one criteria or aesthetic standard that transcends culture?

There is excellence in every era, every genre, and every style of art throughout history. Though art has expanded through the centuries as new materials, insights, and methodologies have been introduced, one cannot say that modern art transcends the art of the past vis-à-vis its aesthetic value. The new does not supplant the old in terms of value.

Indeed, the masterworks of the greatest artists of all time stand out and survive, surpass and outlive their time and culture. Though they may be familiar to us today, they are as fascinating as they ever were, because their expressiveness transcends style or technique.

The reason these works live on is individual to them and due to the specific gifts of their creators. The individual style or technique employed may be much imitated throughout history but lacks the aplomb and originality of the master. This is why painters through the ages look to these geniuses, consider them painters' painters, and attempt to scale the heights they have achieved.

But, in my opinion, and I can certainly be wrong, no one can quite paint the tearful eyes of a Rembrandt, the evanescent fog of a Turner, the potent sunlight of a Monet, or the bravado of a Picasso. These are heights to attempt that can never be surpassed.

14. Why do some people take an interest in art and others don't?

No two humans are alike. Our brains are complex and develop in myriad ways, and what was originally thought to be intelligence is now thought of as plural, intelligences. Visual intelligence is just one of the brain measurements.

Some of us are born with a higher visual intelligence; others develop a strong visual intelligence. Though most of us can see, some of us see more than others, and are more interested in what we see.

The kind of visual intelligence required of an artist is extreme. In my book *The Creative Path*, I described three kinds of seeing: perfunctory, attentive, and engaged. Those individuals possessing perfunctory vision basically use their eyes in a practical manner, naming what they see and navigating the world. Individuals with attentive vision notice more subtleties of vision, and they use for eyes for pleasure. They see more shades of color, texture, rhythm, line, etc., and their greater visual intelligence makes them likely to take an interest in art. Should they decide to become practitioners of art, they would have to raise their visual intelligence to the third level, that of engaged seeing, enabling them to take visual sensations and employ them in creative ways.

I strongly believe that visual intelligence can be taught and nurtured, and that is exactly what I am attempting to accomplish with this book. As you learn these basic principles and then apply them to viewing art, your visual intelligence expands and grows.

15. Does thinking and analyzing art ruin the experience of it?

A complex question. Preconceived ideas can stop us from having a direct experience. If you had come to the conclusion "I love Monet but I hate Picasso," your mind might be somewhat closed when you came up upon a Monet you did not like or a Picasso you loved. Or perhaps you would not permit yourself to change your mind.

So going to look at art without preconceived conclusions is probably a good thing. Being completely open to *finding* the good is the best approach to utilize when viewing art, or really anything, for that matter. Never start with the no.

But that being said, it doesn't follow that you cannot study all the facets of art. The more you know, the wider will be your appreciation field. Study away, but when you get to the museum, toss the opinions out, just take it all in, and look before you leap.

You may find your perceptions and opinions changing as you learn more and look more.

You may start out thinking minimalism is a crock, but when you learn how it arose and what it means, you may even find some beauty in it.

The key is to be open, not uninformed.

16. What is bad art?

Let's put it this way: There is art that strives for expressiveness, authenticity, and originality and there is art that is made for effect, imitation, sentimentality, and sensationalism. Learning to tell the difference is a function of careful and informed viewing.

17. Are there any gender differences in art-making?

This is an interesting topic, and the verdict is not in, as much of art has been dominated by men. In contemporary art, this is less true, as women artists have been and continue to be recognized and their work exhibited and discussed.

There are many women now in art school, studying and teaching art, even demanding disciplines once closed to them, and gender parity in the arts is improving.

As society achieves more acceptance of women as first-class citizens, and recognizes non-gender-identified individuals, the answer to this question may become clear. We still live in a culture with strong gender-associated norms and opinions about what is appropriate for men and women.

The existing gender biases and associations surely and decidedly have an impact on the subjects artists choose and how they depict those subjects, their style and orientation and concerns. As we look at art, this is an element worthy of discussion as we compare works by men and women.

18. Why do I feel more comfortable with representational art?

Most people do feel more comfortable looking at representational art because of the element of familiarity. Whether it is fully representational or semi-abstract, recognizing the subject matter gives us a starting point.

You may refer the image to your impression of the subject. "I like this painting of a sunset. It is extremely intense." "I don't like the way the artist elongated the torso of this figure." "I like the way the artist used blue in the shadow. It is beautiful." We have something to hang our hat on.

With totally nonobjective work, we are lost. What are we looking at? You may admire the colors—"I like that red blotch in the corner"—or the way the paint is applied—"It really feels vibrant." We may look at a minimalist work and have no point of reference at all. "It looks like an empty canvas."

Viewers may associate abstract work with the paintings their five-year-olds bring home from school. "My kid could do that."

The truth is that nonobjective works *are* more difficult to read, and we need to know something about art to evaluate and enjoy these works. Here are some of the questions we might ponder: "Are the shapes symbolic?" "Does the piece suggest a spatial field?" "Is the artist most interested in color, texture, rhythm?" "What kind of music does this piece make me think of?"

The last question is an interesting one. We can accept music as abstract—we use words like *classical* and *romantic* and *folksy* to describe it. But, with the exception of music that contains lyrics, and therefore, subject matter, instrumental music is nonobjective. Yet we find it acceptable.

We can do the same for nonobjective art. We are just in the habit of identifying what we see and naming it. It does take a bit of a stretch to get into abstract art. But our enhanced art vocabulary is sure to help!

19. Is there low art and high art? Can there be a little art in something?

Yes, of course. In a masterpiece, all the elements work together in magnificent harmony. But every work of art is not a masterpiece.

The work can fail in its mission and yet still contain an element that is worthy of praise.

Looking for these exceptional elements is something you will now be able to do, as you read the works of a given artist.

Every artist has something that is his or her specialty, something they do exceptionally well. Look at the laughing figure in a Franz Hals portrait—he nailed that exuberant expression. Bonnard, a wonderful painter, made wonder with his portrayal of water—his bath paintings are a marvel. The playfulness of Klee, the elegance of Modigliani, the ____________________ of ____________________. Look for our games section where you can fill in these blanks as you get into discovering the hallmark of cvcry artist you look at.

You will also notice that not every work of a master painter is a masterpiece. We all, even the greatest of the greats, have our good and bad days. Can you tell the difference?

20. Can there be too much of a good thing?

Yes, sometimes overfamiliarity breeds contempt, and this is an injustice to the artist. When Leonardo da Vinci created the *Mona Lisa*, he never contemplated she would come alive in a television commercial about a credit card. But alas, she has. He never dreamed folks would draw mustaches on her, deface her, and yes, ruin it for everyone.

It takes fresh eyes to enjoy art, and when our eyes have been exposed to ridicule, mockery, and derision, our experience has been spoiled. Just like the artist has to savor the birth of every new work, the viewer needs to look past the old familiar faces, to some unknown and underappreciated artists and their work.

Instead of flocking to the museum to line up and see the popular favorites, I encourage you to enjoy the quieter back rooms of museums and galleries showcasing new work. Your eyes will be freshened and revived, and this will help when you encounter one of the overused, overprinted superstars that are very unfortunately just too familiar to any longer be seen and appreciated.

And one more for good measure: Why does art matter in my life?

Art, all the arts, offer us so much. The practice of the arts and the enjoyment of them are uniquely human endeavors. They require us to be our best selves, to be smart, sensitive, open, clever, empathetic, imaginative, and a host of other adjectives.

The need to express, to individuate, and to share finds its home in the arts. What else would we do with our feelings and thoughts? Where would we put them?

Visual art is just one of the ways to express, but it is a favorite because human beings like to make things. Writing is great, but not concrete enough for many. Acting, dance, all performance is so expressive, but uses the self as material. Music is a gift that enthralls us, but not an ability many possess. Visual art is a maker's art—we craft something that is concrete, can be seen, and lives on after us. This is something many people want to do, and have done throughout history and in all cultures.

The wonder is that every piece of visual art is unique, every artist has his or her own way of tackling the form, and there's no end to what can be conjured. Visual art is just fun to make, and it is also fun to look at.

The viewer of art is at a banquet, with every color, texture, shape, and form laid out to savor, gobble up, and revisit. We don't need art to survive, but it makes our survival really interesting. Whether you are a maker or a viewer, art makes our lives better. And that matters a lot. Enjoy!

Chapter 5
Art Speak: Quotes by Famous Artists

Artists tend to be pretty thoughtful people, and we are fortunate to have some of these thoughts memorialized as "famous quotes." They give us a window into the psychological, philosophical, and practical processes the artist has gone through and what his art means to him, and therefore, to us.

I've selected a few of these quotes and offer them to you with some explanation of why they are important to me and how they may help you to view art in general. This is only a sampling, of course, and there are many others you may find by searching in books and online. They can only enrich your enjoyment of art, and since that's what we are trying to do here, enjoy these and look for more.

On working from life:

"Painting from nature is not copying the object;
it is realizing one's sensations."
—Paul Cézanne

Cézanne tells us the artist reacts to nature and paints his reaction. He is moved by what he sees and that's what we see on the canvas—his preferences and affection for what is before him. Artists don't copy; they read, translate, and reinvent.

On intent:

"I applied streaks and blobs of color onto the canvas with a palette knife,
and I made them sing with all the intensity I could. . . ."
—Vasily Kandinsky

Kandinsky metaphorically uses the word "sing" to describe what he wants his colors and shapes to do. What does it mean for a note of color to "sing"? It means that the pieces of paint are so effectively played that they not only seem vibrantly alive, speak their message, but do it with the flourish of a song.

On the meaning of abstraction:

"The longer you look at an object, the more abstract
it becomes, and, ironically, the more real."
—Lucien Freud

Freud is talking here about a kind of engaged perception the artist utilizes. When he studies an object, it kind of decomposes before his eyes. In thinking about reconstructing it on the canvas, he has to take it apart, and when he does, he sees it as a collection of shapes, lines, colors, and textures. In other words, as an abstraction.

He is not making it up, he is seeing it for what it truly is, what it is made of. This is reality for the artist.

On self-consciousness:

"It took me four years to paint like Raphael,
but a lifetime to paint like a child."
—Pablo Picasso

It would take most of us more than a few years to paint like Raphael, but Picasso was a gifted draftsperson. What he means here is that skill in art is something that can be learned, but the kind of spontaneity, freshness, joie de vivre, and authenticity a child possesses by virtue of his innocence, is much more difficult to achieve as a mature adult than mere skill. It takes a whole undoing of all the lessons we learned to become well-behaved adults to become new again in art.

On finding oneself in art:

"Art is the only way to run away without leaving home."
—Twyla Tharp

This is such a scintillating quote about what being an artist can accomplish. It is at the same time a "voyage of the spirit," or a "vision quest," a "getaway," a "walk-about," an "expedition," and an opportunity to find your true self in the process, as it is a "homecoming."

On how hard it is to be an artist:

"If people knew how hard I worked to get my mastery,
it wouldn't seem so wonderful at all."
—Michelangelo

"Painting is easy when you don't know how,
but very difficult when you do."
—Edgar Degas

Great masters make it seem easy, but they know more than anyone that making art is not easy at all. The nature of visual art is such that we only get to see the last few moments in a very long story, and the final work appears to have sprung to life like magic. This is very misleading and may give people the idea that it is easy to make art. It is not.

It takes years of study and practice especially to learn to draw. Viewers, for the most part, don't get to see all the mistakes, failures, and missed opportunities. Only the artist knows what he's done and not done. No magic, just a lot of hard work and dedication.

On state of mind:

"The works must be conceived with fire in the soul
but executed with clinical coolness."
—Joan Miró

Here's another brilliant statement of what it takes to make great art. You need passion, yes, to conceive, but knowledge and skill to make it happen. This is the great balance of art-making. Too much passion, and the work is a mess; too much care, and it loses its vitality. Hitting that sweet spot—joyous articulation—wow, that's no easy task.

On spontaneity:

"A really good picture looks as if it's happened at once. It's an immediate image. For my own work, when a picture looks labored and overworked . . . I usually throw these out, though I think very often it takes ten of those over-labored efforts to produce one really beautiful wrist motion that is synchronized with your head and heart, and you have it, and therefore it looks as if it were born in a minute."
—Helen Frankenthaler

This is another way to say what Miró said and amplifies how an artist often achieves that look of spontaneity and perfect balance—through many tries. The grand finale is the masterpiece, but it only could have happened because of all those missed attempts. Then the moment comes; the hard work is hidden, and just the reward comes to the fore.

What is painting?:

"Painting is poetry that is seen rather than felt,
and poetry is painting that is felt rather than seen."
—Leonardo da Vinci

Isn't this a brilliant way to explain what painting is—a seen poem? Spectacular! Also his definition of a poem—a felt painting. Genius!

On what art is:

"Painting is just another way of keeping a diary."
—Pablo Picasso

Only a genius like Picasso could be so matter-of-fact with this definition and yet so correct. What is a diary? It is a writing from the heart about one's thought and feelings.

Isn't that what an artist does every day in the studio?

On talent:

"Everyone has talent but not everyone has rags."
—Norman Raeben

This was the opening quote in my book, *The Creative Path: A View from the Studio on the Making of Art*, delivered in art class by my teacher and mentor, Norman Raeben. What he meant by this comment was that artists needed more than talent to create art.

He downplayed talent, as he saw it as just something some had by virtue of skills they had developed or even inherent ability, and focused on what art required of its practitioners—determination, vision, and persistence. Those rags represented getting into the trenches and working at one's art with fervor and unrelenting passion. Talent could be frittered away, make the artist self-conscious or insipid, while hard work mixed with emotional juice was the formula for greatness.

Art is not created by magic; it is a demanding profession indeed.

On how to enjoy art:

"Everyone discusses my art and pretends to understand, as if it were necessary to understand, when it is simply necessary to love."
—Claude Monet

Yes, such a wise statement from a man who had such an extraordinary ability to love. He loved light so much he made countless pictures of the same things just to admire what the light did to color. But for many of us less-talented viewers, whose ability to love may not be as great, let's remember that understanding opens not only the mind. It opens the heart too. When you understand more, you can love more. That's what we're doing here.

On the purpose of art:

"Art is not what you see, but what you make others see."
—Edgar Degas

"The object of art is not to reproduce reality,
but to create a reality of the same intensity."
—Alberto Giacometti

"A true artist is not one who is inspired, but one who inspires others."
—Salvador Dalí

All of these thoughts express the ability of art to educate and enlighten the viewer.

The artist gives us the tools to see things differently, to open our eyes and minds to a new reality. The artist is a trendsetter, and this is expressed well in this quote by the dancer Martha Graham, who said, "No artist is ahead of his time. He *is* his time. It's just that others are behind the times." We can catch up by being intelligent viewers and appreciators of art.

Chapter 6
Looking at Art: General Criteria

The history of art is long and complex and has evolved in fascinating ways. As an artist I am fascinated with the entire range of art that has been created through the centuries. But, alas, I am not an art historian. I approach art as a practitioner and an informed viewer.

My painting teacher, Norman Raeben, used to tell his students that every artist, in a sense, goes through the major movements in his or her own development as an artist, and I think this is true. We begin as primitives and gain sophistication as we grow and practice. We all learn from what has preceded us.

So too with artists throughout history. Art movements arise at a certain time, but they don't end there. Echoes of the major styles and movements show up in contemporary work too, and the purpose of this chapter is to help you recognize these echoes when you see them.

Most books on art appreciation are focused on art history. The author takes you through the major movements or focuses on a specific movement. You learn about the culture of the times in which these works emerged, the biographies of the artists, and the stages of their work.

There are basically two formats in analyzing art: formalism and contextualism. The formalist approach looks at each work in and of itself as an entire world, and the contextual approach evaluates it, as the word suggests, in the context of the place, time, and conditions under which it has emerged. Both are valid and interesting methods for evaluating art, though conclusions will diverge depending on the approach taken to study them.

My approach here to is to somewhat disregard, or at least not focus on, the time and place works of art were created, and to see them as stations on a universal playing field.

Time simply does not exist in our world. All of the artworks we shall examine have many things in common. We will be looking at these commonalities, the threads that weave through all of them.

It goes without saying that learning is evolutionary. One discovery leads to the next and builds upon it. When we look at the art of a certain era, it helps to be cognizant of the worldview out of which it emerged. It is relevant what materials were available to the artist at the time, what economic conditions impacted on his practice, what the mores and culture of his time and place allowed him or forbade him to undertake. This is all interesting and pertinent information.

The question is, can we evaluate the artwork without knowing the context, knowing the personality of the artist, his living conditions, family life, history, whether he married, had children, or lived with his mother? Can we just read what he has given us on the canvas for its own sake, as a world unto itself?

My premise is that we can discern a lot by studying the work even if we don't have all the salient facts about the artist. Perhaps we would admire him more if we knew he was self-taught or extremely poor and be less enchanted if we knew he had every advantage in life. Would we marvel at his colors even more knowing what few pigments were available at the time? Perhaps.

If we are able to acquire this information, we may sigh with a knowing *Ahh*, seeing an additional reason for his methodology or passion. But even without it, we can endeavor to read the work, utilizing what we know about art-making in general, what qualities to look for. We are able to do this because all works of art are made utilizing the elements we have discussed to greater or lesser degree, and understanding these basics, we have a platform to work from, and criteria we can apply to all works.

You have probably heard the idea expressed that instead of giving someone a fish, you will serve him better by teaching him how to fish. So too with this book. Instead of giving you the facts and stories about the art, I am giving you the tools to interpret the work for yourself. Frankly, the facts are so numerous that I could not give them all to you even if I tried. But the concepts, the framework, that I can work with, and you can fill in the details.

I have said that art is communication. That means a dialogue between the artist and his viewer. We can't know exactly what the artist had in mind at the time he created the work. We can guess, based on other facts that are known, but we can't be sure. I have experienced this as I have created a work and then had viewers comment on it. Often they are reading into what I have done based on their own experience. I may have run out of red paint and used blue, and they interpret my use of blue as having a significance I never intended.

So what exactly can the viewer know and what is the dialogue? The artist creates out of a panoply of emotions and thoughts that the viewer can guess at when he sees the final product. He is not necessarily correct. The viewer looks at the work with his or her own array of emotions and thoughts in relating to and evaluating the art. Does the viewer see into the artist's mind?

He may see something, but in truth what he sees into is his own mind. The artist is the catalyst, then, for the emotions and thoughts the viewer experiences, even if those emotions and thoughts diverge from those of the creator.

Art provokes thought and stimulates emotion. This is how art helps us to understand ourselves.

With that in mind, let's talk about ways of looking at art in a general sense.

INTENTION

Before we undertake this discussion about basic artistic approaches and schools of thought, I want to start at the beginning.

You recall that I mentioned what I called the artist's quest, the purpose for which one makes art, and the journey one takes to arrive at it. A little more on this.

Each artwork is driven by what I call intention, and for each artist, that intention is different. Though we all deal with all the complex aspects of art-making, each of us has a special interest in something very personal. We might be fascinated by the quality of light, be obsessed with making a felt line, want to achieve solidity of form, love airiness and delicacy, experience color as a set of complex tastes, have a certain emotion we wish to convey, want to impart a certain idea, have a desire to reduce objects to essences, express a spiritual emanation, make the visual into music, and so on.

These obsessions may morph and change throughout an artist's career, or they may persist throughout. Regardless, what's important for us as appreciators of art is that we recognize them as the artist's intention. What does intention mean?

Intention is the driving force behind the work. It is the reason each artist may address the identical subject and come up with a totally different result. One artist looks at a nude woman and sees a wash of delicate notes, another a woman's inner life, a third a series of shapes in space, and another a political statement about gender.

As you look at art, begin to ask yourself what the artist's intention was, what drove her to make what you see on the canvas. I assure you it wasn't an accident. Read the work and find the intention.

A fellow artist looked at a drawing of mine today in a model session. She saw my figure as an emotional being and said she always saw that in my work. She was reading my drawing and she was simultaneously reading me. I draw with lines and colored shapes, just like all of my fellow artists, but my quest is for verisimilitude of human emotion. You think I am making arms and legs, but in truth I am painting joy and sorrow. That sets my intention to make those lines and shapes in a certain way. Part of this is unconscious and part conscious.

So ask: what set the artist on his course, directed his hand, and made him make the choices he made? What kind of fuel drove the engine? This is knowable and can be read from the work. It's all there—we just have to follow the clues.

POLARITIES OF THOUGHT AND APPROACH

Qualities exist on a continuum. Imagine two poles that are extreme opposites: liberal/conservative, right brain/left brain, classical/romantic, tidy/messy, and so on. These are dichotomies, and every artwork falls somewhere on each of the continuums from one extreme to the other.

Let's use the classical/romantic dichotomy as an example. First, let's define our terms.

We start with **classicism**. According to the *Oxford Dictionary*: "the following of ancient Greek or Roman principles and style in art and literature, generally associated with harmony, restraint, and adherence to recognized standards of form and craftsmanship, especially from the Renaissance to the eighteenth century."

Some of the qualities associated with classicism are symmetry, harmony, idealization.

Classical works are highly finished and perfected and strive for a simplicity, formality, and gracefulness. They may be expressive, but in a cool way that suggests universality rather than individuation.

Now, **romanticism**.

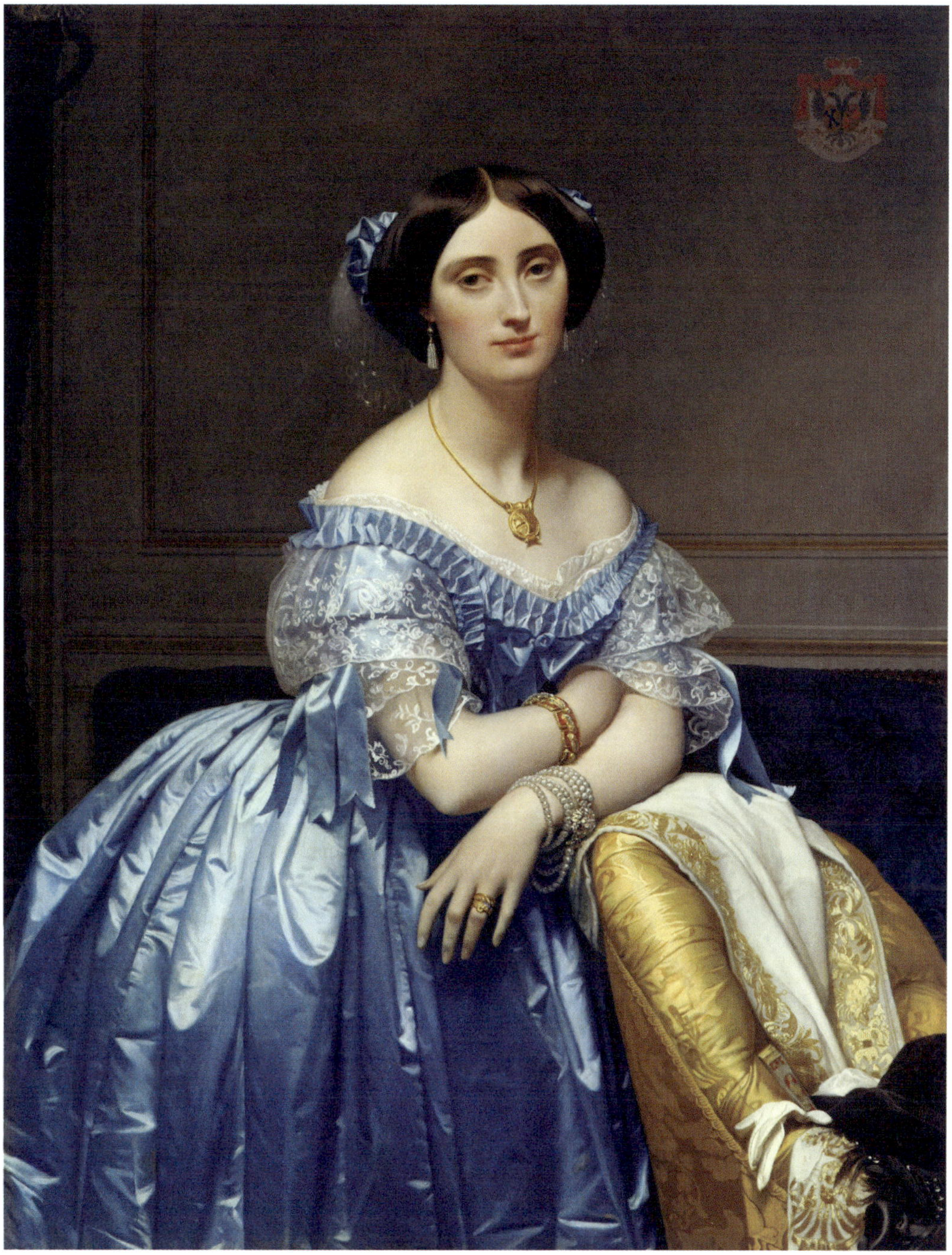

Fig. 19. Jean-Auguste-Dominique Ingres, JOSÉPHINE-ÉLÉONORE-MARIE-PAULINE DE GALARD DE BRASSAC DE BÉARN (1825–1860), PRINCESSE DE BROGLIE.

Oxford Dictionary's definition: "A movement in the arts and literature that originated in the late eighteenth century emphasizing inspiration, informality, subjectivity and the primacy of the individual."

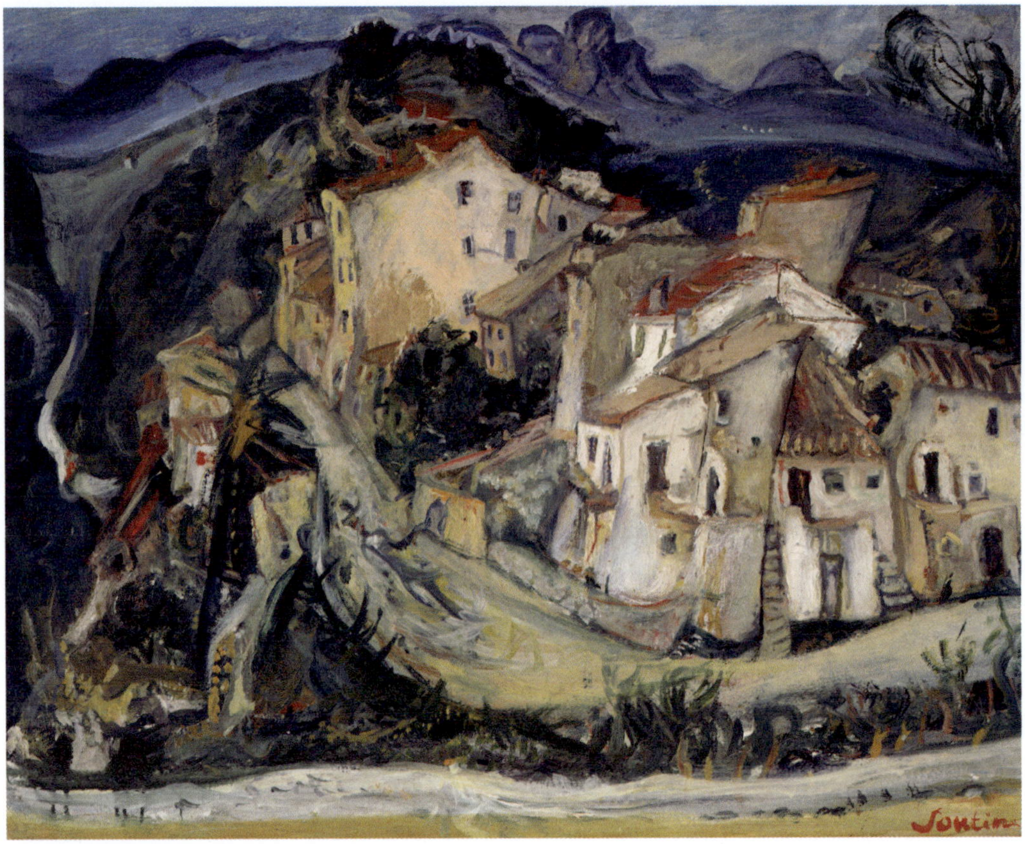

Fig. 20. Chaim Soutine, VIEW OF CAGNES.

Some of the qualities associated with romanticism are asymmetry, particularization, emotiveness, expressiveness, disruption, exaggeration, and even fantasy, the latter as illustrated in this work by Soutine (Fig. 20).

Though the Ingres (Fig. 19) is a figurative painting and the Soutine is a landscape, we can clearly compare their distinguishing characteristics. The Ingres has hard edges, while the Soutine's edges are soft. The Ingres is typified by a sharp clarity, defined areas of color, attention to detail, a static quality, and no apparent brushstrokes. The Soutine, on the other hand, puts forth an animated surface that suggests movement, shapes that seem distorted, and a fluidity of paint with noticeable brushstrokes.

Though these two words, classicism and romanticism, are defined as expressions of specific periods in art history, in fact they exist in every period as expressive opposites: mind and body, thinking and feeling, smooth and rough, etc. They are the north and south poles of art, and every artist exists at a latitude closer to one or the other.

They typify attitudes and approaches and intentions. The classical: to define; the romantic: to express. If an artist strives for simplicity, order, and symmetry, his work can be described as classical. It does not matter whether he is carving a classical nude statue in early Greece or painting a still life in the twentieth century. Either can be described as classical in approach. The terms "classicism" and "neoclassicism" are applied to different periods where a classical approach is paramount.

If an artist strives for emotional content, asymmetry, and drama, his work can be described as romantic. It does not matter whether he is painting a religious scene in the sixteenth century or an abstract confection in the twenty-first. Either can be described as romantic in approach. For both of these terms, we are using them in the broadest sense, not as names of art movements, but rather as general ways of thinking and working.

Remember, all artists are a mix of qualities. They can be 80 percent classical with 20 percent romantic, or vice versa, or their work may have aspects of both approaches fifty-fifty. As you look at art in all periods, this is one of the questions you can pose: classical or romantic. Play our game in the games chapter of this book where you get to rate artists *C* or *R* by percentages.

There are many quality scales we can use to describe art as well as classical/romantic. You can identify artists as primarily left brain or right brain, conceptual or perceptual in focus, with technique that is highly detailed or loose and flowing. All artists from all periods land somewhere on this spectrum, and art periods and styles do as well. If we look at the history of art, we can track the fluctuations as alternating waves where classical approaches dominate followed by romantic ones.

As certain movements in the arts seem to engender their opposites, classical periods in art are often followed by romantic approaches. As an art movement becomes accepted and mainstream, it often brings out artists wanting to break the rules, and the momentum moves to the other end of the spectrum. This flip-flopping of predominating approaches is ongoing.

I compare this to generational flip-flopping in families. We see patterns where stern parents produce rebellious children, and then when these rebels produce their own families, the process reverses and their offspring tend to be more serious and ordered.

Another way to classify this artistic spectrum is with the terms conceptual/perceptual. In the conceptual approach, images arise out of an idea, and in the perceptual, they arise out of the senses. Ask yourself: Is the purpose of this work to illustrate an idea or make a statement? Political art, satirical art, and performance art would fall into this category.

Instead, is the purpose to express an aesthetic value, an emotion? Much of visual art arises out of this intention, just to express a feeling. Think of a painting of a sunset or the stormy seas of Turner or Winslow Homer.

Let's remember that it takes both brain and emotion to create art, so every artwork has elements of both directions. We are speaking of dominance here, not exclusivity.

There are no pure articles. Some political works can be highly expressive. Take the magnificent Picasso *Guernica.* It is a conceptual work because its purpose is to express the horror of war. But the drawing itself with its exaggerated, mannerist contours is highly emotional. So which is it?

Some examples are easier to discern. Think of the Monet water lilies, perceptual painting at its finest. Even here, though, the intention to be true to the light and attempt to paint light itself, not merely lit objects, was revolutionary in its time, a very big idea indeed.

We are all different, and every artist has a unique voice that manifests in many ways. Enjoying art is a function of awareness, and seeing the way each artist deals with the common elements is a major part of understanding art.

It is interesting to notice the manner in which these states of mind manifest in art. Take brushstrokes, for example. Even within a period, you will notice that some artists have a looser way of applying paint, while others eliminate the effect of the strokes altogether.

When an artist makes no attempt to obfuscate his brushstrokes, even reveling in them and the feeling of the paint itself, we call that work **painterly**. Painterly means the emphasis is on the paint, and painterliness is more typical of romantic painters.

To the contrary, if the artist hides his brushstrokes for the sake of a smooth surface, and makes clear boundaries, we might call his approach **linear**. Linear means the emphasis is on the drawing and is more typical of classical painters.

Left-brained or conceptual artists tend to do more planning and predesign studies than their more right-brained or freewheeling counterparts. Painting alla prima, or directly, without preplanning, is another of the insignia of the romantic or perceptual painters.

Notice the shape-making. Are the shapes clearly marked and definitive or vague, more swirling in nature? Line-making as well. Are the lines clean and crisp or wavering and quivering? All these are signposts and indicators of the artist's approach.

As civilization moves through time, these wave motions from restrictive times to more expansive ones come to fruition and assert themselves as art movements. Artists are influenced by the time they live in and often are the vanguard to the next wave of thought and artistic style.

Art is both a reflection of the cultural, political, and economic issues of the time in which it is created, and also a major influence and propellant of change. Looking at art in context is interesting and important study. It is just not our primary focus here. We will occasionally refer to elements and qualities that are more prevalent in a given historical period, and hopefully our discussion of the universal artistic values will not negate, but rather stimulate you in undertaking and valuing the contextual approach as well.

PERSONALITY AND ART

Psychologists, who study the human as a highly developed conscious being, have often tried to discern and then to label the distinct personality types. What is a personality? According to the *Oxford English Dictionary*, a personality is "the combination of characteristics or qualities that form an individual's distinctive character."

Since what we are doing here to is identify the "qualities that form an artwork's individual character," I thought it germane to compare human personality characteristics to the characteristics of an artwork. Of course, it goes without saying that an artwork is not a living being, but it is created by one, and might inherit some of the characteristics of that individual. Can we look at an artwork, therefore, and judge its personality?

Furthermore, will that personality be totally consonant with that of the being that created it? Even though a human may be deemed to possess a quality, he may not always exhibit it. An extrovert may, on a given occasion, be shy. An introvert may go outside his comfort zone, and be suddenly outgoing. The psychologists tell us that personality types are generalizations, not absolute determinants of behavior.

With this caveat in mind, shall we have a go at it? Just for fun. Try to see if we can look at a work of art as indicative of a personality, or actually having a personality?

Our aim here, as we've said, is to find ways of thinking about art, reading it, and evaluating it. To that aim, why not use as many methods and criteria as we can?

I looked to the Myers-Briggs Type Indicator method for determining personality. This is a system developed by Katherine Cook Briggs and her daughter, Isabel Briggs Myers. Their work was a follow-up to that of Carl Jung, who identified four psychological functions humans use to gather and sort information. These are sensation, intuition, feeling, and thinking. Briggs Myers elaborated these and posited sixteen combinations to identify distinct personality types.

Each personality type uses the functions in a slightly different combination, and this explains how they each gather information, use the information they collect, make decisions, and act. Whichever quality is dominant will ultimately impact how the individuals exhibiting this type choose to structure their lives.

The first dichotomy is Introversion vs. Extroversion. Introverts think, then act; extroverts the reverse. Introverts tend to learn in depth; extroverts in breadth. Introverts look within; extroverts without.

How can we see an artwork as introverted or extroverted? An introverted work might be planned and executed sequentially; an extroverted one created without plan, alla prima. An introverted work might be very detailed and exactly rendered; an extroverted one in large irregular swirls, irregular shapes, variegated color, and jagged lines.

The qualities Myers and Briggs discuss vis-à-vis gathering information are Sensing vs. Intuition. People who are dominant in sensing would base their information gathering on what they could see and hear and touch, in other words identifiable empirical information. People dominant in Intuition, on the other hand, would depend more on their imaginations, what they could visualize and theorize, even when not necessarily having the concrete facts.

How could an artwork reflect these two approaches? A sensing work might be drawn from life, an intuitional one from the artist's imagination. A sensing work might be literal, an intuition one more abstract, relying on basic shapes rather than imitated contours. A sensing work might be executed using literal or local color, an intuitional one with experimental, nonliteral, or imagined shades.

When it comes to decision-making, Myers-Briggs types predominate by either thinking, i.e. following rules and being logical, or feeling, using empathy and weighing options more abstractly.

In art, the thinker dominant might come from a more conceptual vein, seeking to express an idea. The feeling-focused artist might draw more from his impressions, and take more license with his rendering. You might see history painters as emerging from the thinking realm, and clearly the Impressionists from the feeling side.

In their last criterion, Judgment vs. Perception, Myers and Briggs posited that those individuals preferring judgment are more likely to seek closure and come to conclusions, where perception-oriented persons might prefer to keep matters more open and fluid. How might this distinction express in art?

Would all abstract art, for instance, be considered to be on the perceptual side while all realistic work on the judgment end? Is this too simplistic? Can an abstract work be a work that stresses judgment and a realistic one a work of perception?

The answer is yes. We need to look more deeply to evaluate the works within genres as subject matter, or the lack thereof, can be treated in many ways. If you see parallels between this method of analysis with what we just discussed vis-à-vis classicism and romanticism, you are correct. The Myers-Briggs differentiations are classifications and, as such, they are variable. Everything is a matter of degree.

Art tends toward one direction or the other, but every work is a unique combination of qualities, just like every human is a unique combination of traits. Let's have fun with this and take some of the sixteen Myers-Briggs personalities and match them with works of art. Keep in mind that I am not matching the psychology characteristics with the artist, but rather with the art.

INTP: The Thinker

(Introvert-Intuitional-Thinker-Perceptive)

Vasily Kandinsky, *Kleine Welten III*

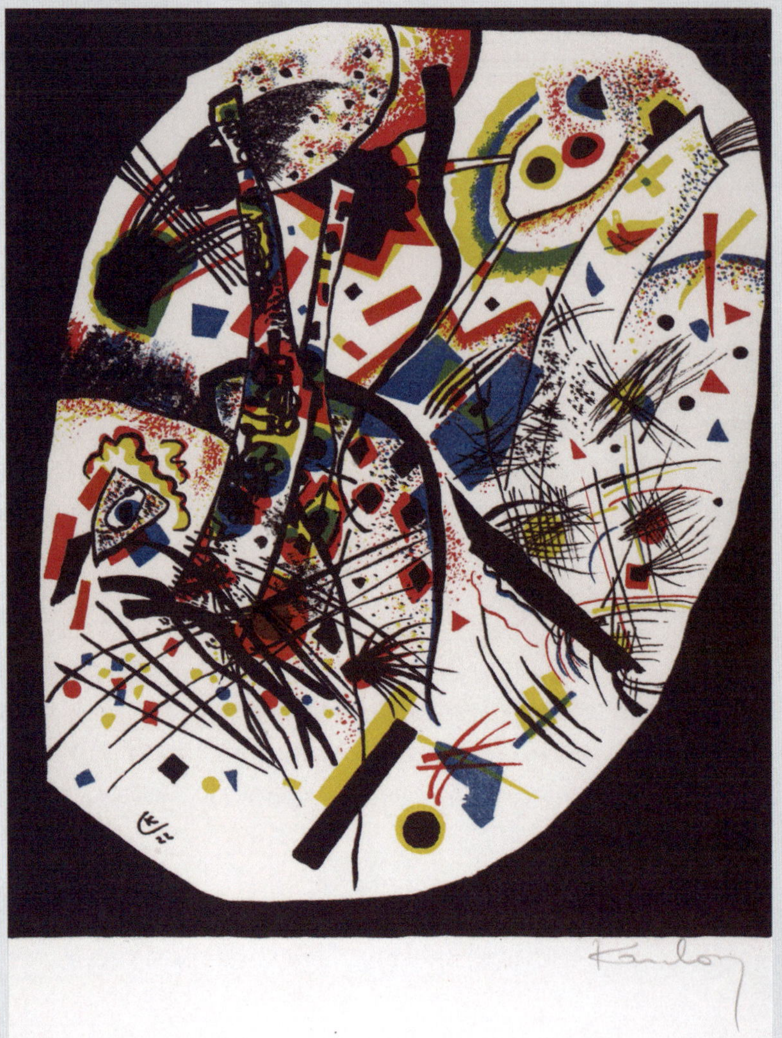

Fig. 21. Vasily Kandinsky, KLEINE WELTEN III.

This work is a composition of shapes in primary colors, and though well thought out and expertly executed, with clean shapes and linear elements, the result is a work that is interesting to look at, even fanciful, analytical without being stiff or somber.

A characteristic of this personality type is to be analytical, contained, and adaptable.

ISFP: The Composer

(Introvert-Sensing-Feeling-Perceptive)

Edgar Degas, *Dancers, Pink and Green*

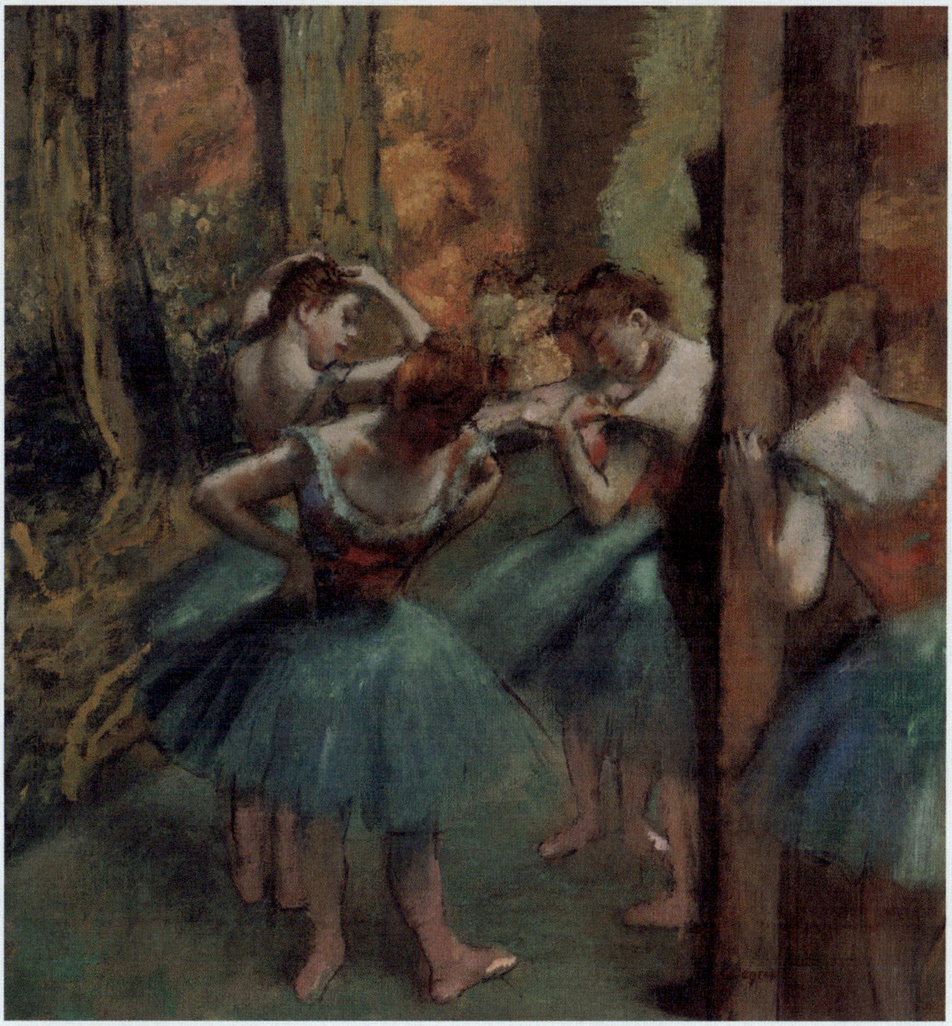

Fig. 22. Edgar Degas, DANCERS, PINK AND GREEN.

Degas and dancers are synonymous as it was a favorite subject, and no one before or after has done it better. He studied the ballerinas in repose and in rehearsal and rendered them with great beauty and heart. His hand was tender, his admiration for their beauty evident in every stroke, as in this simply perfect pastel. Nothing extraneous, but drenched with feeling.

A characteristic of this personality type is sensitivity and kindness.

INFJ: The Counselor

(Introvert-Intuitive-Feeling-Judgment)

Paul Gauguin, *Ia Orana Maria*

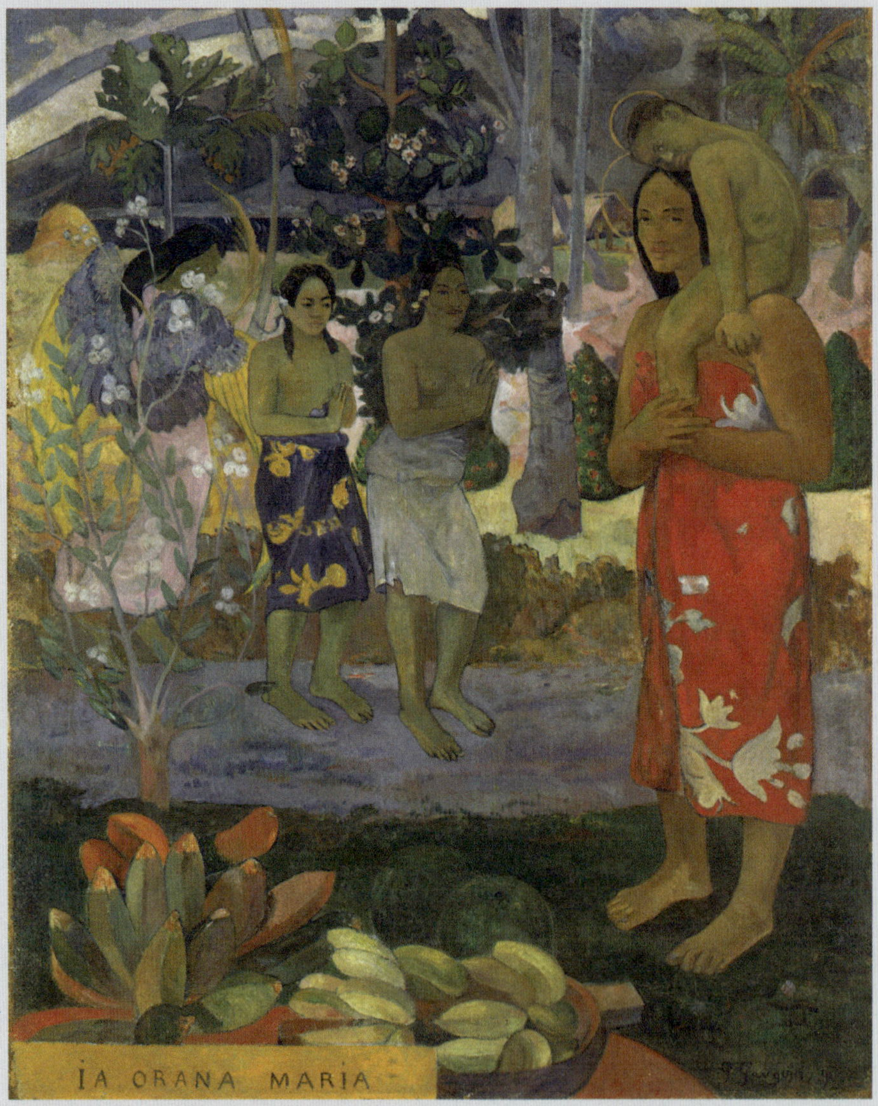

Fig. 23. Paul Gauguin, IA ORANA MARIA.

Paul Gauguin's works are deeply symbolic and emotional, and in fact he is considered a symbolist painter. A characteristic of symbolism is to use imagery that is personal to represent religious or other philosophical ideas. In this work Gauguin depicts Jesus and Mary disguised in Polynesian dress.

A characteristic of this personality is to seek meaning in objects and relationships.

ENFP: The Champion

(Extrovert-Intuitive-Feeling-Perception)

Egon Schiele, *Crouching Nude in Shoes and Black Stockings, Back View*

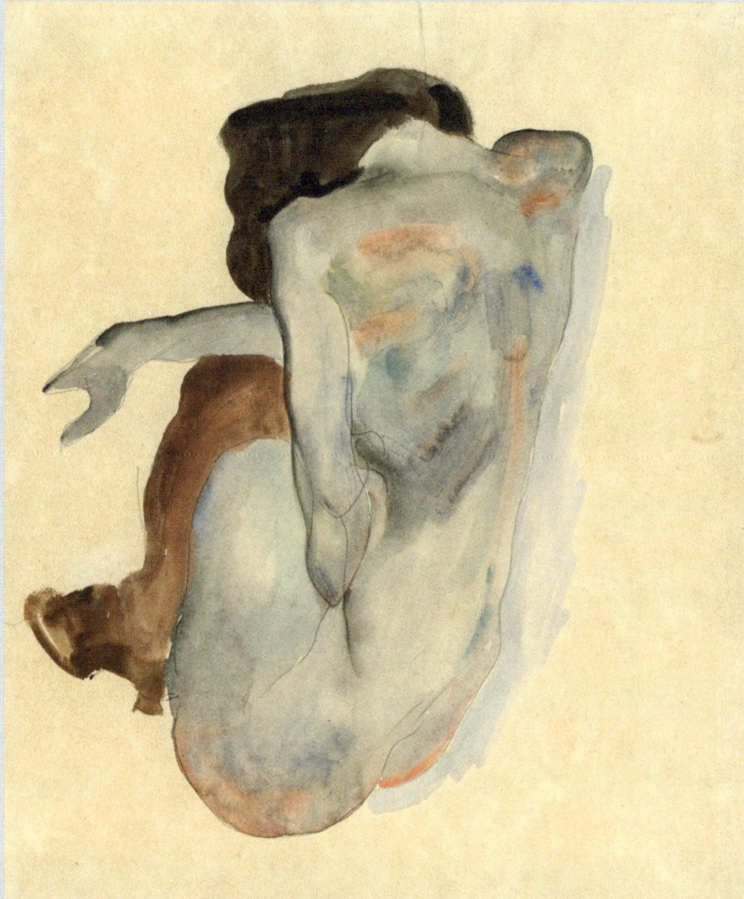

Fig. 24. Egon Schiele, CROUCHING NUDE IN SHOES AND BLACK STOCKINGS, BACK VIEW.

This expressionistic watercolor by Egon Schiele could only have been created with Schiele's emotion and passion for the female form. His work had an unusual sensuality and veered into the erotic. The limpid colors caress the back of this imaginary female and suggest an intense desire to accentuate her femaleness. The position of the model is exaggerated, as is the case with expressionist works such as this, and probably arose out of a drawing session with this model in which the artist, in a sense, let himself go. His drawing is full of feeling.

A characteristic of this personality type is the desire to let things develop and to improvise.

ENTJ: The Commander

(Extrovert-Intuition-Thinking-Judgment)

Jacques-Louis David, *THE DEATH OF MARAT*

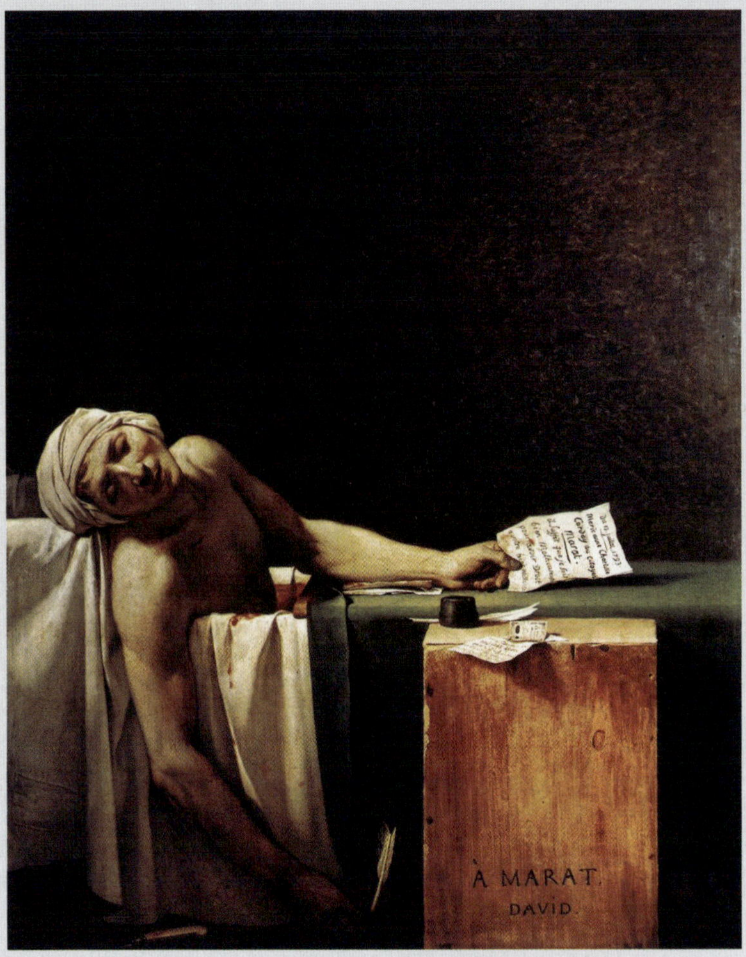

Fig. 25. Jacques-Louis David, THE DEATH OF MARAT.

Neoclassicist David made this painting of the murdered Marat a few months after his assassination. He was a supporter of Marat, a journalist, so this may be considered a political painting. It is notable in this context not because of its subject, but rather the very decisive and deliberate way it was painted and depicts the subject in a most favorable light under the circumstances.

The classical style is very clear in its purpose, the clarity of its line and illustrative mission; David was notable in this regard.

This personality type is characterized by decisiveness and forcefulness.

ISTJ: The Inspector

(Introvert-Sensing-Thinking-Judgment)

Edward Hopper, *Nighthawks*

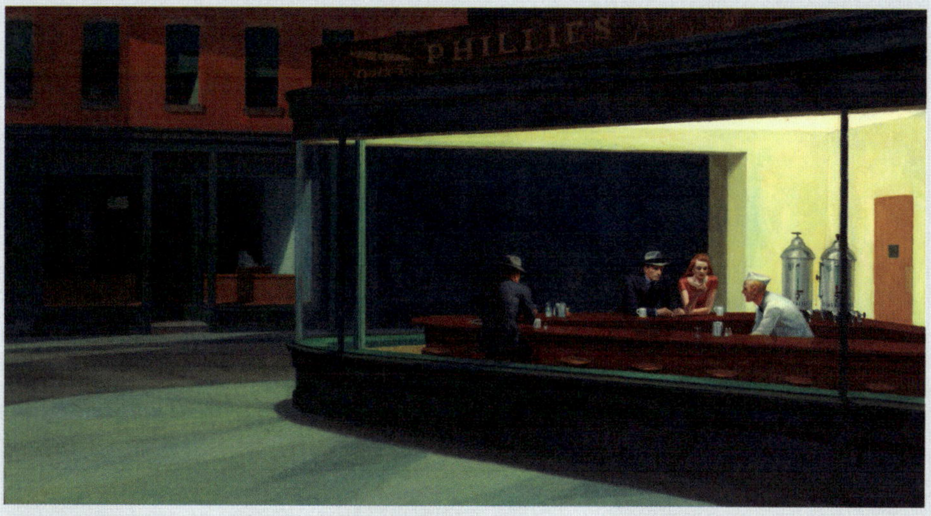

Fig. 26. Edward Hopper, NIGHTHAWKS.

There is something so matter-of-fact about Hopper's style. No muss, no fuss, the paint is flat, colors are local, the mood is undeniable. Hopper is a reporter and is telling us a story. He is asking us to watch these characters without embellishment, and see them just as they are. The facts, ma'am, nothing but the facts. In fact, this very matter-of-factness is what makes this work so compelling.

This personality type is characterized by dependability, organization, and practicality.

ESFP: The Performer

(Extrovert-Sensing-Feeling-Perception)

Mary Cassatt, *Ellen Mary Cassatt*

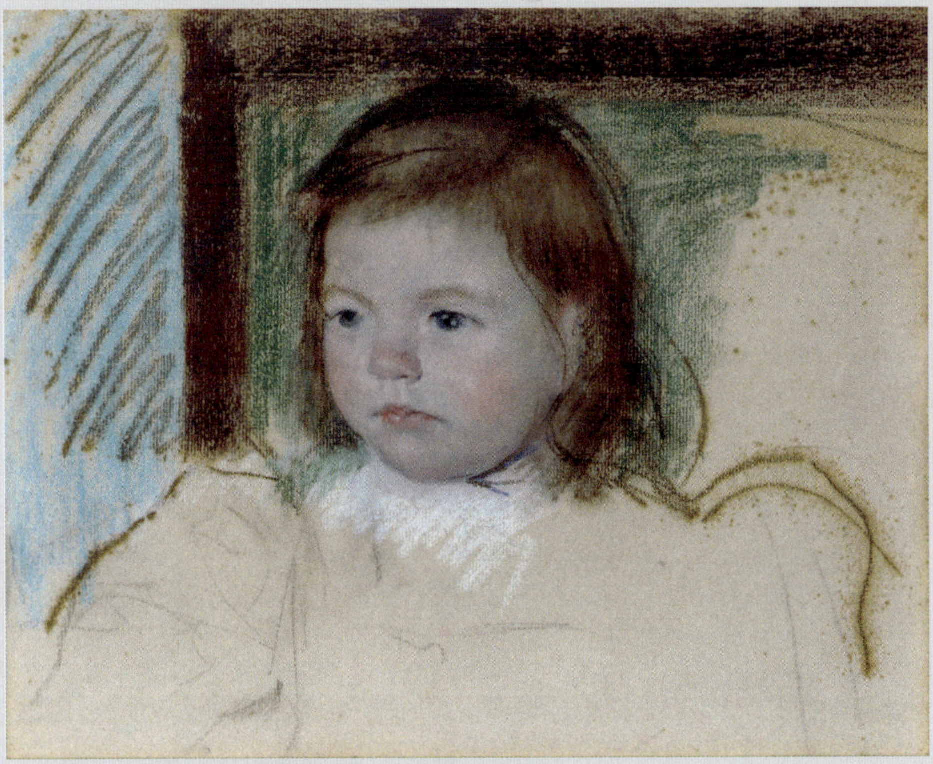

Fig. 27. Mary Cassatt, ELLEN MARY CASSATT.

This lovely little pastel by the American Mary Cassatt is as fresh today as the day it was painted more than a century ago. Cassatt painted women and children with tenderness and an openness that this personality embodies. Here the detailed and tender face of the child is completed with just a few expressive lines and scribble of pastel. But, really, what more could be said to make this better?

This personality type is characterized by exuberance, spontaneity, and accessibility.

ENTP: The Inventor

(Extrovert-Intuition-Thinking-Perception)

Paul Klee, *Drawing Knotted in the Manner of a Net*

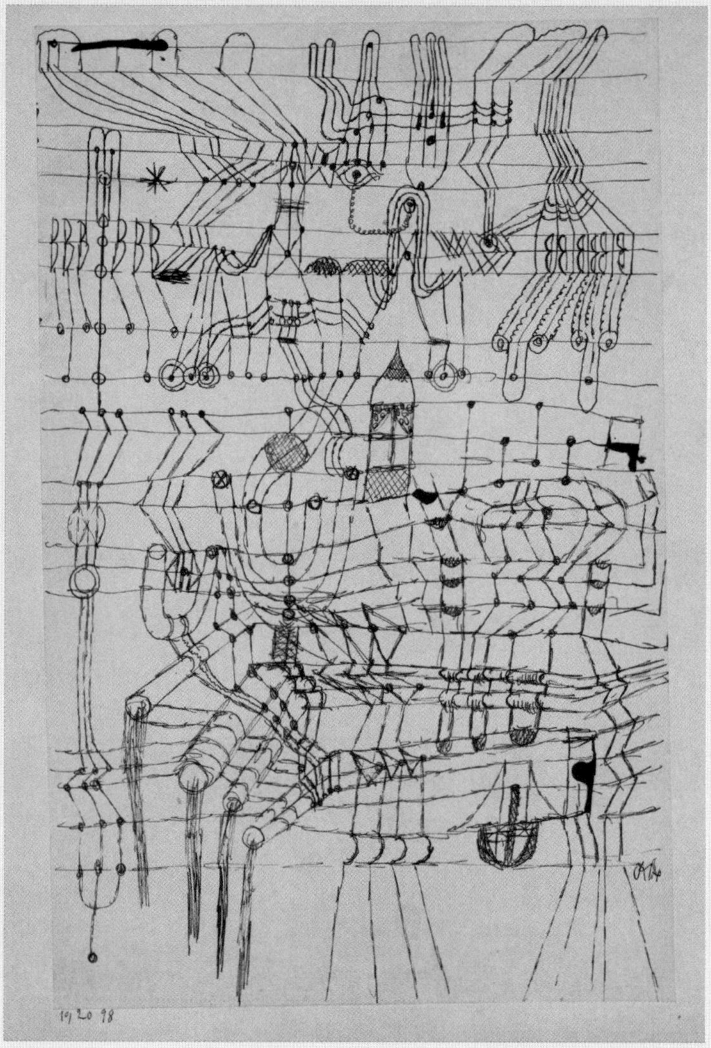

Fig. 28. Paul Klee, DRAWING KNOTTED IN THE MANNER OF A NET.

The title alone of this work shows the inventiveness and creativity of the artist. Klee was a fanciful artist, but not messy or wild—his concoctions and constructions were very well thought-out and executed. His work incorporated play, and he was a freethinker. There is also a delicacy to his line; though it is not weak, it has a carefulness, as if he were executing a well-conceived plan.

This personality type is characterized by outspokenness, conceptual originality, and ingenuousness.

Before I close on this experiment, I want you to know how I classified these eight works according to the Myers-Briggs personality type classifications.

I first chose the work, then asked myself whether the piece seemed to come from an introvert or extrovert origin, whether it was sensory or intuition based, championing thought or feeling, and conclusive or open. I took the four letters, and then looked at the personality type.

Surprising myself, I do think the personalities of the works do pretty much match the descriptions of the personality types. This is interesting, but surely it is possible to use other criteria that might work just as well. Perhaps you can think of some that are even more elucidating. The objective is just to stimulate thought about art.

MODERNITY

One more thing on the broad strokes before we move on to specifics. I want you to become cognizant of certain trends in art through history. These are related to the advance in knowledge about the natural world, a greater technological capability, and the strengthening of the individual over society. As we move into modernity certain trends take hold in art-making. These are:

The march into light. Paintings get generally more conscious of daylight as we move through history. Dark backgrounds get lighter. The value gamut gets shorter.

The simplification of forms. Artists released from copying begin to really look at what they are drawing, painting, and sculpting. They become engaged in analyzing what they see and choosing how to describe or express it. They begin to break the forms into delineated parts. Eventually, it occurs to them to eliminate the forms altogether.

Coloring becomes color. Color comes into its own with the understanding of light, the advent of plein air painting from life outdoors. Artists use color in more expressive ways, multiplying hues. Value gamuts get shorter with more mid tones.

Work gets bigger. Technology makes this possible, but also a larger consciousness, and more freedom. A "why not" takes hold more and more.

The medium becomes the message. Artists begin to explore in depth the possibilities of their medium, letting the medium become the story, not the pretext for the story.

Art gets on the move. The static nature of art is challenged by artists who want to enliven their work through movement. We see the emergence of moving, kinetic forms and new applications like film, video, mobiles, installations, and the incorporation of natural elements like water, light, heat, and sound into art.

The personal becomes paramount. Artists are freed from the requirements of their patrons and societal norms. They realize they can do what they want in the studio. Their work become personal *by design*. It was always personal by virtue of their unique artistic DNA, but now they can make it personal consciously. More and more and ever more rapidly, norms can be shattered and ingenuity reigns. The same is true in sculpture, which follows painting and other forms of visual art.

Think about which period of art interests you the most. Imagine yourself walking through the Metropolitan Museum of Art which contains rooms of art created through the centuries. You can walk through the Ancients, the Greeks and Romans, scoot into the sixteenth century, the seventeenth, the eighteenth, looking at religious scenes, countless history paintings, then dark portraits, see the French, the Dutch, the Spanish, the English, finally the American wing. Everything is getting lighter, airier, the colors are getting brighter. The figures are larger, they are not as ornate, they are getting even lighter and more individuated, even disappearing altogether . . .

Where do you stop, and why? Do you continue into the room with the big abstracts, the pop art, the minimalist works? Do you keep going?

Is it all beginning to make sense, how it happened this way and why? Read on, and by the time we arrive at our last chapter, hopefully we'll be taking that journey with even wiser eyes.

Chapter 7

More Looking: Specific Criteria

So we've looked at the main polarities in approach and matched some art examples with personality types. Now let's consider some of the other things to look for and questions you might consider as you examine a work of visual art:

Was the artist's intent to render the subject realistically, stylistically, or abstractly? One would say **realistic** if the objects are clearly recognizable, the colors are rendered in an imitative way, and the relative size and proportions are close to how they would appear in life, with little exaggeration.

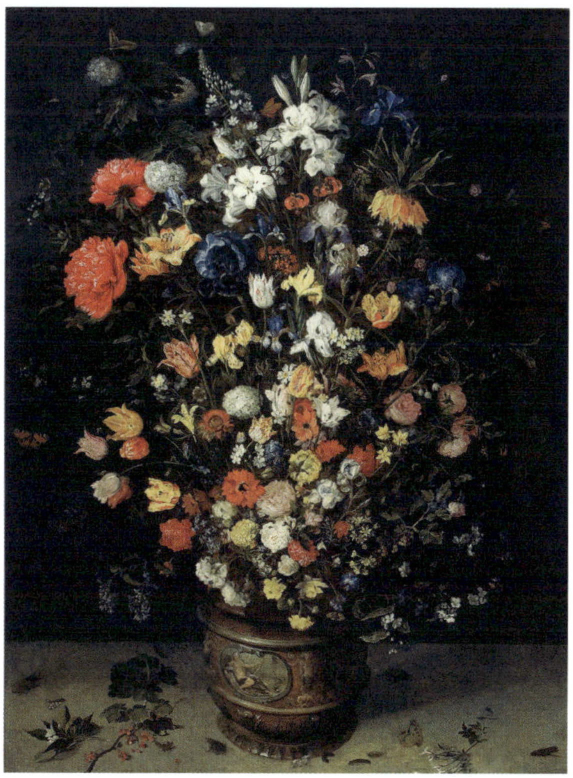

Fig. 29. Jan Brueghel the Elder, BOUQUET OF FLOWERS.

One would say **stylistic** if, though the image is recognizable, proportions are exaggerated, colors are more imaginative than local, there is simplification and less detail in general and the picture is more iconic than descriptive. These flowers by Redon (Fig. 30) would be considered less realistic and more stylized.

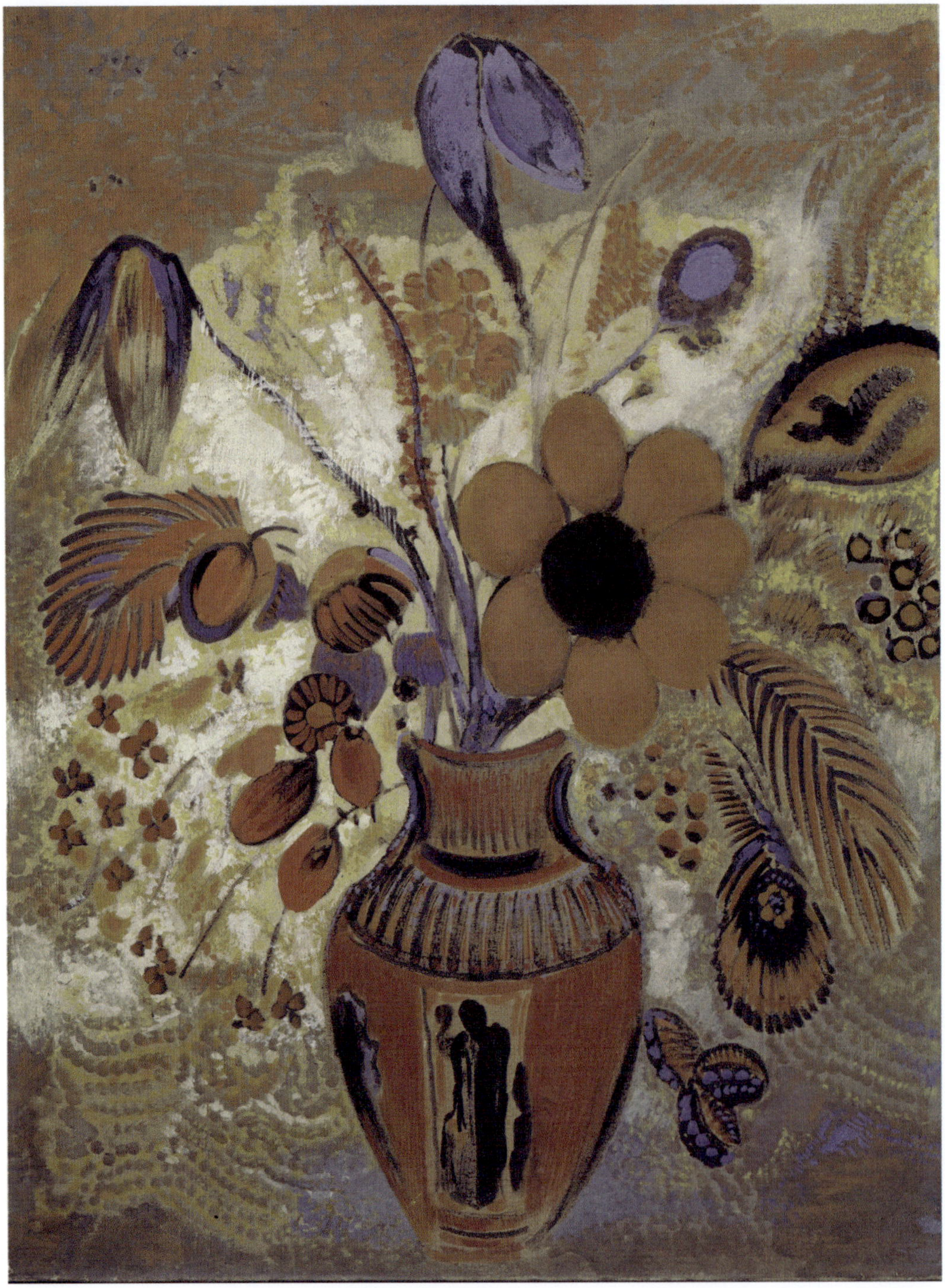

Fig. 30. Odilon Redon, ETRUSCAN VASE WITH FLOWERS.

One would say **semi-abstract** if the objects were recognizable but only barely, with emphasis more on the patterning and design than descriptiveness; and **abstract** if the objects were not recognizable or nameable at all, except in the title perhaps.

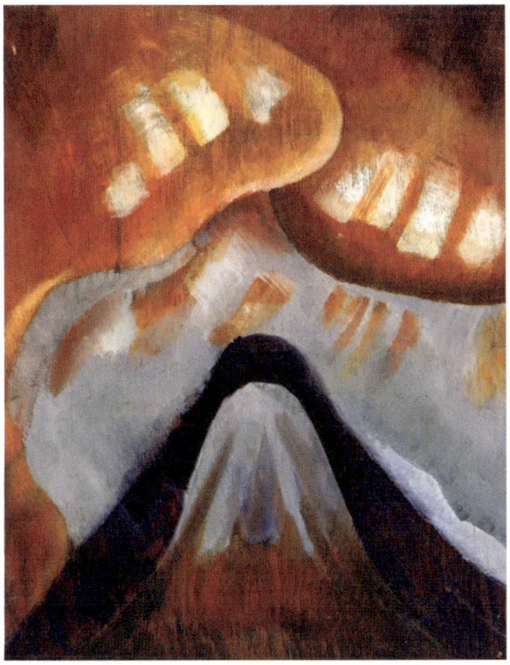

Fig. 31. Arthur Dove, MOUNTAIN AND SKY.

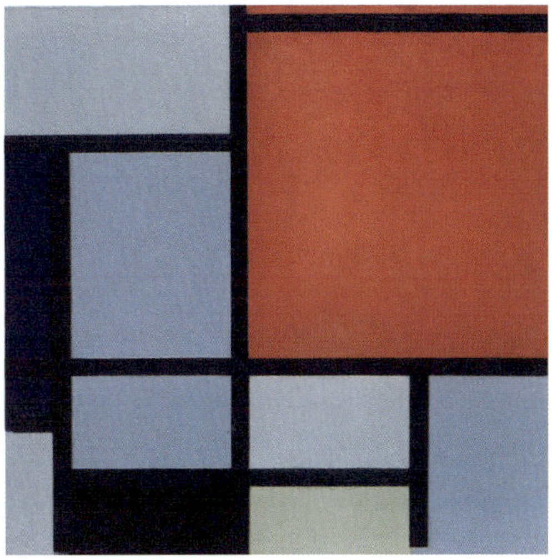

Fig. 32 Piet Mondrian, COMPOSITION.

In the semi-abstract Dove piece (Fig. 31), one has some sense that this might be a landscape, and the title tells us we are looking at mountain and sky. In the abstract Mondrian (Fig. 32), no such references are apparent. The latter was an avant-garde neo-plasticist composition, which we will discuss in more detail later on.

How is the pictorial shape explained and elaborated?

If the picture suggests space, that is, there is an **illusion** that you can see into the distance, how is this achieved? Is it by the relative size of the objects, the intensities of the colors, the blurriness of things far away?

If there no sense of space and everything seems to be on the surface, why did the artist choose this method, and is it effective or just a mistake?

If the space seems to exist but not too deeply, what could have been the thinking of the artist? This was a popular depiction of the Cubists who flattened the space as if sheets of paper were stacked up one on top of the other. This was a different way to describe space than the more realistic "illusion" of deep space.

Here is a good example of the Cubist technique of breaking up the human face into planes as executed by a Czech artist (Fig. 33). It is more decorative than illustrative.

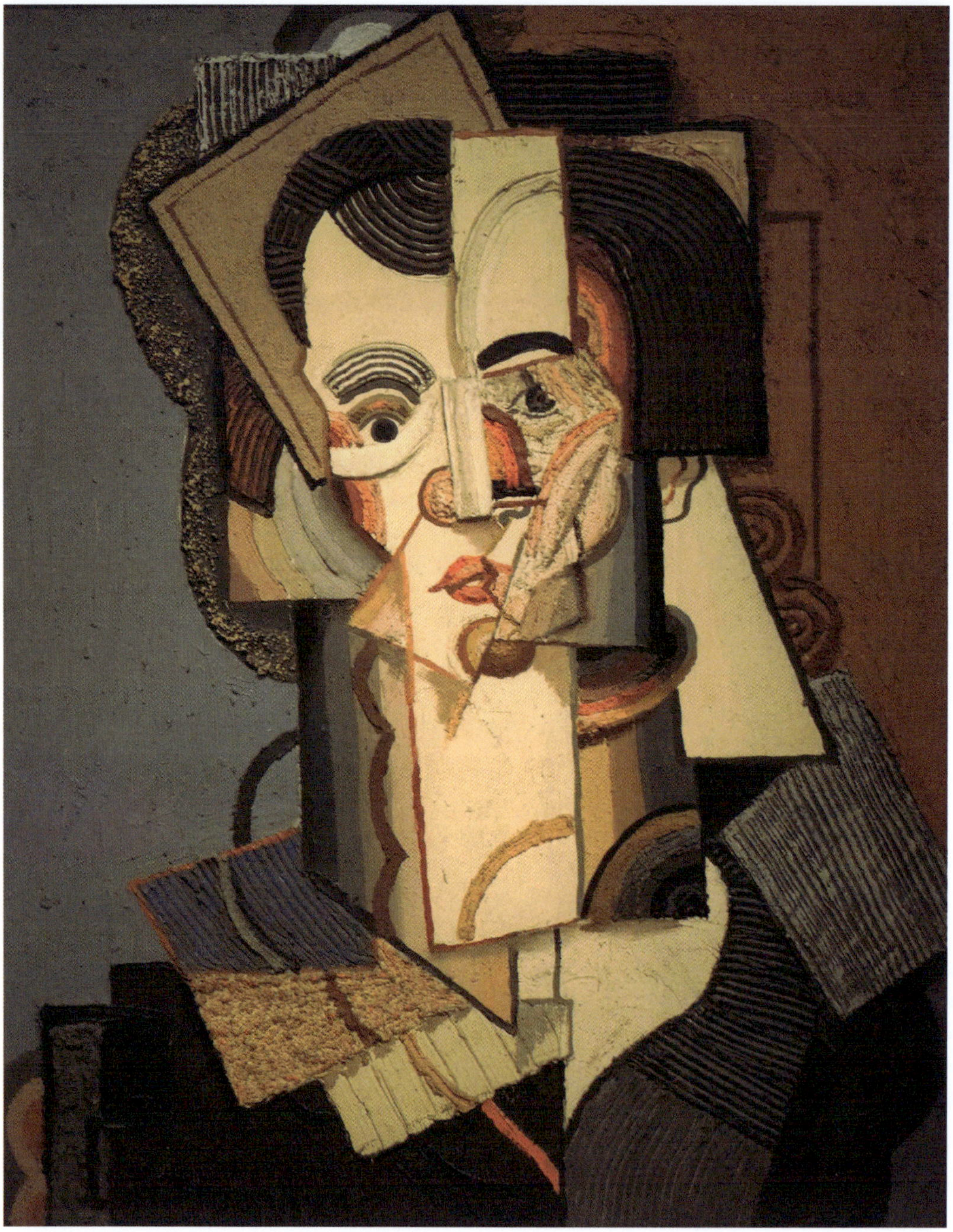

Fig. 33. Antonín Procházka, LADY IN SWEATER.

In abstract painting, space is front and center. With objects eliminated or just barely suggested, the star is the imaginary space the artist has created. No distractions, just space, air, light, and color.

It is a good point to note that when looking at abstract work in general, since objects are not elaborated, the textures, color, and the way the space is explained *are* oftentimes the subjects of the work. And in many cases these elements are emphasized and we can see them for what they are, something we may overlook when we look at realistic work.

POINT OF VIEW

What was the point of view of the artist and why did he choose it?
Every artist throughout time has established a point of view. Every artist drawing the same model in the art studio has an entirely different point of view. The artist chooses a point of view that is most interesting to him.

In most portraits, for instance, the point of view is directly on the frontal view. It makes sense, especially when the portrait was a commission, that the painting show the primary identifying view. But this is not always the case, and how the artist places the subject is an important first statement of the content of the work.

Look, for instance, at this self-portrait by Rembrandt (Fig. 34) on the next page. The artist has more leeway in a self-portrait, of course, as it is not meant to please anyone except the artist.

In this work, Rembrandt paints himself practically in darkness, with much of his face obscured. The light enters from the left and grazes the shoulder, right cheek, and tip of the nose. The painting is moody and compelling; we enjoy finding the face in the shadows. And the light on the cheek feels palpable. Not intended to show character or emotion, this is a painting about light. Quite beautiful in a monochromatic palette, and timeless.

On page 103, in this famous painting by Vermeer, the artist takes up an interesting point of view (Fig. 35). His vantage point is the next room, and we look at the personages through a doorway. Why did he bother with the doorway and details on the neighboring room?

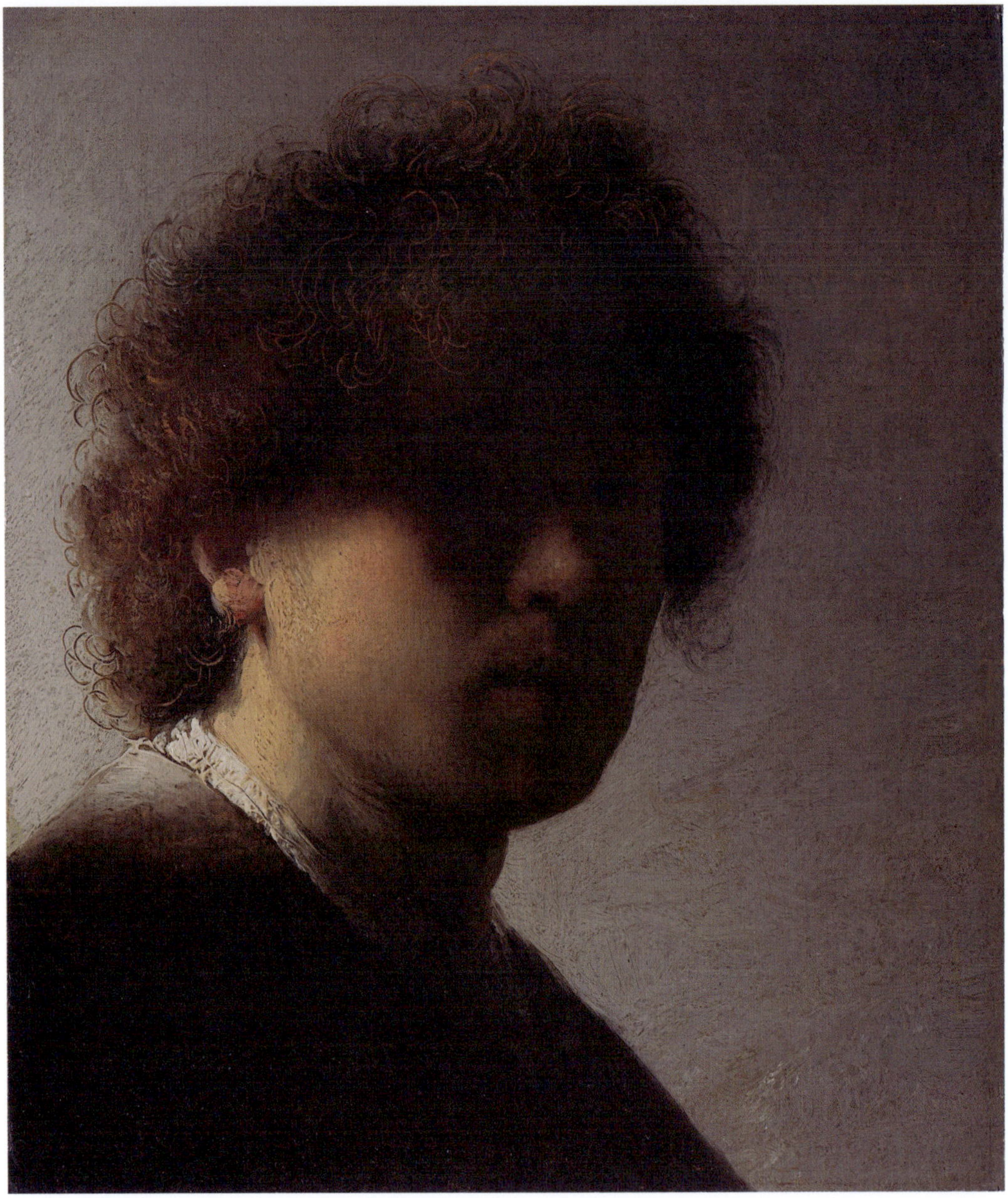

Fig. 34. Rembrandt van Rijn, SELF-PORTRAIT.

The reason is a simple one. We, the viewers are spying on this scene taking place next door. The title tells us the paper the woman is holding in her hand is a love letter. By taking the eye back through the doorway, Vermeer has made us voyeurs and enhanced the effectiveness of his imagery.

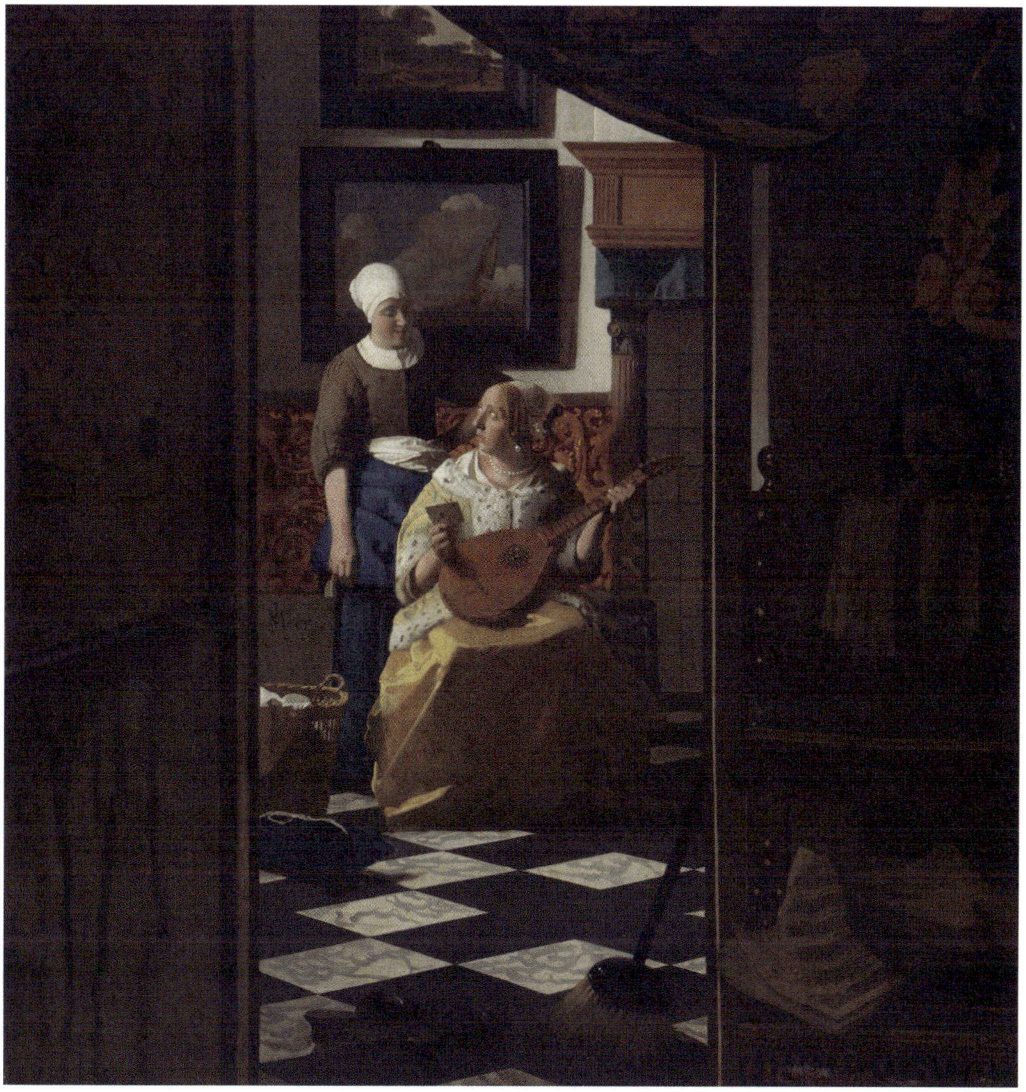

Fig. 35. Johannes Vermeer, THE LOVE LETTER.

Take note of the point of view when you look at art and ponder why the artist chose his stance. The decision was not accidental and to a great extent determined what message the work would impart.

Now think about how radical a decision it was when it occurred to Pablo Picasso and his fellow Cubists that there was no reason they could not simultaneously paint multiple points of view in the same portrait. Picasso was a hurricane of visual ideas, and this was one of them. He did not want to be limited in any way and he found just standing in one spot where one could see just a profile did not pass muster. Why not paint the profile and the frontal view in the same work?

Here's a Cubist portrait of Picasso as executed by Juan Gris (Fig. 36). It seemed fitting to paint the artist's portrait utilizing his own style.

This is a very calculated, well composed, and definitive work, utilizing only a few colors and very deliberately constructed. I especially like the inclusion of the handheld palette with dabs of paint. Notice the shading on each of the broken shards that give them dimension, suggesting form while at the same time breaking it up.

It can take hundreds of years for permission to be granted to do something as remarkable as Picasso suggested. But freedom begets innovation, and once this quintessentially modern artist opened the doors, there was no reason that the figure could not be deconstructed in myriad ways. Look at Marcel Duchamp's fabulous *Nude Descending the Staircase*, Willem de Kooning's oozing nudes, the thin men of Giacometti, so many wonderful, playful, incarnations. Artists were released to enjoy all possible points of view, some even in the same work, and to consider looking at their subjects from above, below, in, and out, without any hesitation.

In Marcel Duchamp's now well-known painting, he shows us a kind of time-lapse picture of the different positions the figure takes when descending the staircase. It is a video in a still-view format. The desire to convey movement is an important dynamic in painting, which is actually a frozen moment. Duchamp discovered an interesting way to exercise the desire to animate the canvas.

Point of view: Something to look for and consider when looking at art.

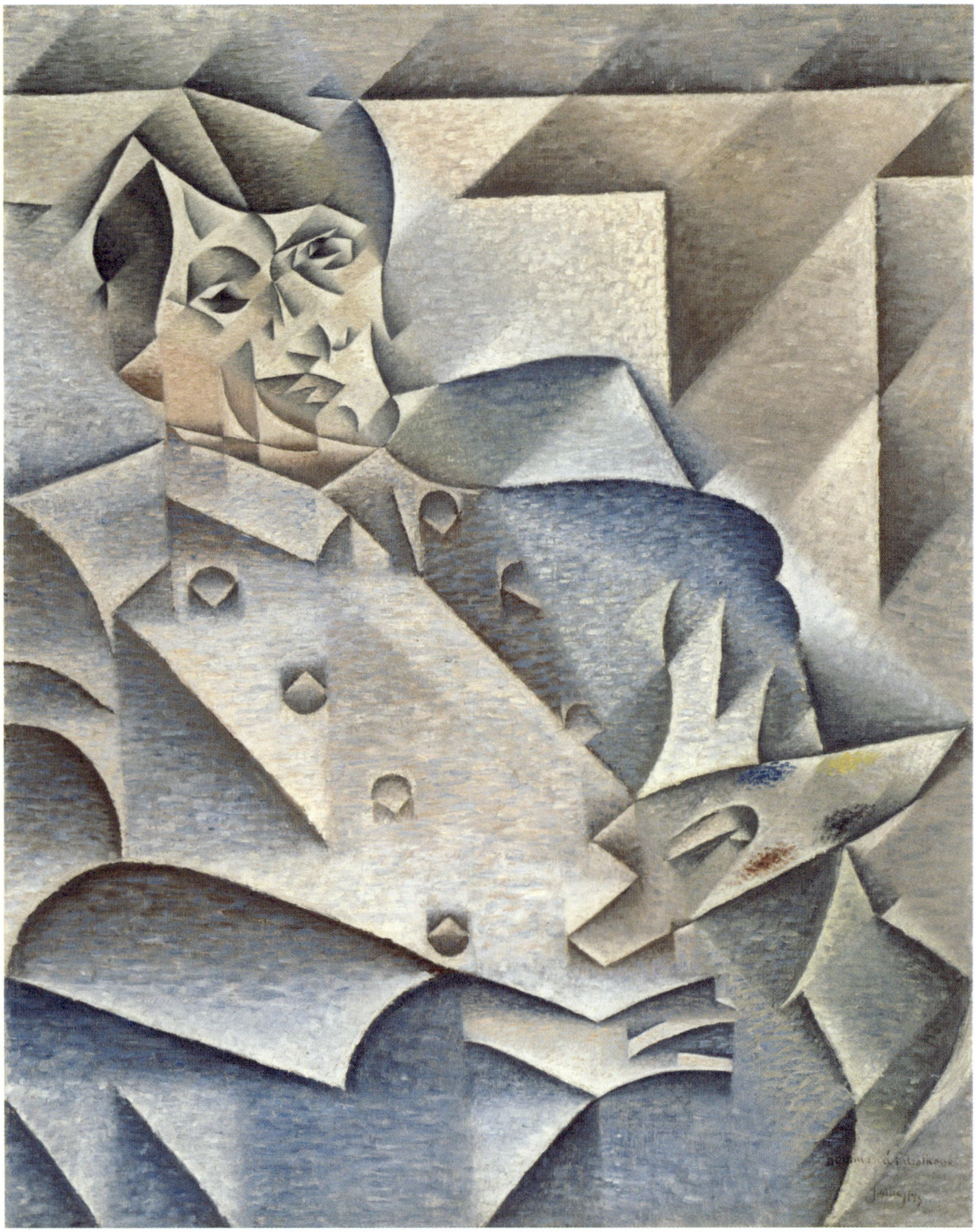

Fig. 36. Juan Gris, PORTRAIT OF PABLO PICASSO.

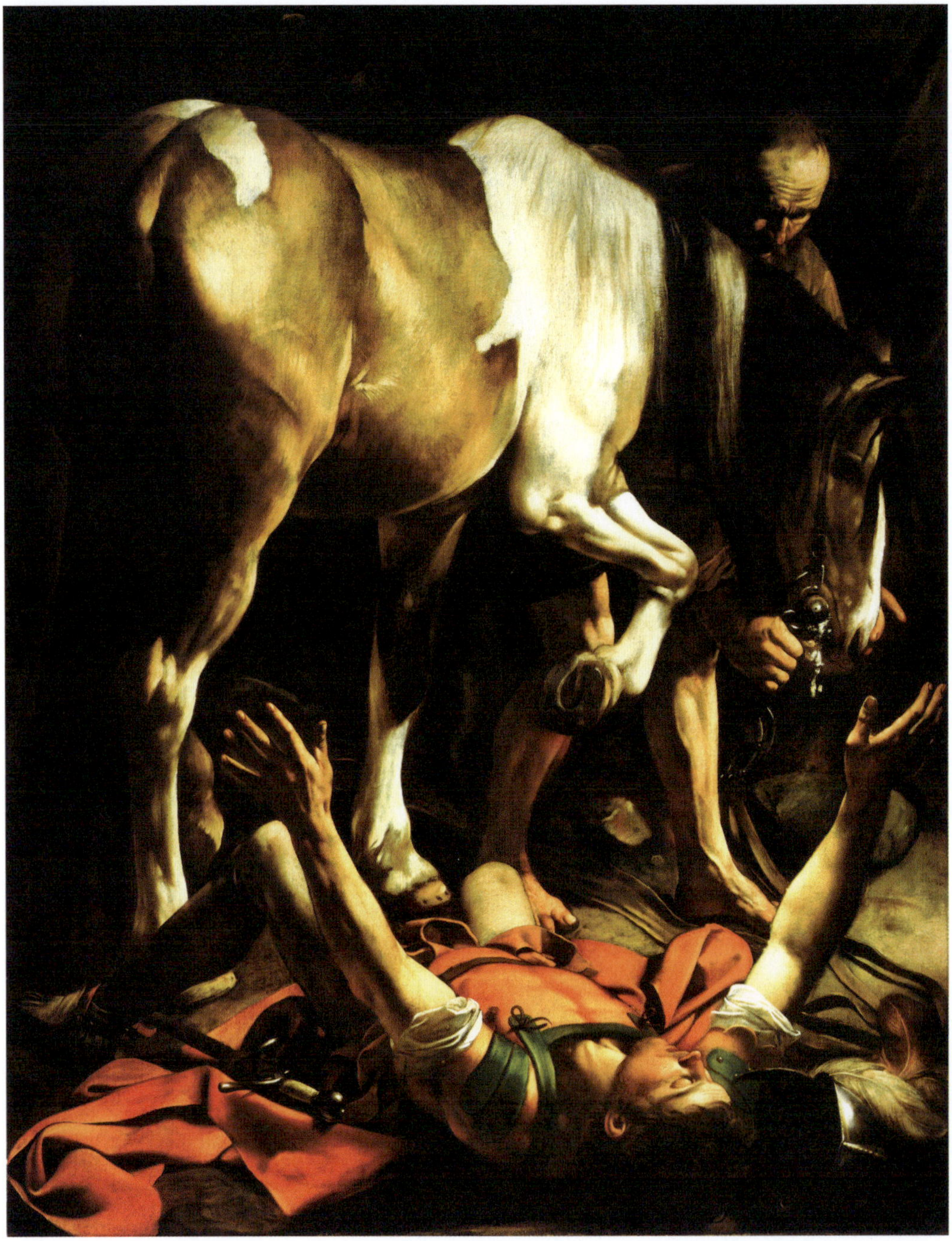

Fig. 37. Michelangelo Merisi da Caravaggio, THE CONVERSION ON THE WAY TO DAMASCUS.

LIGHT

Light. How is it explained?

Space and light are the cornerstones of art. Light is the enabler of all vision. So how do artists explain light in their work?

Many think of civilization as emerging out of the darkness, from ignorance to en**light**enment. When you look at art through the ages, you will see this process come alive. Walk through the museum looking at works through the centuries, and your general impression will be that the light is coming on as you enter modernity. Paintings become lighter and lighter as they march into the future.

Consider this masterpiece by Caravaggio, which depicts the moment Paul becomes aware of the spirit of Jesus Christ and falls off his horse in ecstasy (Fig. 37). It is lit in an imaginative way, far brighter than any moonlight could deliver. It is as if great floodlights were sent down from on high to illuminate the scene.

There are many other examples of dramatic lighting in the art of painting.Visual drama is created by virtue of the juxtaposition of sharp contrasts and a long gamut from light to dark.

On the next page, study this work, painted in 1893, as another example of dramatic lighting (Fig. 38). It is especially effective because the face is cast in shadow and hooded, giving the piece an especially eerie feeling. The artist has heightened the lights and darks to deliver this emotional impact.

In another approach to light, we have the masters of painting whose subject was the light itself and the atmosphere that it permeated. One of these, the sensational painter J. M. W. Turner, was so fascinated with the light that he sought out subjects where effects of light would be most pronounced. Turner adored water, storms, fog, all the world in atmospheric turmoil. Sunsets, volcanoes, explosions; his canvases celebrate the disorder of nature.

On page 109, we have his rendition of a train in the rain, surging through the soupy mess (Fig. 39). Turner chose subjects such as this so he could paint the cacophony of nature. This was a thrilling and challenging assignment for him, his signature and quest.

The greatest masters of light were the Impressionists, for whom light was an obsession. Impressionism, the movement they initiated, became a revolution and changed the palette of the painter in the most significant way.

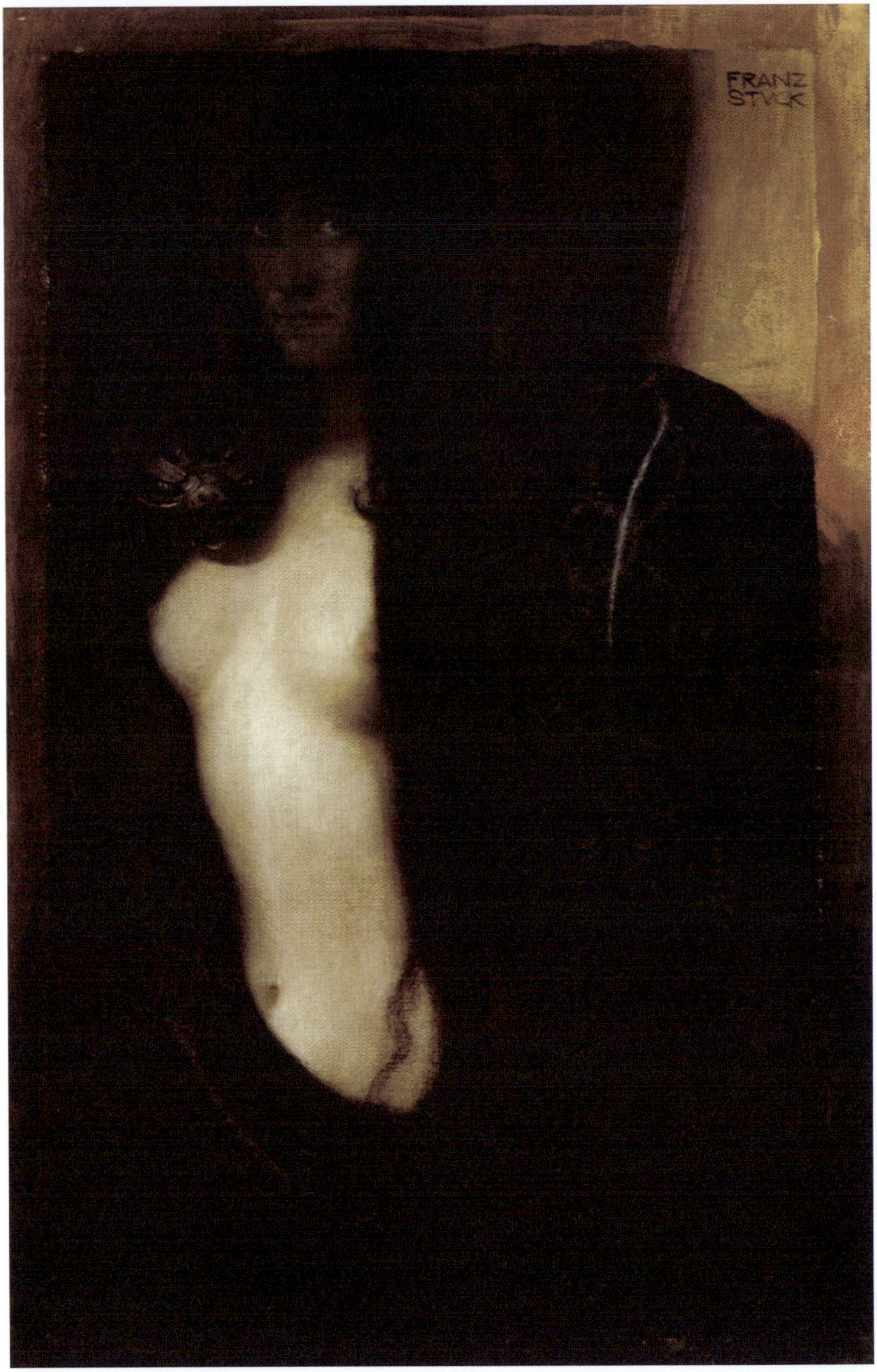

Fig. 38. Franz Stuck, THE SIN.

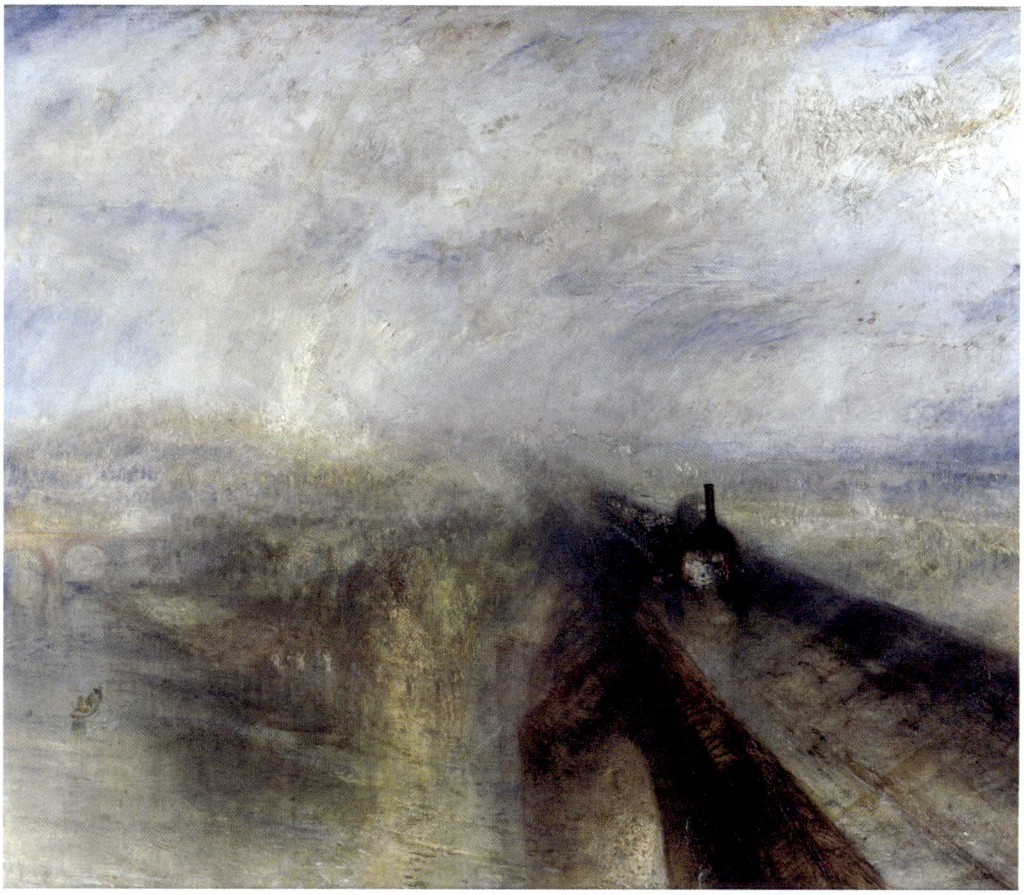

Fig. 39. J. M. W. Turner, RAIN, STEAM AND SPEED—THE GREAT WESTERN RAILWAY.

The painter Monet, known as "the eye," was consumed with the light, so much so that he painted the same scene during different times of the day, just to show how the light influenced the hue and value of the paint. He understood that it is the light that makes all visible, so light became his only subject: the light, the light, and nothing but the light.

For instance, Monet painted over a hundred views of the Thames River, many of the Houses of Parliament, which he worked on from a window at St. Thomas Hospital across the River, as in the example on the next page (Fig. 40). He saw them all as a piece, a panorama of the changes in color due to light conditions. Here we see the view in fog, an example of the atmosphere that Monet loved to paint, his personal obsession.

Impressionism let in the light, and with the light came the color that can only exist in the light, not the dark hues of the past, but the pinks and yellows and baby blues that live in the light. Color was born. The subject matter is a pretext to bask in the color and flavor of the light.

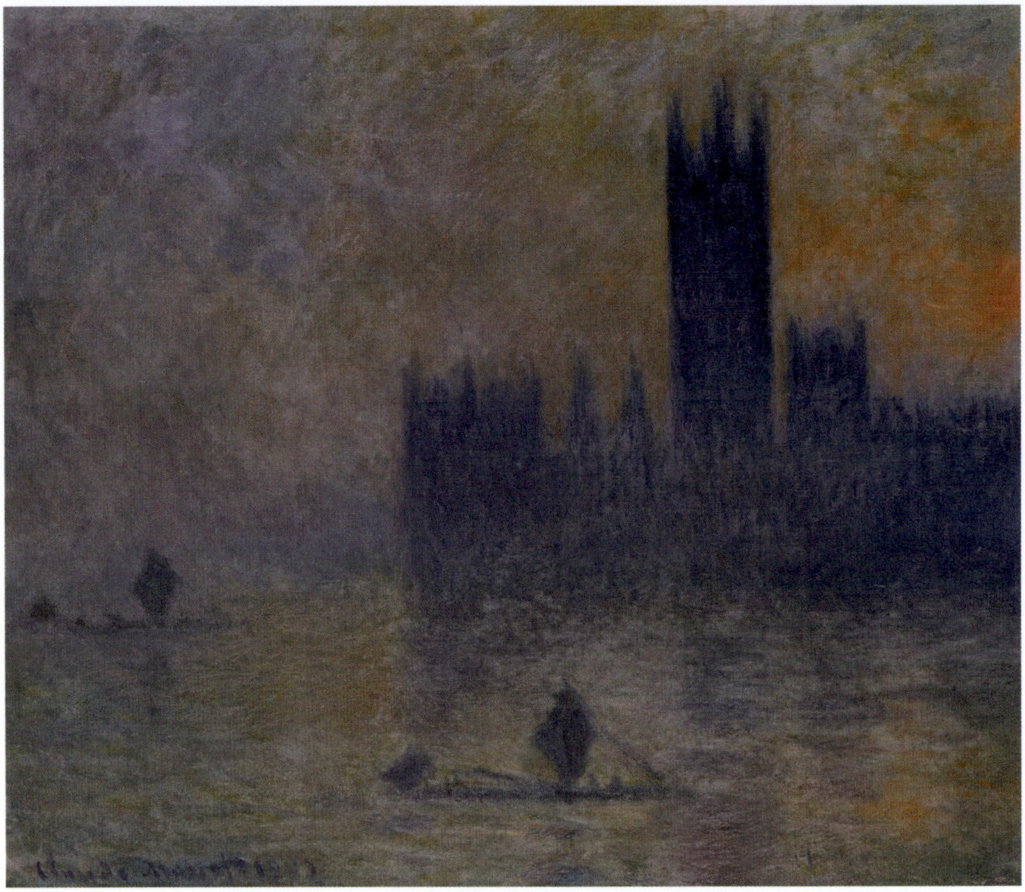

Fig. 40. Claude Monet, THE HOUSES OF PARLIAMENT (EFFECT OF FOG).

Impressionism brought soft, delicate hues referred to as "pastels" into the forefront of painting. These colors express light. Notice the preponderance of pastel colors when you look at Impressionist works and compare them to older works that seem more "lit" than "light-filled."

When objects are lit, the source of the light is identified through the shadows formed when objects block the light. In Impressionism the light permeates all and the shadows, though they do not disappear completely, are expressed as just slightly richer values in vivid hues.

Each of the Impressionist painters had his or her own way of describing the light. Many of their works exist in a kind of dreamy world with beautiful juxtapositions of soft hues. As Impressionism became more mainstream, the Postimpressionists, those painters who followed the initiators, experimented with more deeply intense hues.

One of the American artists of light you may not be aware of was Frederick Carl Frieseke (1874–1939), who lived most of his life in France and is often compared to Renoir. He is considered a Postimpressionist, and his work has been characterized as "decorative Impressionism" as it both explores the effects of sunlight like the Impressionists while also employing a decorative patterning and design. Refer to Figure 41 for an example.

You can almost feel the whiff of breeze that enters through the open door and the afternoon light that creeps into every mixture in this lovely work. Frieseke was in love with the light, and his dedication to it gives the painting a sense of place and time. His touch is loving and affectionate.

In our next sections on atmosphere and color, we will delve further into the expression of light through color. As you look at paintings, establish in your mind how the artist used light, whether the piece looks lit or infused with light, and how the light treatment affected the color palette. Remember that the color is purposeful, not arbitrary.

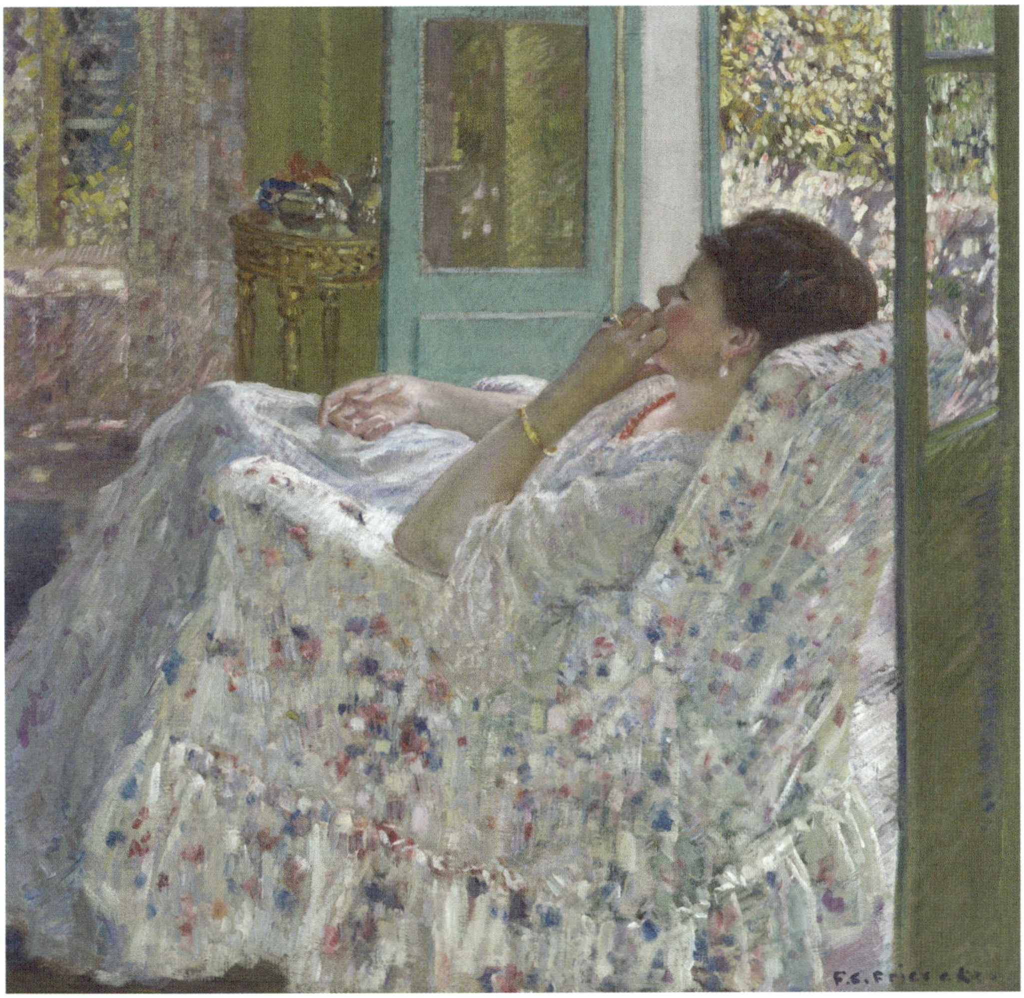

Fig. 41. Frederick Carl Frieseke, AFTERNOON—YELLOW ROOM.

ATMOSPHERE

The air, or what we call atmosphere. How is it explained?

What makes life possible on earth is the air. Our atmosphere permits us to breathe, and therefore, to live. How does an artist, a painter, explain the atmosphere?

As you look at paintings, consider whether the imaginary world created seems to allow for air. If you can say yes, it is probably that the color has been softened to

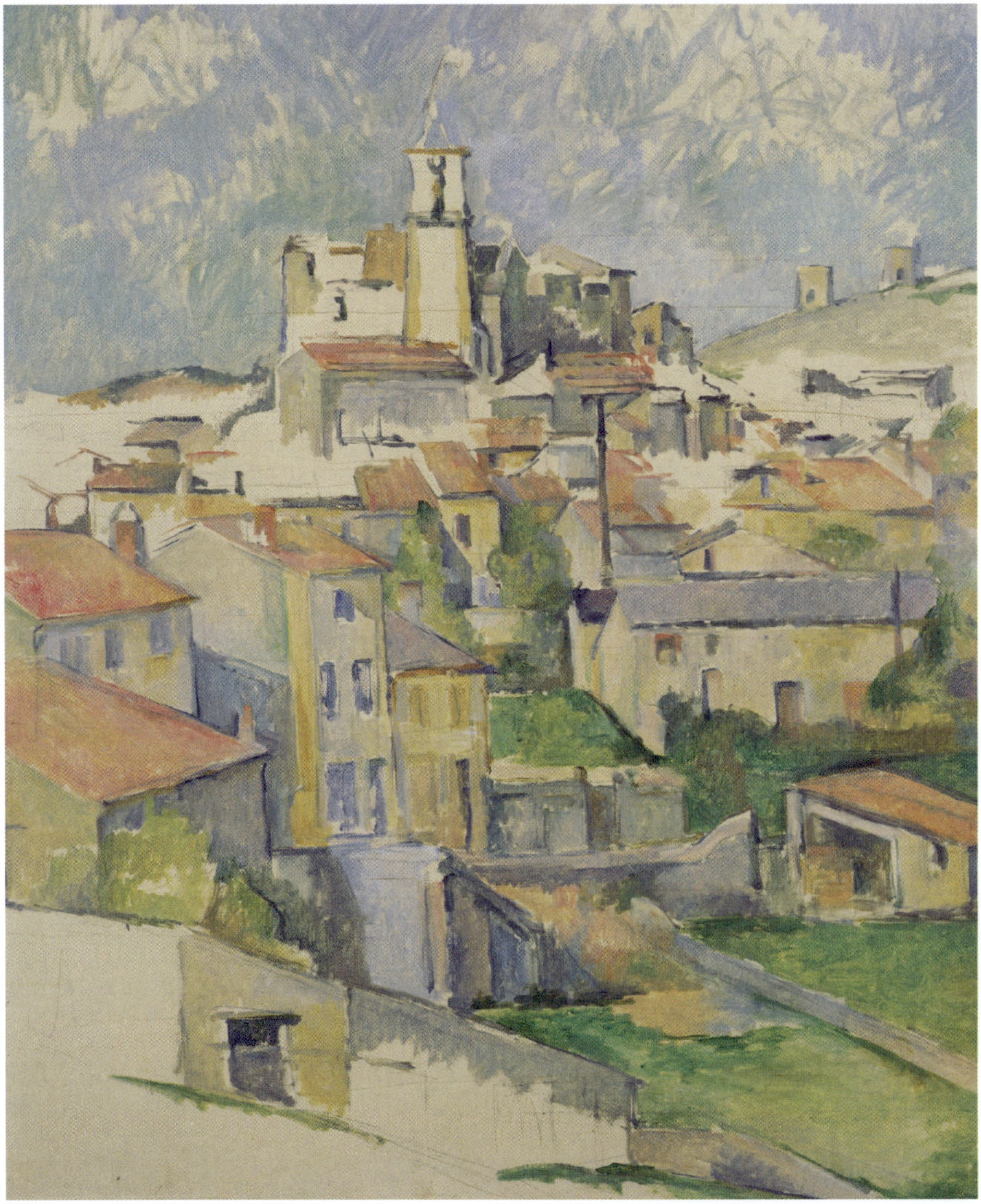

Fig. 42. Paul Cézanne, GARDANNE.

suggest an aerated environment. If the colors are too harsh, they will seem airless, and the picture will appear artificial.

Have a look at this work by Cézanne, a Postimpressionist much revered by other painters (Fig. 42). Notice the soft naturalistic color in this landscape. He is working off a soft neutral tone and casually adds notes of light-filled pastel hues to delineate the landscape. None of his color notes are dark as they are permeated with light and softened by the atmosphere. He has literally visualized the air.

Let's have a look at this 1868 painting by the American Winslow Homer (Fig. 43).

I love this painting for many reasons. Notice again the soft naturalistic color, how the soft blue of the mountains in the background says distance. It's a bright sunny day, and the strong light lands on the horse and the shoulder of the rider while her face covered by the hat is in shadow. The shadow is not black; it is full of color and touched by the light as well—we call this a reflected light.

Remember that when objects are distant from us, we cannot see them clearly, so when the artist blurs the features, he speaks distance, and when he outlines the features, he speaks nearness.

This is the way a painter creates the illusion of the third dimension, with the values, hues, and clarity of the image. And here we have such a consciousness of air that we can almost feel the warmth of the sun and the cool breeze.

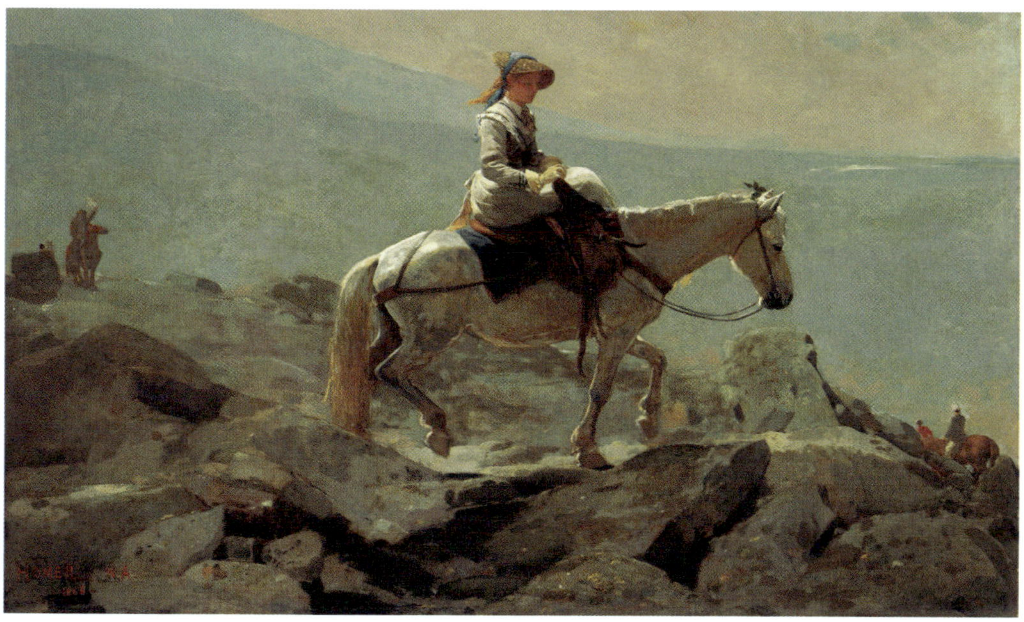

Fig. 43. Winslow Homer, THE BRIDLE PATH, WHITE MOUNTAINS.

Looking for the air will enhance your enjoyment of painting in general, but especially landscape painting, where it is most evident. Take note of how the artist achieved the natural feeling that the place depicted is an earthly place with an atmosphere by virtue of the palette of hues and color that speak of air and light and the way he has composed and delineated the pictorial elements.

COLOR

Let's talk color.

We all love color. If we could not see color and had to live in a black-and-white world, we would feel very sorry for ourselves, wouldn't we?

There are myriad hues, and mixing color is one of the most joyous activities of the artist. Color is one of our expressive tools, and probably the most accessible. Defining space, or drawing, is more difficult than painting and requires more time to learn to do it well. It is heavy brain work. But color, color is the candy box of our emotions.

We use color in imaginative ways in our daily life, in the way we dress, and decorate our homes. We have a sense of a color palette; we "match" colors and have a sense of what goes with what.

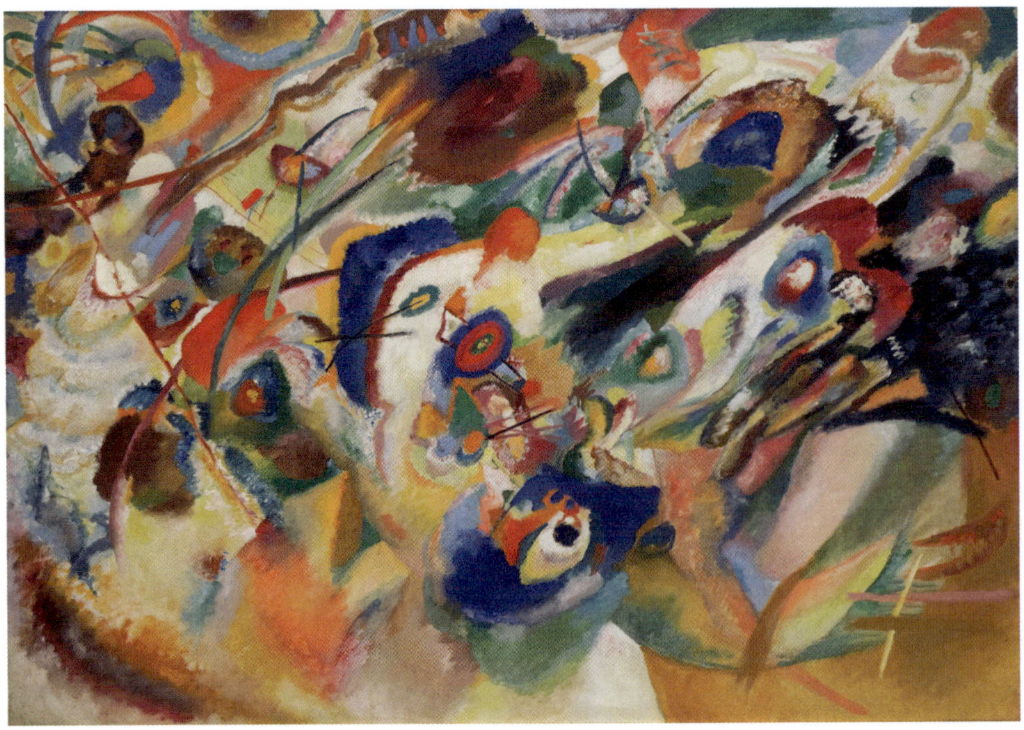

Fig. 44. Vasily Kandinsky, SKETCH II FOR COMPOSITION VII.

A painter uses color in a more elaborate way, not just as decoration, or to make pleasing combinations, but to express the emotions, spatial dynamics, mood, and drama of his work. He may deliberately use colors that do not "match," and that are not pleasing to the eye. They serve a greater purpose in the artwork than to look pretty or please the viewer. They convey a significant message.

So to understand and appreciate the color message, you must look beyond attractiveness and ask yourself how the colors chosen convey a mood, express space, and deliver a specific message. You are reading the colors and the shapes as messages.

You will be decoding them. Ask: Are the colors bright or subdued? Warm or cold? What is the overall tone? Are they bathed in light or sunk in shadow? Are they accurate, do they feel true? Are the colors harsh or soft? Somber or bright? What do the colors tell you about the message the artist was attempting to convey?

Let's look at some of the great colorists and feast our eyes.

Kandinsky gave us a symphony of color in this swirling composition (Fig. 44). He creates a whole dimension out of these floating colored shapes. This is like a delicious feast with sweet and salty colors living together. Think of color as flavors you can taste with your eyes.

A popular subject of the colorist Matisse was a room with an open window. This enabled the artist to depict both the bright outdoors and the cooler indoors in a single work. For a master of color and light, no subject could be more delicious. You will find one of Matisse's windows in our Chapter 9.

Note that windows and doors are popular subjects of painters through the ages. They are particularly resonant subjects for artists, along with mirrors and other optical devices. Artists are fascinated with visual vehicles and anomalies.

A painting is a trip an artist sends you on through imaginary space. Passing through windows and doors makes for particularly interesting visual transit. In a sense, the artist provides a map for your eyes to move through the world of the painting. More on this as we discuss composition.

I'm a tremendous fan of the Nabis (a group of painters following the Impressionists), exemplified by Pierre Bonnard and Édouard Vuillard, both of whom utilized color in a beautiful way. On the next page, in this elegantly composed work by Bonnard, we have the window, bringing in the light (Fig. 45). This is a beautifully and quite deliberately composed work. Note the way the space of the room is defined and the

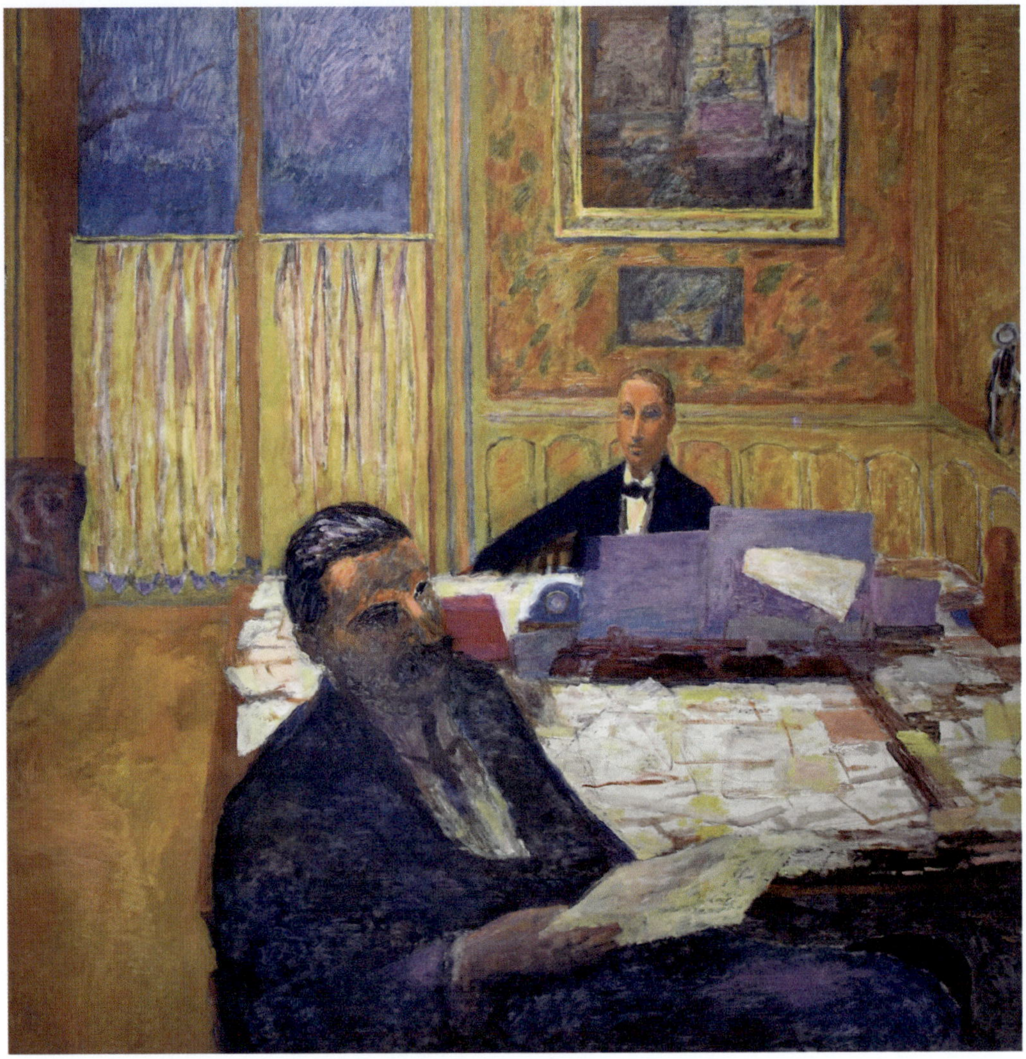

Fig. 45. Pierre Bonnard, THE BROTHERS BERNHEIM-JEUNE.

relative size of the two figures. Note how the painting takes your eye out the window and then back into the room. Note how the orange light on the front figure relates to the other warm notes—the wall, floor, and back figure.

Bonnard's palette here is very selective, and somewhat limited to shades of blue and gold, connected by the white of the papers. The large swaths and blocks of color create the design of the painting. Forget for a moment that you're looking at the illusion of two men seated at a table and look at this painting as a composition of blue and gold. Just lovely!

Nabi painters Bonnard and Vuillard made a kind of contiguous patterning in their works, so much so that they resemble tapestries of light and color. The color is still atmospheric, but richer. For this reason they are considered Postimpressionists and they move us to artists that use color more imaginatively, like Gauguin with his purple skies, and also the Fauves.

The Fauves utilized purer, deeper, less pastel colors and so acquired this nickname, which means "beasts." Their color was considered wild, and is exemplified in works by Derain, Vlaminck, and Matisse for a time, and other practitioners.

Here is an example of a Fauvist style painting by an American artist, who like many of his compatriots of that era, went to Paris to paint and tried his hand at being "one of the wild ones" (Fig. 46). Notice the paucity of black; it had no place in this richly colored world.

Though the Fauvist movement was initiated following Postimpressionism, this does not mean that richly colored painting disappeared from the art of painting once this era passed. Many artists, including contemporary ones, continued to use pure,

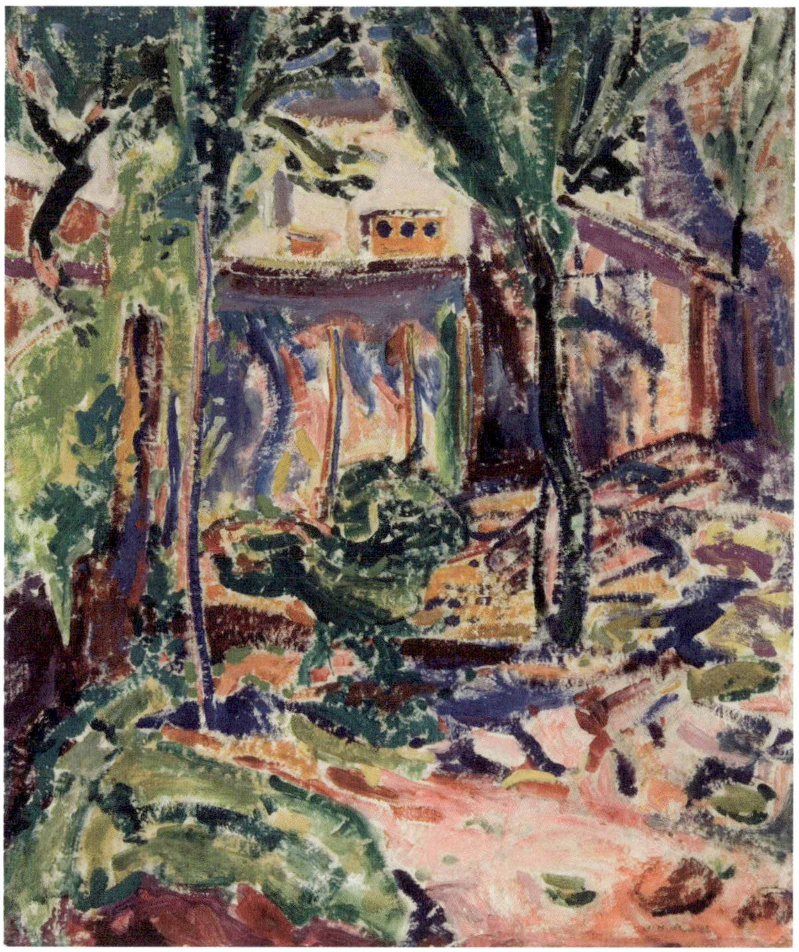

Fig. 46. Alfred Henry Maurer, LANDSCAPE WITH HOUSE.

bright, and even neon colors that are reminiscent of the Fauves. Here is a work by a lesser-known English painter, James Fitton (Fig. 47). I was struck by this self-portrait, executed a year before the artist's death. Both the artist's use of Fauvist color to suggest shadow and his lush purple background, a very unusual color choice, are exceedingly effective.

Remember that the names of movements may help up to understand characteristics of certain types of artwork, but may not be exclusive to a certain time or place.

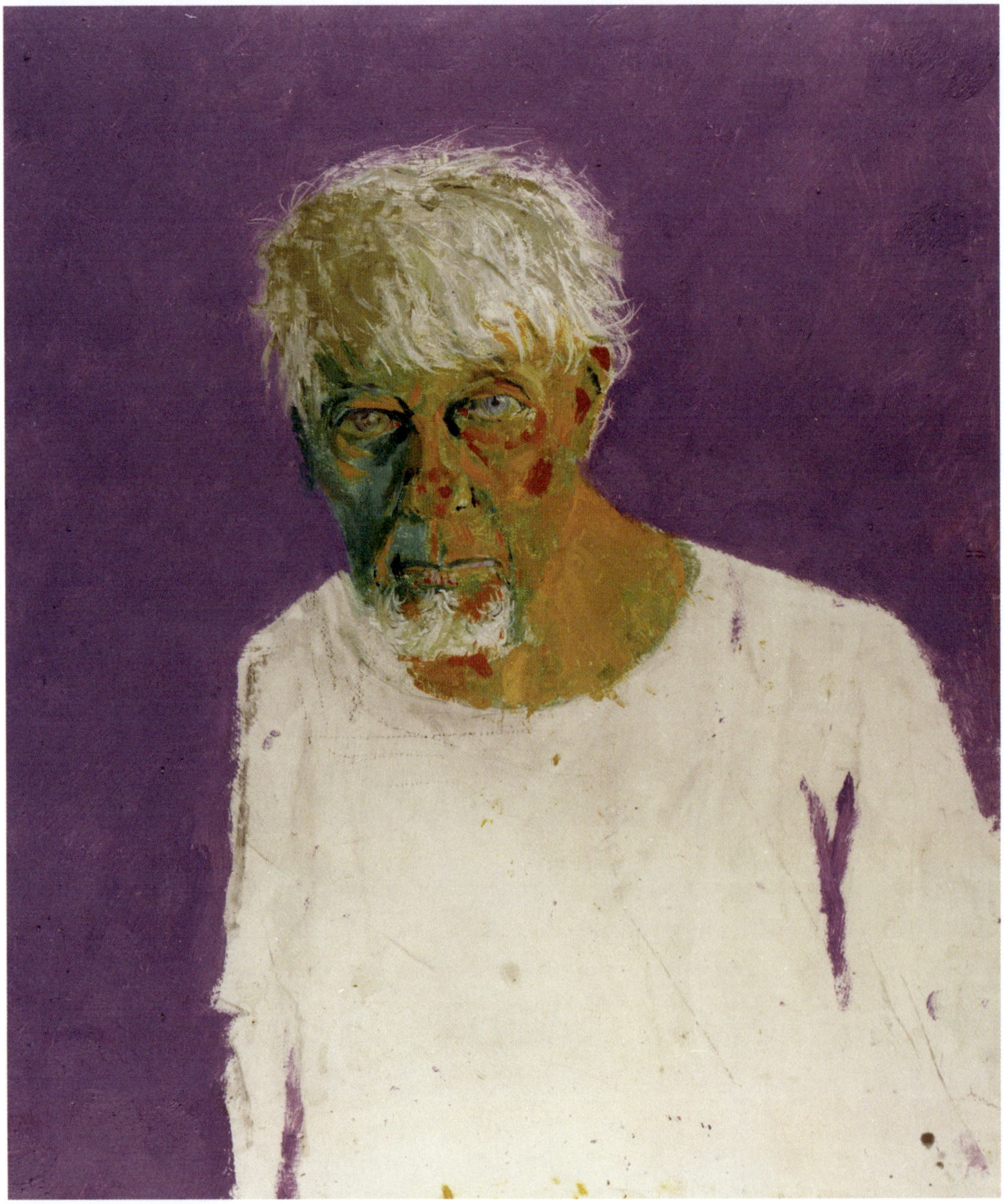

Fig. 47. James Fitton, SELF-PORTRAIT.

There is lots of crossover in the art world—artists from the past whose work seems ultramodern and contemporary artists who specialize in academic realism, like the painter Odd Nerdrum.

Again, the work speaks best for itself. A point for formalism!

I encourage you to look at abstract painters who celebrated color. Look up Rothko, who made simple divisions of the canvas, making it his singular focus. Each note has a different vibration due to the color mixture and the way the paint is applied. Look at Frankenthaler, mistress of delicate washes. Diebenkorn with his geometrical divisions, Hans Hoffman, and many others.

Color plays a leading role in abstract painting. Study color when looking at any work, but pay special attention when you consider an abstract one. Enjoy color as you would a melody in music. Is the color in a major or minor key?

Color is an element in art that we can all relate to. Let's just endeavor to be more specific about what we like or dislike about the coloration in a work of art, and also consider why the artist might have made the color choices he made. Notice the way the color is applied, whether it is transparent or solid, and identify the pattern the color makes.

It is helpful to find adjectives that describe the color you see. Here are a few: pungent, spicy, delicate, hot, sweet, raw, girlish, watery, fragrant, smelly, flowery, sun-kissed, etc.

Get the idea? Your use of language to describe what you see and feel is a creative act, and a way to understand art as an artist yourself. Try it and see what I mean.

COMPOSITION

Composition. Study it.

The way an artist composes his canvas, drawing, or art piece is essential to its success. When you look at a work, try to determine what the artist's focal point is. The focal point is where your eye is driven when you look at the work. It indicates what is most important to the artist, and his composition has directed you to zero in on it.

Whether the work is abstract, semi-abstract, or realistic, it is only offering you a piece of a world. Your eye can imagine where the work leaves off and what would be adjacent. As art students, we are always cautioned against cutting off the object at the perimeter of the work as this would appear awkward. Notice how the artist has sized the objects in the work and where he has elected to cut them. Placement and sizing are important compositional challenges.

Is the design symmetrical or off-center? Does it form a dominant shape, like a square or triangle? Notice the size of objects and their shape. Are they life-size? What about the proportions? Is anything exaggerated?

Artists through the centuries have theorized on what makes a good composition. Vis-à-vis landscape, Renaissance artist John Thomas Smith came up with a proposition called the *rule of thirds*. Dividing a canvas into thirds both vertically and horizontally, he theorized that placing key focal points at these junctures would make for a more effective composition than placing a focal point in the center. The horizon line, for instance could be denoted at either the lower or higher third with the land or sky occupying the balance. Take note of this when you look at landscapes in particular.

Something else to look for in a composition is how the busy and quiet spaces are distributed. What we refer to as *negative space*, the air around an object, is essential to revealing that object and making it of interest. A similar distribution of warm and cool hues and vibrant and subdued tones, also establishes the effectiveness of the composition.

Is the composition static or dynamic? Particularly when figures are represented, a painting represents a freezing of time. This is particularly noticeable when the figures are represented in an animated state—for instance, laughing or dancing. Has the artist succeeded in making the painting naturalistic or does it seem artificial? Is it uncomfortable to look at?

Why did the artist compose the picture the way he did? Can you think of a reason? Is it working, and if so, why?

Here are two examples of artists whose compositions told a story (Figs. 48 and 49). Both of them were painters of intimate interiors, Vermeer in the seventeenth century and Vuillard in the twentieth. Vermeer's compositions depict just two of the rooms in his Delft house, and the decorations and cast of characters repeat. Yet the compositions are so tight and well rendered that they invite us into their world in the most compelling way, as here, where Vermeer permits us to watch him at work.

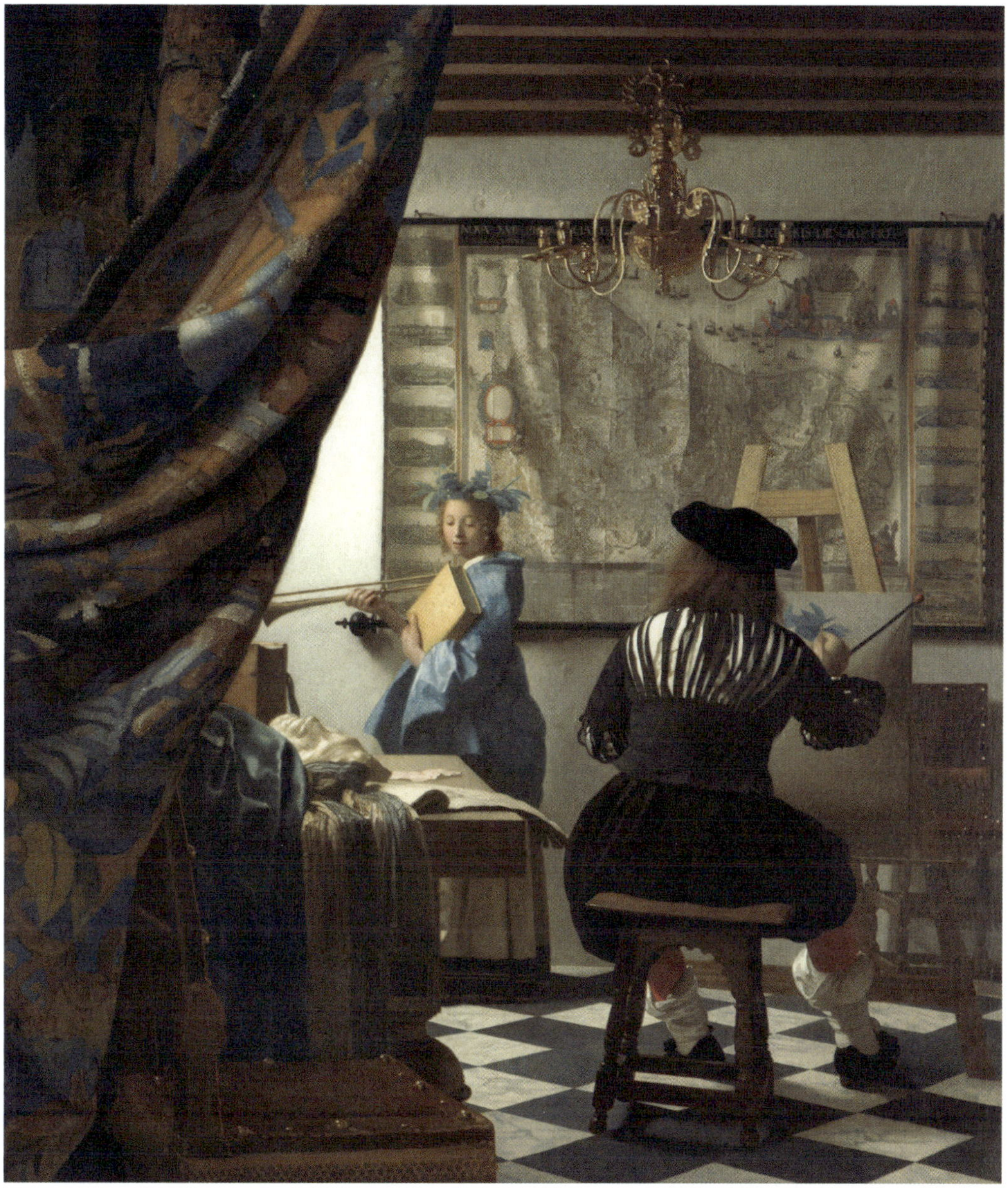

Fig. 48. Johannes Vermeer, THE ART OF PAINTING.

So too three centuries later when Monsieur Vuillard welcomes us into his home on Rue Truffaut to see his mother, with whom he lived to the age of sixty. She ran a corset business, and here she is depicted sewing. His affection for his home is depicted in a tapestry of notes and patterns.

As we travel around the room, our eyes alight on a patch of fabric, a grate outside the window bathed in light, a textured tablecloth, the faded wallpaper, all soaked in the warmth, quiet, and coziness the artist apparently felt in his home. And in the midst of it all, his mother, the center of his universe. Through his artistic choices,

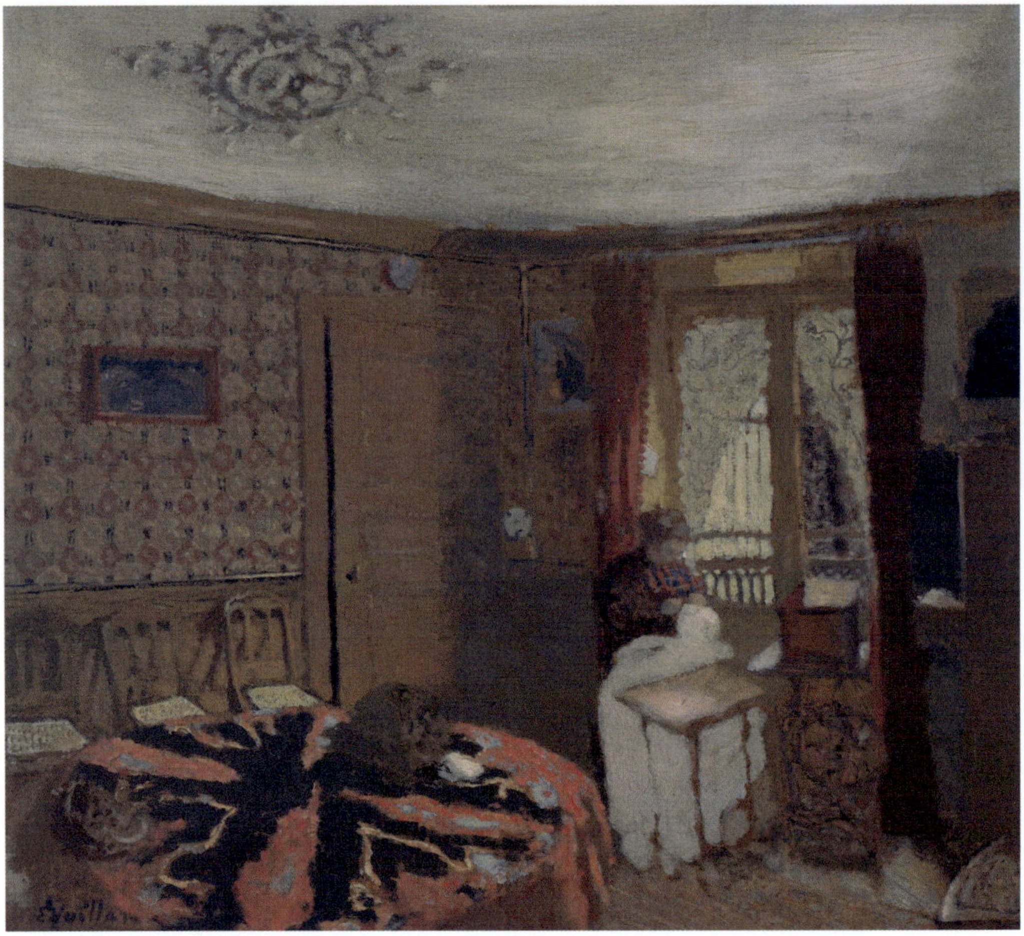

Fig. 49. Édouard Vuillard, MADAME VUILLARD SEWING BY THE WINDOW, RUE TRUFFAUT.

the artist reveals not only his home, but his psyche as well. The inner reality shapes the outer manifestation.

Just to note: Vuillard was a child of Impressionism and a founding member of a group called the Nabis. His brother in art, Pierre Bonnard, joined him in the creation of visual tapestries of light and color in the rooms and gardens where they lived. They are both referred to as "intimists," due to their choice of interiors and family members as subjects of their visionary works.

APPLICATION OF PAINT

Each painter has his or her own way of applying paint and distinct preferences as to how it is best applied. This way of applying the paint becomes a kind of signature for the artist, and in many cases you can recognize a painter's work by the quality of his paint.

Artists have preference for the kind of paint they use, the brand, and the color palette they select. Paint is made with pigment, a liquid that makes it flow, and a binder that holds the ingredients together. The two basic kinds of paint are either water-based or oil-based. Of the paints made with water, we have watercolor, gouache, tempera, and acrylic paint, each having its own qualities and densities. Because water evaporates quickly, water-based paints are quick drying, which makes them difficult to change and manipulate.

Oil-based paint, made with oil, which is slow to dry, is by its nature the most flexible of all and affords the artist the greatest vocabulary with which to work. The paint can be worked, layered, scraped, sanded, and used as a glaze when thinned. It can be laid on thick with a brush or palette knife to create an impasto; it can also be made transparent and translucent.

Pay attention to the quality of the paint when you look at paintings. The little card next to the painting in the museum will usually identify the medium, but after a while you won't need the card. You will recognize the material by its appearance. Does it have a dry or an oily feel? Is it flat or textured?

Can you guess whether the artist used a brush or other device? A palette knife? A rag?

Are there patterns created in the paint? Are colors layered over one another? If so, do you think the artist let the first layer dry and then added the second? What effect does the paint have on the overall look of the painting? How does it express the theme?

Is the paint application tender, rough, fragmented, staccato? What word would you use to describe it?

Notice also the surface of the painting. If it is canvas, is the weave tight or loose? If a solid hard surface, like wood, compare this to the softer fabric surface. Remember that different surfaces accept the paint in a certain way and determine, to a large extent, the look of the piece.

When it comes to paper, just like canvas, there are many different types and weights, and these are usually matched to a material. Smooth surfaces work with inks; rougher papers with charcoal, sanded or textured papers with pastel, etc.

But keep in mind that artists don't always choose the ideal surface or paint for their work for a variety of reasons. It may not have been available at the time or place.

First choice might have been too expensive, so the artist used what we had handy, or could find at lower cost. And sometimes by using an inappropriate material, he may have accidentally discovered a new way of working.

So as you look at surface and application of paint or other material, just note its effectiveness in expressing an idea or emotion. And enjoy it just in and of itself, as you would a beautiful sunset. These materials are just substances the artist uses to express. What the artist has managed to do with the materials is the real story. But it is worthwhile to take note of how the material chosen has allowed the artist to express his personality and preferences.

LOOKING AT SCULPTURE

I've talked a lot about painting, but let's turn now to sculpture. In painting, the artist is working on a flat surface and possibly creating an illusion of depth. In sculpture, he's working with the real thing. As a result, sculpture is made in the round and the sculptor has to imagine his piece working from all angles. You will see sculptors either promenading around their pieces or, if small enough, rotating them on a turntable or other device. The process is a logistical excursion.

Many materials can be and are utilized to make sculpture, both soft and hard. Clay, made of earth, is a wonderful and versatile medium, in that it can be used to both add and subtract elements. A blob added here, one deleted there; it is probably one of the most artist-friendly mediums.

Clay has its difficulties, though. It must be fired to strengthen and harden; large pieces need to be hollowed to withstand forces in the kiln; and glazes used to colorize and texturize the surface are often unpredictable. It is also highly breakable.

Then there's glass, another wonder. Glass, like clay, requires heat to form, either in a glory hole for hot blown glass, with a torch for flame-worked pieces, or a kiln for warm or fused or cast glass. It is highly technical and the artist must memorize complex formulas for heating and cooling (annealing) glass pieces. Disaster can strike, and pieces labored on for weeks and months can be destroyed in an instant, due to miscalculation, using incompatible glasses, or improper, insufficient annealing time. To a certain extent, glass can be reheated and reworked, but not without challenge. Overheating can cause glass to vitrify and lose its shininess.

Then we have all the hard media: marble, wood, metal, and the like, each with its own particular set of issues. Marble is a subtraction medium—the artist chips away, and, for the most part, can't add back the missing chunks. With wood, though addition is possible—wood can be glued, laminated, and assembled—but it has its tricky side too. An organic material, it has weaknesses, knots, and defects that must be taken into account, and these sometimes appear as one is midway through a creation.

As a general rule, the artist must honor the particularities of his material, and work with it, even allowing the material to take the lead and set the tone. Sometimes it works and sometimes not. I sculpted a little Buddha once out of wood, and a knot magnificently appeared in the perfect spot for an eye. But unexpected negatives can arise just as frequently.

Sculptors can and often do combine materials to great effect. And there is a whole branch of sculpture comprised of recycled materials, found objects, and all manner of contraptions and commodities. One of the hallmarks of artistry is the ability to reconfigure and give new life to something discarded as rubbish. To see beauty in the discarded, old, godforsaken detritus of our lives and make it live again as art is a fascination for many artists.

As you look at sculpture, make sure to make the rounds and examine it from every point of view. That is the joy of the art form. Does the piece work, and is it interesting from every angle? Take note of the material the sculptor used and consider why that medium was chosen for this particular piece. Could it have been better in another? Was it created by a process of addition—adding pieces to build the work—or subtraction—cutting away part of something to create the piece?

On the latter subtraction mode, I have said, and other artists have joined me on this, that it feels like the sculpture already exists in the wood or marble or whatever material it is cut out of, and the artist's role is to bring it out, to reveal it.

ARTIST MATERIALS

How do artists choose the medium they prefer?

It is interesting to consider why artists choose the materials they do, why one visual artist decides to be a painter and another a sculptor. Each medium possesses its own set of expressive possibilities, and makes a match with the interests, talents, and abilities of the artists that use them.

Painters create illusions, images, and there is little or no construction involved in their process. Making sculpture involves an engineering problem—the piece has a distribution of weight and issues of gravity, volume, structure, etc. come into play in their creation.

Painting and sculpture are sequential processes. In painting, there is a methodology known as *al primo* or *alla prima* where the painting is completed while the paint is still wet. This type of work might be completed in a single session, or several; what is salient is that the process is continuous, without preparatory steps. This approach is more difficult to achieve in sculpture, which traditionally requires more planning and preparation.

So it is likely that a spontaneous type might choose the art of painting, and someone more able to think procedurally might prefer sculpture. As to the specific choice of medium, this is partly due to availability, accessibility, and exposure to a given material. Artists often try several media and find that one or more are more suitable to their touch or approach, or to the thematic material or subject matter they choose.

I knew a glass artist who was a former baker and found the process of creating glass molds to be similar to that of her former baking and icing activities. A ceramic artist who liked to play in the mud as a child. A wax encaustic worker who found the texture of this medium ideal for her earthly abstractions. A graphic artist who drew the complexities of trees and found no better medium than pencil and charcoal. And so on.

Artists also inherently have a certain preference in terms of scale and proportion. Look at Christo, who needs an entire landscape to create. Or many other environmental artists who think of the earth as their canvas. Every artist has a particularly sized world he or she can manage. It can be tiny for a jewelry artist, or grandiose for an environmental sculptor. The medium not only determines the message; it *is* the message.

OTHER INFLUENCES

Other, nonartistic influences come to account in the choices artists make. Finances, for sure. The ability to work large, for instance, is costly. An artist needs a large space and a significant amount of very expensive materials. A large bank account or benefactor may not be available, so the artist desirous of working large may execute studio pieces instead.

Sometimes health or physical ability is determinative. Artists get old and perhaps can no longer stand to work. I think of Matisse who, diagnosed with cancer in the latter part of his life and only able to work in a seated position, turned from painting to the art of decoupage, or cut-paper collages. His assistant would pre-color the paper and Matisse would cut them. Out of adversity, a stunning new art form!

Success in art makes many choices possible, but the choices informed by lack of success during a lifetime can still be astounding. Here I think of Modigliani, who lived a mere thirty-six years and worked voluminously during his lifetime, but alas, much of his work was lost, discarded, or given away. When he was twenty-six he had a love affair with a Russian poet who had a studio in his building. She was tall, pale, had gray-green eyes, and became Modigliani's muse. This affair was short-lived, but we have forevermore the exquisite object of this artist's desire in his surviving paintings of long-necked, turquoise-eyed women.

And here we must also mention the magnificent painter Vincent van Gogh, who sold only one painting in his lifetime, and whose work posthumously became the most famous and sought after in the history of art. We must ask: Would we have those starry skies if life had gone more smoothly, and success come to the artist when he was alive?

Other skills and abilities play a part in artists' choices too. And this is why knowing the history of an artist is relevant and may color the way you view his or her work. Some examples:

> **Leonardo da Vinci**, of the fifteenth century, known as a painter and sculptor, was also an inventor, skilled in science, music, mathematics, engineering, literature, anatomy, geology, astronomy, botany, writing, history, and cartography. He was truly one of the most remarkable humans who ever lived and the exemplar of the Renaissance man.
>
> **Georges Braque** was a housepainter and decorator before becoming an artist. See how his decorative patterning skill set the tone for his Cubist works.
>
> **Henri de Toulouse-Lautrec**, born into an aristocratic family, suffered from a debilitating condition that left him unusually short, an alcoholic, and a pariah. He turned to prostitutes, who became his models, and his short life ended at the age of thirty-six. His circus characters, and others who inhabited his world, people his exuberant, innovative, and disarming work.
>
> **Paul Gauguin** had a stint as a salesman and even a stockbroker, and in spite of a large family of wife and five children, had such wanderlust that he left

France to live in Martinique, Tahiti, and the Marquesas Islands, and left us with the color of the tropics and the vibrantly rendered individuals who people these islands.

Some other notable day jobs: Mark Rothko taught elementary school; Jackson Pollock was a babysitter; Keith Haring, a busboy; Jasper Johns designed shop windows for Tiffany; Richard Serra had a moving company. And the great Andy Warhol wasn't above designing greeting cards.

One more day job for the books. The artist Julian Schnabel at one time in his life worked as a dishwasher and short-order cook. And what was his signature experiment as an artist? None other than his "plate paintings" where he set paintings on broken ceramic plates. That's putting yourself and your life experiences into your art!

So, to recap, there are multiple reasons and rationales for the choices artists make, some conscious, some not. There's a tendency, when we know the circumstances of an artist's life, to perhaps extrapolate and draw conclusions about the artist's work. These may or may not be accurate.

We have mentioned the very famous Edvard Munch painting *The Scream*.

Munch and his beloved family suffered both physically and mentally, and the artist himself was frail and fraught with anxiety. It is said that his inspiration for the painting occurred one night at sunset while he was walking down a road with two friends. He had an anxiety attack and referred to his experience as a "scream of nature." Does it add to your enjoyment of the painting to know that both a slaughterhouse and an insane asylum that happened to house his sister at the time were within close proximity?

Indeed, many viewers know and identify with the emotion depicted in this work without knowing the conditions that perhaps caused the artist to conjure it. Munch's experience here and the experiences of every artist, both directly and indirectly, are manifest in their works of art. We can read the emotion without knowing its cause.

We opened this discussion with a mention of formalism vs. contextualism. As we continue looking at art and artists in the chapters that follow, our focus will continue in the formalist mode, seeing the work as an entity, a world unto itself, that can be appreciated and enjoyed without reference to the artist's psyche and circumstances. Knowing the context in which the work was created is important information for sure, but not knowing it still allows us to use aesthetic criteria and our own senses to appreciate it.

Chapter 8
Subject and Master: Figurative Art

Pictures tell a story in their own inimitable way. If a thought or idea was totally understandable in words, we would not need pictures, but the truth is that we depend on our eyes to gather much information and to appreciate the world we live in and that artists imagine for us.

We now greatly depend on still photographs and moving images (i.e. film) to fill us in on visual matters. As a result, we do not have the dependency on drawings and paintings to describe what we actually see, a function it performed for centuries. Portraiture, in particular, provided a record of what people actually looked like, and was not only prized, but was an almost essential service.

We turn now to a discussion of the major genres in art: figurative art, landscape, still life, and then on to abstraction and sculpture. There are myriad practitioners in each genre, and I mention only a sampling of the major figures in each. My hope is that you will take this general information and apply it to the viewing of other artists not mentioned here. Though not comprehensive, I lay out some major trends and ways to think about visual art.

Paintings of people, i.e. figurative art, has been and continues to be a subject of fascination for artists. As humans, we continue to be interested in how other humans look, are portrayed, and what emotional qualities they exhibit and bring out in the viewer. The definition and importance of creating a "likeness" has lessened with the advent of the photograph, and figurative art has expanded in every sense.

Early figurative art might be referred to as "history painting," usually detailing a scene from the Bible or an aspect of history and often featuring many individuals, animals, etc. These pictures are "scenes" in a sense, portrayals of people caught in a critical moment.

History painting comes under the banner of "narrative art"—in simple terms, art that tells a story. A cave painting showing the hunt is an example of narrative art, as is the Bayeux Tapestry, which recalls the story of the Norman invasion of England in 1066.

A modern example is the comic book or graphic novel, which tells the story in frames.

A portrait of a single individual, though it may not tell a sequential tale, can also have narrative content. Depending on the pose, attitude, positioning, size, and environment of the person being portrayed, we may draw certain conclusions about the sitter's character, state of mind, demeanor, and life.

To differentiate, a narrative work usually depicts figures in an active format, and a portrait is a likeness or treatment of the sitter usually standing or sitting still.

We cannot be sure that what the painting tells us about the sitter or subject is actually true. The artist has chosen to depict the individual according to his or her preferences and what the artist wants to say about the subject. If you enter an art class and see artists drawing or painting the same model, each rendering will look different, not only because each is rendering the subject from a different point of view, but also because artists make art choices based on who they are and what interests them.

There are many who believe that figurative artists actually make portraits of themselves, and the sitter is only the premise. Indeed, there is a certain truth to this, and if you study the many portraits of a single artist you will find the similarities in the subjects. Sometimes, you may be fortunate to see a photograph of the artist. If you do, relate the artist's facial structure to that of his portrait.

A portrait or figurative work shows the person(s) depicted as frozen in the moment. There is a certain artificiality in this fact, and the painter is aware of it. He or she makes the work over time, but the image is still. I think this is the main reason you will not find many portraits illustrating people smiling, as it seems odd to smile for more than a moment and certainly not for all eternity. Photographers ask their sitters to smile, but painters not so much. This is a curious fact. What do you make of it?

When studying a figurative work, consider the following. Is the depiction naturalistic, stylized, or abstract? Notice the skin tones in particular. Are they what you might expect in a color photograph, or are they strange, a variety of imagined colors? Is there color in the shadows?

What does the pose or position of the sitter tell you about what the artist wanted to tell you about them? Was the artist's purpose to show the sitter in a favorable light? To make the model beautiful? Is there a message in the work? If so, is it political or psychological?

Why did the artist choose to portray this particular subject? Was it just to describe the subject? To make a judgment about the subject? To portray the subject in a humorous way or to make fun of the subject? To exalt the subject? Can you guess the artist's intention by the way the artist has depicted the sitter?

Does the painting have a mood? How would you describe it? Is the person depicted lost in thought, distressed, uncomfortable, excited?

The art of portraiture has many facets. It can be descriptive and just put forward a likeness—much traditional portraiture has this intent. It can be unsettling or mysterious in some way, attempting to say something about the inner life of the subject. Or it can even have an allegorical reference, going beyond the individual, to portray a character that is iconic. As you look at portraits, knowing these distinctions may help you to get more out of the figurative art as you realize that resemblance is only one small component of this art form.

Let's have a look at some of the masters of figurative art through the centuries and talk about some of the special characteristics that made their work so memorable.

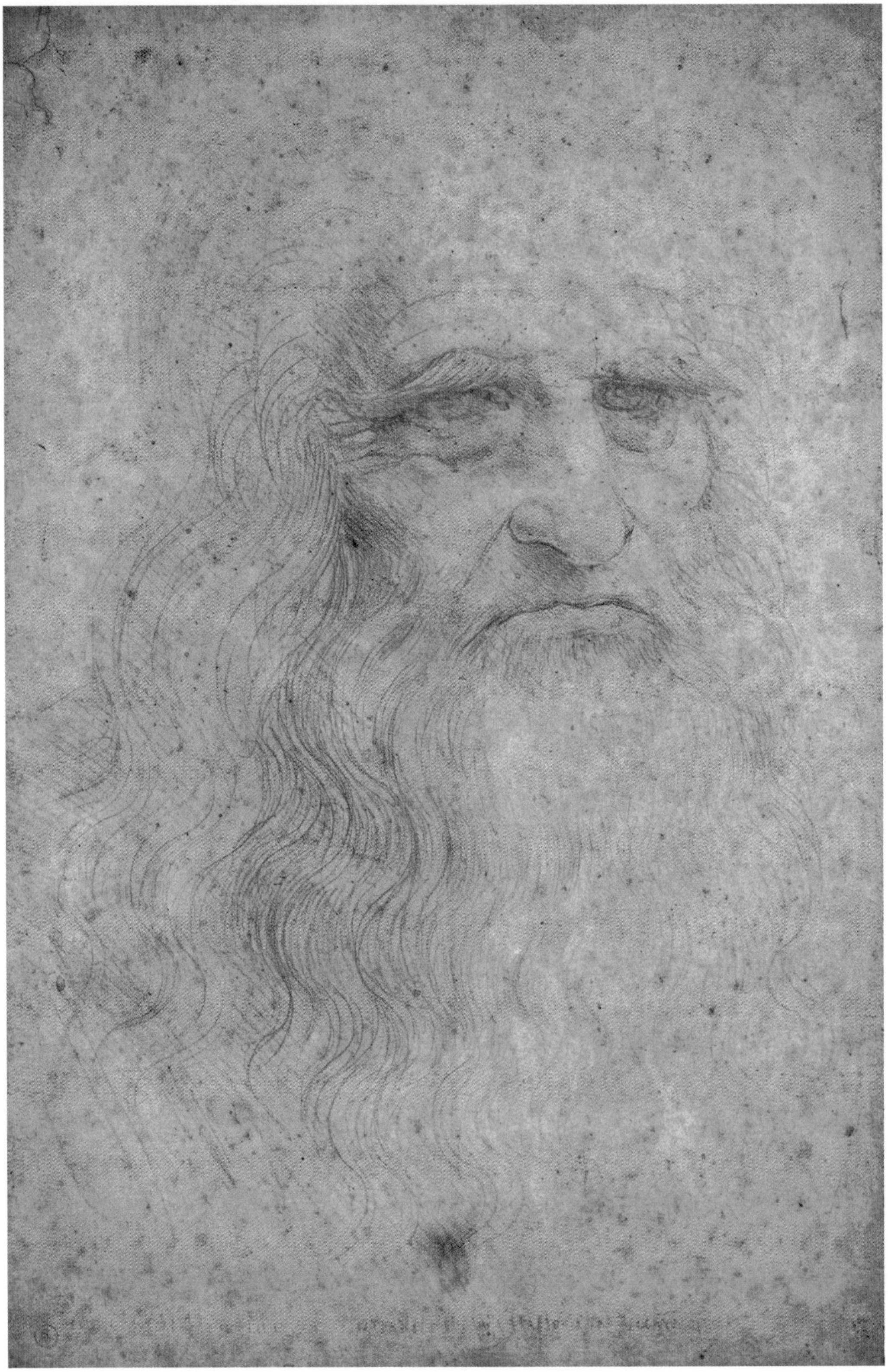

Fig. 50. Leonardo da Vinci, SELF-PORTRAIT.

LEONARDO DA VINCI (1452–1519)

One of the most remarkable humans who ever lived, the "Renaissance man," both artist and scientist, Leonardo created the most famous figurative works in the world, *The Mona Lisa* and *The Last Supper*. Only about fifteen of his paintings still exist, but his name is synonymous with genius.

Why is his *Mona Lisa* so revered? The sitter takes up most of the piece, the colors are drab, the scene behind her resembles a stage set, yet the painting is captivating.

The painting is flat, with no noticeable brushstrokes. She is famous for her mysterious upturned mouth, just the slightest hint of a smile, which suggests a self-satisfaction or perhaps an unrevealed delicious thought. This expression is what makes this painting so interesting, and so alive. It poses a question, something to ponder and wonder about—what is the Giaconda smiling about? This is a question that has been unanswered for more than half a millennium and still continues to amaze.

Sometimes a painting can become so familiar that it can be turned into a joke or used for other commercial purposes that degrade its original intent. When this happens, the work is so tarnished that the true meaning becomes invisible. We cannot unsee the tawdry purpose for which it has been exploited.

Since this is the case for the *Mona Lisa*, we look to a lesser-known work by Leonardo.

Look at this self-portrait he created in 1512 with red chalk only (Fig. 50). It is the size of a piece of copy paper, only 8 × 13 inches. It is amazing for its time as it seems almost modern, something that could be created today. It attests to the power of his genius, which could transcend time. The power of art lives: remember that Leonardo da Vinci lived more than five hundred years ago, and we are still appreciating his work.

Takeaway: Renaissance Genius

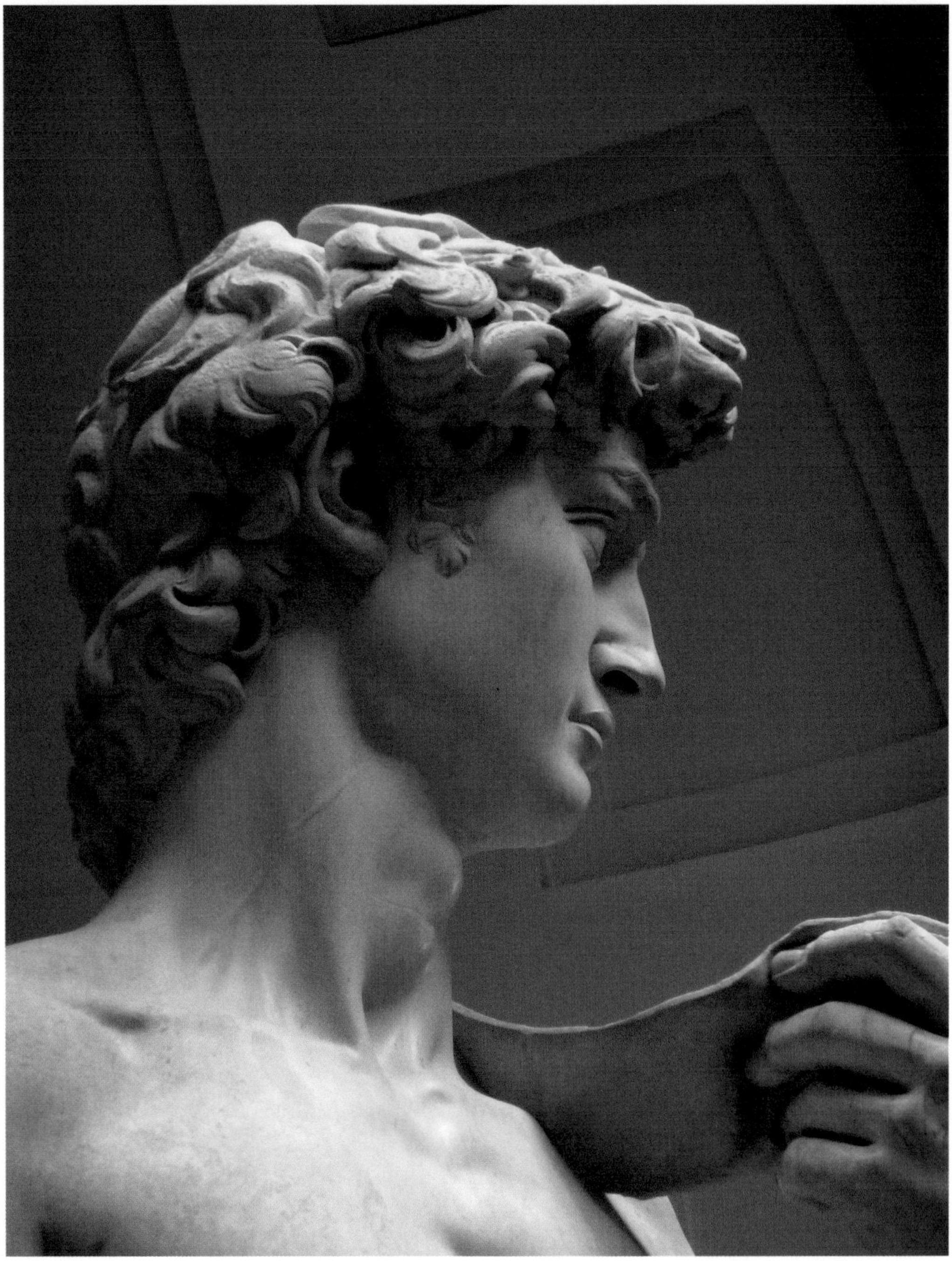

Fig. 51. Michelangelo, DAVID (detail).

MICHELANGELO DI LODOVICO BUONARROTI SIMONI (1475–1564)

Another Renaissance man known by one name only, Michelangelo was the consummate artist, with an artistic skill set so extraordinary that it is difficult to name another so gifted. He reputedly cared little for the pleasures of life, so absorbed was he with his work.

And what he left us are the most memorable sculptures and paintings ever created. They are idealizations with a grounding in a thorough understanding of anatomy and proportion. They are classical, and yet so exquisitely beautiful only a romantic could imagine them.

His *David*, probably the most famous statue in the world, is, quite simply, perfection. This is not a word that is used to describe art, and yet, I can think of no other that would do it justice.

What makes it so "perfect"? we must ask. Giorgio Vasari said of another of Michelangelo's masterpieces, *The Pietà*, that "It is certainly a miracle that a formless block of stone could ever have been reduced to a perfection that nature is scarcely able to create in the flesh."

Understanding of anatomy? Engaged observation? Precision of eye and hand?

Not even these can explain his artistry. Michelangelo idealized the human form and made it into an object of pure beauty. Only the combination of superhuman talent and love could create something this splendid, something rising to the very pinnacle of human achievement.

Takeaway: Idealized Form

TIZIANO VECELLI (TITIAN) (1488–1576)

Titian was known for and is remembered for his sense of color, vivid for this early period, and also his loose brushstrokes. He was a Venetian, and his painting has a beauty and vivacity consonant with that stunningly beautiful corner of the planet. He is considered one of the great portrait painters.

When you stumble upon a Titian in the museum, take note of the richness of his color and remember that the pigments of his day were limited. This will make you even more impressed with the intensity of his color.

Takeaway: Early Colorist

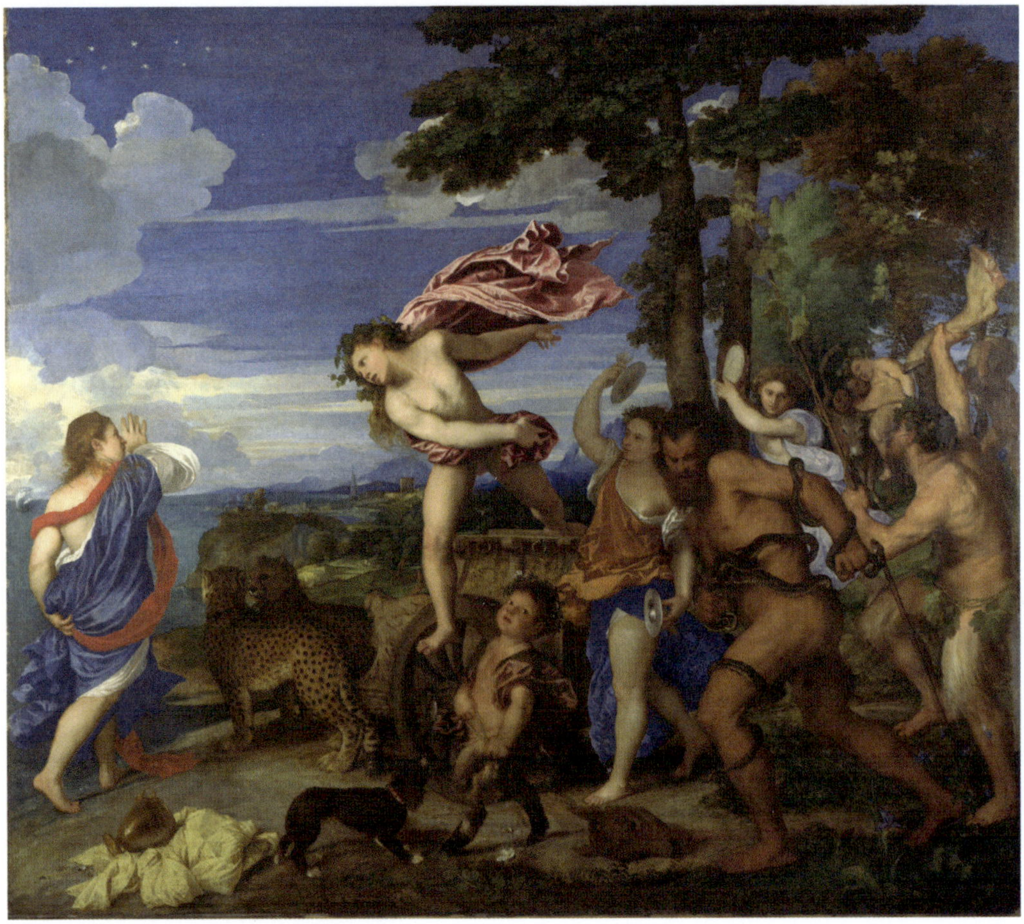

Fig. 52. Titian, BACCHUS AND ARIADNE.

EL GRECO (DOMÉNIKOS THEOTOKÓPOULOS) (1541–1613)

El Greco was a painter whose work is pretty instantaneously recognizable due to its proportion and raw color. He was quite the individualist, ahead of his time, and appreciated more in modern times than in his own. He might even be called an Expressionist, as he deliberately elongated his figures, giving them that unmistakable "El Greco" appearance. Was he a tall man or perhaps a short one who desired to be tall, I wonder?

Remember our conversation about the classical versus the romantic approach. El Greco was definitely in the romantic category, though that word was not utilized in his time. He went in for a rigorous, physical kind of painting and large swaths of color.

El Greco was considered a Mannerist, a kind of iconoclast of the period, reacting against the idealism of classicism, as typified by Michelangelo. Instead of harmony and idealistic beauty, the Mannerist, as typified by El Greco, goes in for exaggeration and asymmetry, for the sake of drama.

As you examine the portraits and other subjects painted by El Greco, think about how modern a painter he was, and how original. One has to leap to the nineteenth and twentieth centuries to find other romantic painters with this kind of imagination, passion, and ingenuity.

Takeaway: Individualist

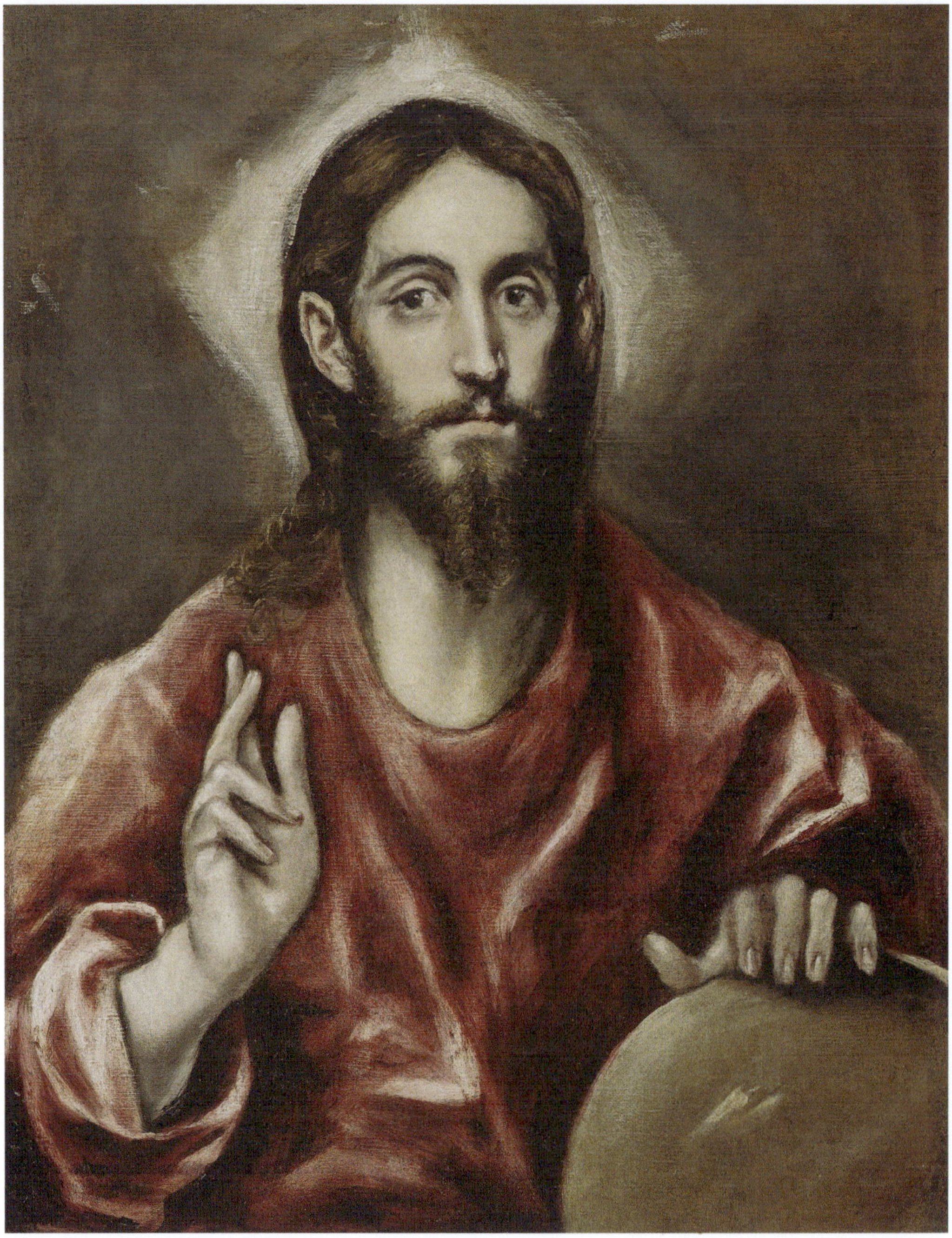

Fig. 53. El Greco, EL SALVADOR.

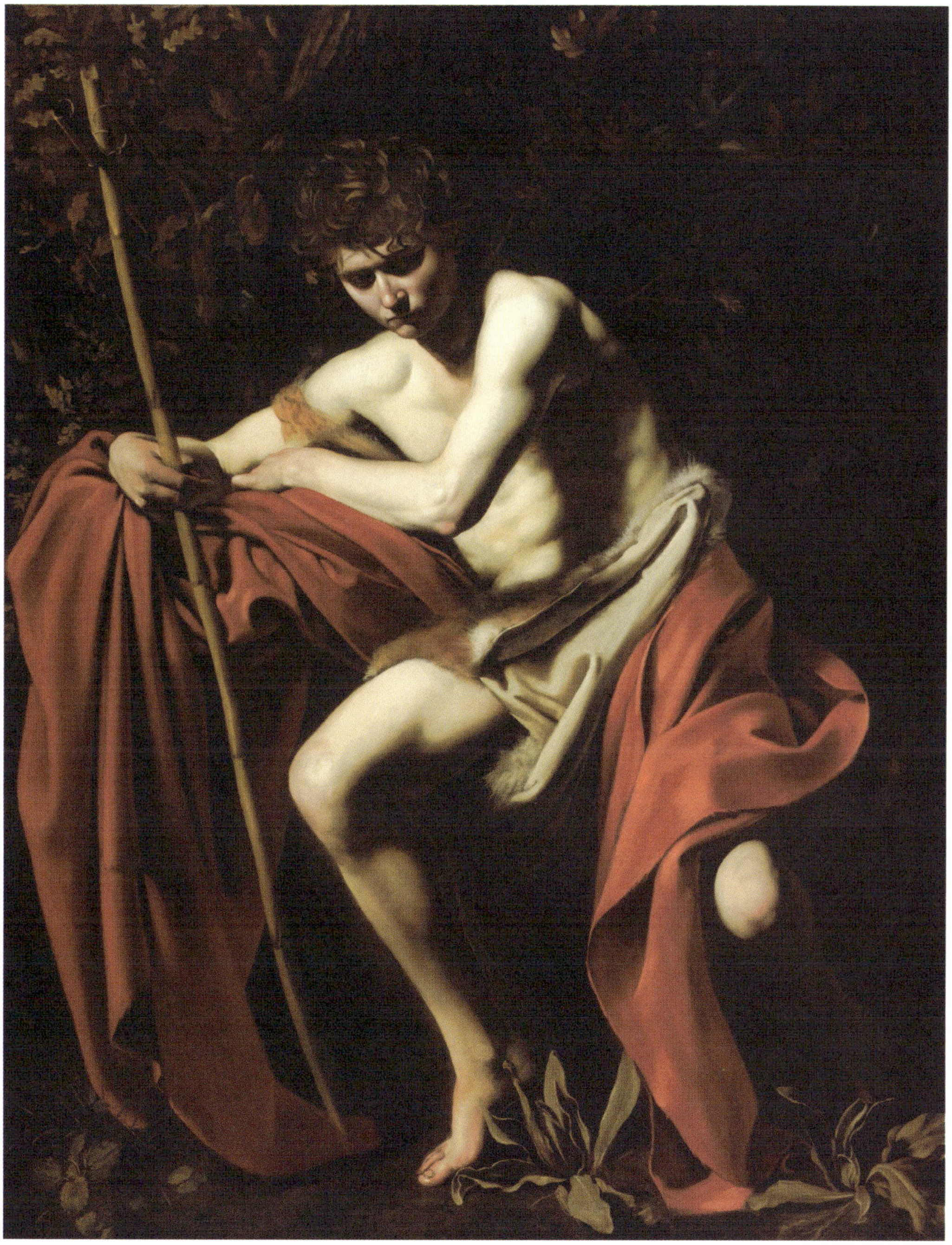

Fig. 54. Michelangelo Merisi da Caravaggio, SAINT JOHN THE BAPTIST IN THE WILDERNESS.

MICHELANGELO MERISI DA CARAVAGGIO (1571–1610)

Ah, Caravaggio, a master of light and shade. He turned on the light in painting in the most significant way. He is credited with inventing a style of extraordinarily dramatic lighting with an extremely long gamut of light to dark values called *tenebrism*. Think of a multi-watt spotlight—even the more radical because he created it at a time when candlelight was the order of the day.

Caravaggio was considered a Baroque artist, which school was descended from the Mannerists, and Caravaggio had a great influence on his fellow painters. With drama and immediacy, Caravaggio was an alla prima painter, working directly onto the canvas.

One can imagine him working feverishly, so full of life and passion are his portraits and scenes. Many painters were inspired by him, down to this day, as he exemplifies the passion of painting itself. His admirers are called the "Caravaggisti," and I daresay I am one of them in spirit.

Caravaggio lived only to the age of thirty-six, but his legacy is long. As you look at his extraordinarily dynamic and dramatic paintings absolutely splashed with a palpable light, think of the artists who followed in his footsteps—Vermeer, Fantin-Latour, Rembrandt, Delacroix—and his modern counterpart, Édouard Manet. Caravaggio's work was magnificent and his influence monumental.

Takeaway: Chiaroscuro

JOHANNES VERMEER (1632–1675)

A Dutch figurative artist, Vermeer's world is a small and very meticulous one. His scenes are set in two of the rooms in his Delft house, and much has been speculated about optical devices he may have utilized in the creation of his amazingly masterful work.

In addition to his careful drawing, he is known for his beautiful application of paint. He used an extensive and expensive palette of pigments including ultramarine blue, not common in the seventeenth century. He built the color with reflected tones from adjacent hues.

This very well-known *Girl with a Pearl Earring* is an example of his extraordinary sensitivity, soft color, and expressive quality. No Impressionist would give you that black background, but it is so beautiful here as it sets off the sweet light on her face and costume.

Only a small sampling of Vermeer's exquisite paintings are known, but his attention to detail is esteemed worldwide. He was a unique voice in portrait painting, never imitated and probably never surpassed.

Takeaway: Exquisite Detail

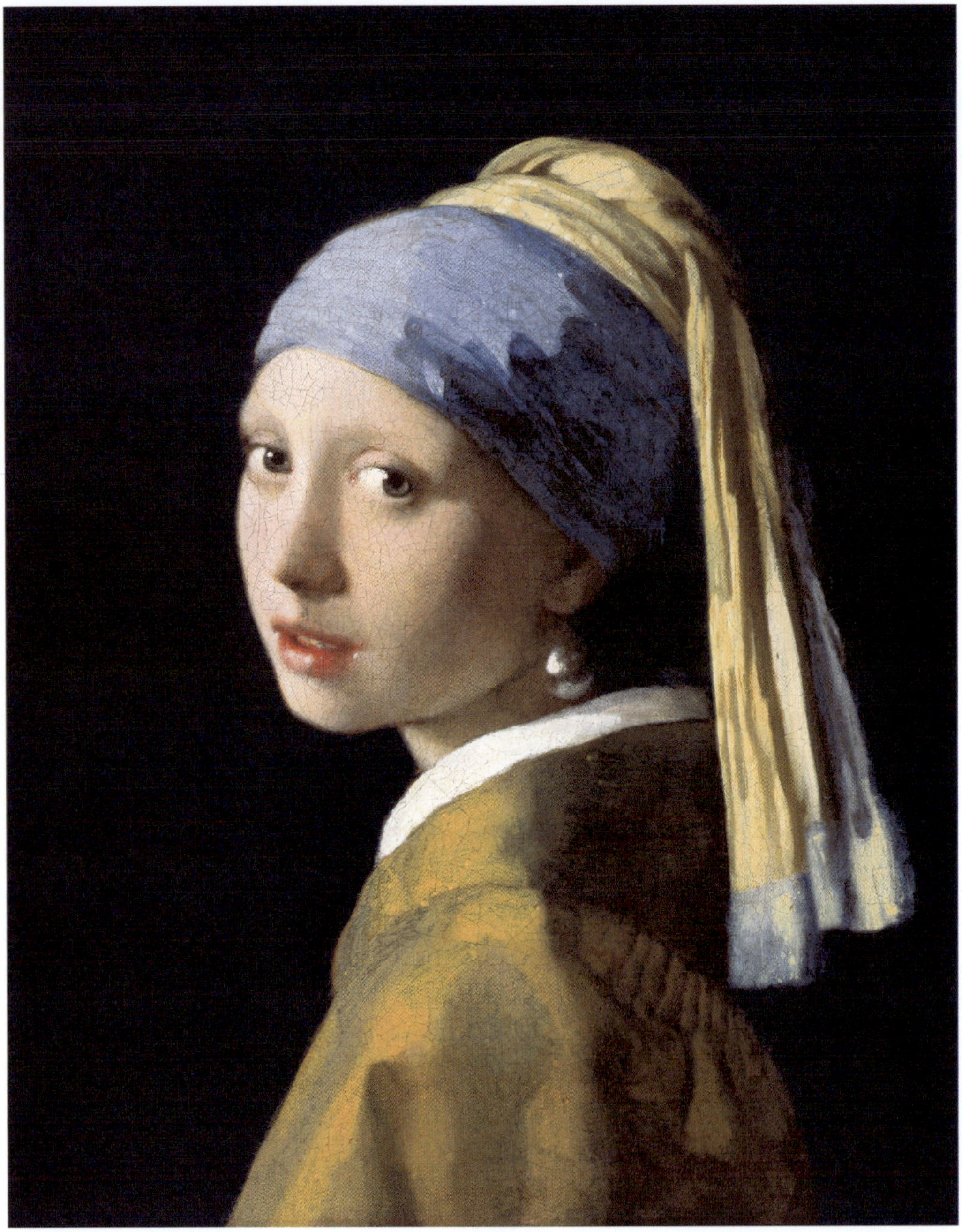

Fig. 55. Johannes Vermeer, GIRL WITH A PEARL EARRING.

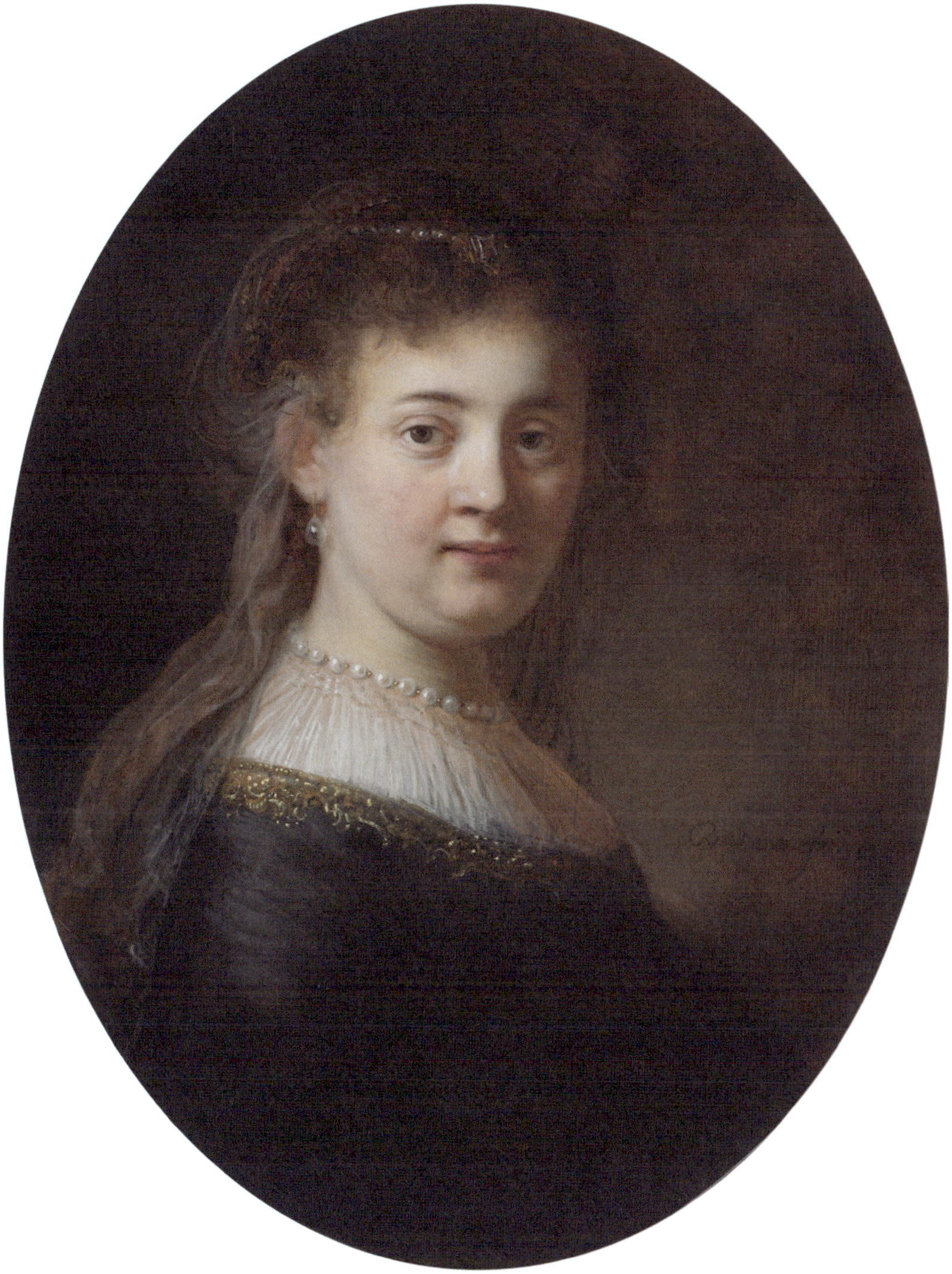

Fig. 56. Rembrandt van Rijn, PORTRAIT OF SASKIA VAN UYLENBURGH (1612–1642).

REMBRANDT HARMENSZOON VAN RIJN (1606–1669)

Without question, Rembrandt was one of the greatest artists of all time, and the quintessential portrait painter. His work was prolific and wide-ranging in subject matter and medium. He was quite literally, a phenom, masterful in all he attempted.

We will look at one of Rembrandt's many self-portraits later in this book, but here we present a painting of his wife, Saskia. Though his mastery as a painter is well-acknowledged, it is his humanity and empathy that set him apart as a master. Though Rembrandt's incredible expertise in portraying the texture of metal and silk is well told here, so much more is captured in this portrait. It is not idealized, but rather suggests the complexity of human emotion.

He truly peers into the souls of his subjects and presents them to us as conflicted individuals. Perhaps because of his enormous skill, he was able to go deeper than other painters in depicting the inner life of his subjects.

Rembrandt was obviously indebted to Caravaggio, from whom he adapted the dramatic use of light and shadow, but in Rembrandt's loving hands, the drama is not for drama's sake, rather the means to present in the "best light" the humanity of his subject. Gone are formalities or the glorifying of the privileged, and in their place the truth and respect due every subject.

Rembrandt's masterful drawing has been described as echoing Asian masters in its freshness, vitality, and clarity. This may be the case, but I have always attributed it to the confidence that only a master of his art form can make possible.

Study the work of Rembrandt for its complexity, authority, and beauty. Try to find how he was able to put so much emotion into his subjects and to capture the viewer so that even today we stand transfixed in amazement as we stand before this work.

Takeaway: Empathetic Expressionism

DIEGO VELÁZQUEZ (1599–1660)

Another giant of the Baroque period, Velázquez was an enormously accomplished court portrait painter who was known primarily for his masterwork *Las Meninas* (Maids of Honor). Much has been written about the genius of this painting, its composition, and point of view.

Velázquez used the long gamut introduced by Caravaggio to dramatic effect, and was another influence on the work of Édouard Manet centuries later. His work was of great interest to other nineteenth- and twentieth-century painters who found his compositions worthy of reinterpretation.

What is it about this work that is so compelling? We take a closer look at it in a later chapter as we try to answer that question.

Takeaway: Composition

JOHN SINGER SARGENT (1856–1925)

We jump to the nineteenth century to the acclaimed work of the American painter John Singer Sargent, a prolific master of the art of portraiture. Another devotee of Velázquez, Sargent's life-size standing portraits echo those of the Spanish master. But he was of another century touched by the light of Impressionism, and this transformed much of Sargent's work.

He liked to paint outdoors, and made myriad watercolor sketches. They have a freshness that may be seen as lacking in the weightier portraits, but sometimes the frivolity entered his figurative work, especially in his outdoor scenes.

Sargent was an extraordinarily skilled maestro of painting, extremely facile, and this perhaps contributed to some of the negative criticism he received from some who found his work clever but perhaps shallow and superficial, created for effect and lacking serious content. Nonetheless, Sargent's reputation has grown and many admire his work as quite elegant. He is surely one of the transitional figures who bring us into the light.

Takeaway: Facility

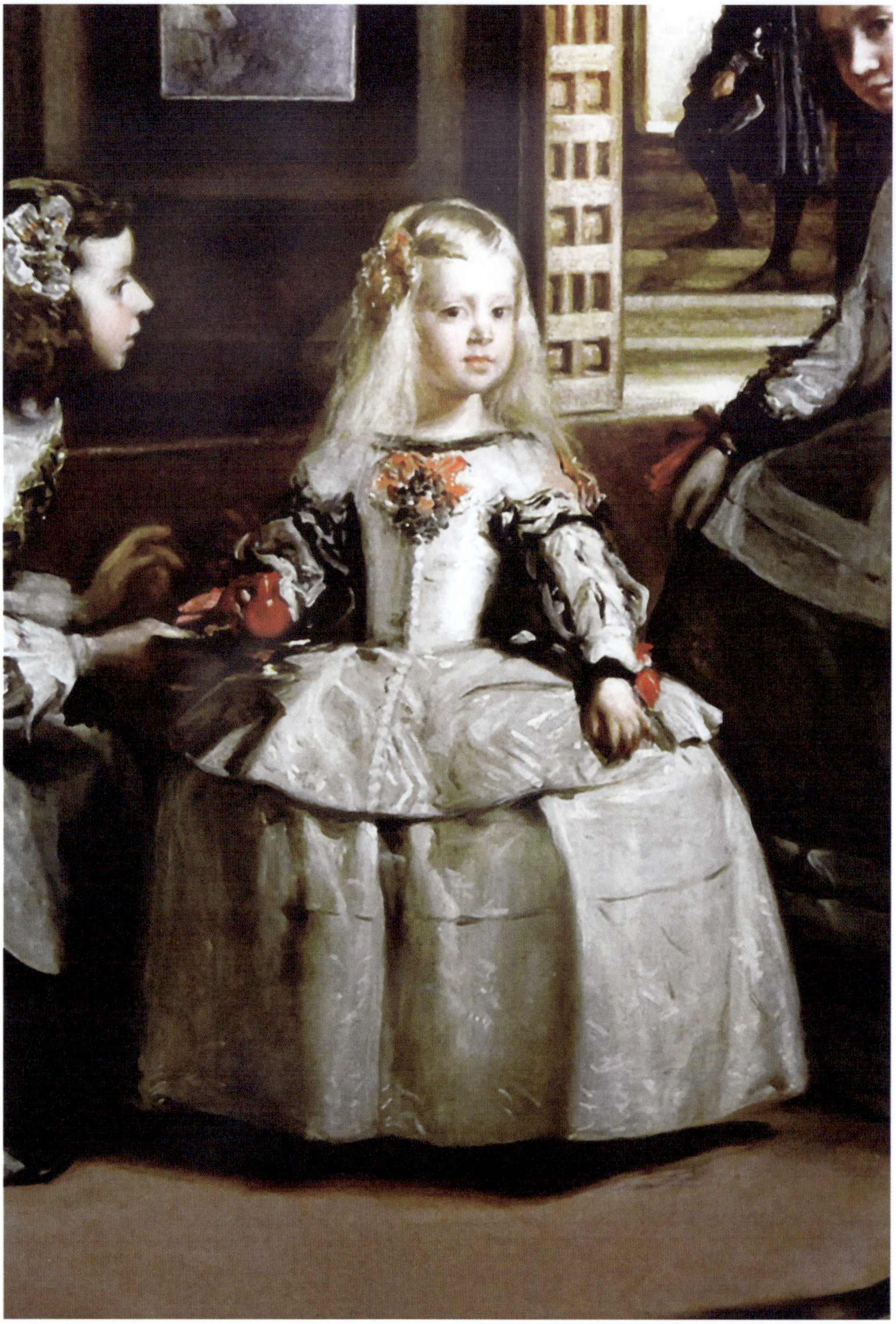

Fig. 57. Diego Velázquez, LAS MENINAS (detail).

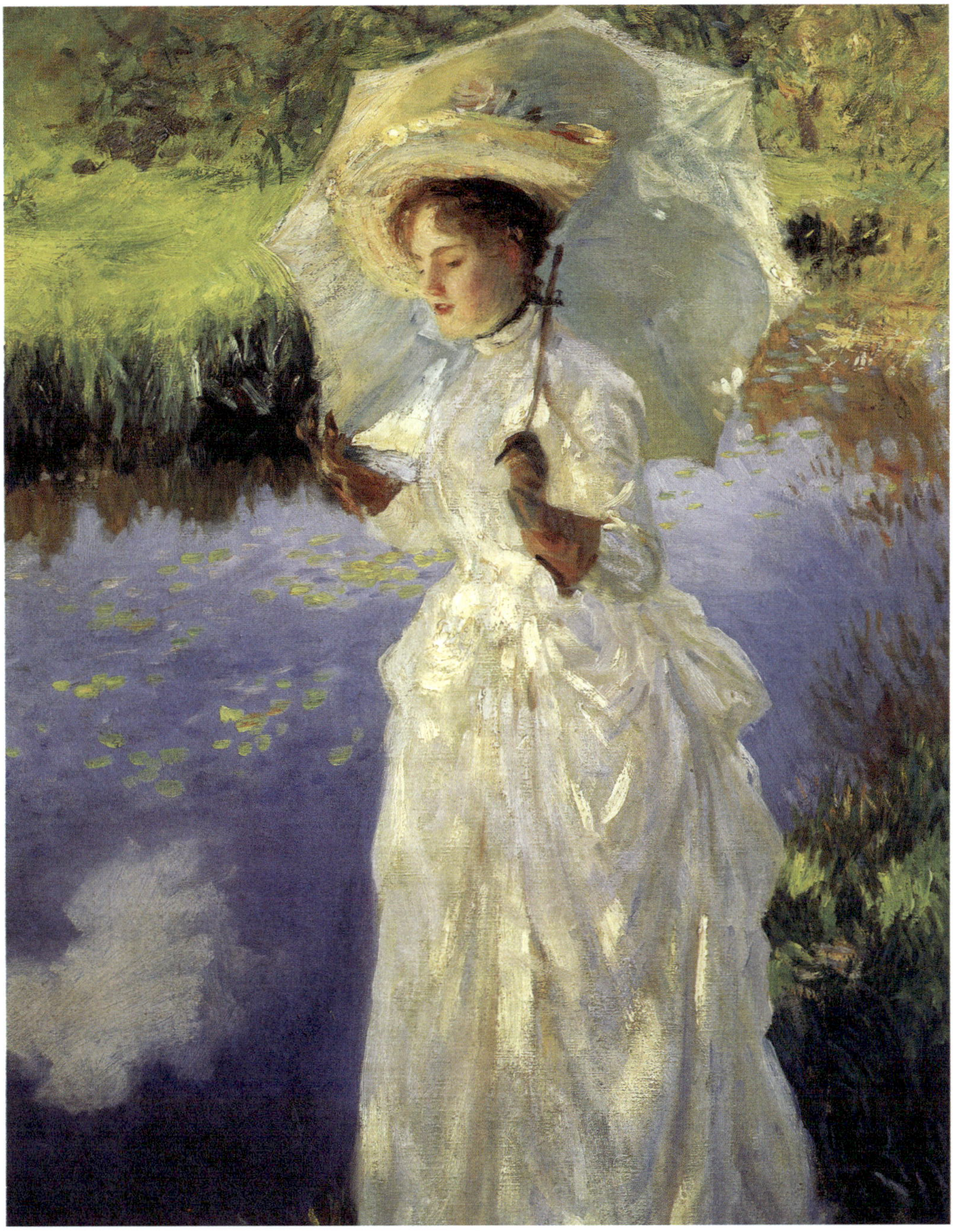

Fig. 58. John Singer Sargent, MORNING WALK.

ÉDOUARD MANET (1832–1883)

The French painter Manet is credited with taking the art of painting into modernity. His beautiful long gamut paintings—I always think of black and white in relation to Manet (his blacks are so intense and luminous)—are in the tradition of the Caravaggisti and the Baroque, but cleaner and more modern, just a step away from Impressionism.

Instead of working in the old-fashioned way from the dark to the light with a medium or dark tone, he worked directly, applying solid paint onto a light ground. This alla prima technique made for a less-worked look. As you look at a Manet and compare it to that of his predecessors, notice the flat paint, the looser drawing, and especially the blacks. The materiality of the paint itself is more noticeable as Manet has moved painting into the expressiveness of the modern world.

Very exciting!

Takeaway: Black and White

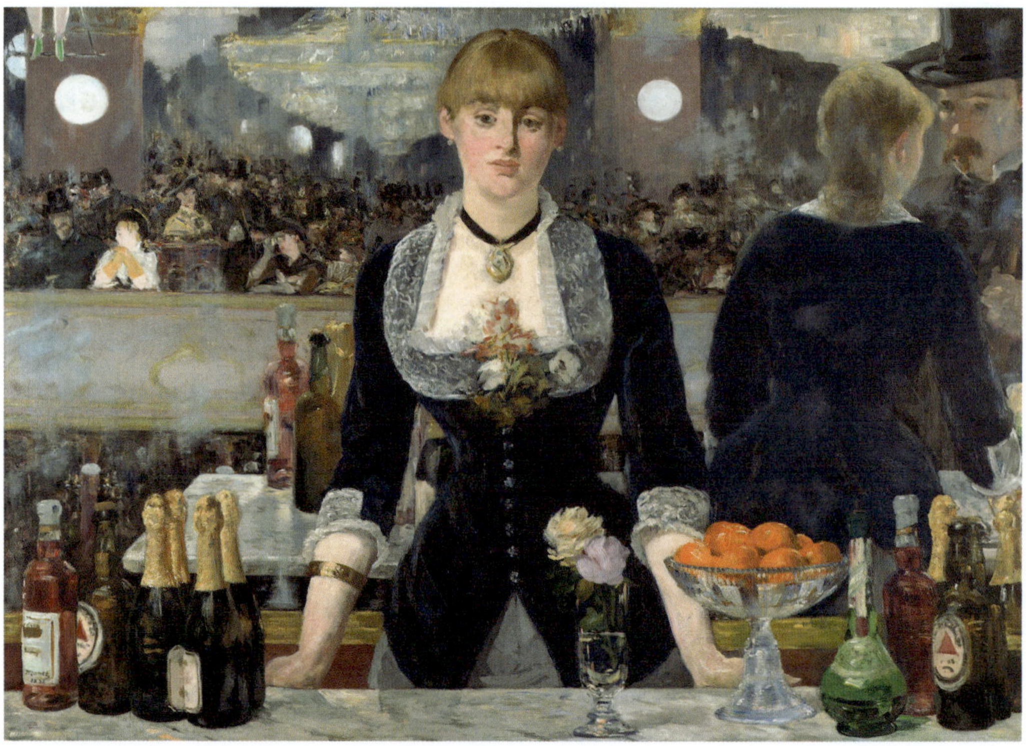

Fig. 59. Édouard Manet, A BAR AT THE FOLIES-BERGÈRE.

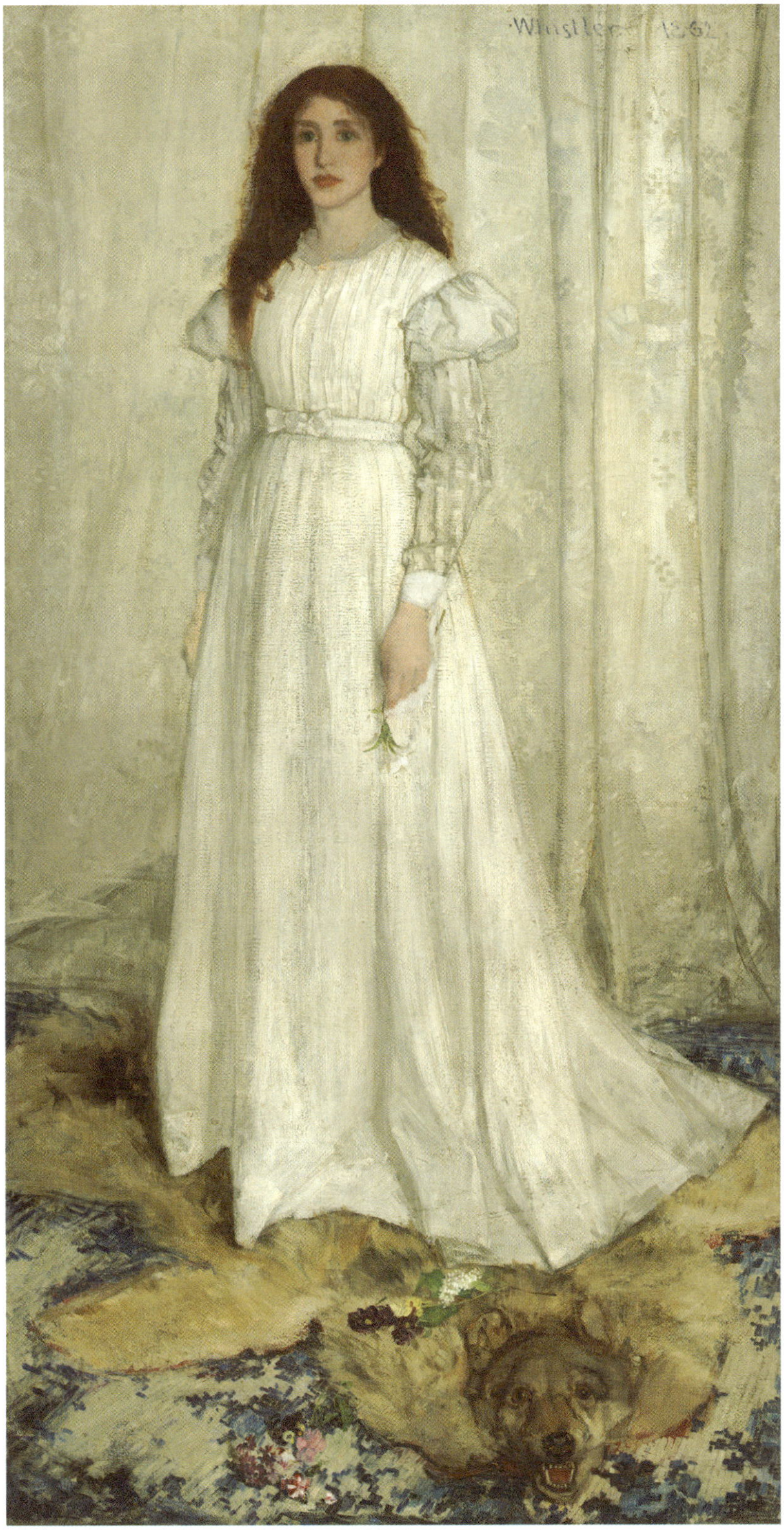

Fig. 60. James Abbott McNeill Whistler, SYMPHONY IN WHITE, NO. 1: THE WHITE GIRL.

JAMES ABBOTT MCNEILL WHISTLER (1834–1903)

Just one generation before Sargent, Whistler was another American artist who lived and worked abroad and was known for his portraits. He is known to have worked very long and deliberately on each work, and there is a calculation and sober appearance to his paintings.

More cerebral than Sargent, Whistler titled many of his works as "arrangements," "harmonies," and "nocturnes," musical terms that give a clue to his approach. The use of these terms suggest that it was Whistler's intent to present his art more as an abstract composition than as a narrative or descriptive work.

His methodology was sober and painstaking as he built his tones up slowly from grays and brown tones. But there is a great solemnness and beauty in his grays and neutrals.

This is an excellent example of how the personality of the artist is reflected in his choices and how these choices become the signature of his work.

Takeaway: Musical Neutrals

GUSTAV KLIMT (1862–1918)

I place the Austrian artist Klimt right after Whistler in this discussion, as he lived and worked just a generation after. But it is an interesting juxtaposition, because you could not find two artists so utterly different in temperament than these two.

I have read that Klimt liked to wear only a robe and sandals with no undergarments. Perhaps he wanted to be unconfined as he quite deliberately and with great aplomb created his wildly and beautifully patterned compositions. They are lush and emotional, even erotic, and full of a passionate exuberance.

Klimt was born into an artistic family (his father was a gold engraver), and his skill at decorative work was considerable. He painted murals and ceilings and designed costumes. This is evident in his exquisitely designed paintings where the figures almost take a back seat to their costumes and elaborate backgrounds. This very beloved painting, *The Kiss*, is illustrative of that concentration.

Klimt's work is just deliciously sensual, colorful, and unmatched in its riotous beauty. Free expression was the credo of the very romantic Klimt.

Takeaway: Sumptuous Patterning

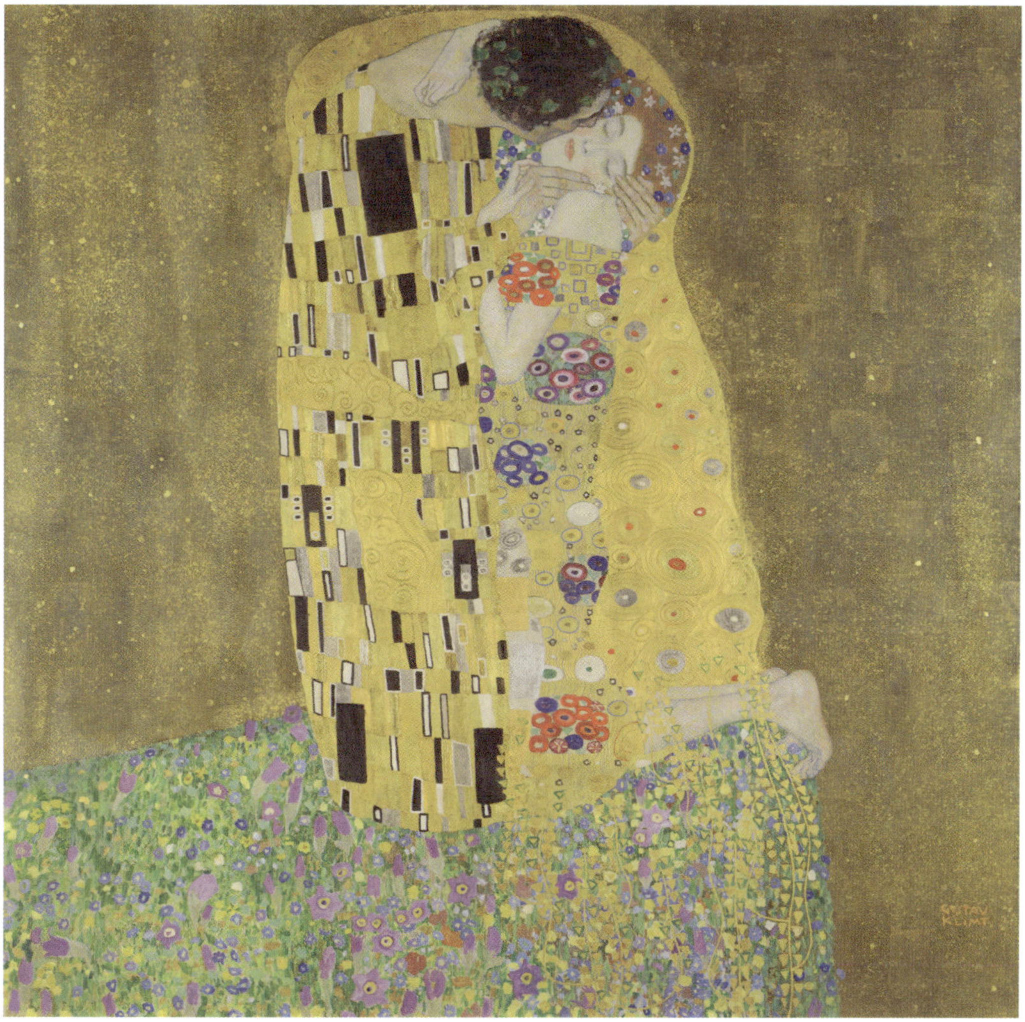

Fig. 61. Gustav Klimt, THE KISS.

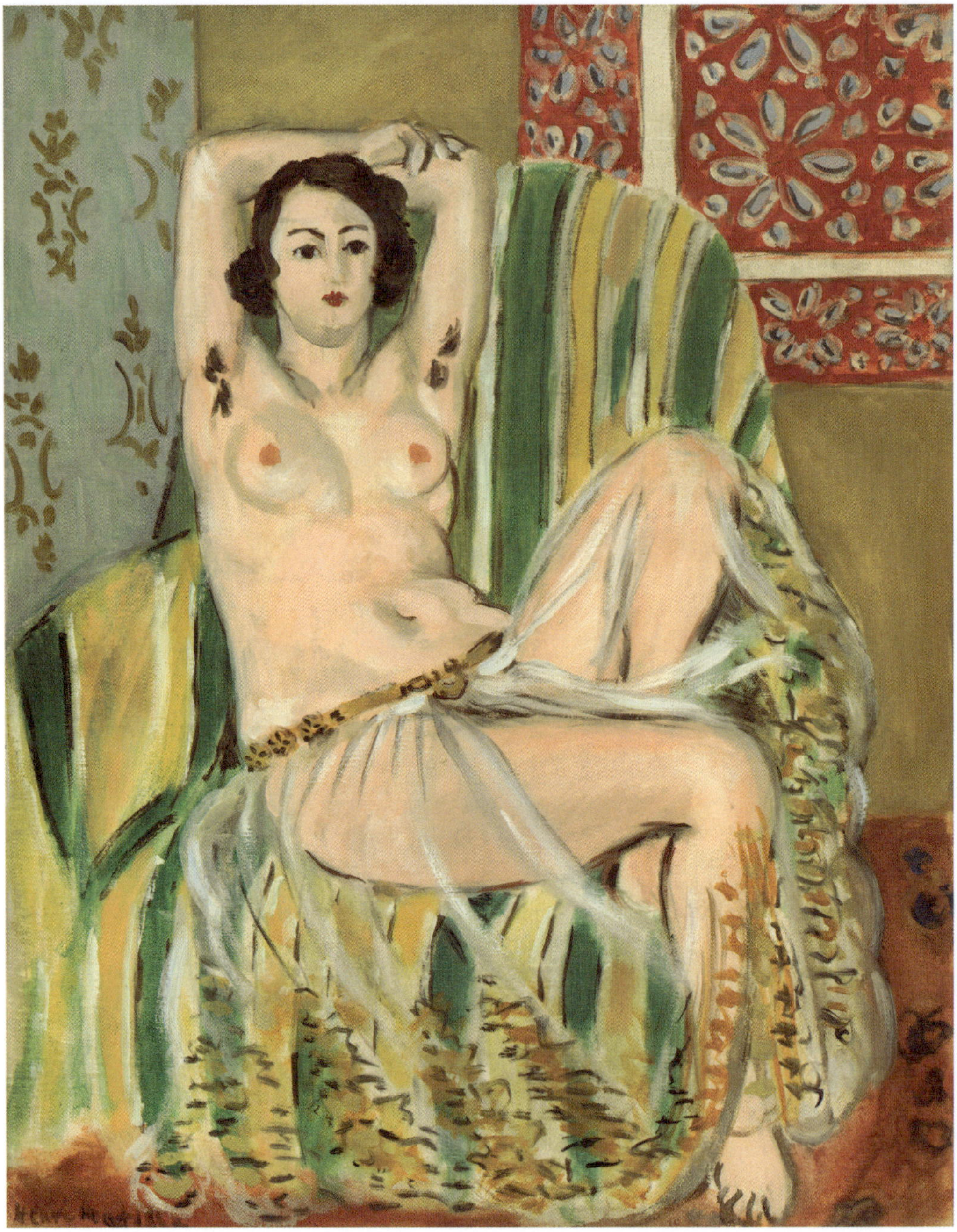

Fig. 62. Henri Matisse, ODALISQUE SEATED WITH ARMS RAISED, GREEN STRIPED CHAIR.

HENRI MATISSE (1868–1954)

Matisse is revered as one of the quintessential modern artists and giants of French art. A key figure in the Fauve movement, he is known for delicious color, his glorious interiors with glimpses of nature through windows and doors, and the marvelous cutouts/decoupage that he championed late in his career.

A consummate artist, Matisse's figurative works, still lifes, and landscapes possess a joyous simplicity with uninhibited color as their mainstay. His sense of composition was first rate, and he is a "painter's painter," much beloved and imitated by artists who followed him.

The painting illustrated here, *Odalisque Seated with Arms Raised, Green Striped Chair*, was one of many he created following a visit to Morocco. It is no surprise that the Moroccan penchant for the arabesque, an ornamental design characteristic of its Moorish culture, would captivate Matisse, who so loved patterning and color. Many of his paintings depict the tapestries, wall hangings, and objects that he collected on this inspiring visit. Even the word "odalisque" which comes from the Turkish *odalik*, meaning chambermaid or harem slave, adds to the fanciful nature of these highly decorative paintings Matisse created as part of his oeuvre. They have a sensuality and a joyousness that is emblematic of the artist.

Late in his life, anxious to continue working but dealing with illness that made it difficult for him to stand and paint, Matisse embarked on the art of decoupage, cutting out shapes and gluing them into designs. His resilience and determination to continue creating left us this remarkable legacy of elegant, sinuous forms cut out of paper, and highly decorative yet highly evocative compositions. Study Matisse for color and composition.

Takeaway: Joyous Color

PABLO PICASSO (1881–1973)

The name Picasso is synonymous with "visual artist." Picasso was a Spaniard who spent most of his life in France, worked in myriad art media, created several art "genres" and "periods," was an absolute fount of creativity, was tireless, and was quite simply a genius.

Some of these "periods" include the "Blue Period," where his figures were highly enhanced with the color blue and had a mournful quality; the "Rose Period," where his fancy turned to rose and pinks, and circus figures and acrobats appeared.

Fascinated with primitive and African art, Picasso then adopted a more stylized approach that imitated these pieces—suffice it to say, with great sophistication. His *Les Demoiselles d'Avignon* dominated this period, and was seen as shocking by his contemporaries, even Mr. Matisse.

Picasso's zest for drawing was the force that catapulted his work from merely expressive, as in the sad Blues and the elegant Roses, toward the African and eventually into Cubism.

He was the great innovator, and his vision led him to break down the object into planes and shapes and to consider, amazingly, the possibility of drawing from more than one point of view at the same time. This was and continues to be recognized as absolutely revolutionary.

Picasso did retreat from the extremism of Cubism to continue to work in what is referred to as a "neoclassical" style. But his genius knew no bounds and it seems impossible to limit or categorize him in any way. He was incredibly prolific, an absolute factory of art, and it is said that he produced as many as 50,000 artworks, including paintings, sculpture, ceramics, drawings, and tapestries.

Few artists have ever possessed the virtuosity and visual vocabulary of Picasso. He was able to draw and paint from memory with ease, something most artists find extremely challenging, and his creativity knew no bounds. He was not inhibited nor afraid to work in the most primitive style, to make pieces that were whimsical as well as classical, to try anything that came to mind and heart. He drew inspiration from the real—from pots and figures and guitars and flowers—but he painted them in a totally nonimitative manner. Picasso was, as many assert, probably the most talented artist who ever lived.

Copyright restrictions have kept me from including Picasso works in this book, but very fortunately, the work here, *Paulo on a Donkey*, created in 1923, has just entered the public domain at the time of writing, and I am able to share it. Let's have a look as it so definitively illustrates the enormous talent Picasso possessed.

Over the course of a sensational career, Picasso worked in almost every media and became expert in many. His imagination knew no bounds. But here we see the foundational elements that made this all possible: exceptional drawing ability, coupled with an inordinate expressiveness. Though this piece lacks the quirkiness, innovation and boldness we associate with Picasso's later works, we can appreciate Picasso's signature here as well. With simple, clean lines, he is able to make us feel the weight, solidity, and gravitational force in the rendering of the child and donkey.

Picasso's artistic choices are spot on. By surrounding the child in a white costume, he focuses our eye on the child's face, which is delicately and beautifully painted. Notice that the child is overly large vis a vis the donkey, but we somehow accept this anomaly. The painter's focus is the child, and the donkey is literally and figuratively his support. Picasso's composition and line impart more than correctness—they make us feel affection for the subject. Only exceptional artistry and vision can accomplish this.

Just a caveat. Though Picasso was a marvelous painter to be sure, his forte was his drawing. Color and a beautiful surface were secondary. I encourage you to get a book on Picasso to study and savor the amazing gifts he had: to draw, capturing the weight, solidity, gravity, dimension, and subtlety of form in his illustrative, realistic works, and to find expressive distortions, humor, playfulness and meaning in his more abstract pieces.

Takeaway: Innovator, Visionary

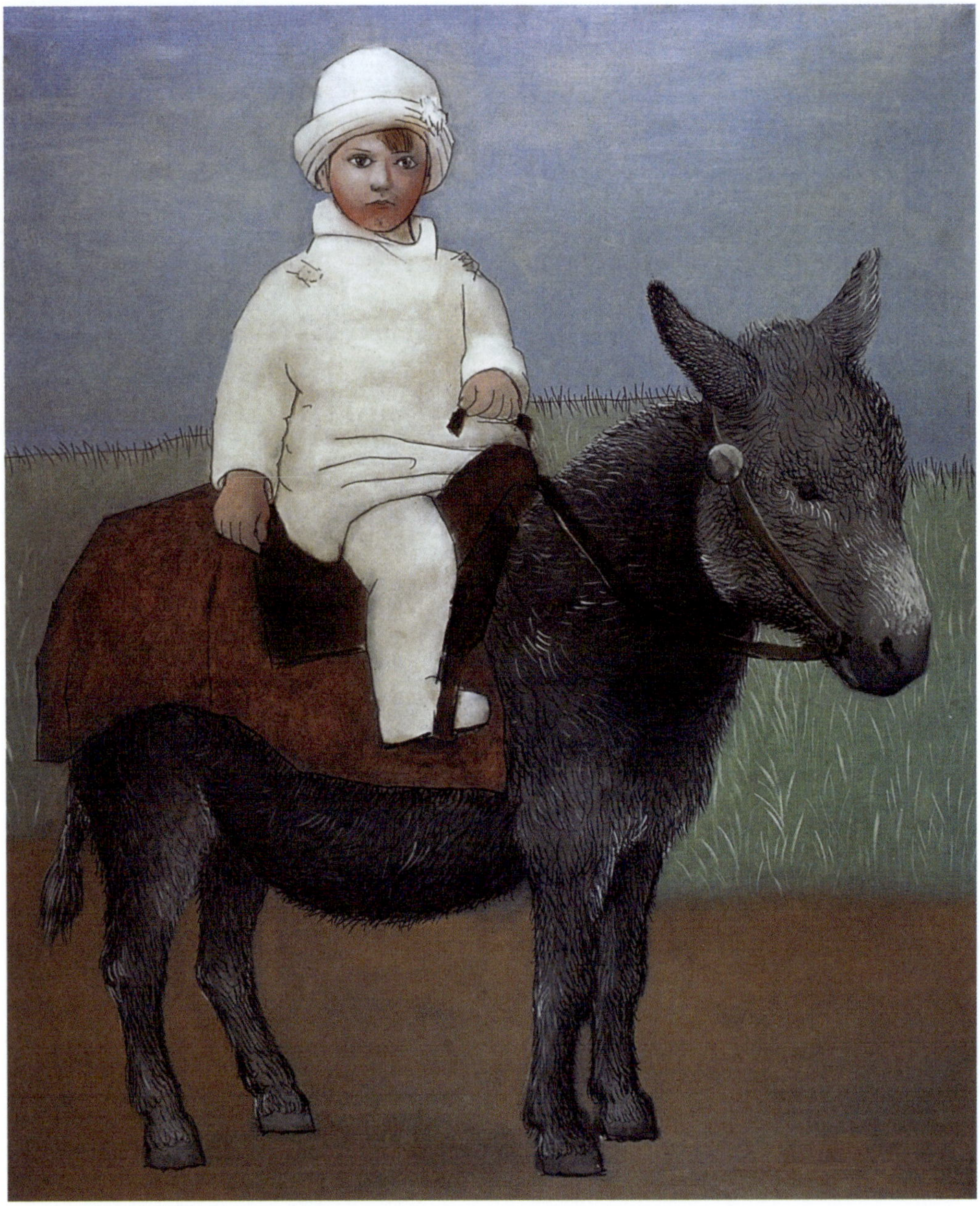

Fig. 63. Pablo Picasso, PAULO ON A DONKEY.

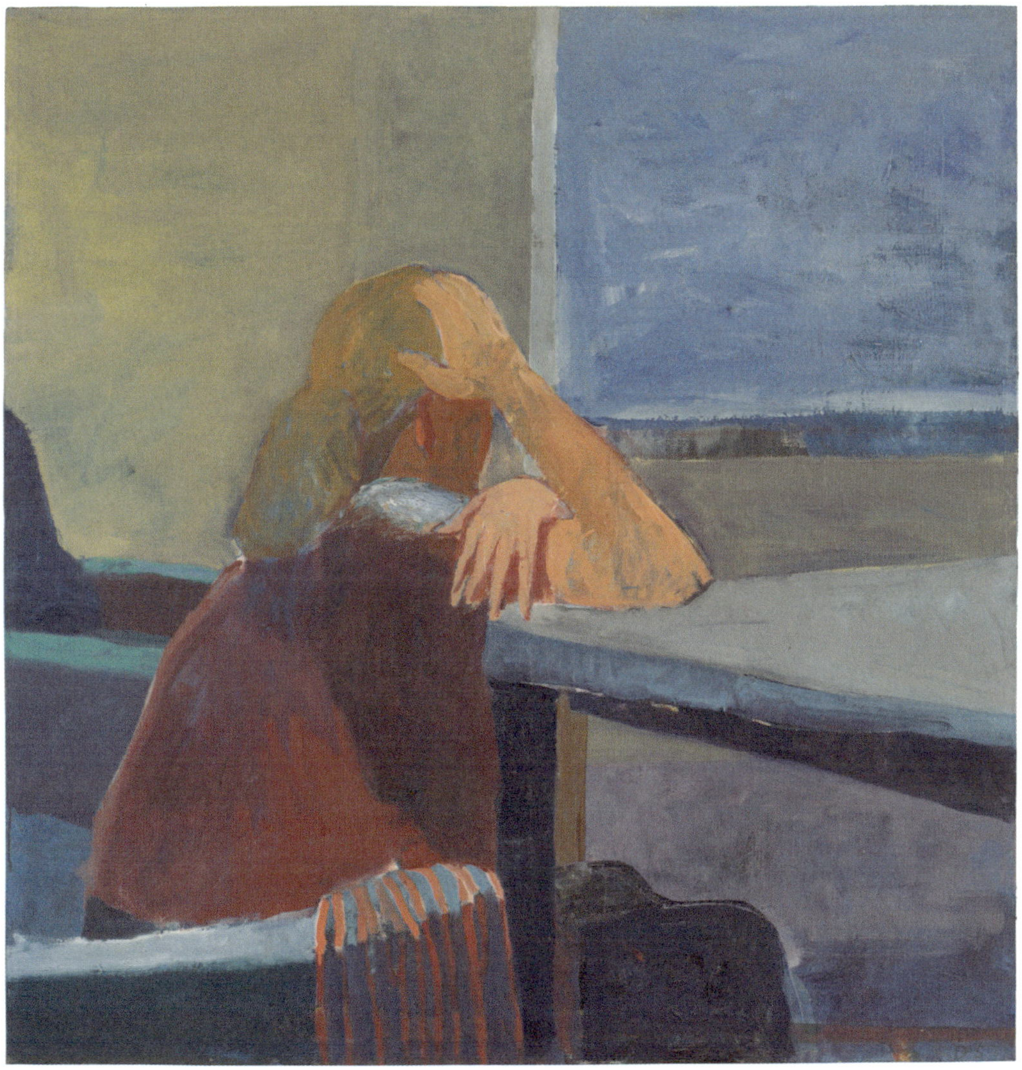

Fig. 64. Richard Diebenkorn, WOMAN IN A WINDOW, 1957, oil on canvas, 59 × 56 inches (149.9 × 142.2 centimeters). Catalogue raisonné no. 2185 © Richard Diebenkorn Foundation.

RICHARD DIEBENKORN (1922–1993)

A California artist best known for his abstract work, Diebenkorn executed many figurative works. In most cases, the figure was a part of the composition and not the star. He often painted the figure from the side or back so her personality would not dominate the work. He was considered one of the Bay Area figurative group of painters.

Diebenkorn is a child of Matisse, and you can see Matisse's influence in his work. Look for composition, large swaths of light filled color, and divisions of color in simple shapes. A really wonderful painter. We will revisit both Matisse and Diebenkorn in the next chapter, on landscape.

Takeaway: Figurative Abstraction

NORMAN ROCKWELL (1894–1978)

You may be surprised to see the very prolific Norman Rockwell included here, as he is widely known as an illustrator, his works having appeared in more than forty books, countless magazine covers, calendars, advertisements, posters, stamps, playing cards, etc., and his art may be considered by some to be sentimental or stamped with the code word "Americana."

I include him because I encourage my readers to look beyond classifications of who is what, and which artists are "serious" and others not, who is "worthy," and all those considered lesser. Here was an artist with the most remarkable skill at drawing, such that his characters pop off the page. He was a visual storyteller.

We have our preferences, yes, and we admire artists for their skill, point of view, sensuality, imagination, a whole host of abilities. Let's keep our minds open to giving credit to all who endeavor in the visual arts, for what they contribute is unique and an invaluable part of the visual art continuum.

Takeaway: Character Drawing

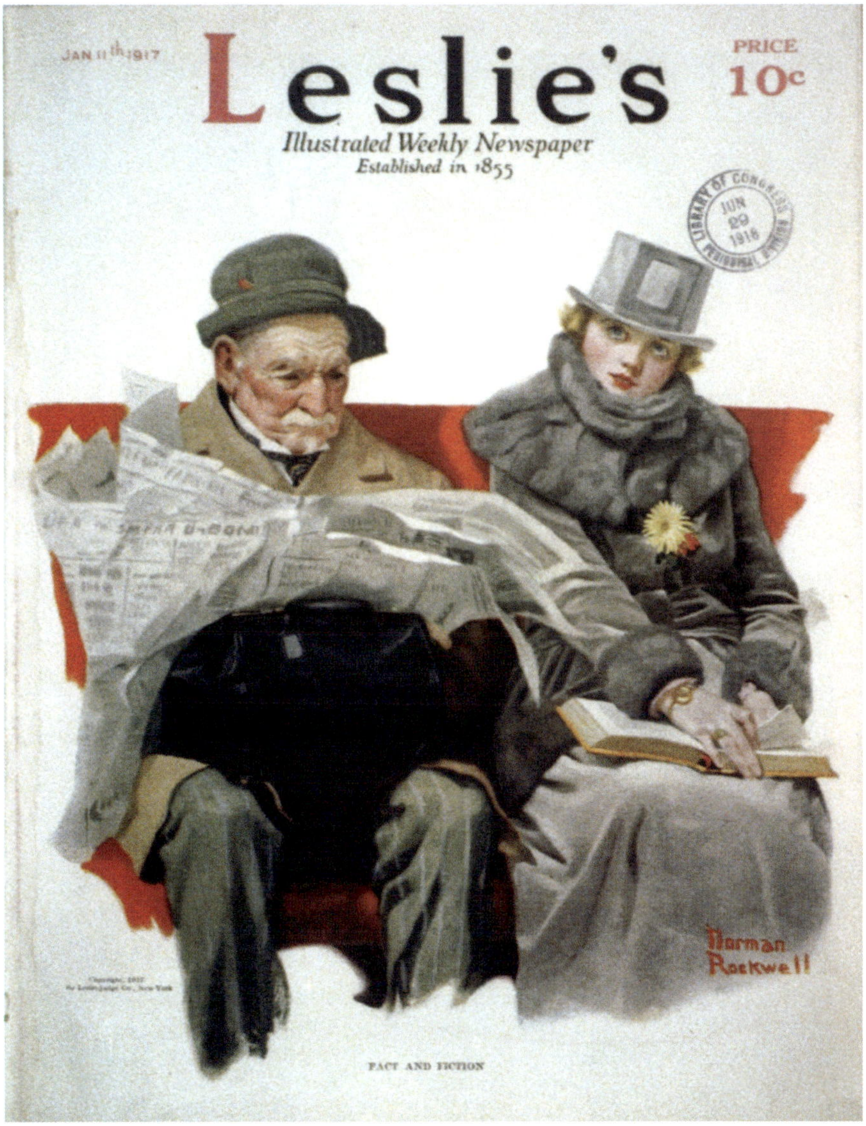

Fig.65 Norman Rockwell, FACT AND FICTION.

WILLEM DE KOONING (1904–1997)

I am ending this section on figurative art with de Kooning, not because he was the last figurative artist, certainly not, but because the figure, and in particular the female figure, is featured so prominently in his work and inaugurated a whole new way of looking at form, or the lack thereof.

De Kooning was one of a group of artists known as the "New York School" who were also considered "abstract expressionists." Some of these artists included Jackson Pollock, Franz Kline, Mark Rothko, Robert Motherwell, Clyfford Still, and Philip Guston, to name a few.

When we think of de Kooning, though, we conjure up visions of his women. De Kooning took a step past Picasso to literally take his women apart, to deconstruct them. Form has evaporated and in its place is a garish scribbled non form, part female, part monster. The subject is almost completely dispensed with, but not quite. More paint than painting, more dribble than paint, but compelling nonetheless. This is a seminal iteration of the figure.

Look up his "Women" series. Do they appeal to you? Do you take them seriously? If not, why?

Takeaway: Deconstruction

Before we leave the genre of figurative art to move on to our next subject, landscape, and as primarily a figurative artist myself, I encourage you to explore the modern exemplars of this most compelling subject. Figurative art runs the gamut from highly idealized work to the gritty, authentic painting styles of several outstanding painters.

Three women exploring the latter include Alice Neel, Marlene Dumas, and Margot Bergman, whose faces and figures are deliberately unpretty, sometimes squashed, distorted, placed in uncomfortable poses, and presenting their unadorned and unabashed humanity.

Another marvelous artist to study and who "tells it like it is" is the incomparable Lucien Freud, whose portraits dip into psychoanalytical territory, so intense was his dissection of his models. He was the grandson of Sigmund Freud and perhaps inherited this tendency for deep analysis. It is reported that he made his models sit for long hours so he could pay proper attention to rendering them. For example, I read that a nude of his completed in 2007 took sixteen months to complete and that he made the model sit for the entire period—some 2,400 hours. That shows an attention to detail few painters employ and borders on obsessive, as does the fact that he is reported to have wiped his brush after every note depicting flesh so that every stroke was slightly different. Nonetheless, the work is astounding.

I admire these "painters of truth" tremendously, as my own work falls into the opposite camp, as I search for an unearthly, glorified beauty and sympathy. Of course, I am not alone in this, and I guide you to search out other, more classical painters, like Kehinde Wiley and Amy Sherald, who recently completed the Obama portraits.

There are many voices, with much to say on this important subject, the human face and figure.

Chapter 9
Subject and Master: Landscape

Landscape, or the depiction of natural scenery like mountains, valleys, vista, trees, and forests, appeared in art first as background to figures and narrative painting, and then eventually as its own stand-alone subject. Now quite popular, painting of landscapes, and all the subcategories like seascapes, cityscapes, riverscapes, moonscapes, etc., are quite favored and collectible.

Landscapes run the gamut from extremely detailed and realistic to the most subtle and abstract and can depict actual or imaginary places. Some are concentrated on the expression of weather, where the actual subject is more atmosphere than place. Landscapes can and have been created in many media. Think of the ink landscapes of the East, and the many watercolor, pastel, and oil landscape pieces executed by Western artists.

It took a while for landscape painting to transition from backdrop to center stage, and for artists to discover plein air painting—actually going outdoors to paint what they see.

Dutch artists began to take landscape seriously in the seventeenth century, and this gained favor in the eighteenth with landowners seeking views of their properties. In the nineteenth century, English landscape painters like Turner and Constable began to give it their all, and the Barbizons actually went outdoors to paint. Inspired by these forerunners, the Impressionists brought the painting of landscapes into the glorious light of day. Simultaneously, a number of American and Canadian artists glorified their own continent in paint.

We turn now to the greats of the art of landscape. I'll be discussing Western artists here, but must make a mention about the Asian contribution to landscape art, which is voluminous and exquisite. In general, Asian landscape art is delicate and elegant, worthy of much attention. Do study it and admire it in all its complexity. But now, to my area of familiarity, the Western practitioners of the art of landscape.

PIETER BRUEGEL THE ELDER (C. 1524–1569)

A member of a family of famous painters, Pieter Bruegel the Elder was a kind of documentarian of the peasant life. His paintings showed people engaged in a variety of their normal activities, many of which were outdoors, so landscape featured largely in these works. He also portrayed individuals in a landscape setting. Bruegel also created a kind of landscape called "world landscape," which shows a small figure in a panoramic environment.

For much of Bruegel's work, landscape took a back seat to the engagement of the figures. Landscape does gain in importance as the figures retreat in size. Do you think the small figures add to the grandeur of the landscape, or not? Asking yourself what the artist was most interested in is a key to understanding his work.

Takeaway: Figures in Landscape

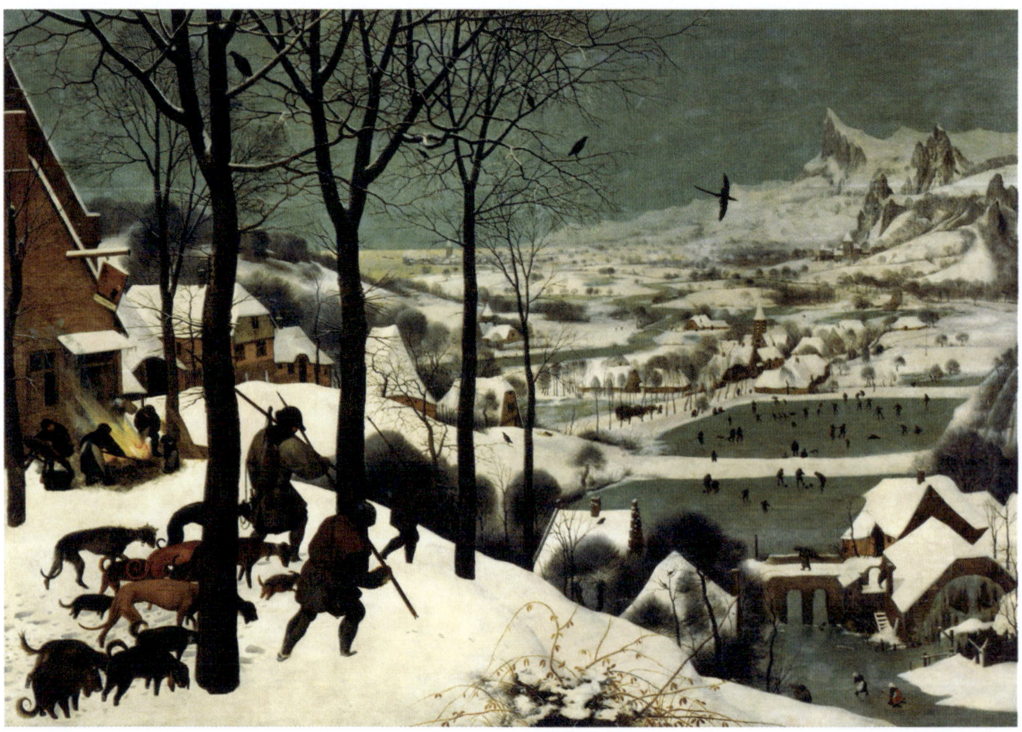

Fig. 66. Pieter Bruegel the Elder, THE HUNTERS IN THE SNOW.

CLAUDE LORRAIN (1600–1682)

A popular French painter of his time, Lorrain had the distinction of introducing the sun into his paintings, remarkably pretty much absent prior to his work. Lorrain did work from life.

Most of Lorrain's landscapes contain figures, but he reportedly had little interest in the figures and added them in an almost compulsory manner. It is reported that he joked that he gave "his figures away for free," suggesting that his preoccupation was the landscape.

There is a stiffness to Lorrain's work, and his pictures seem static, but this did not stop him from being much collected in his lifetime. I read that he retained only four of his paintings, indicating that he was successful in selling most of his output. But we know that does not, in any way, suggest the worth and critical assessment of his contribution. He was surely a devotee of the art of landscape, so rightfully takes his place in this discussion.

Takeaway: Early Landscape for Its Own Sake

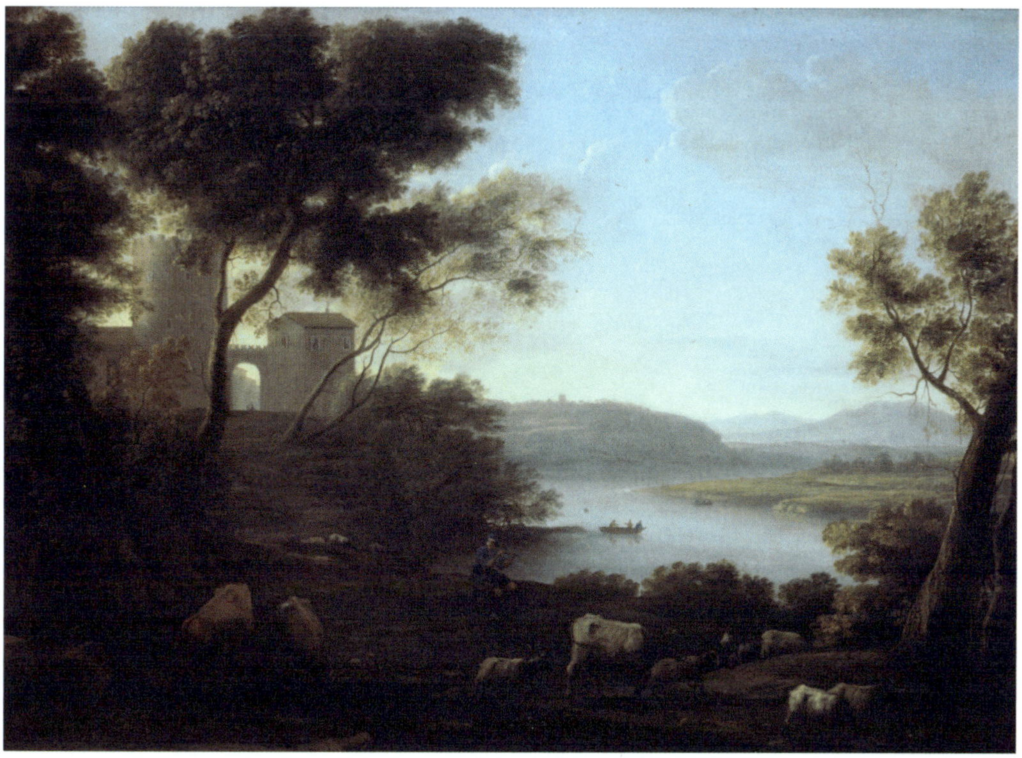

Fig. 67. Claude Lorrain, PASTORAL LANDSCAPE: THE ROMAN CAMPAGNA.

JACOB VAN RUISDAEL (1628–1682)

Another artist popular in his time, Van Ruisdael was Dutch and painted during what is known as the Dutch Golden Age. He hailed from a family of landscape painters.

Van Ruisdael's technique is more vigorous than his predecessors. He used thicker paint, which gave more vitality to his canvases, and carefully studied his subject matter. His trees are less generic than those by former practitioners, as their species would actually be recognizable by scientists. Also notable are the lack of figures and a more potent and developed sky.

His influence on landscape painters was considerable. Turner paid the great compliment of copying Ruisdael's works, as did Constable. Van Gogh was also a great fan and called Ruisdael's work "sublime." Claude Monet was purportedly another devotee.

One can see in Van Ruisdael the beginning of vivid landscape painting. No longer a stage set, his big skies and solid natural forms begin to show the atmosphere that gives landscape painting its reality and potency.

Takeaway: Vigorous Painting

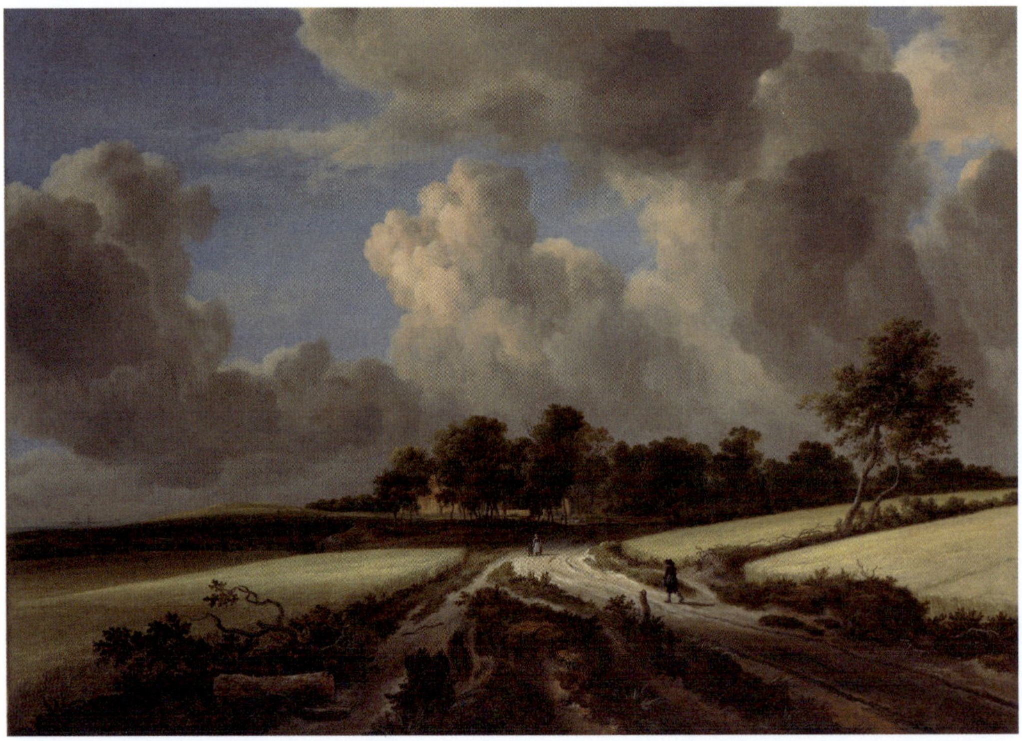

Fig. 68. Jacob van Ruisdael, WHEAT FIELDS.

CASPAR DAVID FRIEDRICH (1774–1840)

Turning to Germany, we encounter Friedrich, a German artist who was instrumental in legitimizing the genre of landscape painting. Purportedly a sufferer of depression, he introduced the subgenre of winter scenes into his artistic lexicon.

When you look at Friedrich's work, you will notice that it has an emotional quality. It is not merely descriptive of trees and mountains and sky. It suggests the majestic quality of landscape and the transformational effect it has on those who contemplate it. It may be called "allegorical" or "metaphysical" in its suggestiveness.

He was spoken of as a man whose work embodied "the tragedy of landscape." Friedrich is in the tradition of Romantic painters who were able to put their feelings into the paint. He is notable for that accomplishment and presaged other landscape artists we discuss here such as Turner, and even Mr. van Gogh, another unhappy soul.

Takeaway: Emotion in Nature

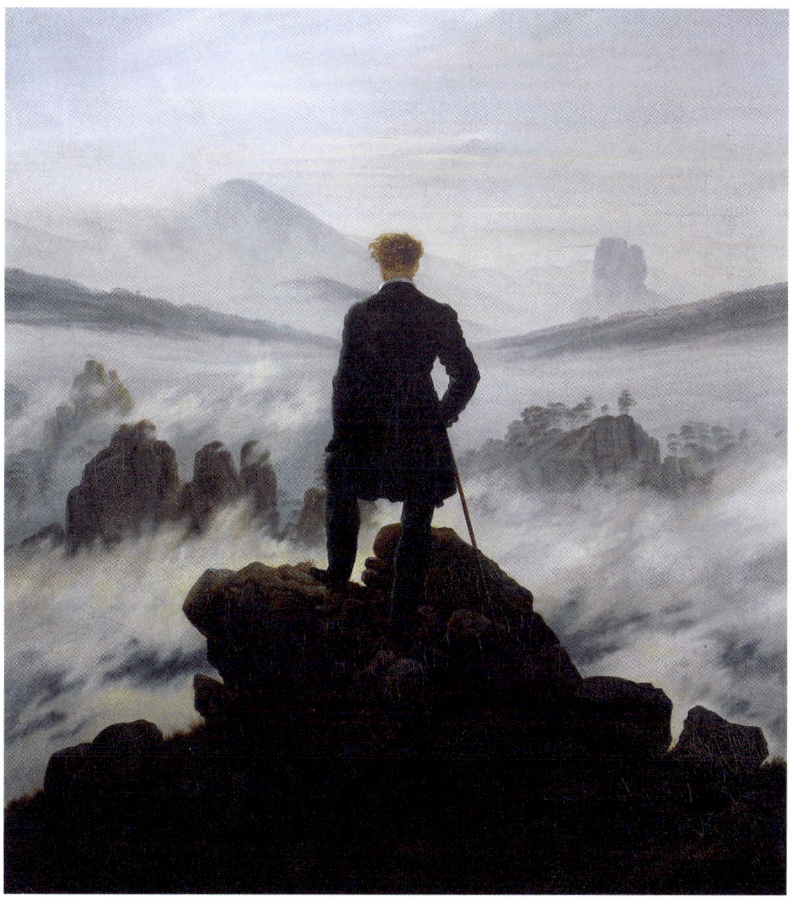

Fig. 69. Caspar David Friedrich, THE WANDERER ABOVE THE SEA OF FOG.

JOHN CONSTABLE (1776–1837)

An English painter, Constable was a student of nature, one of the first to paint in plein air in oil. He had a fresh, al fresco approach, especially to his sketches with their loose brushwork, which was often tamped down in his completed oils. He was a student of the atmosphere, and one can see in his treatment of clouds and seas the fervent fascination with atmospheric effects later enlarged and heralded by Turner.

He was aware not only of natural forms, as were his predecessors, but also of the abstract—light, weather, time of day. A straight line leads from Constable to the Impressionists, who were to loosen the reins even more to let those forms take a back seat to the abstract.

Check out the sky treatment in his famous *Stonehenge* piece; it is as modern as you might expect from a twentieth-century Postimpressionist.

Takeaway: Forerunner

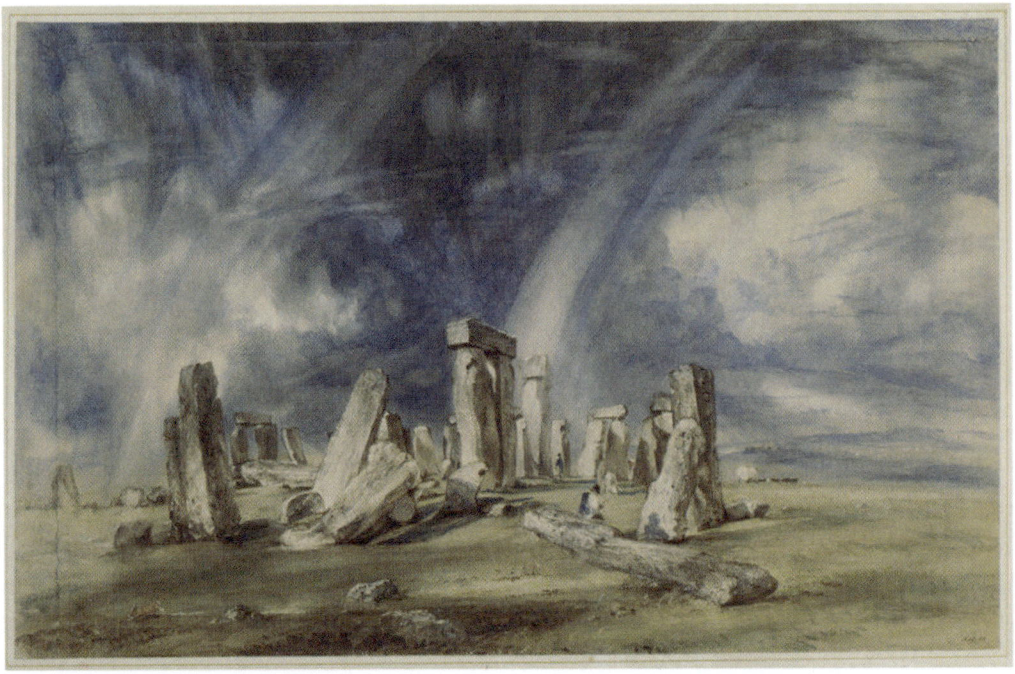

Fig. 70. John Constable, STONEHENGE.

JOSEPH MALLARD WILLIAM TURNER (1775–1851)

What Constable alluded to in his sketches, J. M. W. Turner went at whole hog in his work. His paintings are awash with loose paint, mixed and whitened to create the blur that atmosphere enforces in nature. He was so infatuated with this blur that he turned to painting weather in its extremity—storms, rain, fog, the upheaval caused over water, shipwrecks, and the like.

Turner was as passionate and romantic a painter as any who ever lived. He has left a prodigious amount of work attesting to this passion—over 2,000 paintings and 19,000 drawings and sketches. He was known as "the painter of light," but I would also characterize him as a great dramatist of nature.

Look at Turner's seas in the same way you look at Monet's water lilies. In both cases, they are stand-ins or props for the primary subject—the light itself. Just premises with which to paint the purest of subjects, and the magnificence of painting itself. Staggering!

Takeaway: Light Is Everything

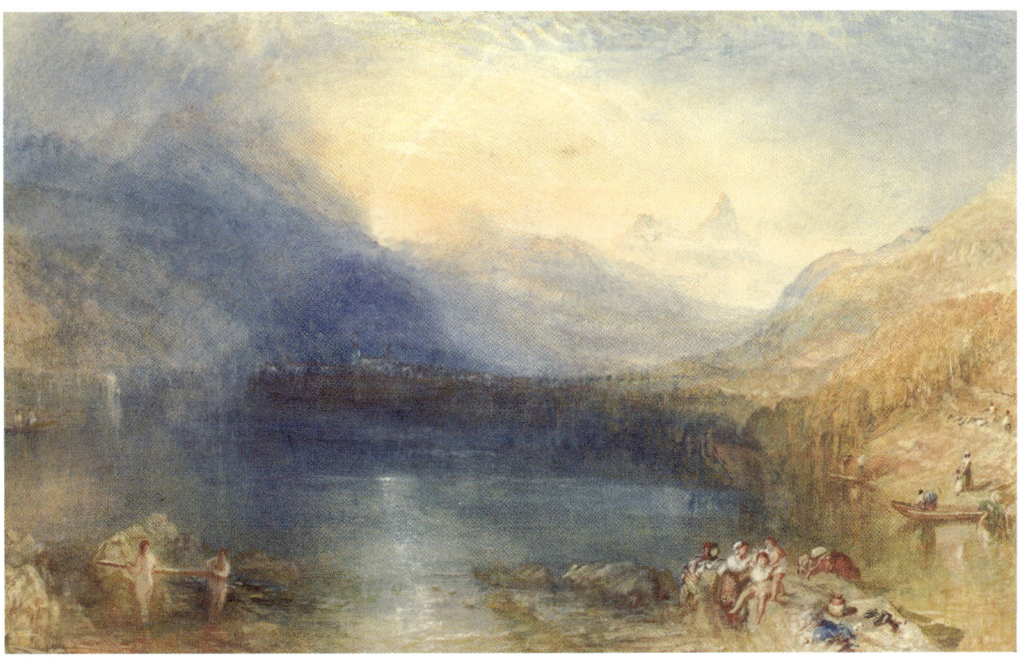

Fig. 71. J. M. W. Turner, THE LAKE OF ZUG.

JEAN-BAPTISTE-CAMILLE COROT (1796–1875)

Corot was a French painter, and there is a direct line from him to Impressionism—he is undoubtedly its precursor. He has a more restrained palette than the Impressionists were to favor, and used silver, brown, and even black in his landscapes—these rarely seen in later Impressionist works. Though he worked en plein air, he also worked from his imagination and later his own photographs.

Corot was a purist, and loved the subtlety of his grayed and minor notes; this in contrast to the Impressionists, who loved intense blues and roses and yellows. Corot was a sober artist, and his soothing landscapes mark him as a classicist. Can you see these qualities in his work, especially when you compare him to the artists that follow? I see him in the Whistler camp.

Just as Monet was to admire Corot and said of him, "There is only one master here—Corot. We are nothing compared to him, nothing." We can admire Corot as well, even if our tastes tend to the romantic rather than the classical.

Takeaway: Classical Beauty

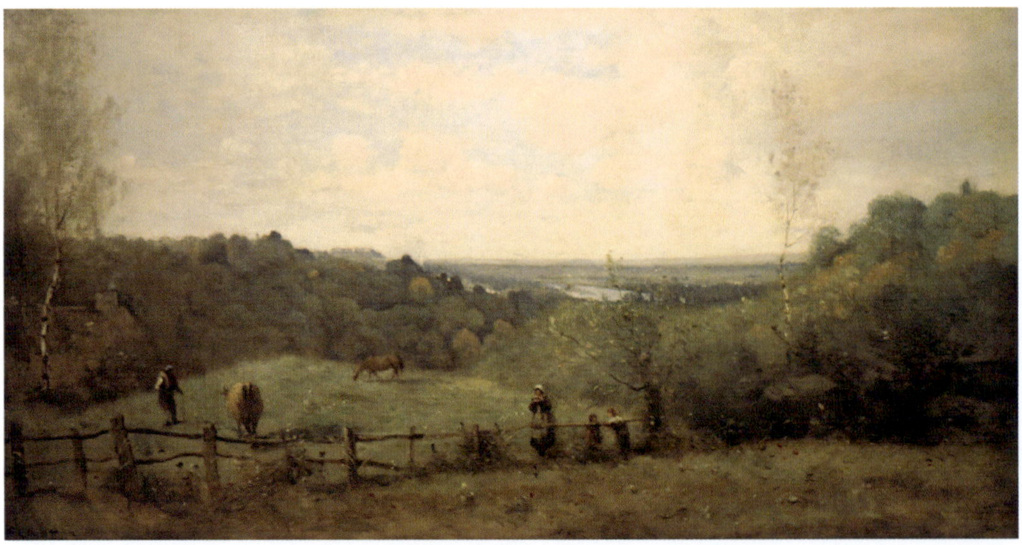

Fig. 72. Jean-Baptiste-Camille Corot, THE HEIGHTS ABOVE SÈVRES.

THOMAS COLE (1801–1848) AND THE HUDSON RIVER SCHOOL

An American, Thomas Cole is the founder of the Hudson River School. He was a romantic painter, and you can see references in his style to that of the German, Caspar David Friedrich, whom we have studied earlier in this chapter. Cole's landscape has that grandiosity that Friedrich went for, a style applauded in the work of many contemporaries and descendants.

After Cole died in 1848, the second generation of Hudson River School artists rose to prominence. They included Frederic Church and Albert Bierstadt, who created the majestic, highly dramatic landscapes we associate with the settlement of the wild American West. The term "luminism" is associated with these painters and characterizes an effect created by dramatic lighting and concealed brushstrokes.

This is not the atmospheric light created in Impressionism—quite the contrary. This is a defined, highly detailed style, which depicts a glorified, idealized, metaphysical nature. It is a far cry from the undefined, light-filled blur of Impressionism.

Takeaway: Glorified Nature

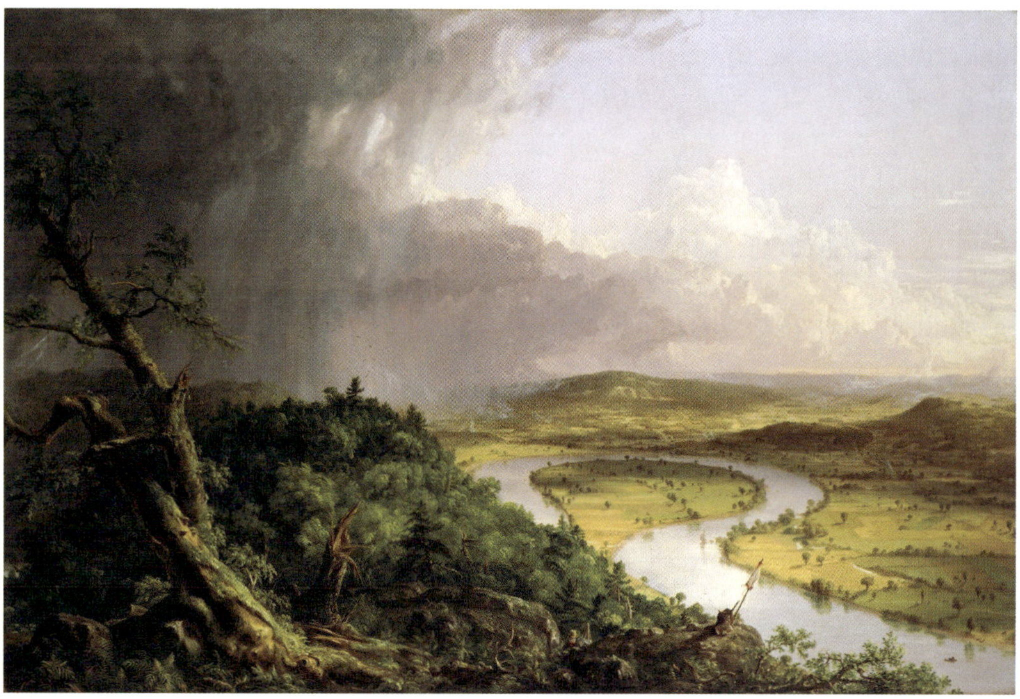

Fig. 73. Thomas Cole, VIEW FROM MOUNT HOLYHOKE, NORTHAMPTON, MASSACHUSETTS, AFTER A THUNDERSTROM—THE OXBOW.

ALFRED SISLEY (1839–1899)

A dedicated landscape painter, Sisley spent most of his life in France and painted the serene locations of the Seine and environs. His painted en plein air and was a decided Impressionist, though his sedate compositions lack the passion of his contemporary, Claude Monet.

Nonetheless, his paintings are simply lovely, filled with sweet notes and a palette of pastel shades. It is interesting to compare these works with those of Monet, the consummate Impressionist, whose ambition and intensity are remembered as the true voice of the movement.

Takeaway: Tranquility

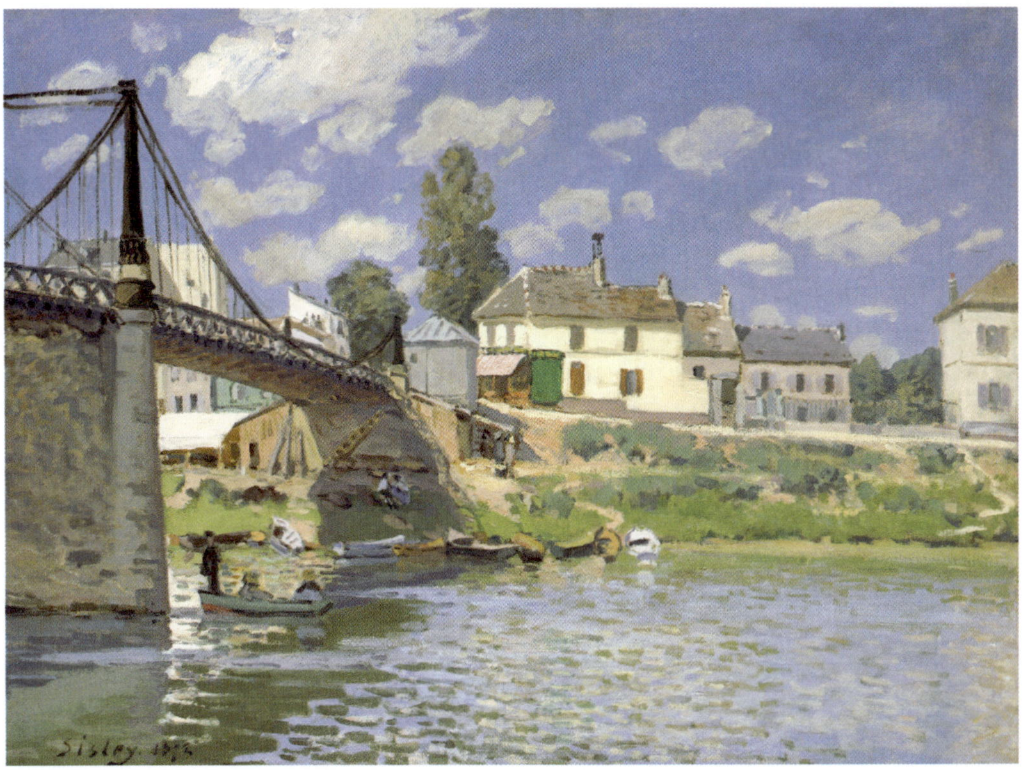

Fig. 74. Alfred Sisley, THE BRIDGE AT VILLENEUVE-LA-GARENNE.

CLAUDE MONET (1840–1926)

The founder and engineer of the movement of Impressionism, Claude Monet was its most expert exemplar. In 1874 he created a painting of sunrise at Le Havre, his hometown, called *Impression, Sunrise*. The painting shows a foggy view of the harbor, and when he was asked to title it, he said, "It couldn't really be taken for a view of Le Havre, and I said: 'Put *Impression*.'"

The name stuck and it came to categorize the work of many artists who studied the light and imbued their studies with the overall feeling of it, eschewing details that were lost in that light. Of these, Monet was the master and ultimate student of light, so much so that he has been referred to as "the eye."

Monet went on to make many studies of the light, often painting the same subject at different times of the day, requiring a different palette for each incarnation. Ultimately, he became so enchanted with the light that he created the Water Lilies series. Painting the pond at his home in Giverny, Monet became lost in the glory of the light as it dappled the flowers in the pond, scumbling the paint to create a tapestry of color. In many of these oils, the subject disappears, evanescing into a sea of color and light. An abstraction.

In the pantheon of painting, Monet stands with a select few geniuses of painting. He surely did not set out to create the movement of Impressionism, still one of the most beloved by students and appreciators of art. Rather, he used his very curious eye to discover a truth, and the importance of that truth created a sensation. Rejected at its introduction as sloppy, unfinished work, the power of Impressionism took hold and inspired generations of artists to follow.

I believe you will find more viewers in the Impressionism rooms of most museums than in the rooms dedicated to art that preceded it and followed it. It continues to captivate viewers for many reasons. These include the joyousness of the color, the looseness of the brushstrokes, and the fact that though objects are recognizable, they are not imitative. Most people seem to prefer these qualities over more dramatic, stiffer, abstract, or conceptual works. What do you think?

Takeaway: Master of the Light

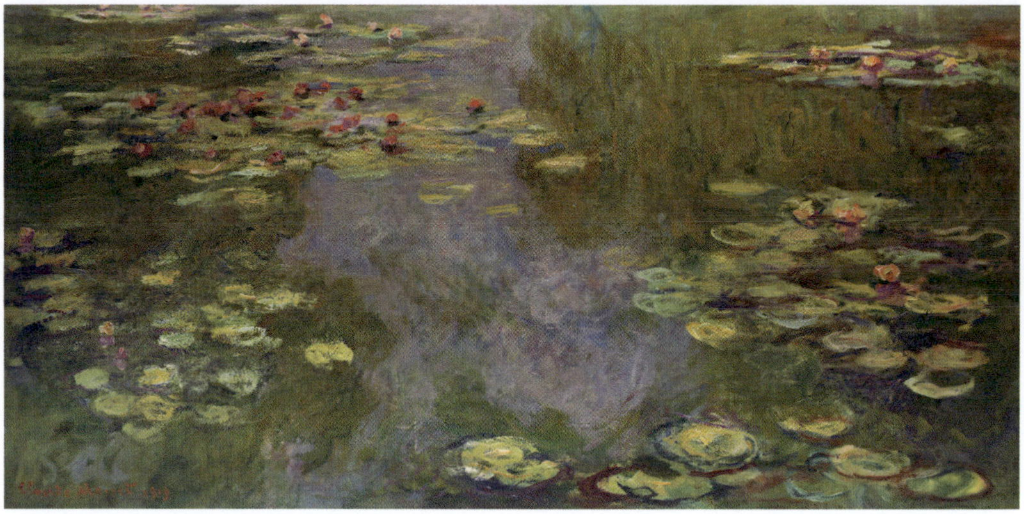

Fig. 75. Claude Monet, WATER LILIES.

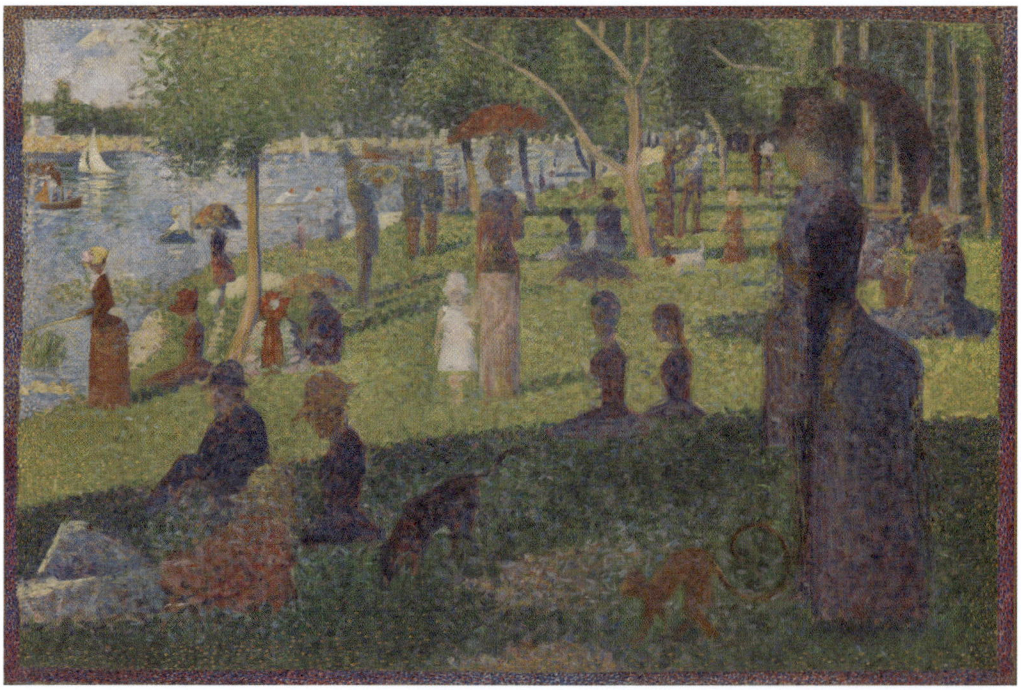

Fig. 76. Georges Seurat, STUDY FOR "A SUNDAY AFTERNOON ON THE ISLAND OF LA GRANDE JATTE."

GEORGES-PIERRE SEURAT (1858–1891)

Monsieur Seurat is considered a Postimpressionist, a movement considered as a bridge between Impressionism and Fauvism. His compatriots include Paul Céezanne, Paul Gauguin, and Vincent van Gogh. These artists, each in his own way, went beyond the airy light concentration of the Impressionists to give their paintings more of an illusion of form. Rather than hewing to the strict rendering of the subject in light, they introduced more expressive elements, like more geometric contouring and more amplified color.

In the case of Seurat, his sense of orderliness and scientific bent created the technique of Pointillism, where tiny dots of color juxtaposed against one another created a vibration of color. Seurat's most famous painting, *A Sunday Afternoon on the Island of La Grande Jatte*, took two years to complete. He did almost sixty studies for this work from life, and the final work is over ten feet wide. The work has a unique look and is undoubtedly a masterpiece of painting.

Was Seurat a romantic or a classicist?

Clearly the latter; his Pointillism technique was a deliberate attempt to use optical laws to create a new effect. Using a quasi-scientific term, Seurat called his process "chromoluminarism." While the Impressionists like Monet used their feelings and powers of observation to create beauty and truth, Seurat searched for a formula that would accomplish that goal.

He sought a color theory that would create harmony in his pictures. Seurat wrote the following: "Art is Harmony. Harmony is the analogy of the contrary and of similar elements of tone, of color and of line. In tone, lighter against darker. In color, the complementary, red-green, orange-blue, yellow-violet. In line, those that form a right angle. The frame is in a harmony that opposes those of the tones, colors, and lines of the picture; these aspects are considered according to their dominance and under the influence of light, in gay, calm, or sad combinations." (Letter to the writer Maurice Beaubourg, 28 August 1890, *Seurat,* London: Phaidon Press, 1965.)

Whatever our own personal bent, we cannot help but admire the patience, love, and dedication that went into Seurat's application of his formulas to art. And the magnificent results of his genius.

Takeaway: Science in Art

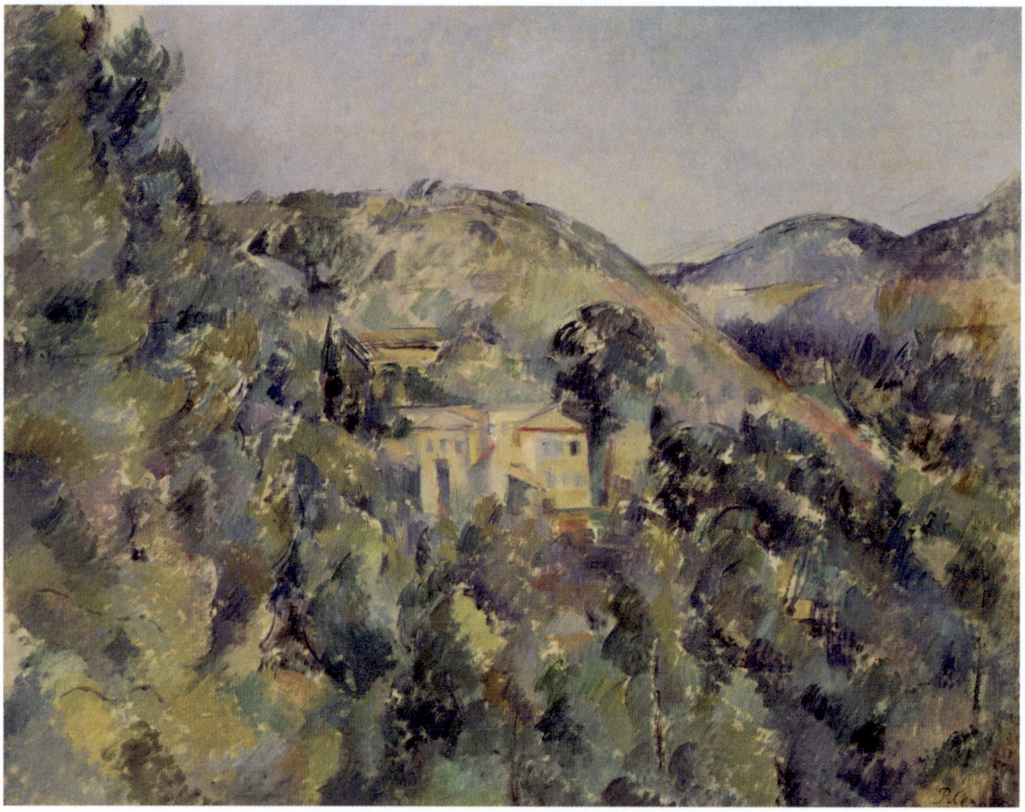

Fig. 77. Paul Cézanne, VIEW OF THE DOMAINE SAINT-JOSEPH.

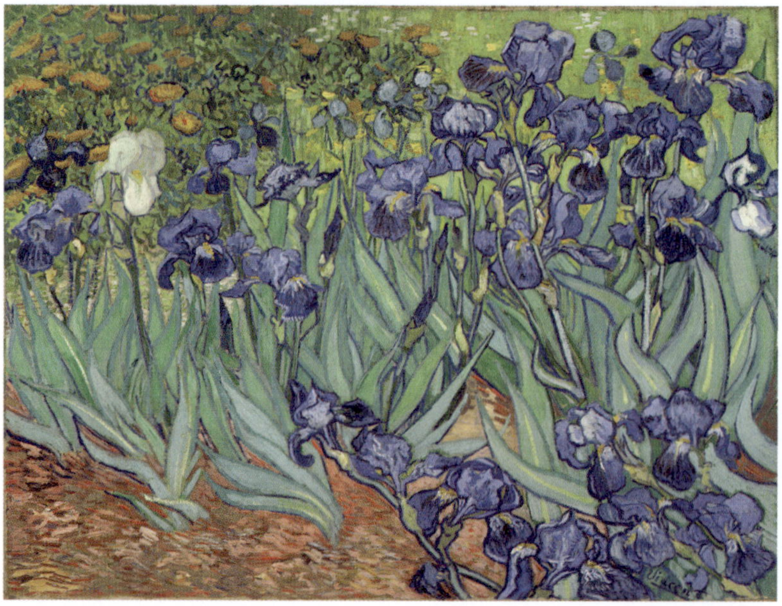

Fig. 78. Vincent van Gogh, IRISES.

PAUL CÉZANNE (1839–1906)

The French painter Cézanne was a kind of "artists' artist," very much respected and revered by artists who recognized his influence. Both Matisse and Picasso referred to him as "father to us all." Cézanne reacted against the airiness of Impressionism, wanting to make more defined forms. He retained the saturated colors used by the Impressionists but painted in a crisper, more delineated manner.

Cézanne was interested in structure and architecture, and to suggest this he made planes of color and simplified geometrical forms. He believed that the forms of nature could be described by the use of three solids—the cube, the sphere, and the cone. This idea was revolutionary, and little did Cézanne realize how far artists of the future would take this idea and move into abstraction.

Other artists who followed him recognized his talent and revered Cézanne for his realization of form. They were to take it a step further, ultimately taking the form apart, flattening it, as in Cubism, and considering drawing from multiple points of view at the same time. In his own way, Cézanne opened the doors to modern art.

Classicist? Yes, definitely. He got down to the basics, sculpting the paint to create more potent forms. There is something very workmanlike about his approach, and though not particularly popular in his time, it proved to have long arms into the future of art.

Takeaway: Architecture of Forms

VINCENT VAN GOGH (1853–1890)

The Postimpressionist Vincent van Gogh, who sold only one painting in his lifetime, and who is now beloved as one of the most popular artists in history, with prices for his works in the hundreds of millions, was a contemporary of Cézanne, but perhaps his opposite.

A true romantic, van Gogh was so full of feeling that he struggled with mental illness most of his life. His paintings are driven by movement, emotion, and passion, as he saw his subjects, even his landscapes and interiors, as riotously alive. He used demonstrable and vivid brushstrokes and bold saturated colors that literally pop, sway, and vibrate.

The vivacity of his work is unparalleled.

We don't know whether it was a disordered mind or distress that animated his work, that made the trees gnarled, the sky violent, the fields swirling, but whatever the reason, the feverish movement thrills us. His genius has made paint electrified and emotionally charged, his compositions magnificent.

Every artist is an individualist, but some are more radically individual than others.

Van Gogh is definitely in this company. We have to wonder whether he recognized this in himself.

Takeaway: Genius of Movement and Texture

HENRI MATISSE (1868–1954)

Though the marvelous Matisse was not predominantly thought of as a landscape painter, landscape plays a definitive, if not starring role, in his paintings. He was fond of painting the landscape through an open window, perhaps because he found it convenient to do so or, more likely, he found that the window provides a natural frame for the view and brings the outdoors *in*. Matisse is very much a designer, eschewing verisimilitude for compositional imperatives.

Like the figurative painting we looked at earlier, this Matisse was made in Morocco. It is a symphony in blues, where the wall of the room, window, sea, and sky all merge. The landscape is most purposefully flattened to enhance the design, although the size of the buildings tell us they are in the distance.

We can see this highly simplified work as a precursor to the more abstract work that would follow later in his career.

Takeaway: Fields of Color

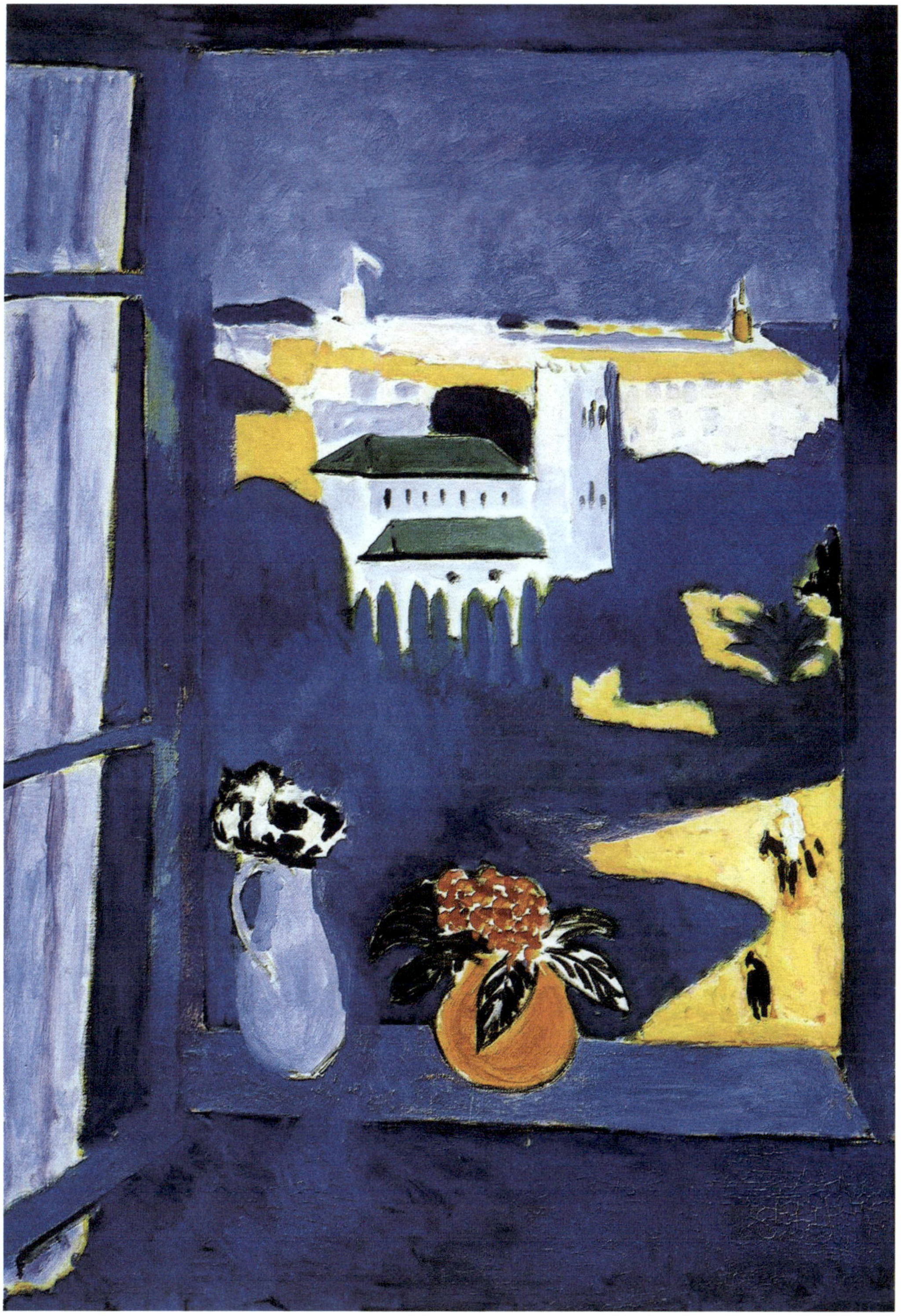

Fig. 79. Henri Matisse, WINDOW AT TANGIER.

SIMPLIFIED LANDSCAPE: THE DOOR TO ABSTRACTION

Remember the rule of thirds? Dividing the horizontal canvas into three sections to create the ideal balance in a work of landscape? Imagine you take a canvas, wider than it is long—in other words, a horizontal—and draw a line across approximately one third from the top, which represents the horizon line, then another approximately a third across from the bottom. Fill the top third with light blue, the middle third with a deeper blue, and the bottom with gold (see Fig. 80). What you have done is it to create an imaginary landscape—here suggesting a seascape—in the most rudimentary way.

Have a gander at this landscape painting by a little-known and short-lived German artist named **August Haake** (1889–1915) (Fig. 81). It is not signed but has been verified to be a Haake because of the two holes at the top of the canvas. The artist carried his work strung from the two holes on the back of a bicycle and characteristically made the holes his calling card. I offer it as an example of a simplified

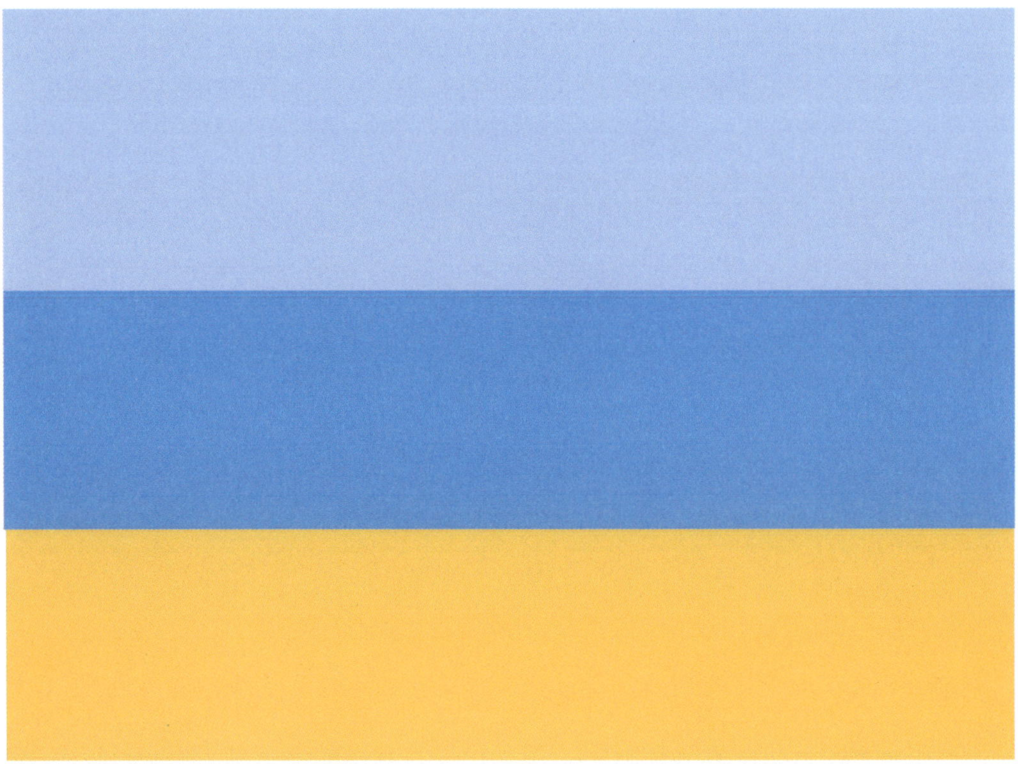

Fig. 80. Simplified landscape (illustration).

landscape: just three textured bands of color. You can easily see how the next leap would be to something even less detailed and more abstract.

Many wonderful artists moved a step further to create paintings that function both as landscape and abstraction or include aspects of nature in an abstract format. In the simplification process, other properties come to the fore. The beauty of the paint itself, transparencies, texture, subtle gradations of value, geometry, patterning, and the like.

This type of work has also been referred to as "lyrical abstraction." I encourage you to look up the following seminal artists of the twentieth century and study their work. (Generally, these artists' works are still under copyright protection, so I am unable to include them in this book. Still, you should be able to find a nice sampling of their pieces online.) Surely you will find traces or suggestions of natural forms or landscape, not identified or described, but rather felt and imagined. A bit about them:

Hans Hoffman (1880–1966) was a well-known artist and art teacher, whose students included Helen Frankenthaler, Lee Krasner, Joan Mitchell. and Larry Rivers. He believed that abstract art had its origin in nature and in the spiritual

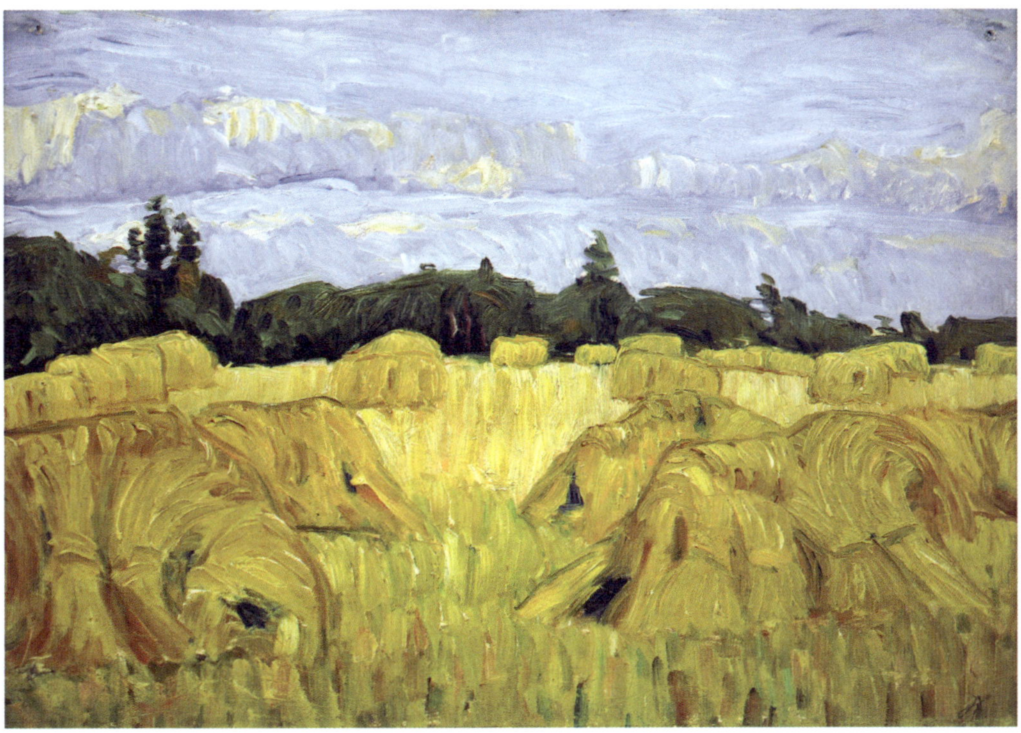

Fig. 81. August Haake, FIELD WITH SHEAFS.

character of art. He was concerned with pictorial structure and famous for his theory of **push-pull.**

This theory elaborated how an abstract artist could **pull** parts of his picture forward and **push** others back, thereby creating spatial relationships and a context of pictorial space.

This is not unlike what I have described as the artist imagining his line going into and out of imaginary space. The difference was that Hoffman elaborated the methodology and applied it to the abstract artist.

Hoffman's own work emphasized primary colors and simple shapes.

Joan Mitchell (1925–1992), an American who lived and worked in France most of her life, also took inspiration from landscape for her vibrant and vigorous abstract paintings. Her work is in the domain of what we call **gestural abstraction** by virtue of her very sensitive and vibrant mark-making. She loved Henri Matisse, and I would daresay most of the lyricists of abstraction concurred.

Look up examples of Mitchell's abstractions. It is noted that Mitchell described her abstract paintings as "remembered landscapes." Though her starting point may have been a memory of landscape, she obviously went on to develop them into more abstract compositions, obscuring the landscape references, or at least changing them.

It does seem easier to remember a landscape than a still life or figurative subject, doesn't it? One can imagine broad areas of sky, grass, sea, and sand morphing into colored shapes and linear texture with little specific drawing. Landscape to abstraction—a natural connection.

Milton Avery (1885–1965). The American painter Milton Avery was a lyrical painter, also very much in the tradition of Henri Matisse. His poetic and lyrical landscapes are simply lovely, almost childlike in their simplicity. He was a colorist par excellence, and his canvases are a feast for the eyes. He made simple divisions and used big swaths of luscious color.

Mark Rothko (1903–1970). Eighteen years younger than Avery, Rothko, an American painter of Russian Jewish descent, was influenced by Avery's simplified, stylized landscapes and made works reminiscent of them early in his career. Later on he went even further to concentrate on color and eventually, to throw all references away and bask in the nuances of color and texture.

His later works contain bands of vibrating masses of color, which he applied using a variety of secret ingredients to create a spiritual glow and reverberation.

Looking at a work featuring three bands of color, can you not see how the rule of thirds had taken a modern form turning landscape into pure abstraction?

Helen Frankenthaler (1928–2011). One among Hans Hoffman's cadre of students, she invented color field painting, a bathing of the canvas in a close range of hues. She, like a compatriot Rothko, adored color, and she applied it on a raw canvas with thin paint that made the oil saturate and the raw pigment rest and reverberate on the surface. She later abandoned this technique and actually worked with acrylic paint, which is more plastic and bright.

A doyenne of color, Frankenthaler explored its many facets throughout her illustrious career and created some really lovely pieces. Her compositions are just a hop, skip, and a jump from landscape. You'll find them by googling her name.

Richard Diebenkorn (1922–1993) was a member of the Bay Area Figurative School, a group of painters in and around San Francisco. Another devotee of Matisse, Diebenkorn's early figurative works are stunning and show elements that would later manifest in his abstract work—a division into simple shapes, an emphasis on coloration, and the blending of the figure into a pattern.

In the 1960s Diebenkorn's attention turned to more abstract works, and he is well known for his series entitled *Ocean Park* in which he painted the hills and dales and shapes he peered at from his Santa Monica studios, just blocks from the Pacific Ocean (see Fig. 82 on the next page). He produced 145 of these paintings of the sweet light of this area. A colorist, he translated the landscape into a collection of simple shapes of light.

What makes these works so special is that, as a highly perceptual painter, he is still connected to the quality of the beautiful light. He tells us with the tender aerated colors and iridescent hues that we are close to the ocean. One of the works in this collection appears on the next page.

Was he a landscape painter? Yes, certainly. His landscape encompassed the buildings, the sea, and the streets of his California home, which he reduced to this poetic geometric collection of atmospheric colors. They are a sight to behold.

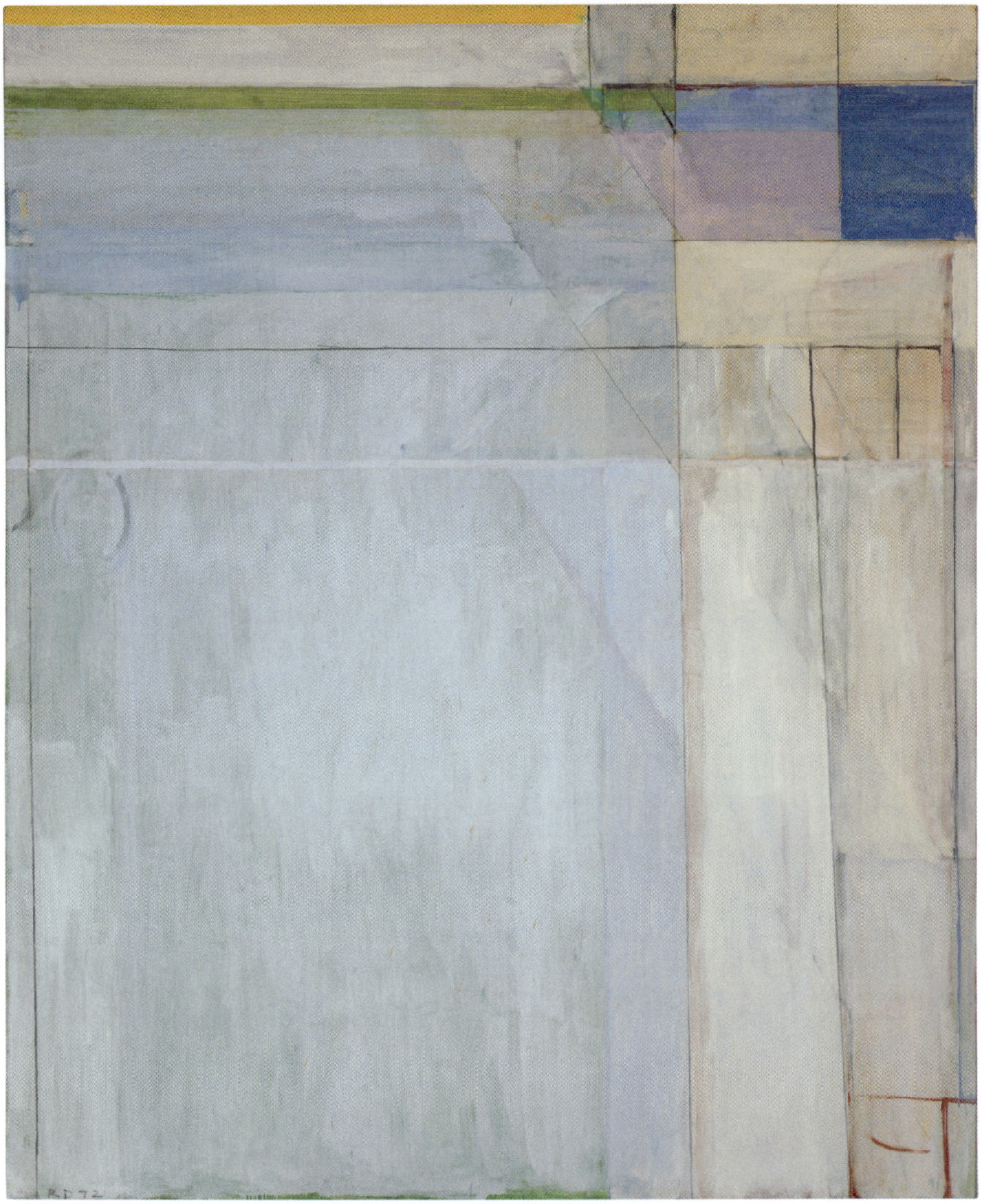

Fig. 82. Richard Diebenkorn, OCEAN PARK #54, 1972, oil and charcoal on canvas, 100 × 81 inches (254 × 205.4 centimeters). Catalogue raisonné no. 4117 © Richard Diebenkorn Foundation.

I hope you have enjoyed this abbreviated visit to some of the highlights of landscape painting. It continues to be quite a popular subject and quite varied in its interpretation. I encourage you to delve into other shining lights in the genre. Here are some distinct voices that stand out yet have much company. Have a look at these and search further for favorites of your own.

I'm a great fan of the Canadian painter **Tom Thomson** (1877–1917) and a group of landscape painters who followed him and collaborated to form what is known as the "Group of Seven." They worked in the early years of the twentieth century and did some vivid, highly animated paintings of their Canadian surroundings. Worth a look.

More current are a whole slew of painters interpreting landscape in unique, very personal ways. Trading in river scenes for swimming pools, backyards, and gardens, you will surely enjoy the sensual works of **David Hockney** (1937–present), a British artist, who often paints and draws with an iPad, along with his large canvases.

On the other end of the spectrum, you will find a Latvian American artist, **Vija Celmins** (1938–present), who projects a somber, neutral, and impersonal view of nature. No gaily painted palm trees in her world. Her preference is for incredibly detailed renderings of the more mundane natural forms—rocks, deserts, and spider webs. For her, romanticism is anathema, hyperreality her cause célèbre. The revolt against the "beautiful" is a predominant force in other genres as well; we examine this further in our review of abstraction in chapter 11.

Another painter of landscape worth perusing is **Gerhard Richter** (1932–present), whose attention to texture is as fervent as that of Celmins but in a much more painterly and colorful format. He is another good example of the landscape-abstraction connection. A counterpoint to Richter is the Swedish artist, **Joakim Allgulander** (1965–present), who offers sleek, textured but clarified images that are very sculptural.

The popularity of landscape painting is considerable, and contemporary landscape painters have achieved startling prices for their work. One example of this is the Scottish painter, **Peter Doig** (1959–present), who in 2015, achieved a price for his work *Swamped* that topped $25 million. Few contemporary artists ever approach such an astounding sum; nonetheless, it is just one testament to the depth and breadth of landscape in art and its perceived value to art collectors.

Chapter 10
Subject and Master: Still Life

The French Academy in the seventeenth century created a hierarchy of subjects for painting. The most lofty was history painting, followed by portraiture, scenes of daily life, landscape, and lastly, still life. The preference for the depiction of human beings was clear, dropping landscape and still life, two genres that did not include people, to the bottom.

Still life, the depiction of objects, both natural and manufactured, has nonetheless proved to be a popular subject for painters through the ages. Part of the reason is the accessibility of objects and the ability to arrange them as a subject under fixed conditions. The changing light means that landscape painters working en plein air must constantly adapt to these conditions as the light waxes and wanes, changing the color of everything they see.

The arranged still life objects could remain ad infinitum in a fixed place in the studio, available for long hours of study. No model fees or squirming figures to interrupt the artist's work. The resulting works have proved of interest to art collectors as well, being potentially quite decorative.

In addition to its accessibility, still life is a wonderful subject for students of art.

It enables the student to practice the rendering of the various textures and reflective qualities of cloth, wood, glass, ceramic, as well as delicate substances like flowers etc. It offers an excellent format for studying shape and line, and for composing a canvas. In a sense the artist practices composition by not only painting the still life but also by setting it up to be painted.

The eighteenth-century Dutch painters were much interested in this subject matter and rendered it realistically. An example is this Chardin table with a variety of objects created in 1769 (see Fig. 83 on the next page). Again, notice the variety of textures the artist was able to imitate including the shine on the fish, wooden tabletop, glass

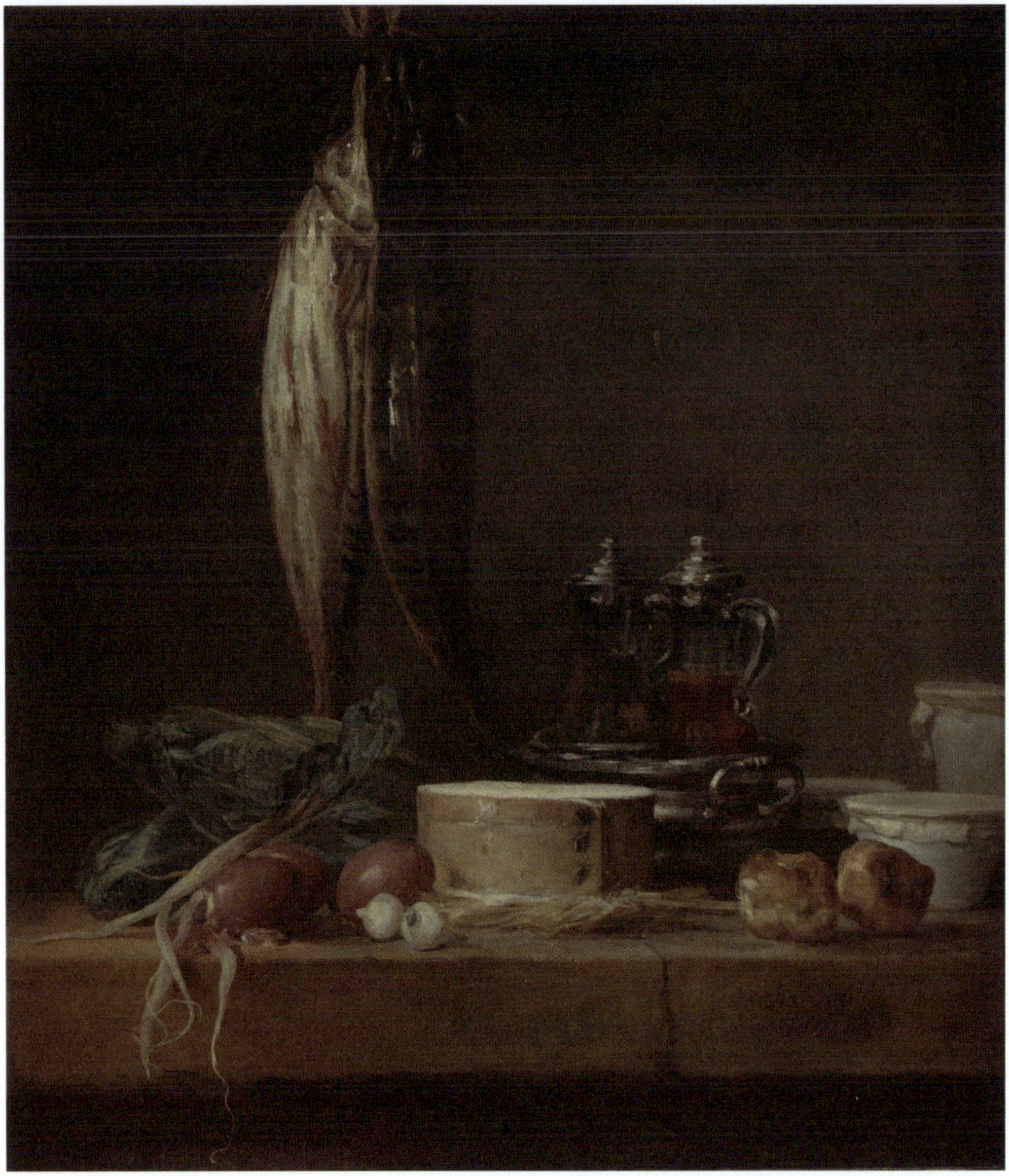

Fig. 83. Jean-Baptiste-Siméon Chardin, STILL LIFE WITH FISH, VEGETABLES, GOUGÈRES, POTS, AND CRUETS ON A TABLE.

jugs, and the glint of light on the metal tops. The objects were undoubtedly chosen because of the multitude of surfaces the artist wished to re-create.

Here is another example of a popular subject in still life painting: flowers (Fig. 84). This next piece was created in the nineteenth century by the artist Henri Fantin-Latour, also in a realistic vein. Notice how the plain grainy neutral background sets off the ornate flowers. We call this a "foil" in painting, the quiet that sets off the main interest in a painting and by doing so, invigorates it.

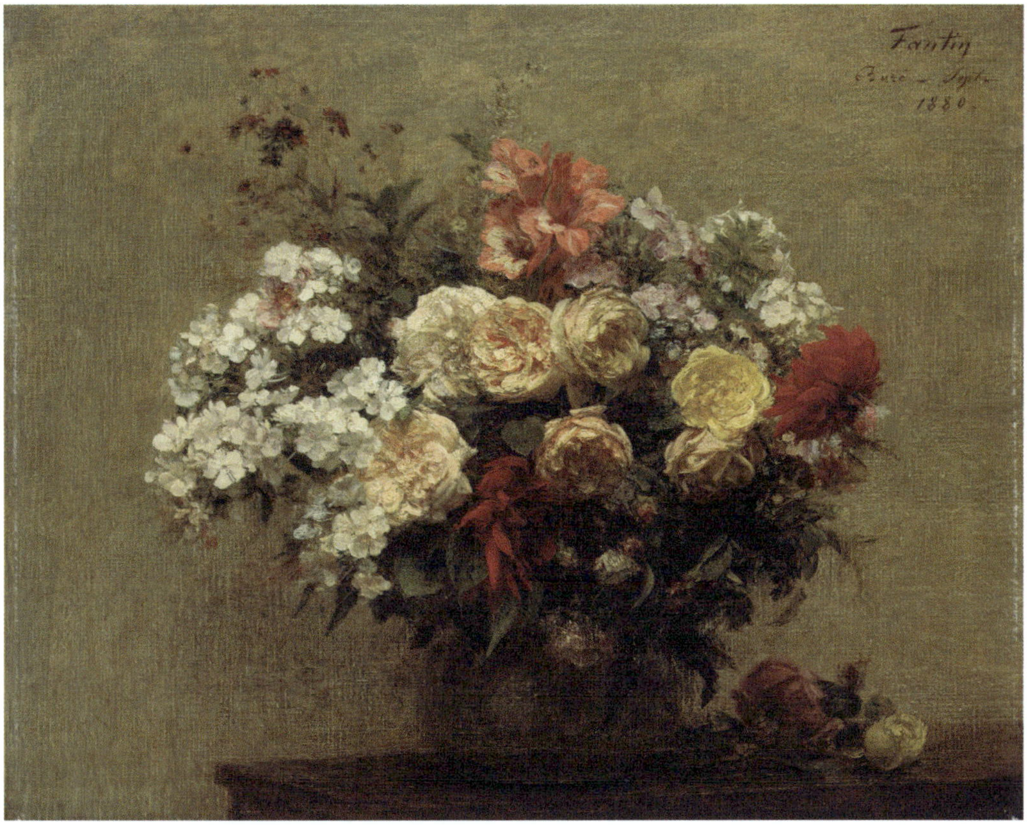

Fig. 84. Henri Fantin-Latour, SUMMER FLOWERS.

As we look at more modern treatments of still life, relate them to these realistic paintings. The creative possibilities of still life came into their own in the twentieth century as artists took the subject to an entirely new plateau.

You have Gauguin's homage to van Gogh with his *Still Life with Sunflowers*, some wonderful works by the Nabis, the examinations of the Cubists and the Fauves, the intensive work on the subject by Cézanne and many others who made the subject matter their own. We'll take a look at how these and other artists brought still life as subject matter from its former lowly status to the height of creativity and experimentation.

Probably no artist is more associated with fruit than Paul Cézanne (see Fig. 85 on the next page). He was an avid painter of still lifes, and fruit—representing the sphere—resided happily in many of them. He broke his objects into their component parts, absorbed as he was in creating their form. Cézanne didn't just copy the objects, he also studied and analyzed them. Breaking simple objects into the facets or planes that comprise three-dimensional form is a precursor to the Cubist technique. In Cubism, the objects were further disguised as the genre probed the anatomy of the object.

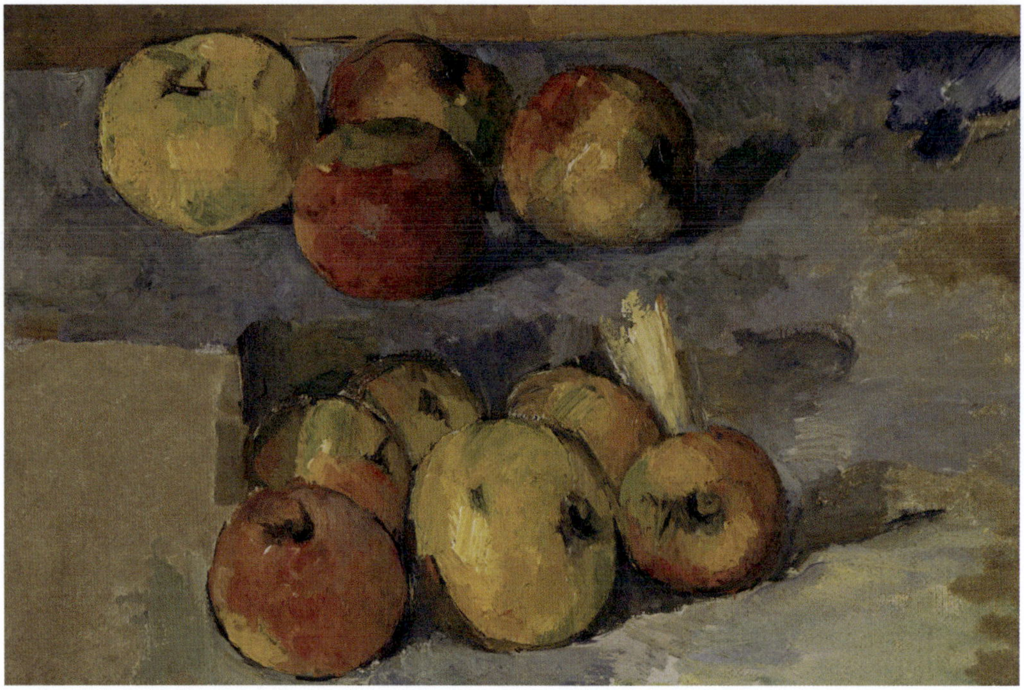

Fig. 85. Paul Cézanne, APPLES.

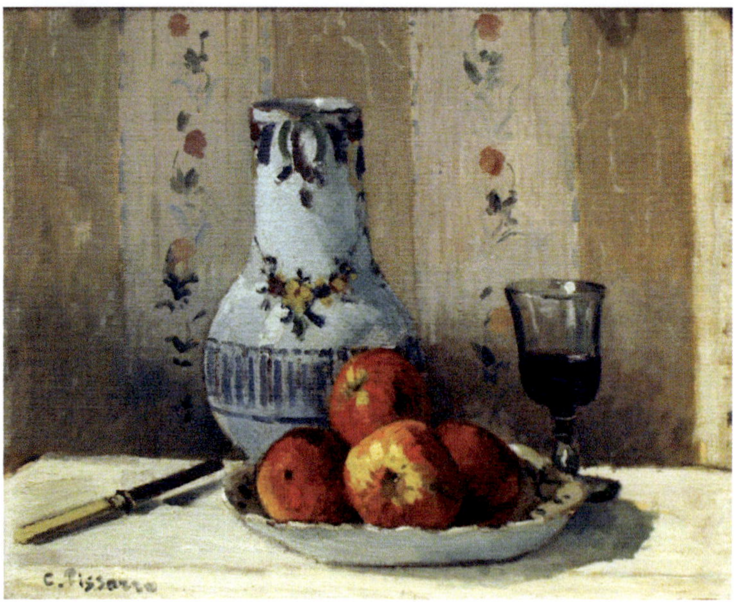

Fig. 86. Camille Pissarro, STILL LIFE WITH APPLES AND PITCHER.

Other artists of the period followed Cézanne's lead. Here is a painting by the artist Pissarro that features some orangey apples in the context of some soft decorative painting (Fig 86). This is a simple work that describes the still life as it appears, with good drawing and effective painting, but no distortions of any kind.

Now have a look at this very complex Cubist work by Juan Gris (Fig. 87). He was following the work of Picasso and Georges Braque, who, as a former housepainter, incorporated decorative motifs into his still life compositions. Here Gris compresses the illusion of space, and brings the trees outside and the grate in front of the window right into the picture plane. Imagine boards of wood (flat planes) laid one atop the other, creating three dimensions in the build. This technique replaced using linear perspective to accomplish depth. By virtue of these stacking planes, he brings all the elements into the foreground. It makes for a fascinating and very decorative design.

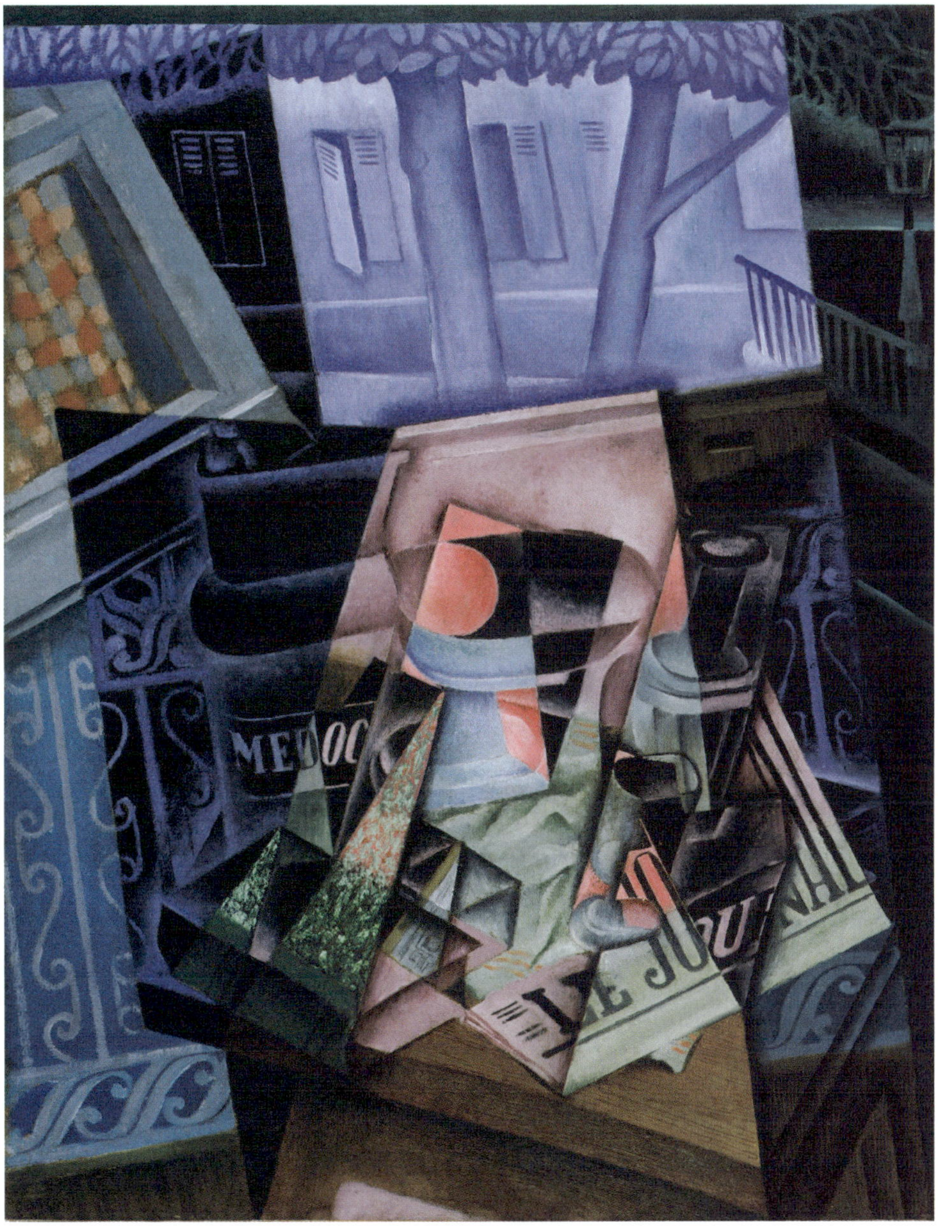

Fig. 87. Juan Gris, STILL LIFE BEFORE AN OPEN WINDOW, PLACE RAVIGNAN.

Now compare these van Gogh sunflowers (Fig. 88) with the realistic Fantin-Latour flowers we just looked at (Fig. 84). Firstly, both the flowers and the background say *light*. No dramatic long gamut as in the Fantin-Latour. We have a simplicity and also an expressive quality. The flowers point in different directions and we even have one that is drooping. The van Gogh flowers actually have a personality! This is something that is possible once an artist gives himself permission not to imitate, and to speak with his paint from the heart. Even a pot can be personal!

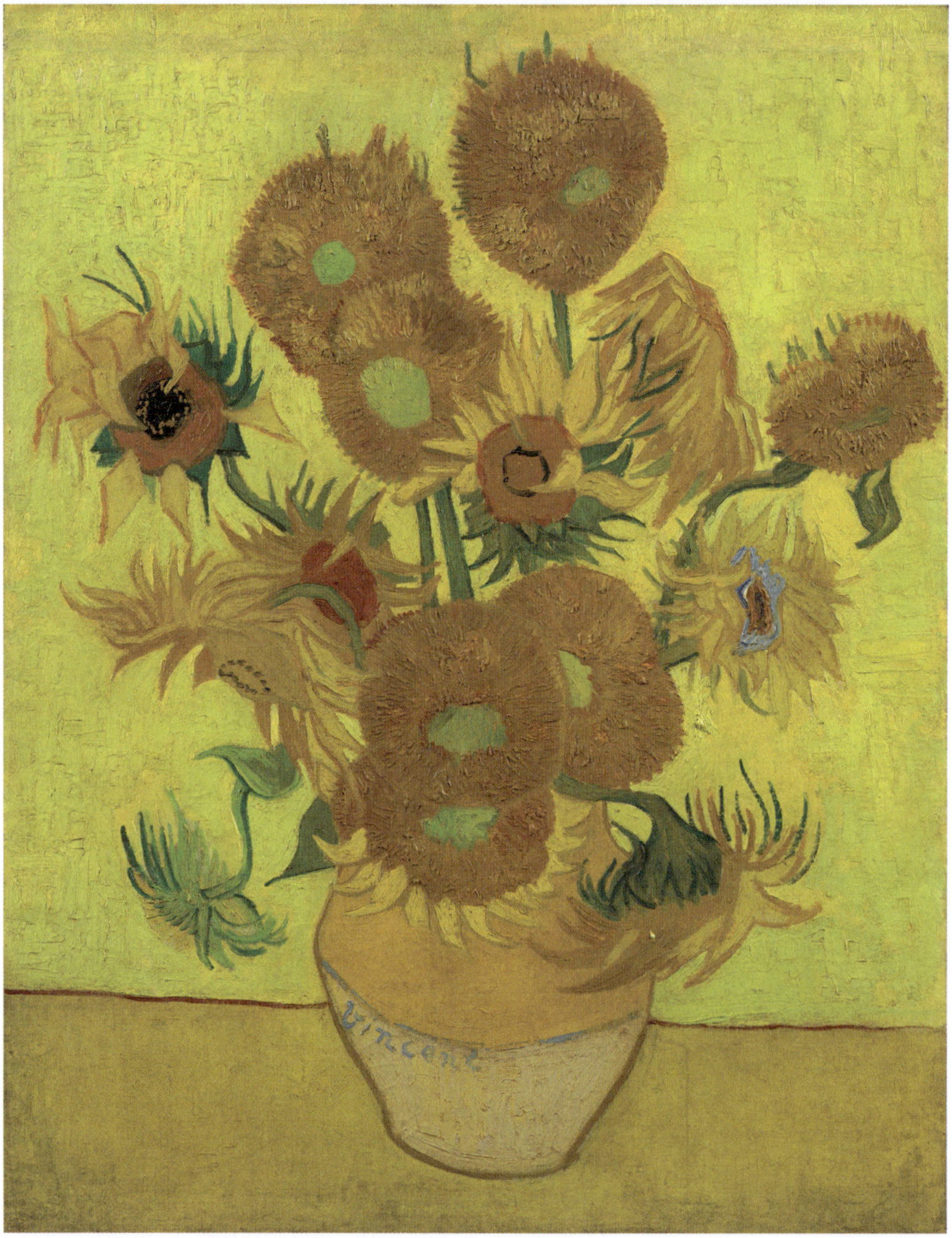

Fig. 88. Vincent van Gogh, FOURTEEN SUNFLOWERS IN A VASE.

I've mentioned that for an artist, the setting up of the still life is the beginning of the creative process of creating it. Choices determine outcome. Have a look here at the studio still life setup of the artist Giorgio Morandi, who eschewed complicated and elaborate still life motifs and simply lined up a few bottles, vases, and bowls on a surface and painted them without fanfare (Fig. 89).

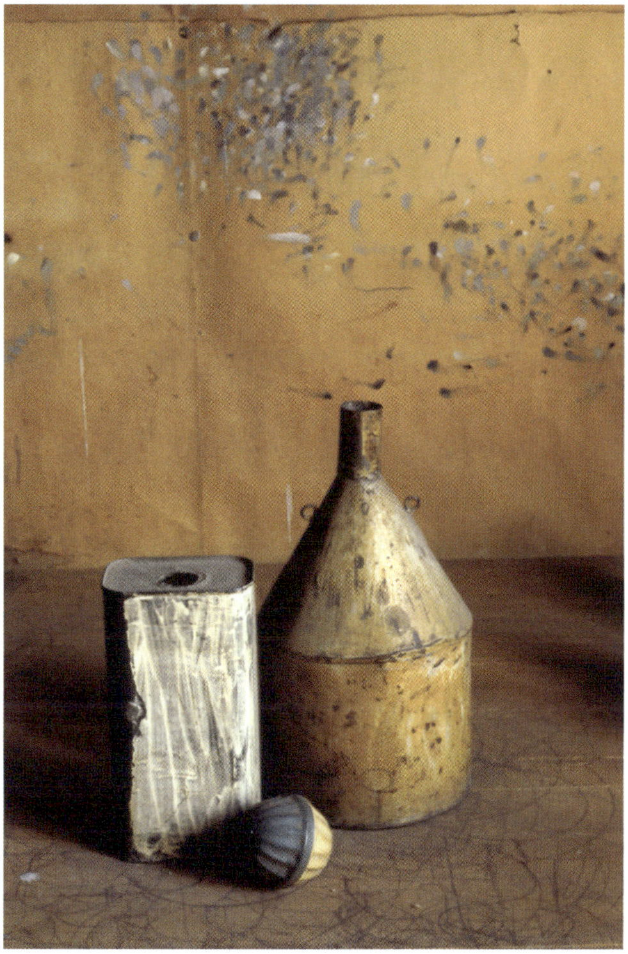

Fig. 89. Paolo Monti, MORANDI STUDIO.

Morandi took the ceremony and decorative aspects out of still life and concentrated on simple, tonal portrayals of ordinary objects. Morandi went for very minor key hues existing in a very neutral zone. As goes the genre of still life, you might call him a minimalist. The desire for simplicity is a great mark of modernism and certainly a trend, as you can see, as art-making moves through time.

Just as figurative work and landscape veered into the abstract, so did the art of still life. From Morandi's simplification, we move on to other simplifications and finally to abstraction.

Another modern development was for artists to actually attach objects to their artworks. The art of collage, a modern method of cutting, tearing, and placing different materials—paper, fabric, natural materials—onto a surface eventually transformed into the art of assemblage, when these attachments themselves were three-dimensional. Assemblage is considered a relief, but if the materials attached are significant, the assemblage can be considered a sculpture.

Works of this type are also referred to as mixed media. Artists like Jasper Johns, Robert Rauschenberg, and Kurt Schwitters are known for inserting all manner of objects into their work. One of Rauschenberg's work even included a taxidermy pheasant!

Robert Rauschenberg's experimentation with collage and assemblage was groundbreaking. He called these works "combines" for obvious reasons, as they were composed of painted elements plus junk he picked up on the streets of New York and integrated into his compositions. He commented that these found objects were revitalized in the context of these paintings/sculptures.

Once started, an idea or technique can become an obsession and even become impetus for a whole new way of thinking. When Rauschenberg dripped red paint across a quilt and then stretched it as a canvas, as he did in his piece *The Bed*, was he crossing over into performance art? More on this as we continue.

Here's a Rauschenberg collage (Fig. 90), and though not featuring much in the way of actual objects, it is a fascinating composite of images. Figuring out how they are related, both visually and narratively, is quite a puzzle. Modern painters like Rauschenberg are aware they are concocting an imaginary space. The rules of the "realism" road—creating a recognizable illusion—do not apply. Here, I love the simple box structures along with the classical imagery. Do you concur?

As with most experiments, one thing usually leads to another. So too in art. Inserting actual materials and objects into or on top of a painted surface was certainly not the end of the story. Once objects are introduced into play, they next move off that flat surface into space, and we have sculpture composed of found objects and mixed media. A big "why not?" enters the zeitgeist. Here is Degas putting an actual cloth skirt on his bronze form of a young dancer (Fig. 91).

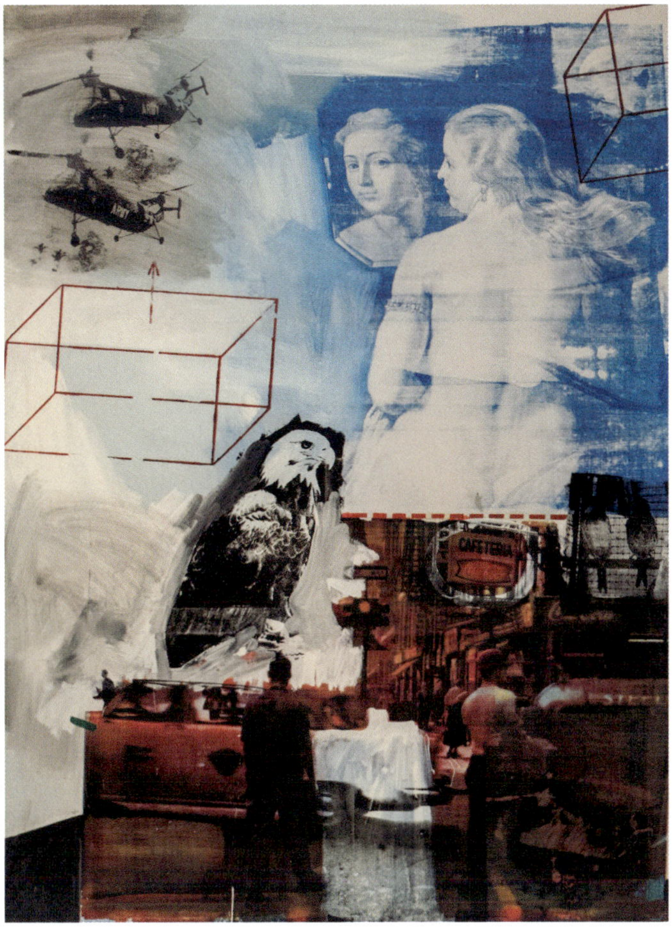

Fig. 90. Robert Rauschenberg, TRACER.

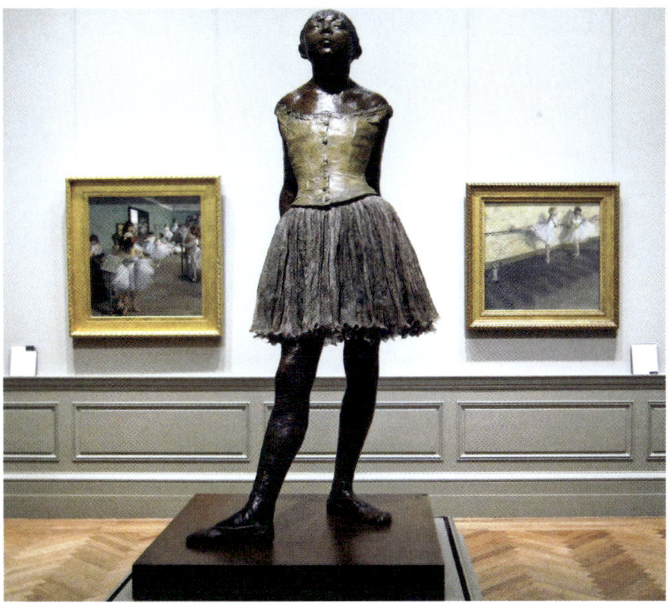

Fig. 91. Edgar Degas, LITTLE FOURTEEN-YEAR-OLD DANCER.

Artists see objects, sometimes just detritus, as suggestive of something they wish to portray, or find just such an interesting form that they devise a whole piece around it. Searching for these little treasures is a major part of the practice of many artists who become denizens of thrift shops, scrap heaps, and storage warehouses. Here is a contemporary sculpture that incorporates doll parts, old clockworks, and polyester resin (Fig. 92). Great fun!

Ultimately artists move off the wall and past sculpture altogether to conceive of entire rooms filled with objects as their canvas, sometimes with a living person inhabiting them, as they create **installations**. We discuss this in more detail in the next chapter.

It is undeniable that artists are doing all of us a great service, taking the discarded, unusable refuse of modern life and turning it into art. Now if only we could do the same with all the plastic filling up our oceans. . . .

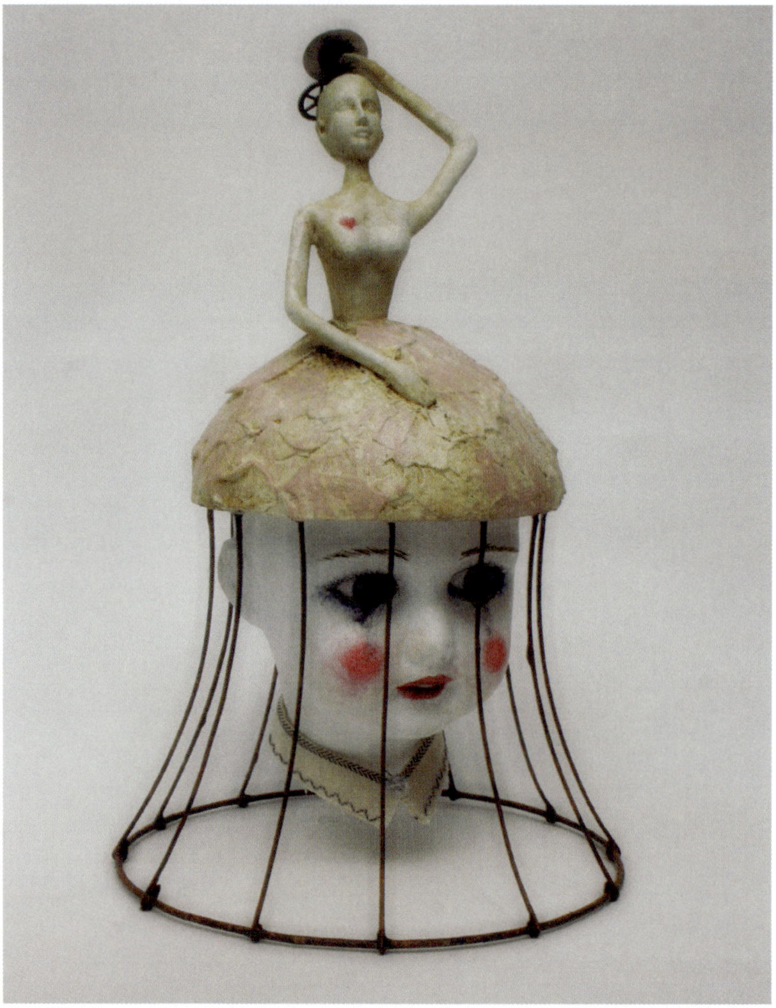

Fig. 92. Jeylina Ever, ORLANDO.

Chapter 11

Subject and Master: Abstraction

Abstract art detaches itself from the illusion of anything real. It may arise from the examination of an object, but the artist is not compelled to make a visual reference to that object in his work. If he makes some reference, and either simplifies or stylizes it, but it is still recognizable, we say that the work is semi-abstract.

Sometimes abstract artists will tell you what inspired them to create the composition, or what they used as source material in the title of the work. Sometimes they will leave the inspiration ambiguous and they will refer to the work as *Opus 22* or some such.

Before the nineteenth century and the advent of the camera, creating illusions of actual objects seemed necessary and important. But once you could take a perfect image of something with a camera, doing so lost its appeal for many creative people. This liberated artists to make compositions of colors and shapes in myriad varieties.

What motivated artists to move past the object was not only due to the advent of a device—the camera—that could do the job for them. Artists gradually through history became aware of the many ways they could not only imitate but comment on their subject. Taking those artistic licenses by simplifying objects, drawing from multiple points of view, exaggerating proportions, etc. all are precursors to doing away with the object altogether.

When art is liberated from the object, when the pot disappears, what remains as subject? What is left are all the abstract qualities that make that pot apparent, all the qualities of light, air, space, movement, color, rhythm, etc. You have mood, flavor, rhythm, texture. Like music, you have something suggestive, not described; something felt, not identified. Many see visual abstraction as a kind of visual music. Think of Whistler, who even gave his compositions musical titles.

When you think of the arts—music, literature, dance, theater, visual art—many of these are "abstract" by their very nature. Music and dance certainly are abstract forms—they may suggest, but do not describe, themes and motifs. Literature and theater can be naturalistic and depict actual events, but they can also be abstract especially in poetic form, but also in prose and theater format.

So why was abstract visual art seen as such a departure?

Many of the artists who were captivated by abstract art did so partly for ideological reasons. They wanted to show rather than describe and they saw abstraction as a purer way to do so. They saw details as a distraction from the poetic or imaginative realities they strove for.

Suffice it to say, artists discovered many ways to create abstract act, some of which were of such interest that they became movements, and many undertook the call. We will look at some of these and some of the greatest practitioners of abstract art.

Vasily Kandinsky (1866–1944) is credited with producing the first 100 percent abstract painting. He was a thinker and theorist, developing theories about painting that he then elaborated in his work. His road to abstraction was gradual, as you might expect, and I have read that his conversion to abstraction occurred in a most unusual manner. While he was out for a stroll, it is told, his student went about tidying the studio. While doing so, she turned one of his paintings on its side. When returning to the studio and viewing this piece, it is reported that Kandinsky fell to his knees, crying at the beauty of this composition, now revealed just as a composition, and not as a depiction of an object. This proved revelatory.

While Kandinsky was having his awakening, many other artists experienced similar calls to abstraction, and this manifested in many different ways. Imagine for a moment that you have lived by a set of rules and regulations your entire life, and then one day you are told that the rules no longer apply. In a sense, this is what occurred when the rules of color and form were permitted to expire. Artists no longer had to make illusions, and this unleashed an explosion of creative excursions.

To put the emergence of abstract art in perspective, so you understand how and why it arose, here is a quick voyage from Postimpressionism to the present. We're traveling fast here, so hang on for the ride.

From Postimpressionism (1880s), our next stop is **FAUVISM** (1890s), where heightened and brightened color violated naturalistic treatment. The Fauves went to town with an enthusiastic display for vigorous painting and bright primary colors.

Some of the practitioners include Matisse, Derain, Dufy, Vlaminck, and Marquet. Fauvism represented an enthusiastic liberation for these artists; it was a relatively short-lived movement at the time, though bright color would be revived in later movements like Pop and Op Art.

Next comes **CUBISM** (1900s), where the object is broken and the rules of perspective are replaced by multiple points of view and stacked planes.

Cubism was an important movement in painting and sculpture and represented a major shift in thought that had both philosophical and scientific components. It took art into an entirely new purpose and sphere away from the creation of visual illusions into an analytical framework.

To depict multiple points of view in the same work meant that artists were no longer bound to spatial and temporal limitations and could exist in the past, present, and future simultaneously. As you can imagine, this thinking not only changed the look of painting and sculpture but stretched into other art forms like literature and architecture and gave permission to their practitioners to experiment with entirely different verbal and literal structures.

Cubism arose out of several influences, including artists' studies of stylistic primitive art, which suggested a simplification of facets or planes and the use of clearly defined shapes. The breaking up of forms by Cezanne was also an influence. Artist exemplars of Cubism include Picasso, Braque, Gris, Delaunay, Léger, and others.

Cubism is a distinctly modern phenomenon related to a shift in consciousness away from the literal and illusionist tradition to an analytical one. Did it in turn influence scientific theories like Einstein's theory of relativity? Probably, yes.

In art as well, Cubism started an outpouring of new visual ideas. Once the image, the illusion, was broken, many artists found ways to express the new disorder. Conventions flew out the window and new movements were created.

There was **FUTURISM** (1910s), an Italian movement, which incorporated machinelike forms and dynamic design, a kind of fast-paced movement, exemplified by Boccioni and Severini. These artists fell in love with industry, which typified modernity, and rejected organic shapes, which they found traditional and boring.

SUPREMATISM (1910s): This was a Russian version of Futurism led by Malevich, which had a different focus. Also forsaking the illusion of the past, this movement aimed to devise a supremely perfect abstract shape to supplant it.

Eschewing complex forms, the Suprematists strove to reduce their imagery to geometric forms—the square, rectangle, and circle. This was a theory of reductionism that had a spiritual context. Purity was the goal.

They did away with all the trappings of realism. Was anything left?

CONSTRUCTIVISM (1910s): This offshoot of Suprematism in Russia built on the geometrical forms, but without the spiritual imprint. This form was an amalgam of the geometrical married to images with an industrial or technological slant. Kind of Suprematism meets Futurism, Russian style. This was perhaps more in keeping with the Communist revolutionary story.

EXPRESSIONISM (1905–1920): Artists who rejected the real in favor of the abstract basically fell into two camps—those on the hyper-strict side who chose minimalist, often geometric shapes, and others with a spiritual bent who chose spontaneous brushwork and vivid, musical shapes that were exciting and emotional. The latter group were called Expressionists.

Think about how these two forms harken back to our discussion of classicism vs. romanticism, with the geometrical artists clearly on the classical side and the expressionists as modern romantics.

In Germany, the Expressionists were represented by two groups: Die Brucke (translates as "The Bridge"), led by Kirshner, and The Blue Rider, led by Kandinsky. Though the groups had different approaches, they shared the desire to express universal truths in an abstract fashion. Kandinsky evolved a lexicon of forms and colors, noting and theorizing the meaning of each. He was very interested in musical forms, and his work has a musical quality.

It is interesting to note that Expressionism was a movement that promoted the release of spiritual and emotional yearnings, and as such, was much vilified by the Fascist forces in Germany. Hitler equated Expressionist works with cultural degeneracy.

Expressionism was an important force in the twentieth century and lives on today. Some of the greatest painters would likely consider themselves in this category. It represents a worldview that is an umbrella for many types of expression. Can you think of a few artists who might call themselves Expressionists?

DADAISM (1910s): Dada was a movement by iconoclasts who challenged bourgeois society and made art as a form of protest. This was exemplified by Marcel Duchamp, who famously exhibited a urinal as art (Fig. 93).

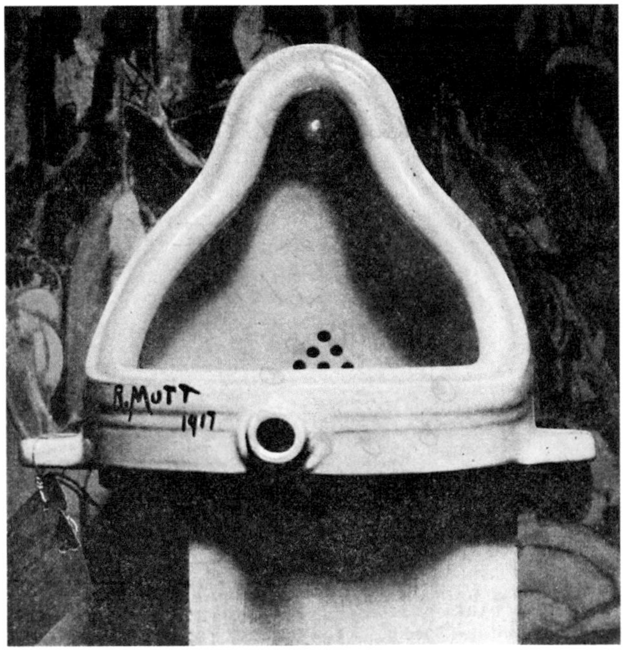

Fig. 93. Marcel Duchamp, FOUNTAIN.

Why in the world would Duchamp do this? It was a professional joke with a message, a statement, and a question about the practices of the art establishment. Duchamp submitted a urinal, which he had purchased and signed "R. Mutt 1917," to an exhibition of the Society of Independent Artists in 1917, which permitted anyone to contribute a work, provided they paid for membership ($1) and annual dues ($5). By doing so, he was challenging the democratization of art. In the end, the board decided not to show the Duchamp creation, and Duchamp furthered his joke by inviting the famed photographer Alfred Stieglitz to immortalize it.

Later in this chapter we'll look at other works of "conceptual art" whose purpose is to make a statement, protest, or otherwise turn the art world on its head.

What did "Dada" mean? The French word is a term for a hobbyhorse, and it is not clear how this term came to be employed by the artist community. Perhaps it was chosen by accident (some say a German artist, Richard Huelsenbeck, randomly picked it out of a dictionary) or to suggest a childish nonsense word. In any case, the name stuck and defined these works of anti-art, or at least anti-conventional art.

Dada arose after World War I and was also seen as an anti-war reaction. One of the techniques employed by the Dadaists was collage. Artists such as Max Ernst glued actual objects into their compositions, rather than just depicting them. The

Cubists did this as well. Dadaists also pioneered the introduction of words into their compositions, blending literature and visual art.

DE STIJL (1920s): A Dutch minimalist and reductionist movement, De Stijl means "The Style." De Stijl artists promoted purity and only the essentials in art-making, limiting themselves to only straight lines, rectangular shapes, and black, gray, and white plus the primary colors. This movement is also referred to as neoplasticism. It spilled over into architecture, and Mies van der Rohe was a primary proponent.

De Stijl painters were led by Mondrian, who was a theorist, much like Kandinsky. His geometrical patterns were not random or simply decorative. They had a significance that he codified. Lines and colors represented cosmic forces and energy. Verticals came from the sun's rays; horizontals represented the earth moving around it. Each color delivered a message. This is what we call conceptual art, visual art that is derived from an idea and which aims to depict that idea, especially symbolically.

Echoes of De Stijl are still evident today as a design theme reflected in architecture, interior design, and furniture.

SURREALISM (1920s): As opposed to movements breaking with realism totally, the surrealists just expanded the definition, creating images of implausible dreamlike scenarios, filled with visual non-sequiturs and distortions. Surrealism was certainly informed by Freud's writings on dreams and the unconscious. The interest in alternative realities took form not only in art as exemplified in the work of Salvador Dalí and others, but also in literature.

One can think of the Surrealists as detaching their paintings from the literal while still keeping the semblance of the object. It is a breaking away from the local and the familiar, from logic itself. Though not a move into abstraction, Surrealism was a modernist movement and brought the vocabulary of visual art into new dimensions. It continues to be felt today, particularly in the medium of literature, as in magical realism, and also in film, a medium particularly well-suited to the depiction of other realities.

ABSTRACT EXPRESSIONISM (1940s): A particularly American art movement that emerged in the 1940s and 1950s, it was expressed as a variety of incarnations in the work of its many adherents. The title is the umbrella under which many different interpretations came to life. Expressionism = emotional intensity + Abstraction = denial of the actual or figurative.

The Abstract Expressionists took a step further than the Futurists, Surrealists, and Cubists. They dispensed with the object altogether, for the sake of more direct and powerful expression. As Jay Meuser, a California abstract painter, declared, and the abstract artists agreed: "It is far better to capture the glorious spirit of the sea than to paint all of its tiny ripples."

So instead of details, we have essences. We have spontaneity. We have the subconscious. We have the spiritual. These are the icons of the abstract expressionists whether they are made manifest by the drips and splatters of Jackson Pollock, the saturated color of Rothko, the austerity of Agnes Martin, the black marks of Motherwell and Kline, or the furiously scribbled women of de Kooning.

Have a look at a work by Arshile Gorky, an Armenian artist, a survivor of Armenian genocide, who subsequently lived and worked in the United States (Fig. 94). His work leaps from a Surrealist bent into Abstract Expressionism, as typified by this work.

Gorky apparently was a practitioner of the Surrealist idea of "automatic" writing, a kind of drawing where the hand is supposedly directed by the unconscious, to make resonant lines that evoke memories or dreams. Reviewers read some of the lines in this work as Armenian plows, which evoke his very troubled past.

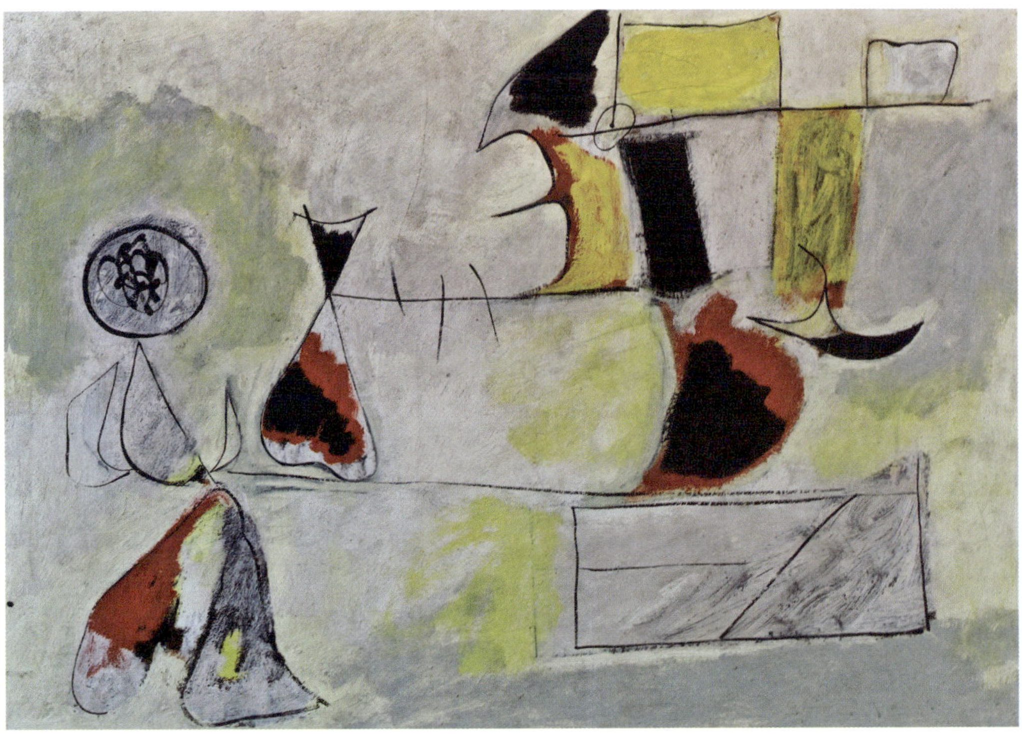

Fig. 94. Arshile Gorky, GARDEN OF WISH FULFILLMENT.

Though his work was well received, Gorky suffered many life crises, including the loss of fifteen of his works in a plane crash, and eventually killed himself.

The mainly American artists who took up this art genre in mid twentieth century were a feisty lot. The aim was to go abstract but to inject emotion into their often explosive work. These are not tame compositions of juxtaposed shapes. They are a riot of color and often feature thick and loose application of paint.

Do not be fooled that these works were carelessly or casually made. Quite the contrary. Though they appear spontaneous, many are carefully planned and executed. The Abstract Expressionists, for the most part, went big, as large canvases seemed necessary to contain the expressive intensity of these artists.

Ask yourself this. When you see and feel these large works by the Abstract Expressionists, does this change your critical perception of smaller works by the forerunners, say the Impressionists? Do these Impressionist works, radical in their own time, seem tame in comparison? Does that make you like them less or more?

COLOR FIELD PAINTING (1950s): With narrative eliminated, color took a front seat in Abstract Expressionism. One of the subgenres of Abstract Expressionism was Color Field painting, where swaths of color were the subject. Utilizing unprimed, and therefore absorbent canvas, artists like Gorky, Rothko, and Frankenthaler were able to produce what is referred to as *stain* paintings

In these works, the highly pigmented color creates a vibrancy and a vibratory effect that makes these works almost glow. Hans Hoffman, a painter and theorist, wrote about this art form and influenced other painters like Morris Louis and Kenneth Noland, admirers of the luscious colors of Helen Frankenthaler. An aside here: I met Ms. Frankenthaler in a Miami Museum in 2009, at an exhibition of her work. She was quite the grand dame of abstract painting even then.

OP and **POP** (1960s): Two deviations from realism came about in the 1950s and 1960s called Op and Pop. Op Art is a genre that produced interesting optical illusions and was a fashion in art for a time, and Pop Art is the crossover of popular images, many from commercial art and advertising materials to fine art.

Both of these art forms are a reaction against the lyrical and romantic canvases of the Abstract Expressionists. As we discussed previously, seesawing from classical to romantic art forms is a trend throughout the history of Western art. Whenever there is something that artists latch on to as gospel, there arises a group of artists to defy and counteract their manifesto.

Both Op and Pop did just that, making fun, in a way of the spiritualism of the Color Fielders and deliberately desanctifying images with the importation of what were considered less worthy images—ads, comic book characters, the flag (à la Jasper Johns).

They poke fun at, ridicule even, the emotionalism and high-mindedness of the Abstract Expressionists, pooh-poohing their seriousness and self-consciousness.

These movements, especially Pop Art, harken back to Dadaism, as protest movements in art. Have a look at the iconoclast Andy Warhol and his *Oxidation* series. Harking back to the Duchamp urinal, in these Warhol's works, he actually uses urine as an art medium. Don't laugh—the effects are really quite startling, and even, yes . . . beautiful.

MINIMALISM (1970s): Minimalism, which came about in the 1960s and 1970s, was a movement that took the reductive trends of abstract act to the end of the line. Trying to get down to the most general, least specific, artists eschewed any decoration, reacting again to what they saw as the "extravagance" of Abstract Expressionism.

You may be dismayed as you view these paintings, which appear almost as blank canvases, white on white or black on black, and ask yourself whether this is art.

My suggestion would be to understand these works in the context of the different movements that preceded and followed it. Remember that art is both percept and concept, vision and thought. These minimalist works are expressions of a thought, indeed a whole belief system. Whether or not your appreciate them in a formalist sense, as individual works of art, you can relate to them in the contextual one—as stops on the train of ideas in art.

SUMMING UP ABSTRACTION

With artists eschewing objects, the third dimension undefined, and perspective forsaken, we are left with the basics—line and shape. These can be tightly conceived and reductive, or loose and painterly. In the former category, we looked at Futurism, Suprematism, Constructivism, De Stijl, Minimalism, Op and Pop, and in the latter, Expressionism, Abstract Expressionism, and Color Field. We also have Dada and Surrealism, which were both protestations against the regularity of the realistic art form.

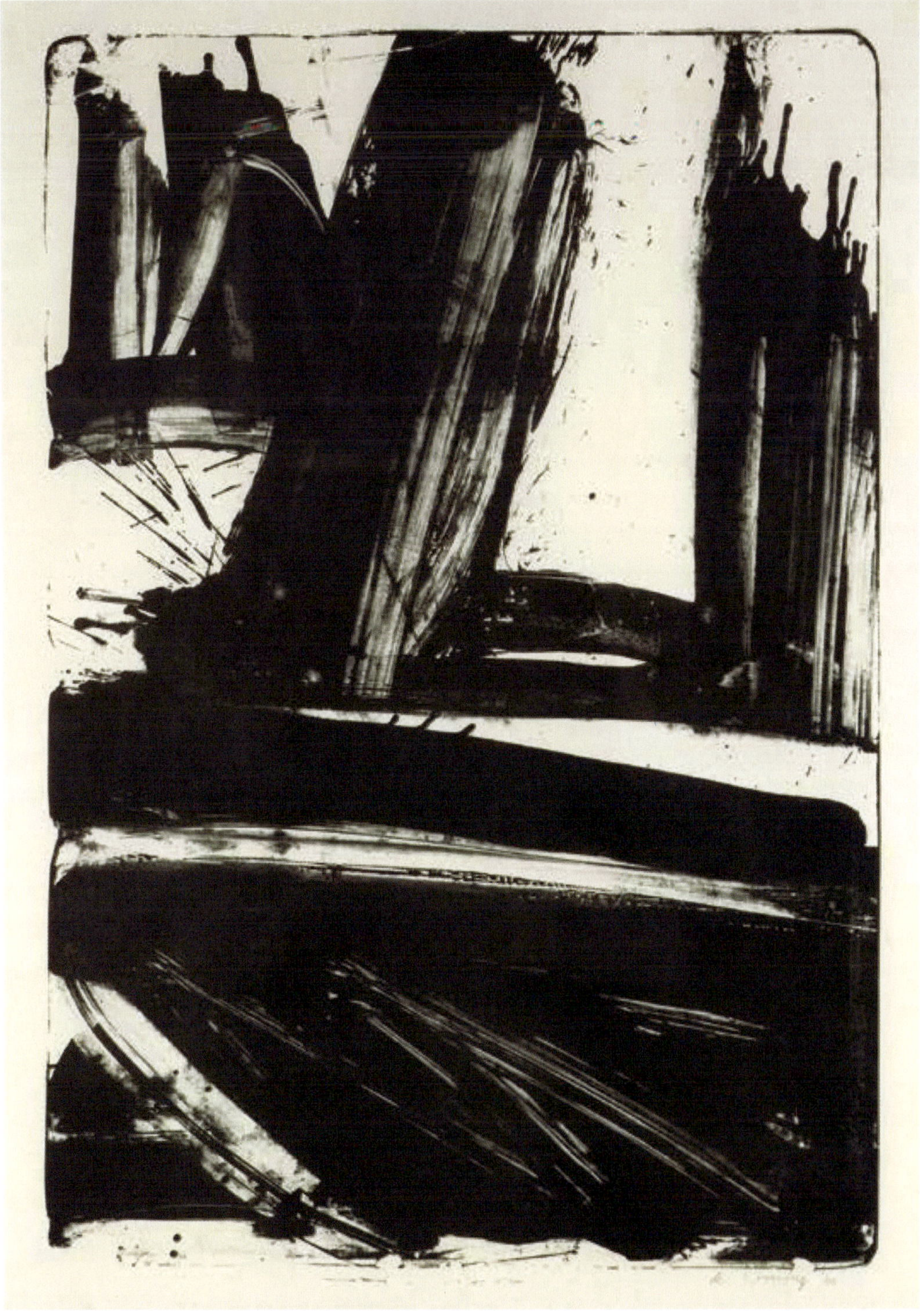

Fig. 95. Willem de Kooning, WAVES #1.

Look at this simple lithograph called *Waves #1* by Willem de Kooning, Abstract Expressionist par excellence (Fig. 95).

What is it? Is it an "impression" or an "expression" of waves? As per Dictionary.com, an impression is "an idea, feeling, or opinion about something or someone, especially one formed without conscious thought or on the basis of little evidence." What is an expression? Answer: "The process of making known one's thoughts or feelings."

Does it matter which word we use?

The picture is a depiction of an emotion stirred or suggested by waves. Not the description of the wave, but the emotion it engenders. That is abstraction in a nutshell.

The catalyst for abstraction was the great movement of Cubism, which broke open the doors to modern art. When permission was granted to change the object, naturally eliminating it altogether was not far behind. Driven by the desire to express, and permission granted, the train begins moving down an inevitable track. The artist Malevich explained his purpose as the conveyance of "the primacy of pure feeling in creative art."

Quite a ride indeed, and it's not over yet!

As we leave this list of the movements of abstraction, a few definitions:

WHAT IS CONCEPTUAL ART?

Conceptual art, sometime referred to as "conceptualism," is art in which the idea has taken precedence over other concerns like materials used, techniques, aesthetic values, emotional resonance, or skill in execution. It takes issue with the assumption that art is a special object created by especially gifted individuals called "artists." You can see how the Duchamp *Fountain* was therefore considered a work of conceptual art.

On the next page is another example of "conceptual art," a work exhibited by the English group Art & Language (they put out a magazine called *Art-Language: The Journal of Conceptual Art*) and hung in the Tate Gallery (Fig. 96).

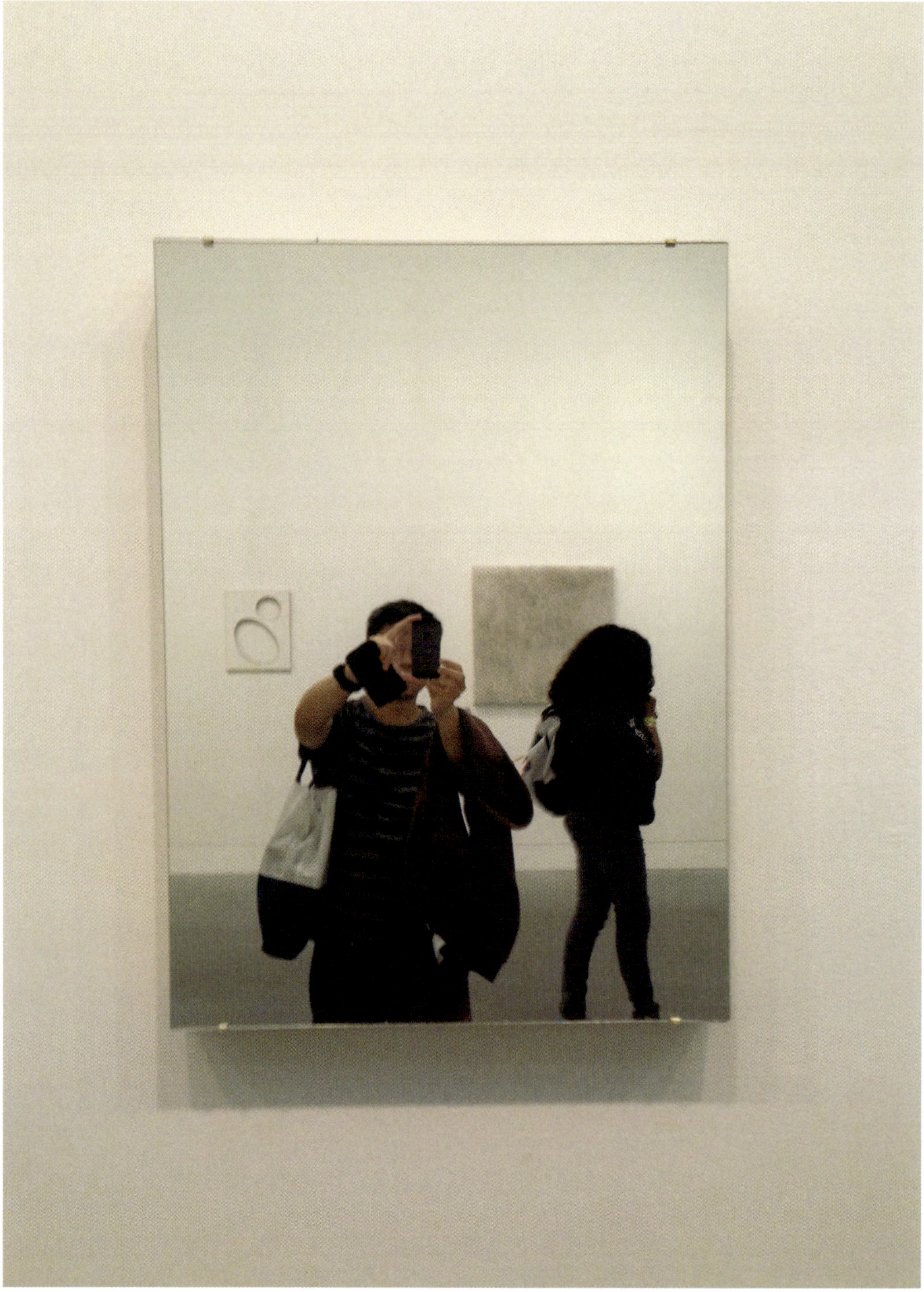

Fig. 96. Art & Language, UNTITLED PAINTING.

It is a mirror attached to a canvas. What's the point? Just that there is no such thing as art, or rather, anything can be art, even your reflection in a canvas. Just by hanging on the wall of a museum, it achieves the status of art. Whether you agree with this or not doesn't matter. This is a visualization of an idea—a work of conceptual art.

Very recently, it was in the press that the artist Banksy embedded a shredder in the frame of an artwork he put up for auction, which was activated after the piece was sold. The shredder proceeded to destroy part of the work. This act took the artwork into the realm of conceptual art, as the destruction of the work was the art, not the artwork itself.

Since ideas are usually expressed with language, you will find that words play a big part in conceptual art, and can be substituted for canvas, paint, and brush. Another example of conceptual art was actually a volume of words created by the artist Yoko Ono, a very interesting conceptual art–maker. Her book, *Grapefruit*, can be read as a book of poems, or as "an event score," a text that crosses over into a musical form. The poems are ideas that can be read as instructions, or as abstract, nonliteral pieces of art.

You can clearly see how conceptual art moved art out the realm of a static form observed by a still viewer into an event-based activity in which the viewer might participate. Ergo, installations, performance art, and other interactive forms.

WHAT IS MODERN ART?

Modern art includes art produced from about the 1860s to the 1970s. From Vincent van Gogh, Paul Cézanne, Georges Braque, Pablo Picasso, Henri Matisse, and their fellow adventurers into color and the break-up of forms . . . through Surrealism, Abstract Expressionism, Pop and Op, and all the movements we have heretofore mentioned.

A continuum of artists using their personal artistic voices to make visual art.

WHAT IS CONTEMPORARY ART?

Contemporary art is the art of today, and classifications of it may be a bit fuzzy. Art from about the 1970s on to today can be considered contemporary. This may be confusing because the words "modern" and "contemporary" are synonyms, but in art parlance Modern started with Postimpressionism and goes through the 1960s, and Contemporary is what follows.

THEN, WHAT IS POSTMODERN?

All work that is *Contemporary* may not be considered *postmodern*, though the reverse is usually true. Postmodern art includes some practices that extend purely visual art into other spheres and includes conceptual art, performance art, installation art, and multimedia art.

To clarify, there are contemporary artists who still work in a traditional manner, and many who incorporate representation into their work. Not every contemporary artist is an abstract artist, nor is he or she a postmodern artist.

What then, are some of the characteristics of postmodernism?

- **Use of text:** Sometimes called bricolage, text may figure as an important element.
- **Collage and mixed media**: Use of media in different ways and combination of media.
- **Hybridization of low and high arts**: Mixing imagery and materials from what was formerly referred to as high, or fine, art and low art, or kitsch.
- **Taking art of the past into a modern context**.

Once again, you can clearly see how postmodernism is a further breaking down of norms and traditions. Modern art did away with the object in abstraction, yes, but postmodernism opens up the barriers even further to say that you can use the object, but in a totally revamped and revitalized manner.

It is even more of an "anything goes" mentality than any of the movements of modernism because the strict adherence to any style, manner, medium, or approach is no longer a requirement in postmodernism. You can be a realist and glue popcorn to your canvas, or you don't even have to have a canvas, you can glue it to yourself and stand in a gallery as the work of art.

Let's have a look here at some of these activities postmodernism made part of art practice:

ACTION PAINTING (A.K.A. GESTURAL ABSTRACTION)

Postmodernist artists like Jackson Pollock, Willem de Kooning, and Franz Kline took another step forward in tossing away the object when they made the physical act of painting the driving force of the work itself. The theory was that the subconscious mind could express itself directly by the artist freeing himself to work

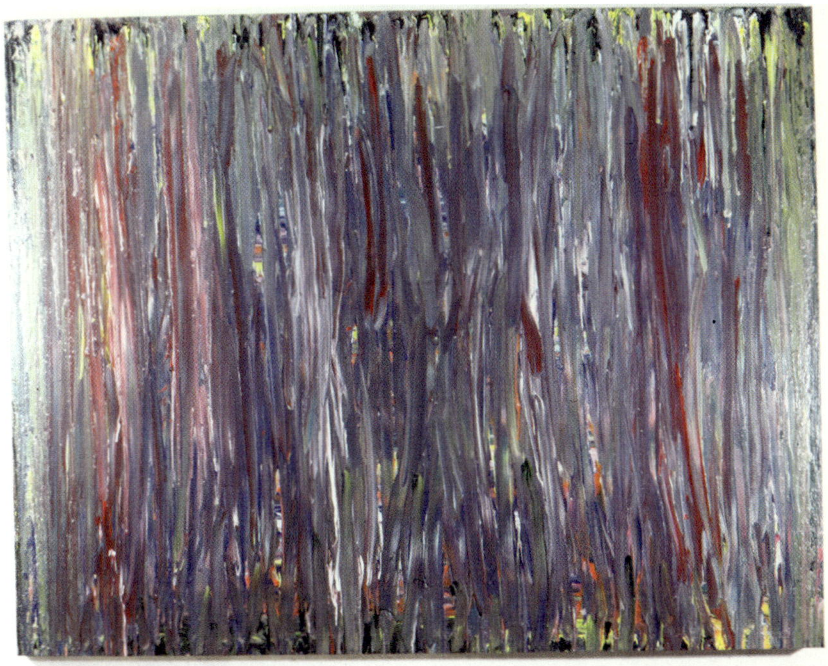

Fig. 97. Frank James Graham, UNTITLED.

without thought, to dribble, spray, whip, and literally throw the paint upon the canvas. The idea was to work directly and to throw caution and care to the four winds. What was left on the canvas was the moment, pure unadulterated emotion.

Here's an example of an action painting (Fig. 97).

The story here is quite simply, the paint. No objects, no dreams, no marks even. Just the paint in action. No wonder he didn't give it a title!

Of course, one thing always leads to another, and this je ne sais quoi approach of action painting led to other attempts by artists to liberate themselves not only from the object, but the canvas itself. Who needed a picture, after all? Enter performance art, happenings, and installations.

PERFORMANCE ART

In a sense, the action painters were putting on a bit of a performance. No longer standing tall at the easel, brush in hand, they became dancers and acrobats painting on the floor, walls, bobbing and weaving as they flung the paint willy-nilly.

So it is not surprising that it occurred to them that it was the performance itself that was the art, making what was on the canvas or paper almost irrelevant.

You may wonder what performance art has in common with theater. Is it the same thing?

Not exactly. Theater performances are created as entertainment, though they may be thought-provoking. They usually have a narrative with scripted lines that are repeated in each performance. To the contrary, performance art projects a concept through performance, but it usually is not scripted, and may involve interaction with an audience.

Performance art can be challenging or startling and suggest new ideas to audiences. Because of the connections to theater, some performance artists prefer the terms *live art* or *interventions* or *intermedia* to describe their work as visual art, not dramatic art.

To differentiate performance art even further, events that are planned without any script at all can be referred to as *happenings*. With the artists and the audience participating and interacting, each happening is a unique occurrence.

Art forms evolve, as we have described, with one movement giving momentum to the next. But this is not to say that art practices of the past disappear. Though they may not be prominent, artists continue to work in realistic, Impressionistic, Expressionistic, semi-abstract, and fully abstract modalities, all at the same time. There are artists who make their own paint as artists did in the fifteenth century, or who continue to draw with the detailed crosshatching of the Renaissance draftsmen. Fashions and preferences move on, but many stay to linger in the zeitgeist of the past.

Abstraction blew the roof off art, but many artists continue with traditions, and many abstract artists like to render realistic work at times in their career. The most important thing abstraction left us was to make individuality the birthright of every artist.

As you view the creative explorations of the modernists, try to savor that individuality without judgment. Not all the iterations may be successful; some movements were short-lived and faded away, but all were manifestations of the unlimited possibilities of visual art and the ability of the human mind and heart to conjure imagery.

Knowing the historical path artists have followed is the story of the growth of consciousness, and the release of the human spirit. Continue to be amazed at the diversity, power, and expressive potential of the artists of the recent past and today as they open the definition of what is art to include some never before imagined imaginings.

Savor the old and await the new! In our last chapter, we shall have a guess at what that future in art has in store for us.

Chapter 12
Subject and Master: Sculpture and Other Artistic Practices

Sculpture, generally speaking, is visual art that is created in three dimensions: width, height, and depth. It can be flat, with a raised surface, and if so, we call it a relief. It can be freestanding, and therefore be viewed in the round. It can be suspended, as a mobile, or lie on the ground, on earth or in water. It can be made of any of a host of materials, and/or a combination of materials.

These might include hard materials like stone, concrete, metal, wood, etc., or soft materials like fabric. Sculpture may be formed by applying heat to change its physical form, like clay, which is formed as a soft material and then hardened when extreme heat is applied in a kiln; or glass, which goes from a solid to a liquid state as heat is applied and then back into a solid state as it anneals or cools.

Sculpture can be made utilizing a variety of techniques relative to the material being employed. It can be formed by the process of subtraction, as for instance, the chipping away at a block of stone, or grinding, cutting, or sanding away chunks and slivers of wood. It can likewise be formed by the process of addition, as in assembling found objects or pieces of materials and gluing or tying them together.

In many instances, sculpture is created by applying both subtractive and additive methods, as in building a work out of clay by adding clay, modeling it, and then carving pieces of it away. It can also be created by a process referred to as casting, where a mold is made from what is called the positive, and then another substance is poured into that mold and subjected to heat to make it conform. Examples of casting materials include bronze and glass, the latter often referred to as pâte de verre or glass paste.

In addition to the traditional materials used in the creation of sculpture, modern artists have created works utilizing light (light sculpture); sound (sound sculpture); earth (environmental sculpture or land art); and moving forms (kinetic sculpture); as well as installations that may include many objects and forms. Using distressed objects as elements in sculpture (found art or recycled art) is quite common, as artists find the whimsy and beauty in these repurposed parts of utilitarian objects.

Once a sculpture has been formed, or during the forming process, various techniques can be utilized to distress, color, emboss, stamp, texture, or paint the surface. Even though sculpture can be colored, color does not have the enormous significance in sculpture that it enjoys in the art of painting, except perhaps in glass-making and ceramics. In historic works, the paint has often worn off or faded as—more often than in painting—the surface has been exposed to the elements. Form is the sine qua non of sculpture.

Sculpture has been made in every era from prehistoric times to the present, with practices and styles mirroring the movements in painting and other forms of two-dimensional visual art. Many painters also create sculptures as a significant part of their oeuvre.

Sculpture, by its nature, is less of an alla prima activity like painting. It is often more time-consuming and requires multiple steps to create. It involves engineering, as making the three-dimensional object balanced and conforming to gravitational forces may be no simple matter. Artists working to reduce a solid piece of stone or wood can easily chip too much away; it takes careful execution to permit an image to emerge out of a solid block.

Subjecting materials to extreme heat also makes the results precarious. Ceramic glazes often surprise as they emerge from the kiln, and glass that is not properly and strategically annealed or cooled may later crack. It takes lots of practice and patience to achieve dependable results with these processes. Even masterful artists often encounter unforeseen accidents in sculpture formation.

What are the criteria for evaluating a work of sculpture? To answer this, consider the qualities of solid forms: They have weight, volume, texture, dimension, proportion, energy, balance, substance, direction, occupy space, may have planes, shapes, suggest flow or movement. They can be expressive, suggestive, elegant, monumental, powerful, emotionally resonant, have character, etc. We admire works of sculpture for these many reasons, as they possess qualities we admire. Each work has these ingredients in different combinations and priorities.

There is much agreement as to the most loved and treasured sculptures ever created. They have the qualities we most admire to a great extent. Let's have a look at a few of them as examples of aesthetic principles and consider their attributes and particular strengths.

Aside from the fact that this sculpture of Nefertiti is so old, and so beautifully preserved, it is considered an extraordinarily beautiful work, a symbol of everlasting feminine beauty (Fig. 98).

What makes it so? A delicacy, expert craftsmanship, and elegance. Though the headdress appears oversized compared to the shoulder width, it gives the piece a majesty that says *Queen*.

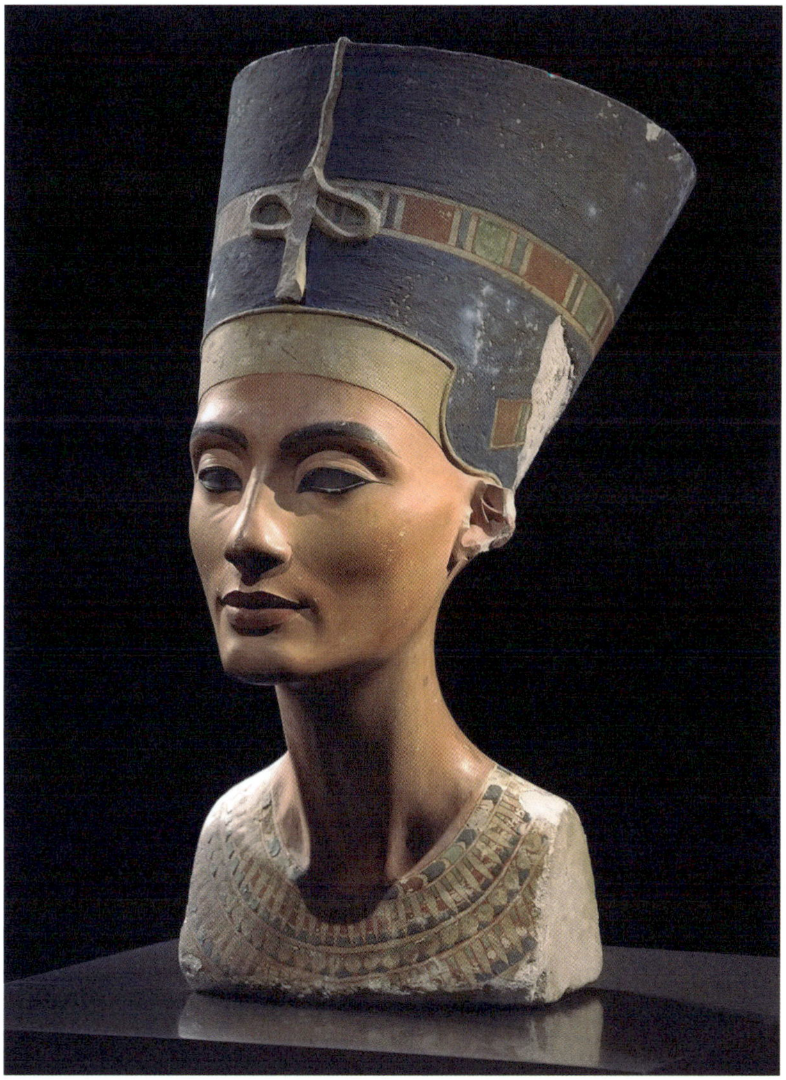

Fig. 98. Thutmose, BUST OF NEFERTITI.

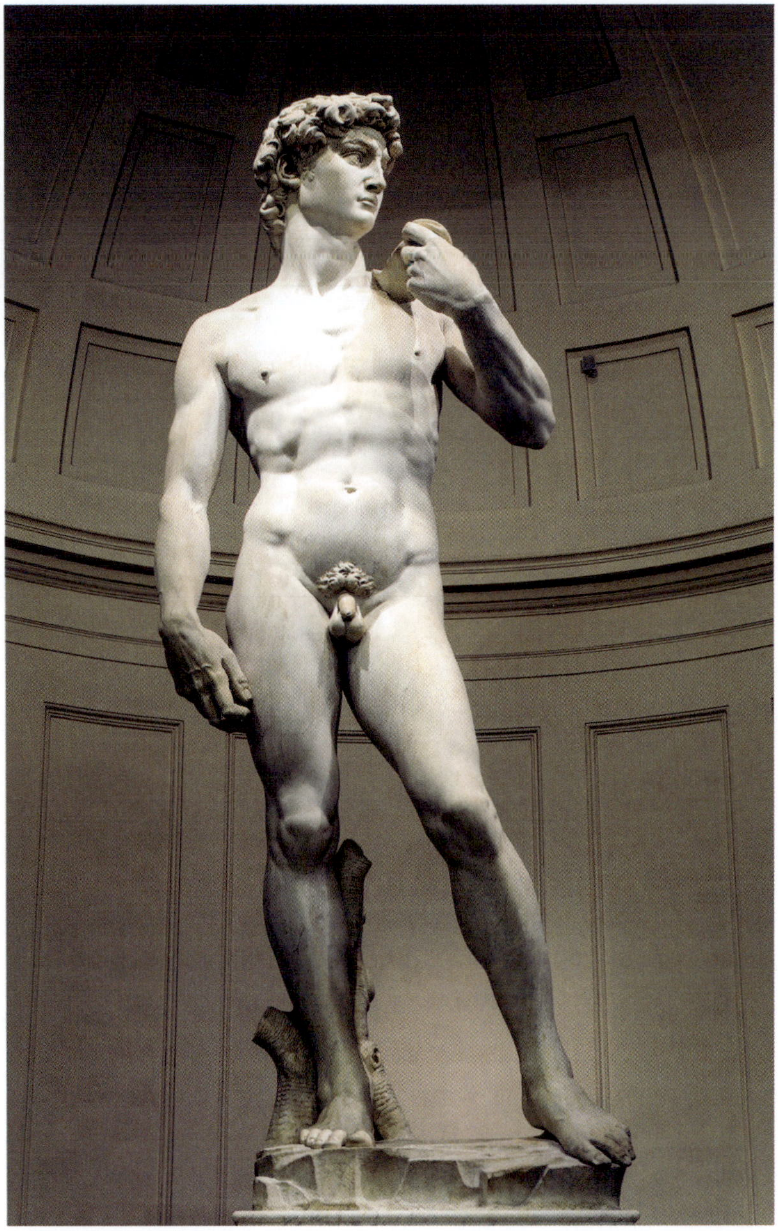

Fig. 99. Michelangelo, DAVID.

Probably the most iconic sculpture ever created, the *David* has it all: proportion, superb craftsmanship, and expressiveness (Fig. 99). It is a Renaissance version of the Greek tradition of standing male nudes. The contrapposto pose—with weight shifted to one side—gives a naturalism to the figure and is further accentuated by the counter-position of the head.

Though an accurate portrayal, it is also idealized and is a symbol of male beauty, heroism, and strength. It represents the Platonic form of the male—pure perfection.

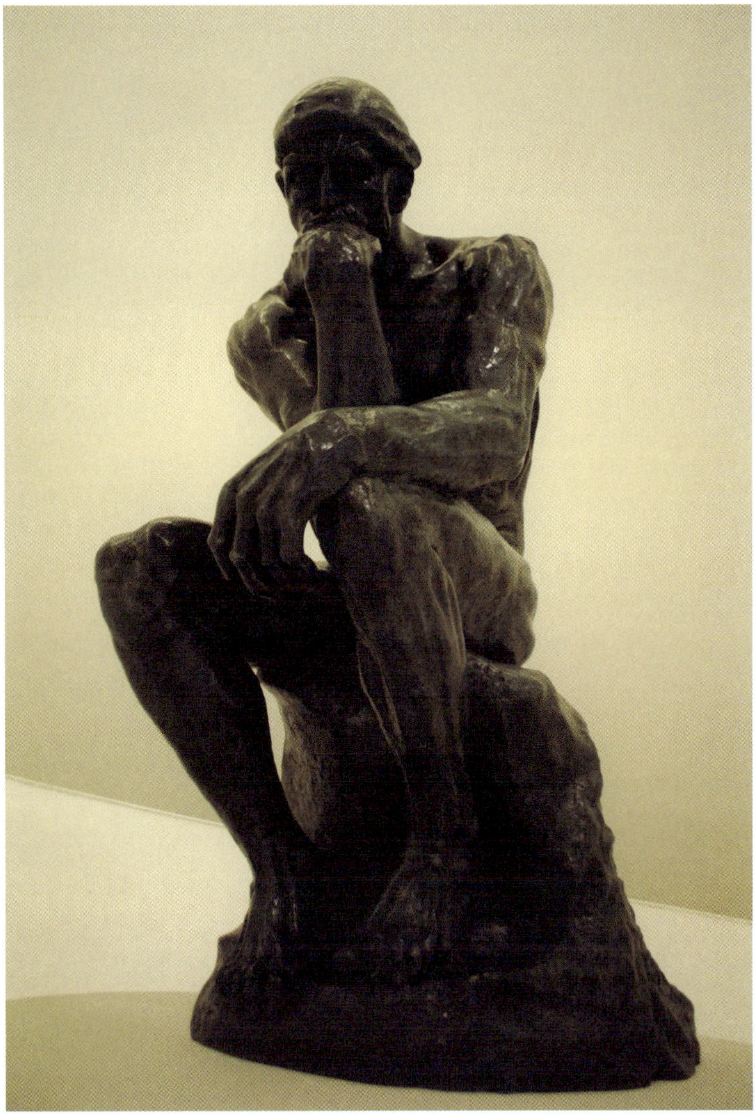

Fig. 100. Auguste Rodin, THE THINKER.

As opposed to the *Nefertiti* and the *David*, idealized objects of adoration, *The Thinker* has an expressive crudeness that makes this piece so evocative (Fig. 100). *The Thinker* is every man, and it is his character and very human pose that captures our interest and our attention.

The sculptor Rodin originally conceived of what was to become *The Thinker* as originally a work called *The Poet*, representing Dante observing what he had wrought. After exhibition in 1888, the image proved popular, with a wider symbolism than the artist had intended. As suggestive of a man lost in thought and contemplating action, it caught on, and many copies of *The Thinker* can now be found around the world. It is representative of the ability of an artwork to become iconic.

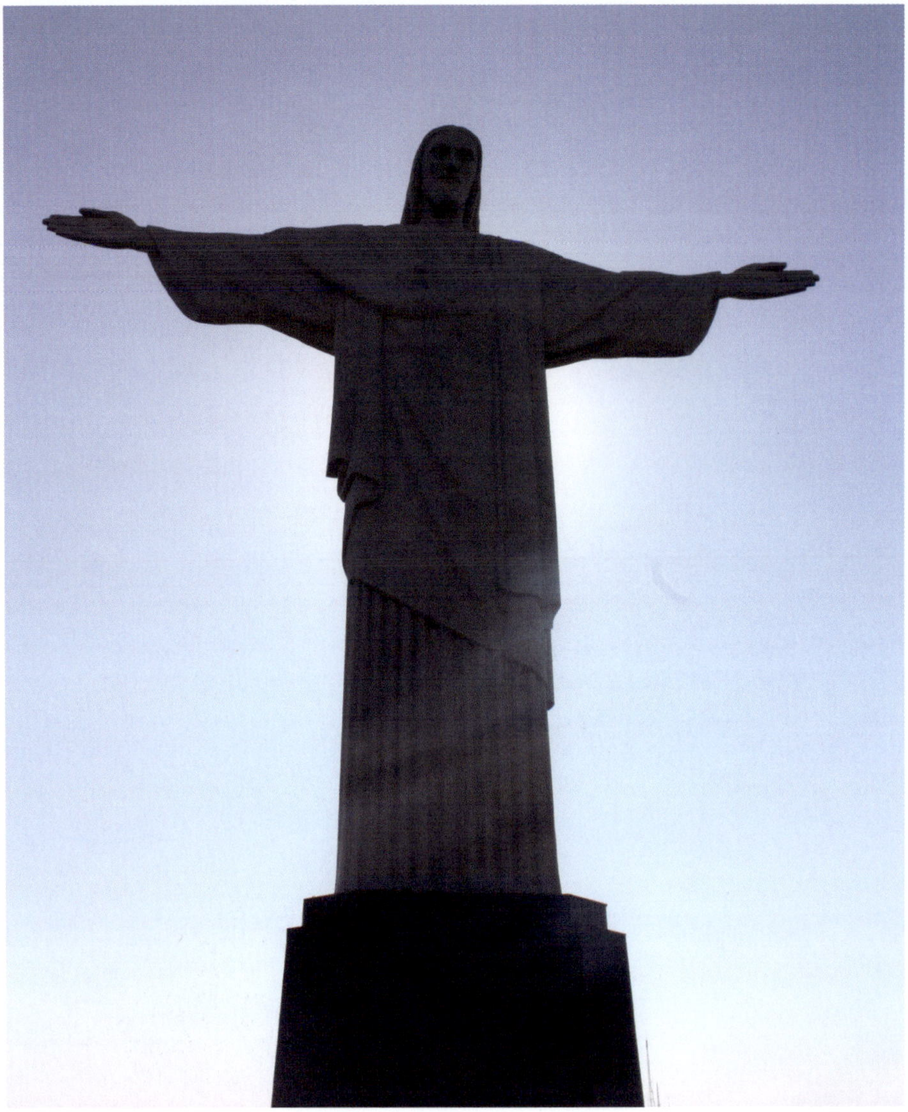

Fig. 101. Paul Landowski, CHRIST THE REDEEMER.

Size and positioning of sculpture can have a powerful effect and make an otherwise ordinary work seem dramatic. Millions flock to Rio de Janeiro to see the sculpture of *Christ the Redeemer* by Paul Landowski (Fig. 101). Its monumentality is a factor (the sculpture is 98 feet tall and 91 feet wide and weighs 635 tons), but it is the majesty of its environment makes it even more compelling. The figure takes on a gravitas as the expansive blue sky and sparkling sun dramatizes the spirituality of this image. The attempt to inspire awe was the driving force of this artwork.

Consider scale and environment when you look at art. Also lighting and presentation, like framing. A great artwork can be diminished by its setting, just as a lesser one can be enhanced. Something to think about.

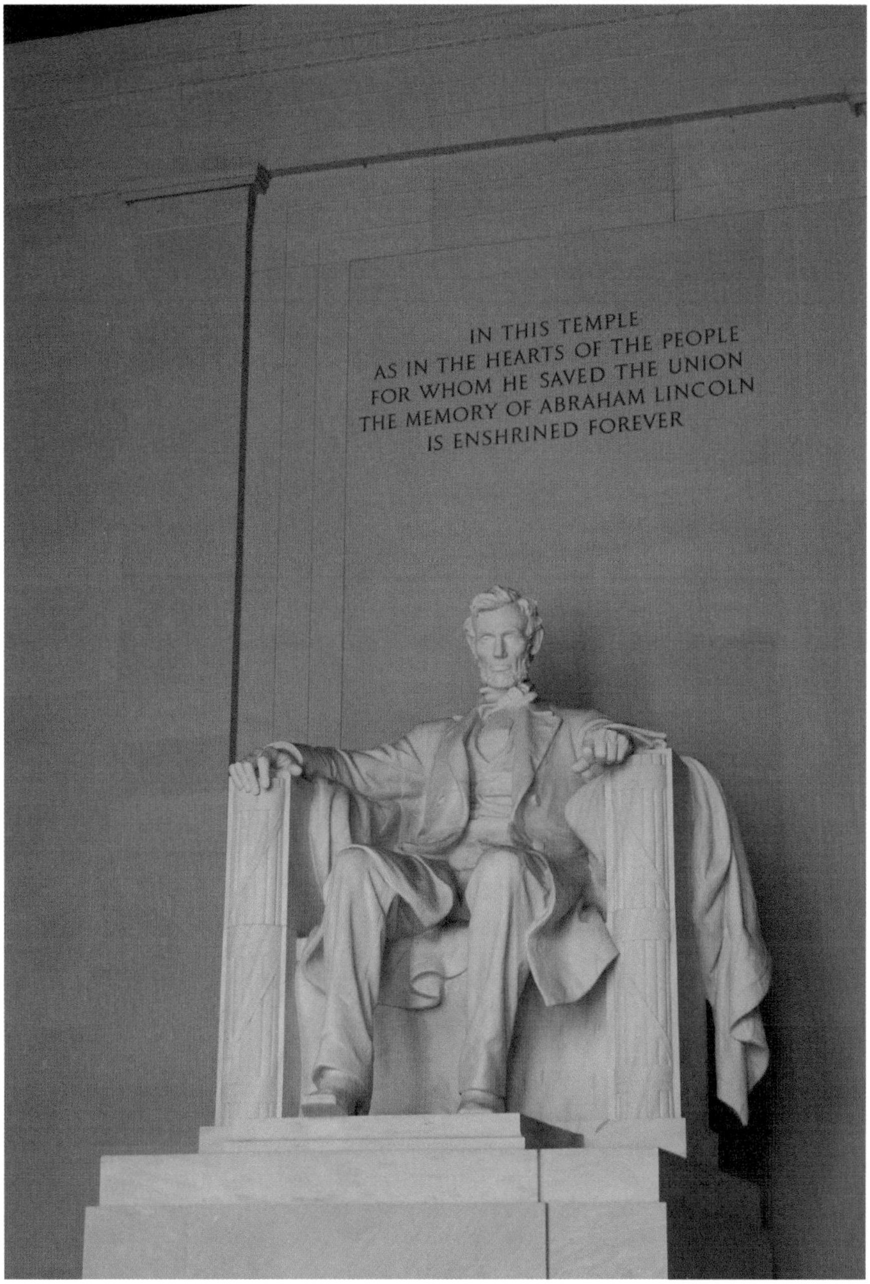

Fig. 102. Daniel Chester French, LINCOLN MEMORIAL.

Consider the portrait sculpture of Lincoln that graces the Lincoln Memorial in Washington, DC (Fig. 102). The weight of Lincoln's mission and the gravity of his contribution is embodied in the downcast look of the man in this enormous chair. The viewer cannot help but feel the importance of the subject. Once again, the placement of the sculpture in the Lincoln Memorial is critical to its impact. As you climb the stairs to greet it, the viewer is struck by its presence. The size alone makes the viewer feel insignificant.

Many well-known painters were also masters in the art of sculpture. Picasso, Braque, Degas, Matisse, and others elaborated their two-dimensional vocabulary into three dimensions. Picasso was a master of found art, utilizing all kinds of materials and objects in his whimsical sculpture and also elaborating a huge body of work in ceramics.

Degas's passion for ballerinas and horses found form in his many bronzes. Though Matisse's exuberant paintings were his calling card, he made many bronzes of simplified organic forms. Braque, the Cubist, expressed his Cubist philosophy in his reliefs and sculptures.

Just as modern painting moved away from the depiction of the actual object, so did modern sculpture. Sculptors were released to express the emotion of their subjects in simpler, more direct ways by eschewing details. Expressions of pure space and interlocking shapes replaced naturalistic carvings. And sculptors became aware of the negative space in creating related forms with the space between them as significant as the solid masses. The so-called "holes" are actually part of the total work, as "air" became, in essence, a material.

Let's discuss some of the masters of modern sculpture, and isolate the characteristics that make their works interesting, and their contributions to sculpture significant. Two major modern masters, both articulating biomorphic forms, were the artists Constantin Brancusi and Jean Arp.

Considered by many the father of modern sculpture, **Constantin Brancusi** (1876–1957) said this about his work: "There are idiots who define my work as abstract; yet what they call abstract is what is most realistic. What is real is not the appearance, but the idea, the essence of things."

His highly simplified forms get down to the "nitty-gritty" by eliminating unnecessary details and paring these forms down to the emotional essence of what he was trying to express. They never depart completely from the subject, and many of his stylized and reduced forms have become iconic representations, like his piece, *The Kiss*.

Jean Arp (1886–1966) was a contemporary of Brancusi and a consummate artist who worked in many media; his biomorphic sculptures suggest but do not define organic forms. In fact, he referred to his works as "organic abstractions." As opposed to Brancusi, whose subject is easily recognizable in his simplified pieces, Arp created the form first and only then titled or named it.

His work *Cloud Shepherd,* a bronze, created in the latter part of his career, is a good example of his desire to allude to natural forms but not specify them, as here you might see reminiscences of a sheep, a shepherd, or even a cloud (Fig. 103). The sculpture is all of these, a symbolic form, a life created by the artist. The naming follows the creation.

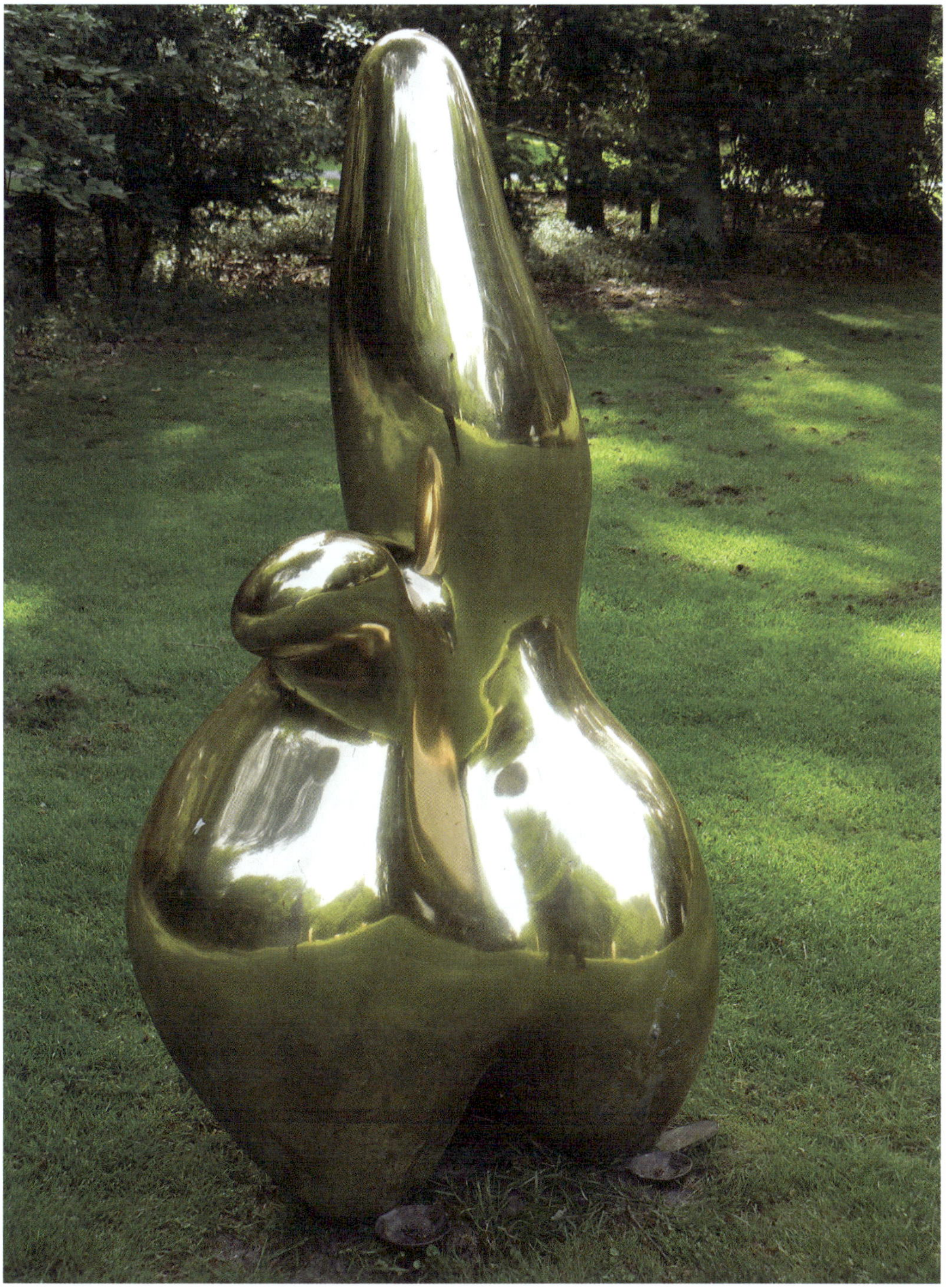

Fig. 103 Jean Arp, CLOUD SHEPHERD.

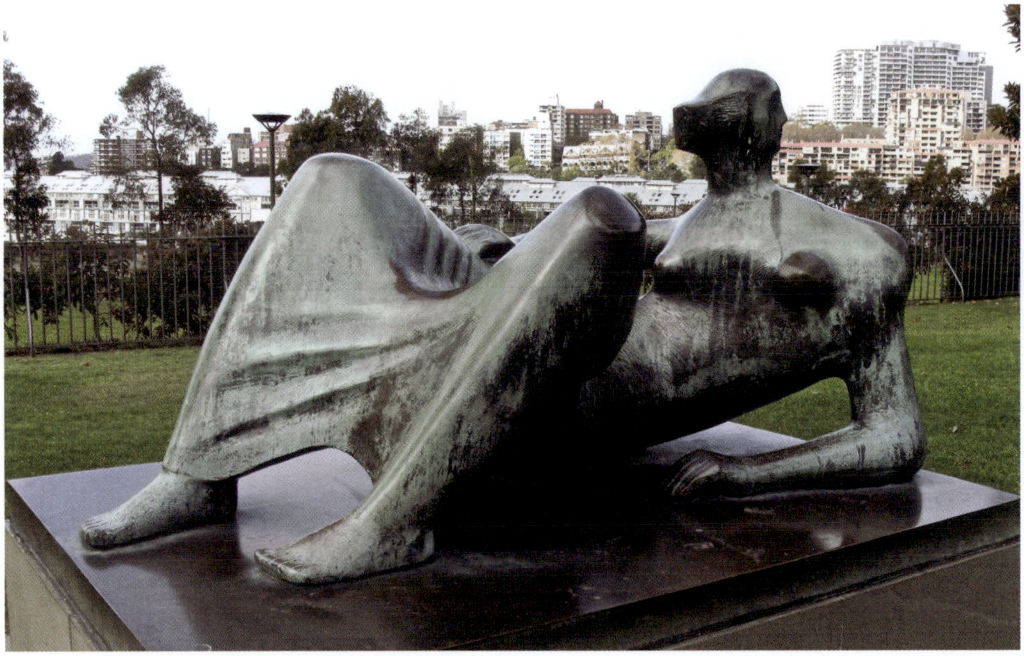

Fig. 104. Henry Moore, RECLINING FIGURE: ANGLES.

Look at this sculpture by the wonderful artist **Henry Moore** (1898–1986) (Fig. 104). We are looking at a female form simplified to her essence. Moore created biomorphic forms, organic shapes suggesting animal, human, body, or any living being that we can identify with. He removed the particularities of identity to give them a universal impact. There is nothing idealized about the Moore figures at all.

They are fascinating to view in the round: when you chance upon a Moore sculpture, make sure to circle it, stopping to pause and examine the work from every viewpoint. With a Moore piece, I always feel that I am looking at many works of art in one. This is one of the attributes of a great work of sculpture.

Moore is also associated with sculptures that are created in parts where the negative space is an important unifying force.

Search Google and have a look at Moore's psychological opposite, **Alberto Giacometti**, a sculptor who is known mainly for his highly exaggerated thin forms. They also speak to the subject of human existence, but in an entirely different way. Giacometti's figures express the frailty and tentativeness of life, where Moore expresses the hedonism and suchness of life. Both were highly expressive masters of the art of sculpture.

Modernist sculpture paralleled developments and movements in modernist painting. Many artists known for their painting dabbled in the art of sculpture, and expressed similar themes, approaches, and qualities.

Let's look at two examples.

First we have one of twenty-five carvings by the painter Modigliani that he made after meeting the sculptor Brancusi in 1909 (Fig. 105). Notice that his preference for the elegantly long-necked woman carries over into the sculpture.

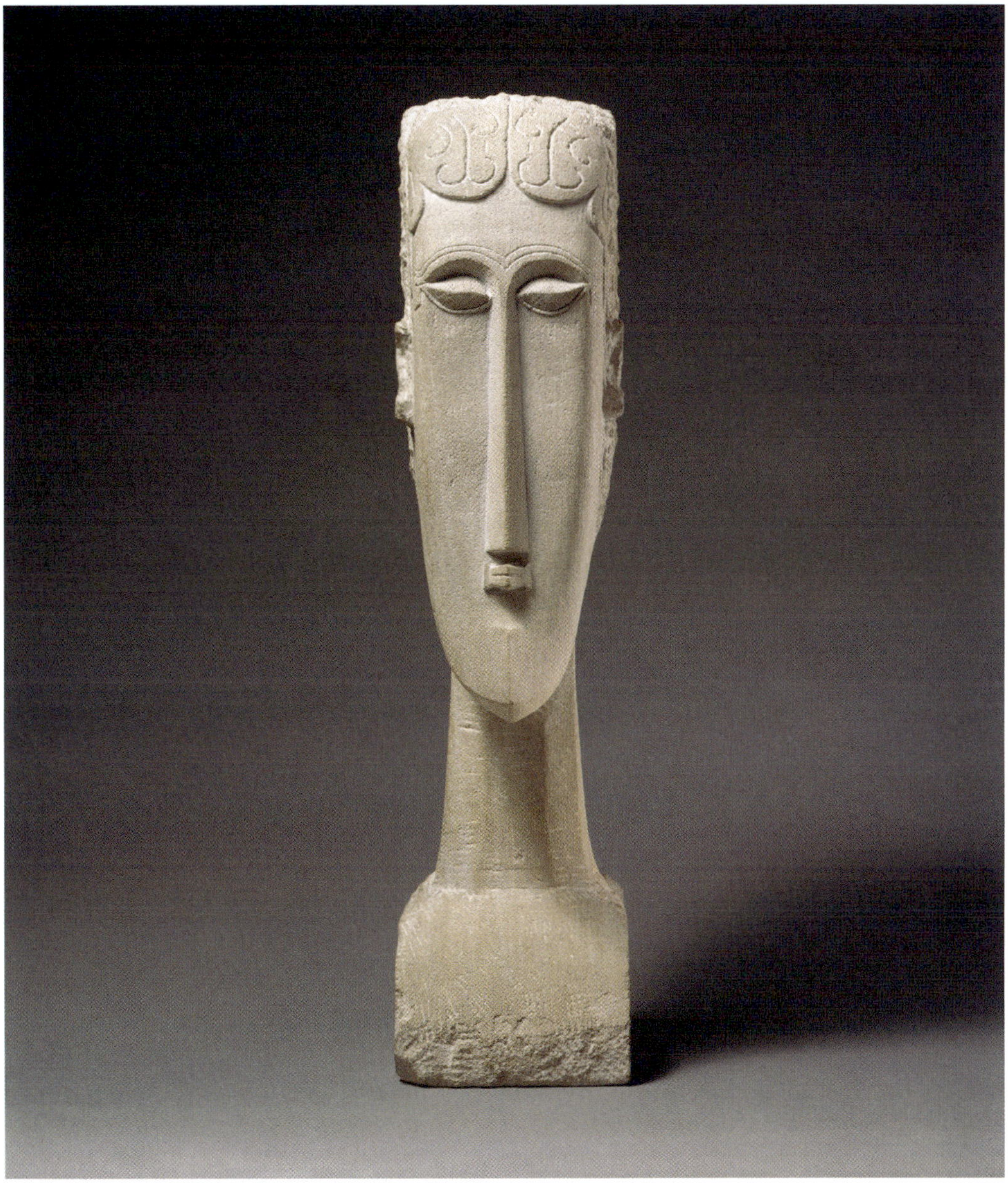

Fig. 105. Amedeo Modigliani, WOMAN'S HEAD.

In this second example, a bronze by the Italian Futurist Umberto Boccioni, the title tells the tale (Fig. 106). Called *Antigraceful* by the artist, here he depicts his mother in a particularly unsettling style.

The artist is quoted as saying, "We must smash, demolish, and destroy our traditional harmony, which makes us fall into a gracefulness created by timid and sentimental cubs." He does just that here, by breaking his sculpture into Cubist planes and jaggedly distorting her face.

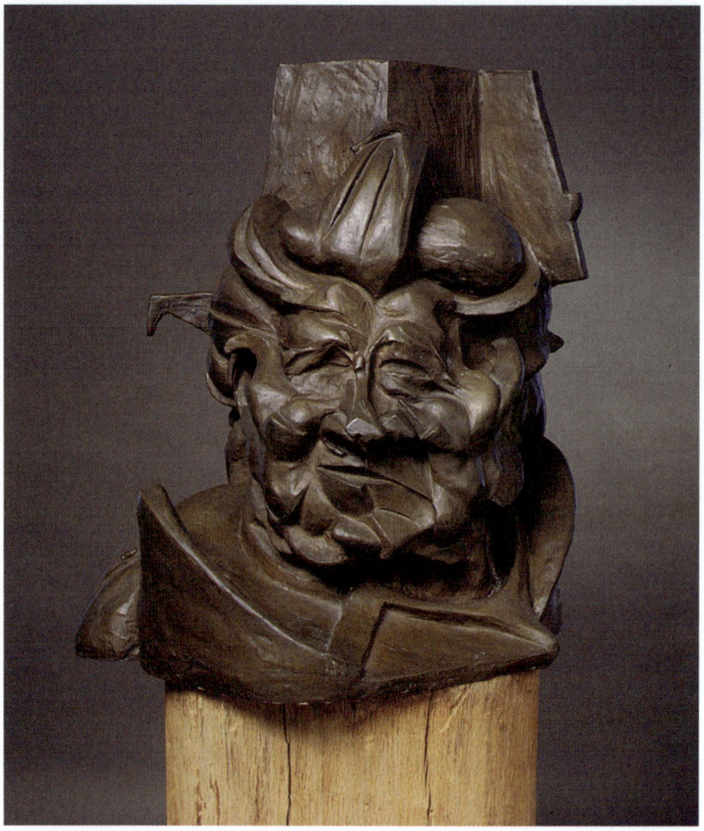

Fig. 106. Umberto Boccioni, ANTIGRACEFUL.

CONTEMPORARY SCULPTORS

Following these artists of the early twentieth century, sculptors began to take advantage of a host of new materials available to them—resins, plastics, concrete, steel, etc. They also began to work on a larger scale and to make works that are married to architecture and landscape and which that become environments in and of themselves.

Some even are interactive, or are so large that people can actually enter and tour them.

Here are examples of just a few contemporary sculptors to give you a sampling. If sculpture is your passion, I encourage you to seek out some of the wonderful contemporary work being accomplished as public art, or gracing parks, cemeteries, public plazas, lobbies, and other spaces.

Deborah Butterfield (1949–present)

Born on the day of the seventy-fifth running of the Kentucky Derby, the contemporary sculptor Deborah Butterfield has made horses her primary subject. She has written that she sees the horse as one might a self-portrait, imbuing them, as she does, with emotional gravitas.

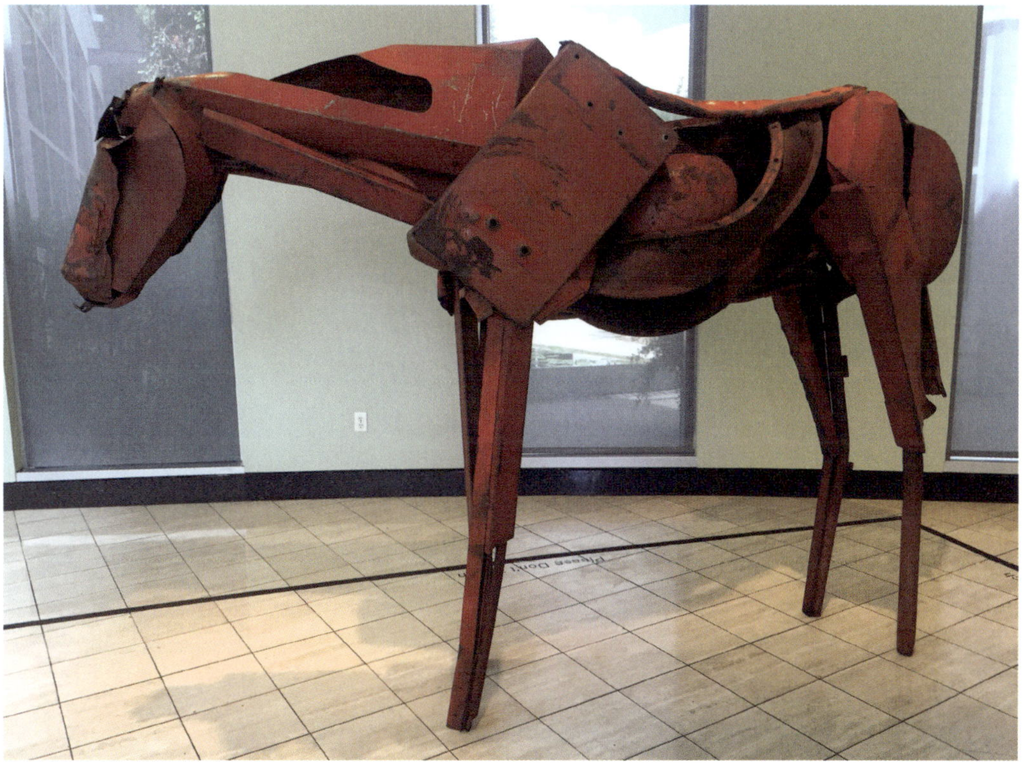

Fig. 107. Deborah Butterfield, RORY.

David Smith (1906–1965)

Smith was an Abstract Expressionist known for large steel sculptures. He actually worked with many materials including wood, coral, wire, and metal. He may have inaugurated the use of welding in sculpture in the United States, now ubiquitous in the medium.

Cesar Baldaccini (1921–1998)

A French sculptor, he used scrap metal and junk in his early works, then graduated to crushing cars and other objects with a hydraulic crushing machine. He followed this up with work in plastics, pouring polyurethane and using molten crystal.

Anthony Caro (1924–2013)

The Englishman Caro was an assembler of metal forms, mostly found and then combined in interesting ways.

Caro began this work after meeting David Smith. Previously he had been a student of Henry Moore and had produced more figurative works and heads; he later returned to the figurative after the abstract work for which he is famous.

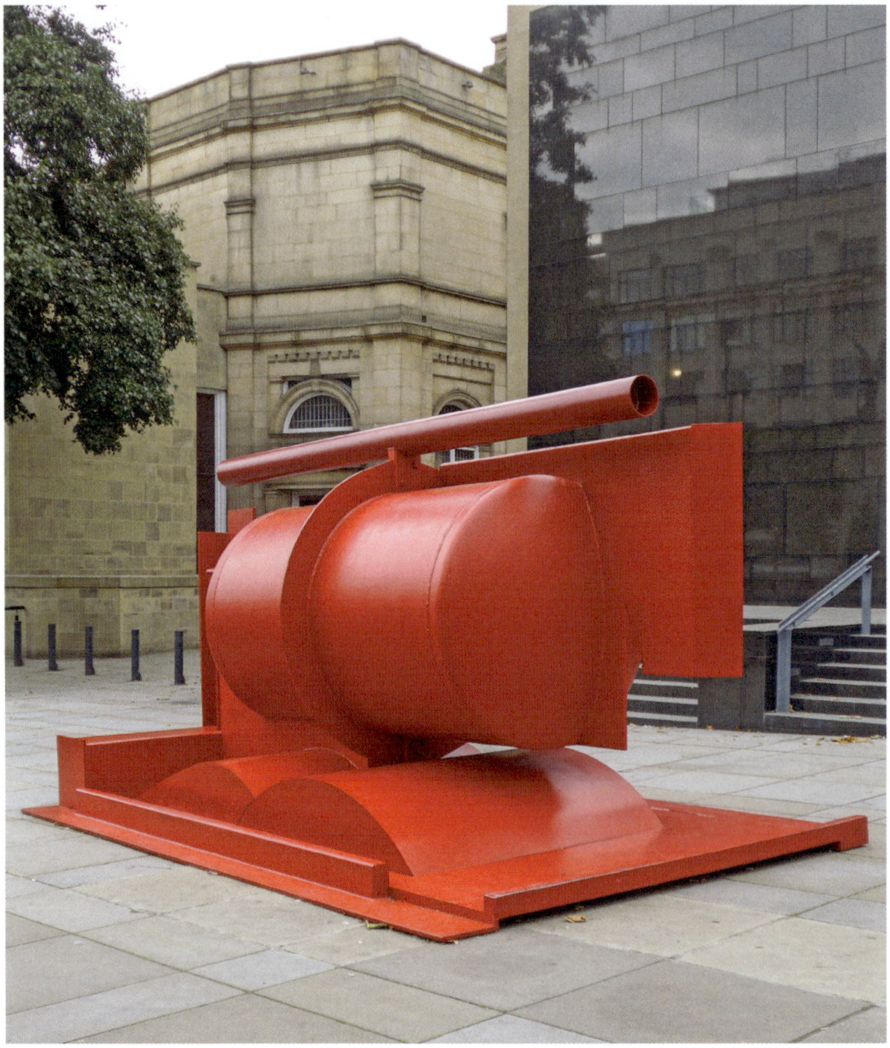

Fig. 108. Anthony Caro, AURORA.

Robert Rauschenberg (1925–2008)

An all-around artist, primarily a painter, Rauschenberg's work became sculpture with the advent of his "combines." Gathering trash and found objects from the New York City streets, be began to pile them onto his canvases, creating three-dimensional assemblages. He got quite elaborate in what could be attached, even going so far as to add taxidermy animal parts.

Mark di Suvero (1933–present)

His large abstract constructions necessitated the use of a modern crane to move and position the structural steel and heavy wooden beams that comprise his sculpture, some of which move and sway.

This type of large abstract work is often utilized for place-making—in plazas, entrances to important buildings, parks etc., once unheard of, now a familiar addition to the landscape.

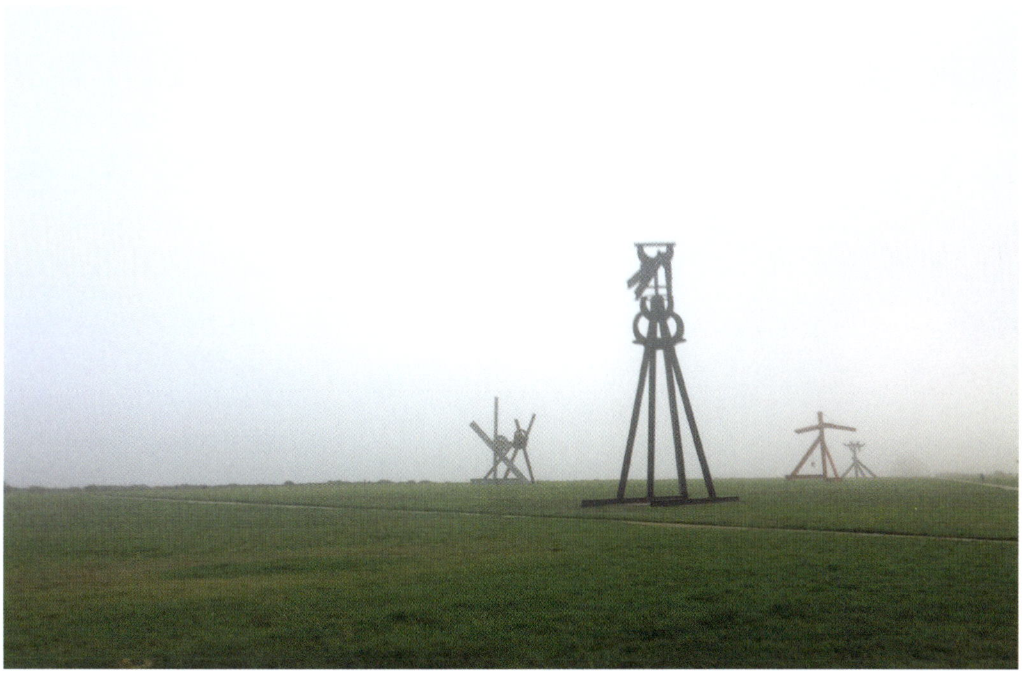

Fig. 109. Mark di Suvero, (sculptures left to right) OLD BUDDY, DREAMCATCHER, MOTHER PEACE, and HURU.

Richard Serra (1938–present)

Another sculptor thinking big, Serra has utilized fiberglass and rubber, molten lead, lead sheets, and steel beams. His work is minimalist, but grandiose in scale. A sculpture he made in 2011 in Qatar was eighty feet high. One of the effects of these enormous sculptures is their effect on the humans that can stand beside or within them. The scale itself carries the emotional message.

Anish Kapoor (1954–present)

A British sculptor, born in India, Kapoor's sculptures cross the line into architecture. This is not only because of their scale, but the fact that many of them are experiential—they can be entered and one can move through them. The concept of *viewer* is expanded to that of *participant.*

Kapoor started with biomorphic forms made of limestone and marble, plaster and pigment. He then worked with highly polished mirror-like stainless steel. These create reflections that become part of the sculpture. Color is a factor in his work, and he even made a sculpture utilizing colored water. Also in his toolbox: red wax suggesting blood; rust; the concept of change as the sculptures grow and morph in real time. Kapoor has removed another of the former qualities of sculpture: its static nature. A true innovator, his sculpture is architecture is theater.

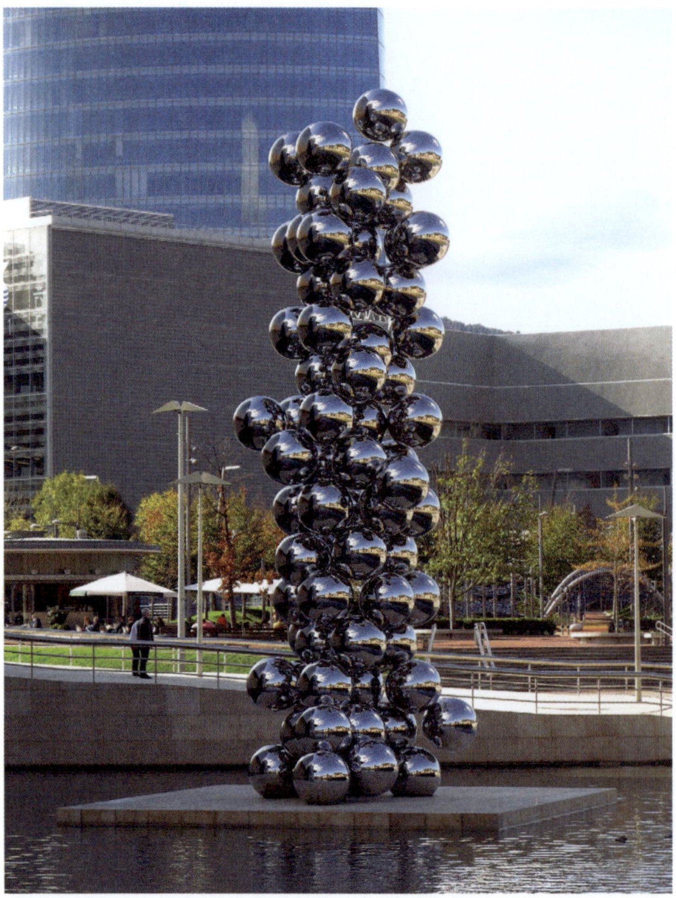

Fig. 110. Anish Kapoor, TALL TREE AND THE EYE.

In many ways sculpture is more available and accessible to the art lover because it is often installed outside and in public spaces. Today, the popularity of public art as a component of new structures and venues is making sculpture part of our everyday experience. We celebrate the inclusion of art where it is available to everyone to enjoy. In our final chapter on the future of art, you can read my commentary on the place of art in a world undergoing severe climate impact.

PHOTOGRAPHY, PRINTMAKING, AND OTHER PAPER MEDIA, ETC.

In addition to drawing and painting, the primary media of two-dimensional art, there are several other forms we need mention. The art of photography, growing in popularity, is one of these, as is the art of printmaking, and other media on paper, as is paper-making itself, collage and mixed media, the latter of which we have mentioned in passing but we reiterate in this context. Today we also have digital art, art that is made or enhanced on the computer.

Photography is a rather late entry into the art world, and it is now recognized as a significant art medium, with many photographers recognized as important artists.

Photography is often used as an illustrative or commercial medium, so discerning which photographs stand on their own as art is a matter of discussion.

The use of the camera by itself does not disqualify a photograph from being art, as it is a tool like many others that artists use. It's what one does with the tool that matters, of course. Though the camera takes the picture, it is the photographer who chooses the subject, calculates the light, the angle of vision, and the many other aspects that make the eventual image important and interesting.

Because photography records actual moments in time, photography has a particular resonance—the ability to stir memory and make history meaningful. On the next page, look at this photograph by the famous photographer Alfred Stieglitz (Fig. 111). Called *A Snapshot, Paris*, it has the quality of a painting or sculpture, something stressed by the artist who wanted his beloved medium to achieve the same status as these. He and other "art photographers" who concurred, have managed to establish photography as a bona fide fine art medium.

Some of the many exceptional artist-photographers of the past include Andres Kertesz (1894–1985), whose photographs from interesting points of view influenced many painters, like Vuillard and Bonnard; Brassaï (1899–1984), another Hungarian whose visions of Paris, especially at night, became emblematic of the city.

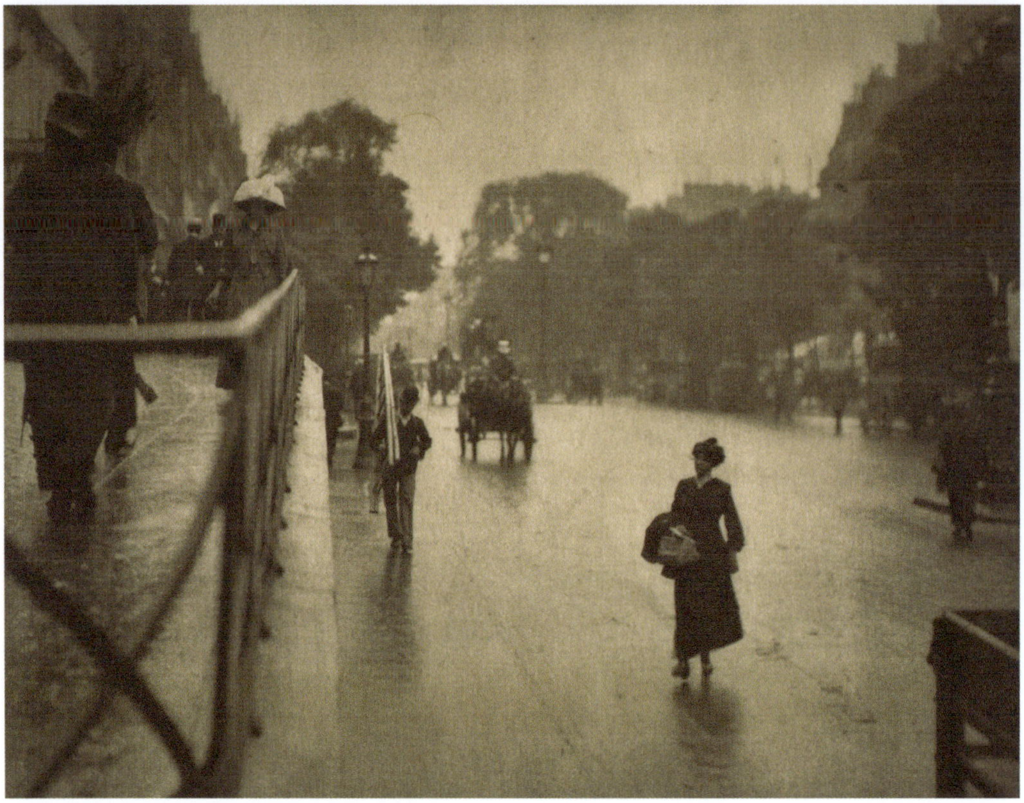

Fig. 111. Alfred Stieglitz, A SNAPSHOT, PARIS.

Another French street photographer, Henri Cartier-Bresson (1908–2004), who photographed in many European cities, said this about his craft: "Photography is not like painting. There is a creative fraction of a second when you are taking a picture. Your eye must see a composition or an expression that life offers you, and you must know with intuition when to click the camera. That is the moment the photographer is creative." Today, since photos can be manipulated digitally, clicking the camera is only the starting point in the creation of a work of art.

Like painters, photographers choose genres within which to express themselves. Memorable photographers in the portrait genre include Alfred Stieglitz (1864–1946); Richard Avedon (1923–2004), fashion photographer par excellence; Eve Arnold (1912–2012); and Diane Arbus (1923–1971). For journalistic themes, some of the names to remember include Robert Capa (1913–1954); Larry Burrows (1924–1971); and Walker Evans (1893–1975); and in landscape photography Edward Weston (1886–1958) and the legendary Ansel Adams (1902–1984). I encourage you to seek out the many artists who did and continue to work in the medium of photography.

I won't elaborate on the marvelous practitioners in collage or printmaking or other forms here, but remind you that these approaches and media each have their magic properties and offer artists an opportunity for different types of expression. They have been utilized by painters and sculptors as essential parts of their language of art-making.

As an artist who has tried many if not all of them, I can tell you a few of their secrets:

COLLAGE is a layering technique and marvelous for practicing composition and breaking out of the artist's comfort zone. The most innovative pieces can be made from moving around the pieces of the puzzle until a new picture appears. Unlike the painting medium, which covers and changes what has come before, in collage the artist can manipulate the parts and not commit herself until she is satisfied with the arrangement.

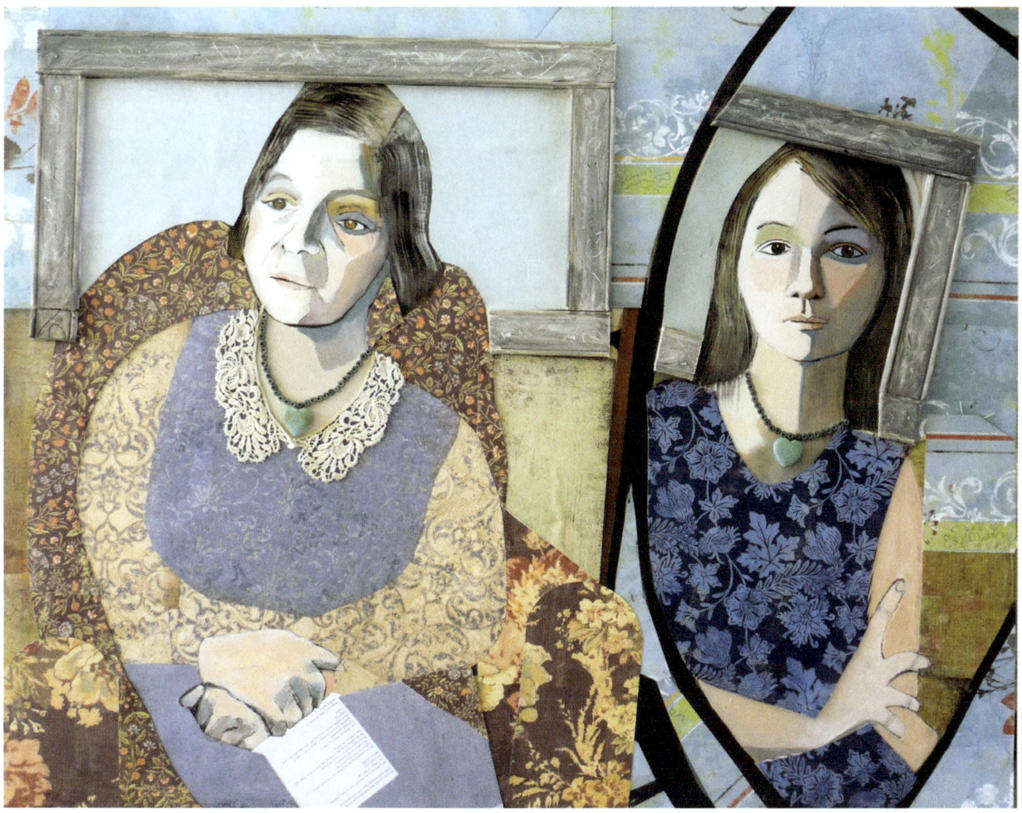

Fig. 112. Carolyn Schlam, REFLECT/REFRACT.

Here's a recent collage of mine that depicts an older woman and the reflection of her younger self in a mirror (Fig. 112). Of course, the image is in her mind, aroused by the poem she holds in her hand. Somehow mixing the materials in this way makes an interesting subject even more interesting to look at. Do you agree or not?

Some interesting collage artists to look up include Kurt Schwitters, Romare Bearden, May Ray, Hannah Hoch, and Joseph Cornell for assemblage.

DECOUPAGE is a variant of collage and involves pasting cutouts into design motifs; Matisse was famous for his late-life decoupage. It is a highly decorative medium, and, like collage, very graphic and eye-catching.

PRINTMAKING is an indirect medium where one prepares a plate and then prints the image in reverse. It is great fun and always a surprise to see the result. Of course, the print can be further manipulated by adding colors and shapes to it directly once it emerges from the press.

MIXED MEDIA describes work that includes two or more media. It can be ceramic and glass, watercolor and pencil, oil paint and collage, really any combination.

Since oil and water don't mix, using oil-based and water-based materials in the same work is a lark. You might remember your kindergarten project called crayon resist, where you used a wax or oil crayon to make a colorful design and then covered it with water-based ink or paint that filled in all of the cracks, but resisted the wax or oil. We would call this mixed media.

Many artists dabble in these techniques as each possesses its own expressive vocabulary. Though we have just scratched the surface here, I hope you will look up artists working in all these media, and discover how they are mixing them in ever more fascinating ways. There's a lot to see and appreciate.

Chapter 13
A Closer Look: Decoding Works of Art

Qualities are by their very nature subjective. A quality is both a trait of something and a standard against which things can be measured. When we evaluate art, we are both describing the characteristics of the work and measuring the work against other similar pieces, either by genre or period. All of this is a matter of opinion and can be debated endlessly.

In thinking about the various qualities (as in traits) we can use to define art, I came up with a list of words. Then in reviewing these words, I tried to find master categories under which they could be classified. These categories too are subjective, and are certainly debatable. You may want to challenge my categorizations and come up with your own. Mine are:

SKILL: ability or expertise in execution
- Qualities in this category would include: ambitiousness, drawing ability, painting ability, harmoniousness, verisimilitude, facility

ORIGINALITY: imaginative indicatives
- Qualities in this category would include: freshness, timelessness, surprise, symbolism, cleverness, humor, whimsy, playfulness, uniqueness, progressiveness, imagination

EMOTIONAL EXPRESSIVENESS: power to move feelings
- Qualities in this category would include: mood, authenticity, intensity, sentiment, subtlety, poignancy, tenderness, power

VISUAL EFFECT: pleasing nature or attractiveness
- Qualities in this category would include: light expression, coloration, illusion of space, delicacy, flavor, brightness, rhythm, vibrancy, lyricism, texture, vivacity, naturalism

DESIGN: aspects of composition and structure
- Qualities in this category would include: patterning, composition, sophistication, movement, simplicity, distortion

MEANING: Power to provoke thought

- Qualities in this category would include: character, elevation of theme, resonance, depth, iconography

In my attempt to classify terms, let me state that artworks possess many qualities at the same time. They can be original and intense, skillfully made and subtle, have both movement and harmonious design, and so on. I offer the classifications only to make you think and sort them into categories that may be easily remembered. You can then begin to apply them to the artworks you see.

In many cases, though artworks have many qualities, the works and the artists who make them come to be defined by a specific quality. We think of Matisse as a colorist, Picasso as an original, Klimt as a master of patterning. We love van Gogh for the vibrancy of his work and Degas for his lyricism.

You may put this all in the category of semantics, but we use words to help us explain what we see, and the more words we have at our disposal, the more exact we can be. If it helps you that I have allocated the terms in this way, I am glad.

For all the major elements of art, there are a variety of adjectives you may find to more accurately describe them. I'll name a few. See if you can think of five more for each:

LINES can be fluid, flowing, hesitant, bold, deliberate, felt, swirling, thin, thick, bold, meandering, variegated;
COLOR can be warm, cold, sweet, salty, pungent, major or minor key, bright, primary, pastel, subtle, watery, earthy, iridescent, metallic, vivid, intense, saturated;
TEXTURE can be smooth, rough, sandy, jagged, rocky, satiny, pebbled, irregular, luscious, gooey;
SHAPES can be geometrical, vertical, horizontal, mechanical, organic, rounded, elongated, shrunken, distorted, simple;
LIGHT can be dramatic, subtle, heightened, pronounced, warm, cold, harsh, reflected, tender;
SPACE can be deep, shallow, distorted, intimate, monumental.

According to Thesaurus.com, here are some of the synonyms for the word "beautiful":

admirable, alluring, angelic, appealing, beauteous, bewitching, charming, classy, comely, cute, dazzling, delicate, delightful, divine, elegant, enticing, excellent, exquisite, fair, fascinating, fine, foxy, good-looking, gorgeous, gracious, grand, handsome, ideal, lovely, magnificent, marvelous, nice, pleasing, pretty, pulchritudinous, radiant, ravishing, refined, resplendent, shapely, sightly, splendid, statuesque, stunning, sublime, superb, symmetrical, wonderful, well-formed.

If you think this is a lot, here are some of the synonyms for the word "expressive":

articulate, clear, direct, eloquent, fluent, glib, intelligible, loquacious, lucid, smooth, succinct, well-spoken, alive, allegorical, animated, appearing, ardent, artless, brilliant, canny, charged, cogent, communicative, colorful, complete, considerable, convincing, crafty, deep, demonstrating, denotional, descriptive, displaying, dramatic, easy, effective, effortless, emotional emphatic, energetic, enthusiastic, evidential, excitable, explanatory, explicit, extended, extraordinary, facile, faithful, fastidious, fervent, flexible, flowing, forceful, frank, graphic, gushing, identifying, idiosyncratic, illustrative, imaginative, impressive, incisive, indicating, individual, ingenious, intense, interactive, knowing, lifelike, lively, loving, marked, masterly, materializing, meaning, meaningful, metaphorical, mettlesome, mournful, moving, naming, narrative, natural, open, passionate, pathetic, peculiar, picturesque, pithy, plain, plastic, poetic, poignant, pointed, polished, powerful, pregnant, private, profound, radical, ready, realistic, responsive, revealing, rhetorical, rich, romantic, sad, secret, sensational, sensible, sensitive, sentimental, shocking, showing showy, shrewd, significant, signifying, sincere, slick, stylish, sly, soft, speaking, spirited, startling, stimulating, stirring, striking, strong, substantial, sudden, susceptible, symbolic, sympathetic, talkative, talking, telling, tender, theatric, thoughtful, touching, transferred, true, typical, understanding, vivacious, vivid, vocal, voluble, warm, weighty, wily, mobile, allusive, figurative, communicatory, revelatory, silver-tongued, loaded, breathtaking, thought-provoking, diagnostic, informative, trenchant, nonverbal, persuasive, unambiguous, connotational, connotative, implicative, intentional, conspiratorial, definable, delineative, depictive, demonstrative, designative, extensional, referential, noticeable, emblematic, symbolical, evocative, interpretable, expositive, expository, extroverted, figural, forcible, impressible, impressionable, impressionistic, linguistic, lyrical, major, one-on-one, meaty, naturalistic, oratorical, provocative, oversensitive, pictorial, readable, semiotic, thin-skinned, sententious, significative, soulful, stylistic, touchy-feely, fraught, indicatory, high-flying, alive to, associational, denominative, evincive, exhibitive, expositional, facund, histrionical, ideographic, illocutionary, incarnating, marrowy, paralinguistic, presentional, semantic, signalizing, significatory, telltale, theophanic, well-drawn, full of meaning, full of substance, pregnant with meaning, disclosive, revelational, promulgatory, impassionable, without skin, epiphanic, manifestative, heart-touching.

You may quarrel with many of these synonyms for *beautiful* and *expressive*, especially those that seem lesser, like *nice* and *cute*. These would not be attributed to artwork in a complimentary way. You may quarrel with others like *symmetrical* or *fraught* as you may not find these characteristics to be representative of "beauty" or "expressiveness." It is interesting to note how many more synonyms popped up for "expressive" over "beautiful" as the former is assuredly a bigger tent.

Think about this a bit and apply it when you look at art. It may open your mind when you look at a work that is not conventionally "beautiful" and yet is highly "expressive."

Your new definition of beauty may expand as your eyes open.

I offer these terms to you to encourage you to widen your vocabulary so you have the tools to describe what you feel when you look at art, or come to a conclusion about many things you see and do. I suggest that widening your vocabulary will also widen your point of view and make your opinions more considered and better expressed,

Now let's put this vocabulary to work to look at some works of art.

1. EXPERTISE AND HOMAGE

The female reclining nude has been a popular theme in Western painting for centuries. This is the case even though one rarely sees a painting of a nude displayed outside of a museum and, in fact, it is one of the more difficult subjects to sell. Nonetheless, the subject is fascinating to artists for many reasons. Drawing groups that draw and paint the nude form are available everywhere, and countless artists continue to produce works in this genre.

Let's have a look at some of the notable reclining nudes through history, each strongly influenced by their predecessors. This is a subject that is not going away anytime soon.

Certain artworks that become iconic not only inspire legions of viewers, they also inspire other artists as well, and their work invites imitation and reincarnation. Such is the case with this work by the remarkable master of the Venetian Renaissance known as Titian.

He stands out in art history as one of the greats, recognized in his time, and revered ever since. Titian's versatility and mastery, especially as to color, have made him one of the most copied artists.

Venus of Urbino, Titian's painting of a reclining nude (see Fig. 113 on the next page), is actually based on a work by Giorgione, a friend of Titian. Giorgione created his work titled *The Sleeping Venus* in 1510, the year of his death, and the work was actually completed by Titian (see Fig. 114 on the next page). More than twenty years later, Titian created his own version, which we are now examining. The background is changed as Titian's version is an interior scene. However, the position of the female form in the foreground of both paintings is almost identical. The Titian nude, however is shown very much awake.

The Titian *Venus* is actually quite coquettish—remember the date of this work is 1534—and might be considered brazen, as there is no attempt to conceal her sensuality. Was this a painting made of a young woman with no idealization or mythical content? Just a nude? It appears so.

The setting is a palace and we see a dog and two women looking into a chest, perhaps seeking clothes for the naked woman. The work was made for a commission by the Duke of Urbino to celebrate his marriage.

Aside from the flagrancy of the subject matter, what is there to like about this nude? It is painted with a long gamut and the dark of the background makes the brightly lit nude even more curvaceous and solid, as do the draperies, which feel like silk. All of the other elements combine to set off the center of interest, the beautiful display of the female form.

The *Venus of Urbino* was much appreciated by artists to follow Titian. It was imitated by Velázquez in 1647 in his *Rokeby Venus* and by Goya in 1797 in his work *The Nude Maja* (see Fig. 115 on page 239).

And then by many other artists, most notably by Édouard Manet in his 1863 painting called *Olympia* (see Fig. 116 on page 239).

Manet's painting was considered scandalous when it was first shown, this largely because it was considered a painting of a prostitute. References in the painting allude to this, like the orchid in her hair, as does the title—"Olympia" was a name used to refer to prostitutes at the time.

But this is no concern to us, just a blip in history. What we do want to look at are the aesthetic elements that characterize this work and distinguish it from the Titian. First similarities: both works are painted in a long gamut—this was a characteristic of Manet, who did wonders with black. The poses are also similar.

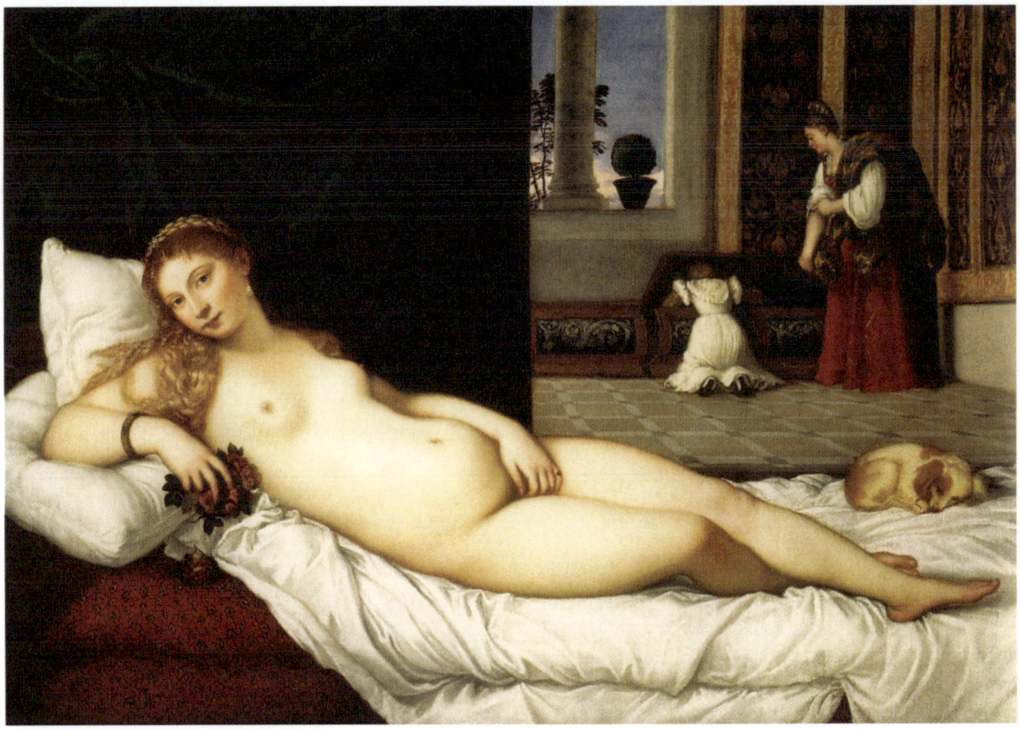

Fig. 113. Titian, VENUS OF URBINO.

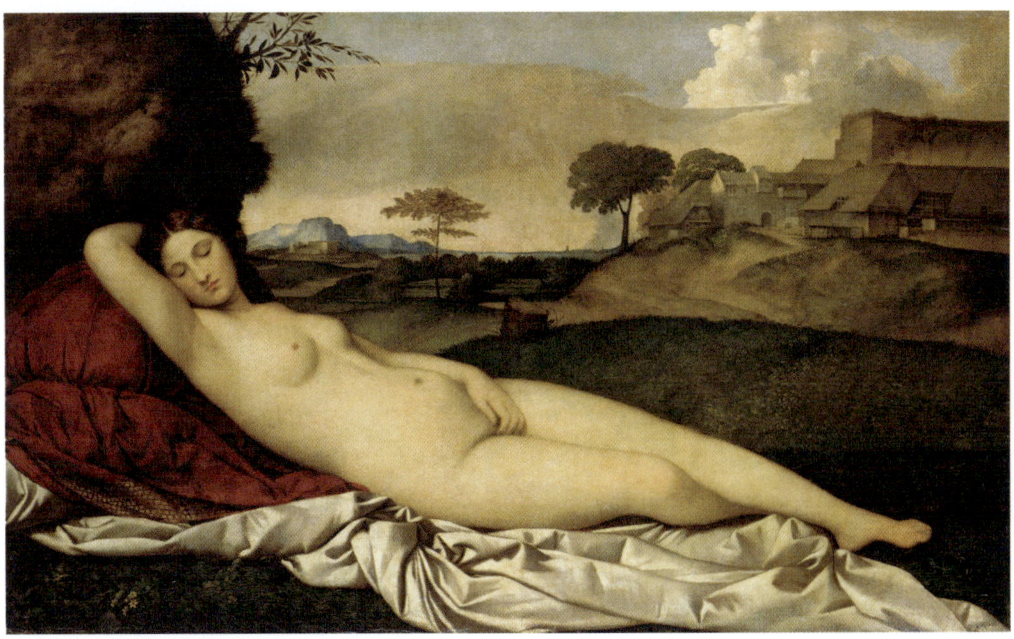

Fig. 114. Giorgione, SLEEPING VENUS.

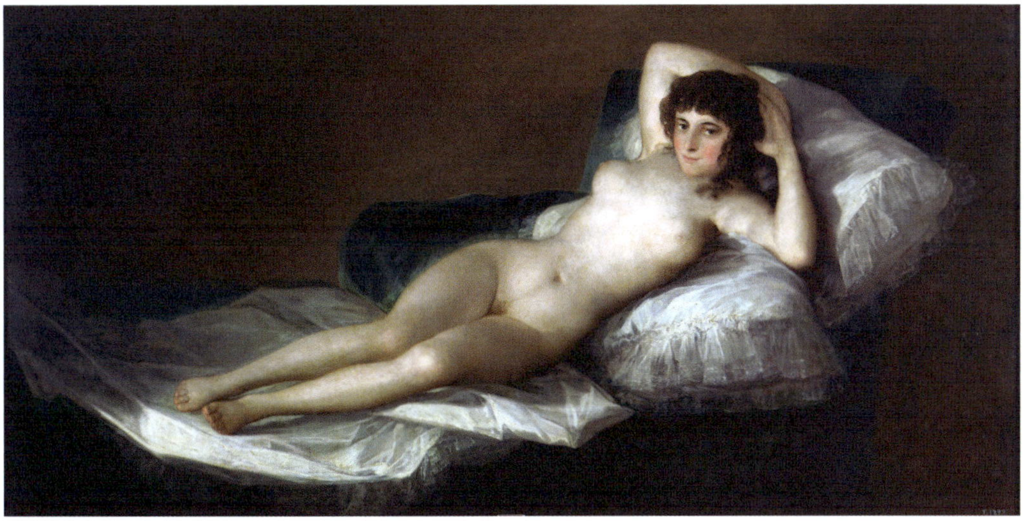

Fig. 115. Francisco Goya, THE NUDE MAJA.

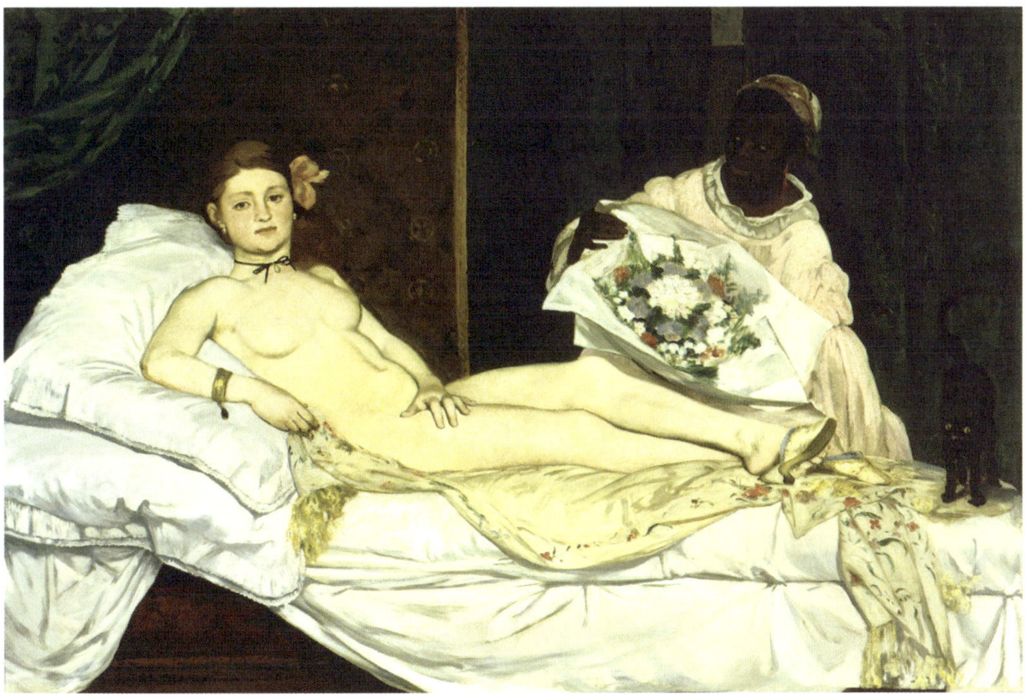

Fig. 116. Édouard Manet, OLYMPIA.

But what we have in the Manet is a shortened foreground, with the Maid painted much larger. This makes the painting more intimate and at the same time more pronounced; the maids in the Titian seeming extraneous and included just for narrative purposes. In the Manet there are no distractions and the composition therefore feels more unified. I find it very satisfying and much more inviting to look at.

I also have the impression that the light is natural, provided by daylight, this from the skin tones, whereas the Titian seems artificially lit. This consciousness of the softening effect of daylight was a characteristic of the Impressionists, and Manet was a precursor to that consciousness.

QUESTIONS. Think on these:

- Why is the reclining nude such a popular subject?
- Do you find one of these works to be superior, and if so, why?
- Can you look at a nude in the same way you look at a painting of a bowl of fruit?
- Is a nude a subject that would interest you as a painter or sculptor?

2. ART ABOUT ART

For many artists, a main subject of art is art itself. We like to reflect on what we are doing.

On the next page, this painting by Velázquez (Fig. 117) is one of the most studied in art history and many consider it a masterpiece, a few even the most important painting of all time! Containing eleven figures and more than ten feet long, it was a complex compositional challenge for the artist. It is actually very enigmatic and quite cleverly composed. Though it appears to be a study of the five-year-old child who takes center stage—the Infanta Margaret Theresa—closer study shows otherwise.

It actually depicts the artist Velázquez painting the King and Queen as they pose for a portrait. The sitters are the viewers, not the subject. We are looking at this scene from their point of view. We see either their reflection or that of the painting the artist is making of them reflected in the mirror in the background. The Infanta, her maids, the two dwarfs, the chaperone, bodyguard, and Queen's chamberlain stand before the King and Queen, perhaps there for their entertainment.

So what are we looking at? We are looking at the portraitist, not the portrait; the scene is reversed. The main subject becomes the little girl who has the benefit of standing directly in the light emanating from the window on the right.

In this example, you can see that every work of art tells a story. And every story has a point of view. Velázquez turned portrait painting on its head here. The purported subjects, the King and Queen, are the spectators, and the main event is the little girl there to distract them.

Not an easy task to make nine figures live in the same world, be sized correctly vis-à-vis their position, and to make it all believable. This work is considered a tour de force. Following Velázquez's accomplishment, many artists attempted copies and adaptations, as did John Singer Sargent in his considerably less complex work (see Fig. 118 on page 243).

With only four figures, Sargent's task was less daunting, but the composition here is excellent and worthy of study. The four girls define the foreground, middle ground, and background, and the white dresses link and ease your eye's travel from one to the other. The dark empty spaces provide the quiet necessary for the figures to dominate and stand their ground. Really wonderful composition on this basically square format.

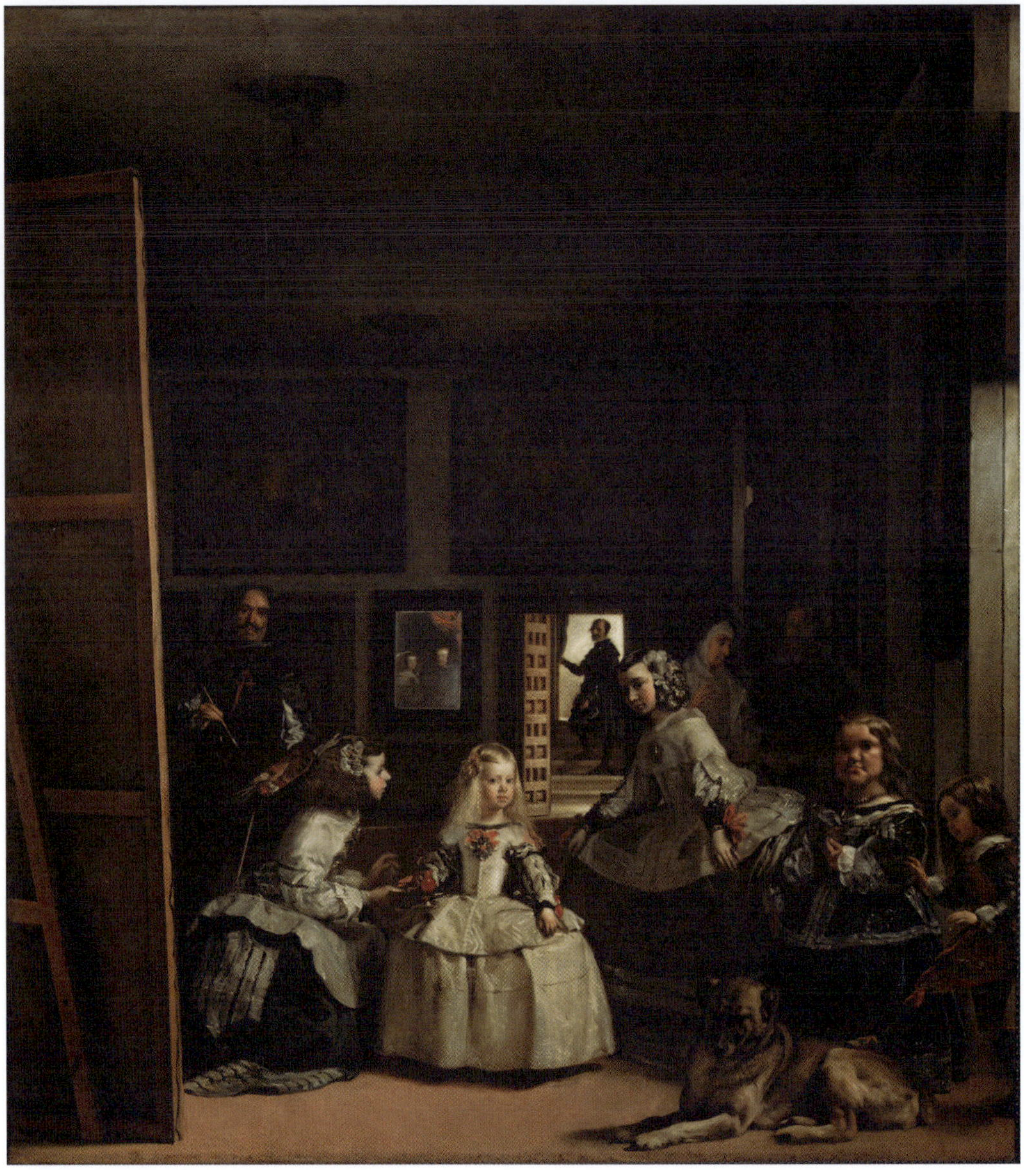

Fig. 117. Diego Velázquez, LAS MENINAS.

Pablo Picasso was so enthralled with the Velázquez work that he made fifty-eight studies after *Las Meninas*, organizing and reorganizing the composition to his liking. In a five-month period he ripped *Las Meninas* apart and put it back together again, as if he could only comprehend its magic in this way. One can only imagine the feverish pace at which he created these works.

The Picasso *Meninas* are all now in the Museu Picasso in Barcelona. Worth a visit for sure to marvel at his ingenuity. I visited myself last summer, and only one thing was missing—a photo of the actual Velázquez work. How anyone could understand

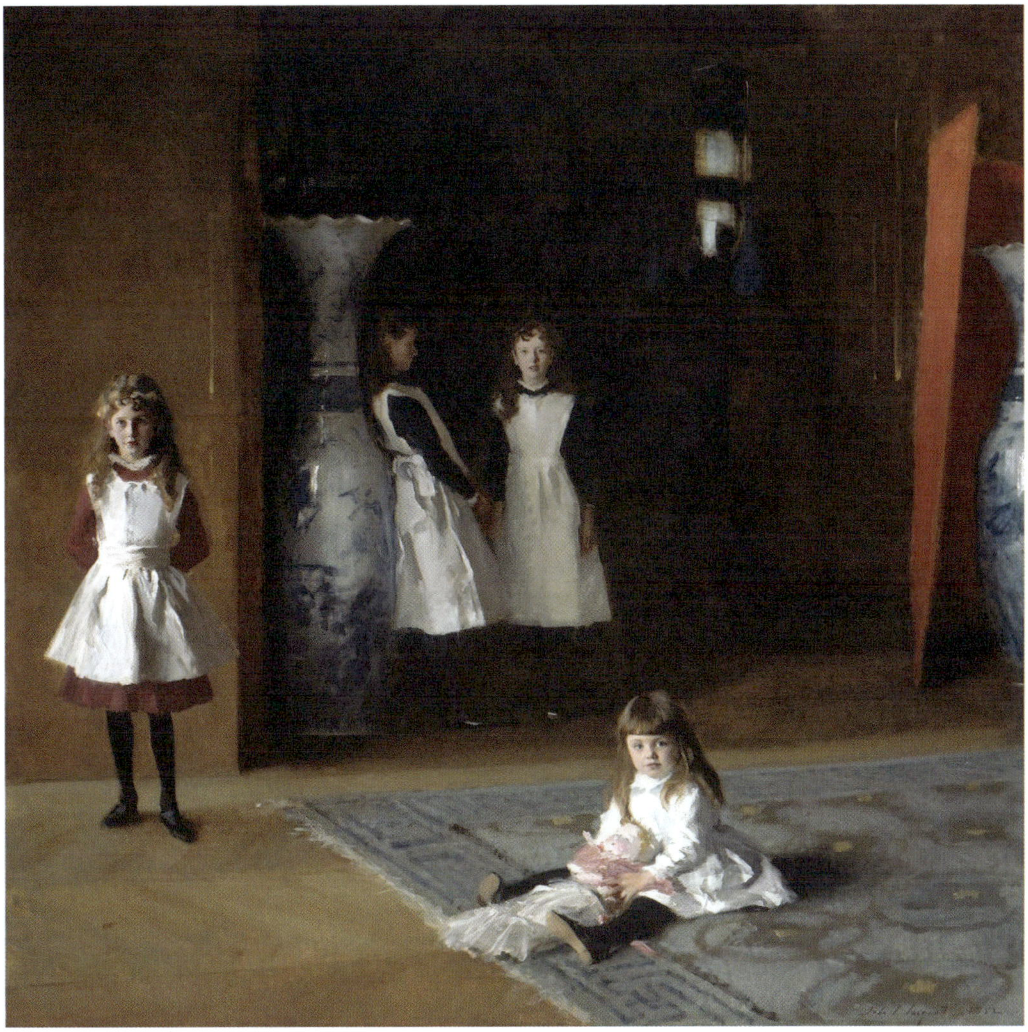

Fig. 118. John Singer Sargent, THE DAUGHTERS OF EDWARD DARLEY BOIT.

these fifty-eight works without seeing what they are drawn from is a mystery. Bring a photo of the Velázquez when you visit—all the museumgoers will flock around you.

Other artists also found the work enthralling and worthy of reinterpretation. The figure of the Infanta itself has been much copied and re-created in myriad ways. On the next page are two examples: an abstracted sculpture by the sculptor Manolo Valdés (Fig. 119) and a photographic take on the Infanta by the contemporary photographer Jacqueline Roberts (Fig. 120).

You will see this phenomenon many times throughout art history—artists taking inspiration from great works that preceded them. Imitation is said to be the greatest form of flattery, and here that is certainly true. Translating an inspiring

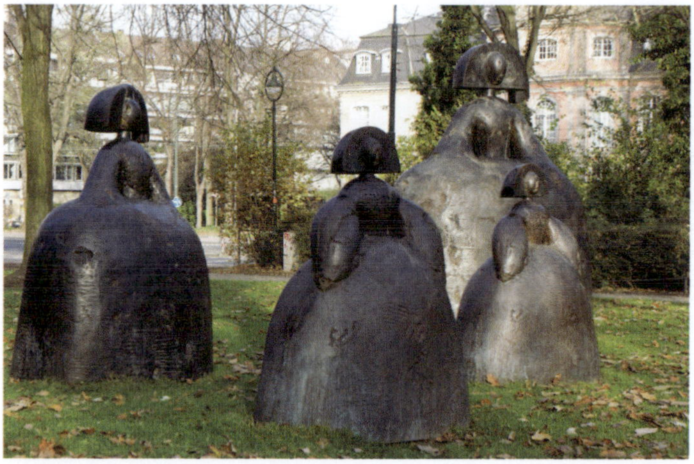

Fig. 119. Manolo Valdés, LAS MENINAS.

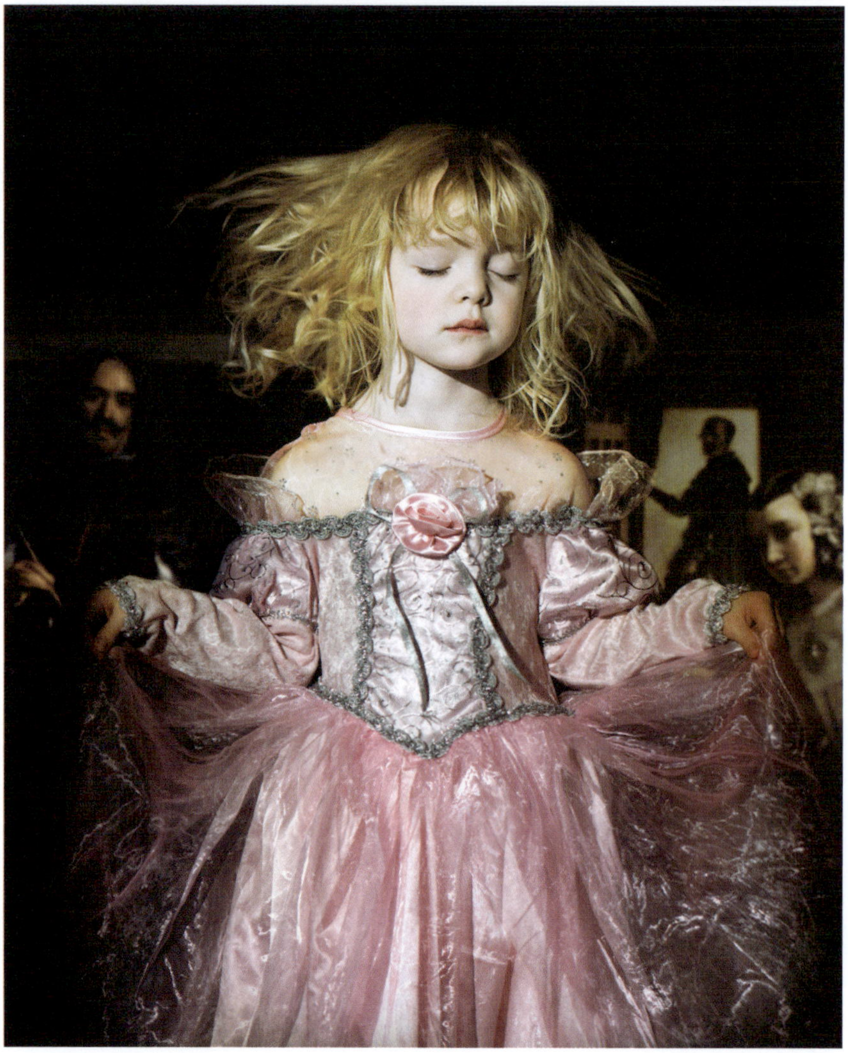

Fig. 120. Jacqueline Roberts, A MENINAS DREAM.

work from one medium to another honors the originator and allows the inspiration to be reborn.

Many have the impression, a misconception truly, that artists work primarily from their imaginations and just "make things up." In truth, we use a whole panoply of sources and prompts—actual observation from life, photographs, ideas, music, and yes, the work of artists that have preceded us who continue to challenge us.

QUESTIONS. Reflections on *Las Meninas*:

- Why do you think *Las Meninas* is an important painting?
- Why do you think so many artists were interested in copying or interpreting it?
- Does it inspire you, and how would you interpret it?
- If not, what work have you seen by any artist that you would like to reinterpret?

3. THE MANY FACETS OF THE SELF-PORTRAIT

The self-portrait has long been a subject of painters. Either lacking a suitable model, wanting to experiment, or desiring to cast oneself for posterity, painters have often used their own visages as convenient subjects. What they choose to accentuate is both an expression of their style and a window into how they view themselves.

Self-portraits have been created in every style, genre, medium, and palette over the centuries.

Just as every individual has a self-perception—some positive, some negative, some self-effacing and others narcissistic, artists have revealed themselves to us in this fascinating way. From pure realism, where the artist shows you his stately visage, like Rembrandt, all the way to today, when artists like Jimmy Wright (Fig. 121) offer you their self-image without artifice, and full of emotion, the self-portrait lives on as an important theme in art.

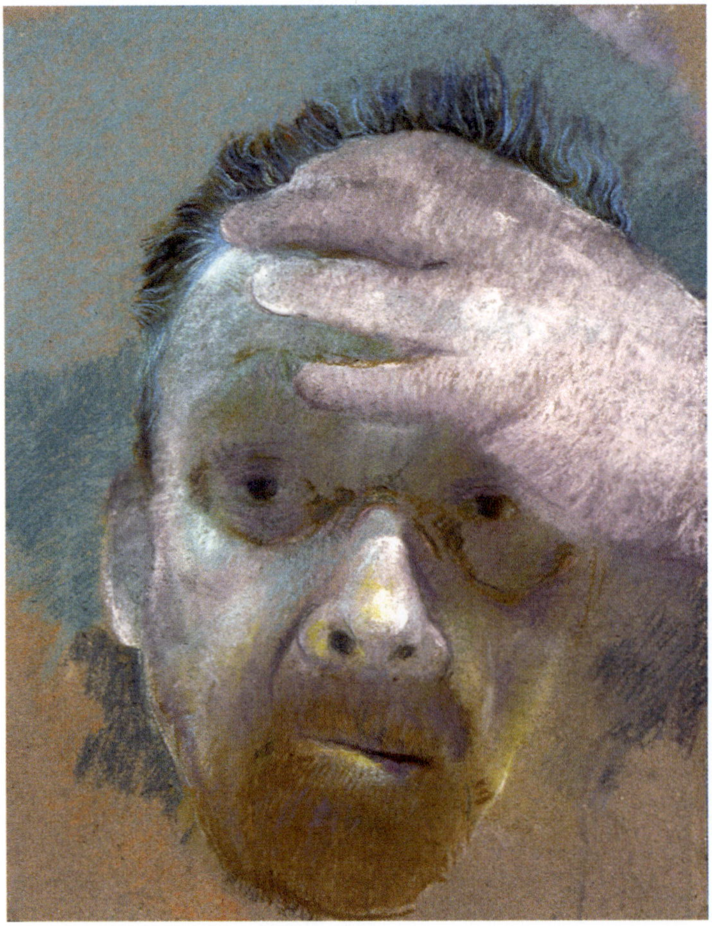

Fig. 121. Jimmy Wright, SELF #4.

The self-portrait remains one of the most interesting subjects in art. Since it is not created to please a sitter, it may be a truer reflection of an artist's point of view. With this in mind, let's have a look at some of the most interesting self-portraitists.

The master painter known as Rembrandt painted some forty self-portraits in oil during his career as well as etchings and drawings. This particular one (Fig. 122) was done at the latter part of his career after a hiatus of seven years, during which time he turned to other subjects. He was forty-six years old when this portrait was painted.

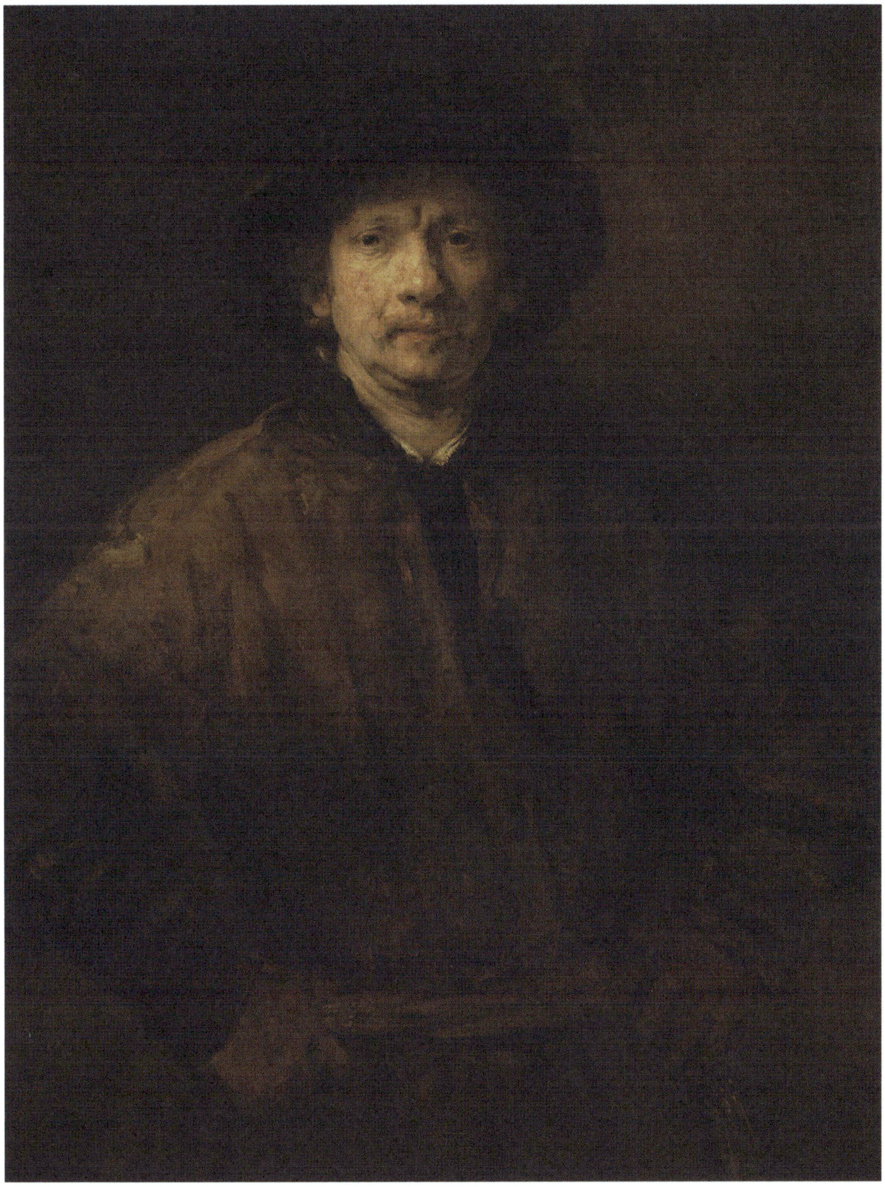

Fig. 122. Rembrandt van Rijn, LARGE SELF-PORTRAIT.

As with many self-portraits, Rembrandt accomplished his by looking at himself in a mirror. Of course there is some license taken as he is shown here with his hands on his hips, not in the act of painting. This may be a reason many of the portraits do not show hands, or just note them in a cursory manner. An artist of today could have someone take his photograph and then execute the portrait from the photo. If working from life with the mirror, the image will always be reversed, and position somewhat altered.

Why did Rembrandt paint so many self-portraits? One might assume that the self-portrait as subject gave him the opportunity for full artistic integrity. With no need to please the subject as one might be required to do when executing a commissioned portrait, he was free to paint as he wished. He was making the self-portraits presumably just for himself.

In fact, since he was such a well-regarded artist of his time, it is reported that the self-portraits were much in demand by collectors, and in fact, only a handful of the works remained in his family collection. Regardless of this, I think we can still assume that they were not made necessarily to please his public. This makes them even more interesting for study, as we can assume they represented the purest intentions of the artist. Rembrandt paints himself in his studio clothes, it is thought, because in another drawing illustrating these same garments, they are noted as his customary working dress.

Okay, now let's discuss the work. Only a faintness of light on the chest and shoulder has the figure emerging from the deep brown tone. The tone is rich and warm. Light enters from one direction, casting much of the figure in shadow.

There are no distractions in the background or dress. All attention is on the head, which is splashed with a warm golden light. The light carves the head out of the shadows. The expression is forthright yet somber. The gaze is intense.

The paint is skillfully applied, the brushwork not particularly pronounced. The figure has a solidity, feels weighted. The bright light on one side of the face is heightened as the light on the dress is subdued; this gives prominence to the head and face.

What makes this self-portrait captivating? Can you isolate what it is that makes a Rembrandt portrait rise above those of his peers?

In my estimation, it is the lack of bravado, yet the extreme confidence that makes these portraits outstanding. They have that physical solidity, yes, but more than that, they have a humanity, an empathy, that gives a deeper reality, a view perhaps into the soul of the artist. What a complex human being he was!

Peer into the eyes and face of this portrait and you can leap back to a moment in the seventeenth century when it was painted. It has such immediacy, doesn't it? You can hardly believe it was made over 360 years ago.

Other artists, perhaps not as humble and understated as Rembrandt, expressed themselves more dramatically, shall we say, as in this painting by the artist Courbet a few centuries later (Fig. 123). The long gamut and extreme lighting is reminiscent of Caravaggio, and this might be considered a Romantic work. Even the signature in red says *drama*.

This is a quite unusual presentation of the self. What do you think the artist was saying about himself?

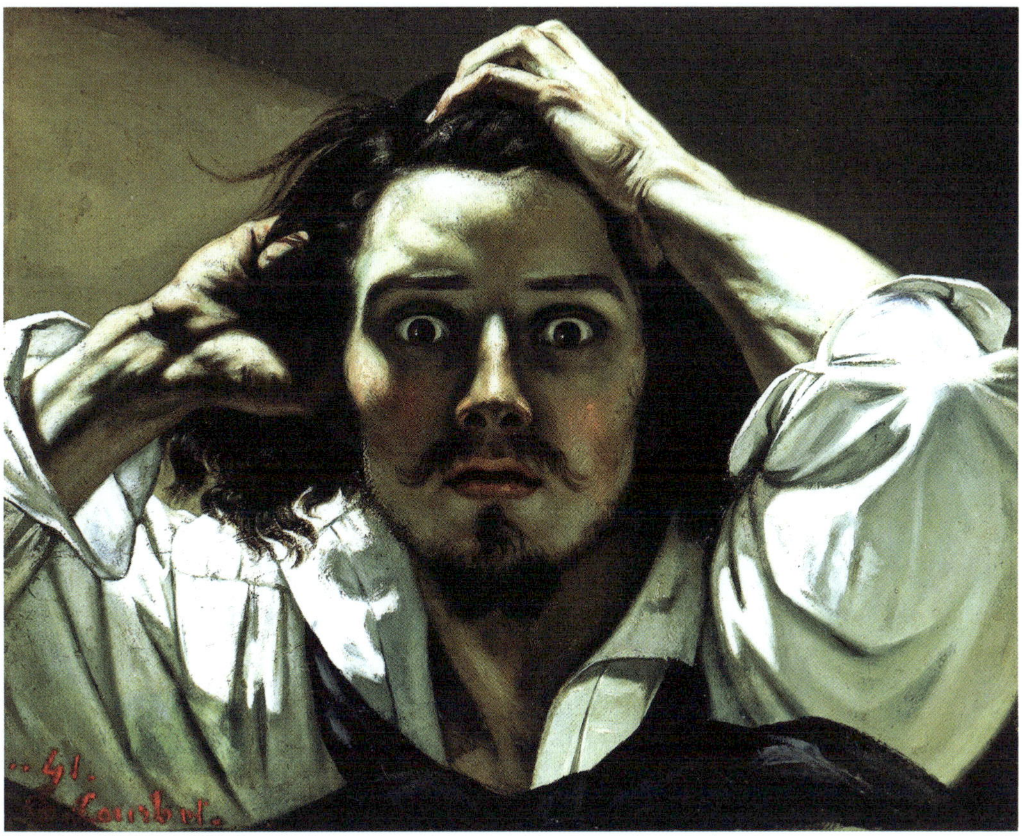

Fig. 123. Gustave Courbet, THE DESPERATE MAN.

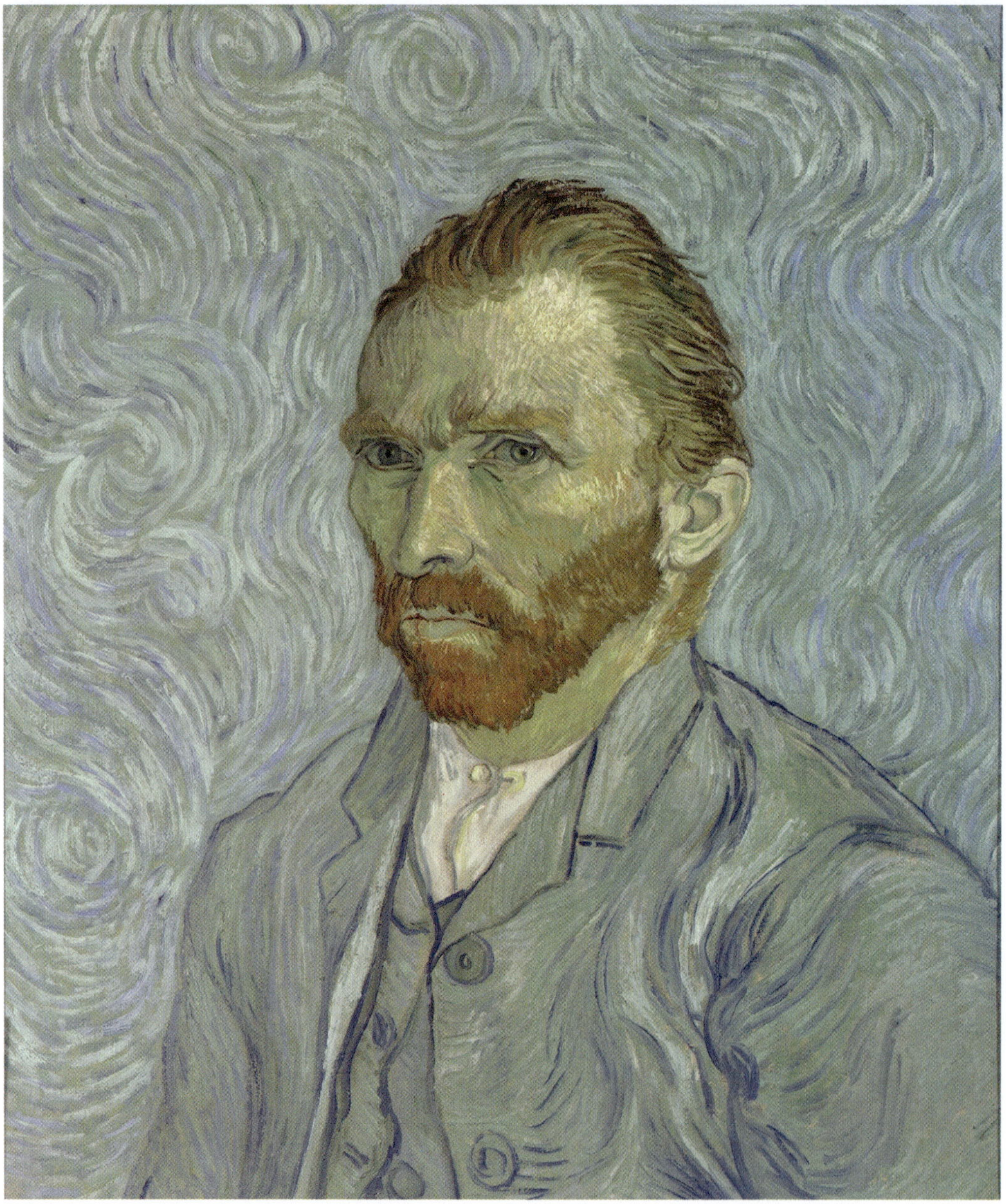

Fig. 124. Vincent van Gogh, SELF-PORTRAIT.

The much more modest Vincent van Gogh presented a much more sober view of himself in his self-portrait (Fig. 124). The distress exhibited in this, either the last or next-to-last self-portrait painted by the artist, is not dramatic, as the portrait is executed in soft middle tones, but it speaks a kind of resolute sadness. Van Gogh did many self-portraits as he often could not afford models. We still have the swirling texture of the background, which suggests turbulence, but the quiet colors have the effect of toning the piece down and making it feel harmonious. Overall I find this to be a very flattering portrait of a man who sees himself without artifice or guile.

Now that your interest has been stimulated by looking at these self-portraits, look for them in books and museums. Check out the very personal symbolic portraits of Frida Kahlo, the myriad self-interpretations by Andy Warhol, the photographs of Cindy Sherman, and many other practitioners of this genre.

QUESTIONS. A few to ponder:

- Why do you think the self-portrait is a popular subject for artists?
- In your opinion, what makes a self-portrait interesting?
- Which is your favorite of the works shown here, and why?
- How would you paint your own self-portrait, and what would you feature?

4. SPIRITUALITY IN ART

When we think of Francisco Goya, a romantic late-eighteenth century Spanish painter, our first association is probably with one of his masterful Maja figures reclined on a settee. He was a great portraitist and considered a bridge between the old masters and the moderns.

But artists often surprise us and step outside of their comfortable box for one reason or another. They try another subject or enter into a dark period or a light one, or make loose sketches when they are known for tight finished compositions. Though they may exemplify their time and age, sometimes they depart into the future or the past and make something that seems to have come from another time.

So with this piece, one of several Goya painted directly on to the walls of his house in the later years of his life (Fig. 125). He did not make these paintings, subsequently labeled *The Black Paintings* for exhibition, and they remained on the walls of the house for some seventy years until they were removed and transferred onto canvas under the direction of a Prado curator. There they remain.

What an opportunity we have to see work that was created by an artist but not meant for show. The title was not chosen by the artist and is merely descriptive. I daresay that if I showed you this painting and asked you to guess when it was made, you would guess it to be a contemporary piece. The history paintings of the time were filled with colorful figures. And here we have a dramatically simple composition of a dog's head peering into the vastness of space. What does this painting tell us?

We see only the head of the dog, which suggests that the creature is stuck. It looks up imploringly into the vastness of space perhaps hoping to be saved. The sky takes up most of the picture; its vastness makes the dog seem even more lost and pitiful.

This is a deeply emotional visual experience describing pathos and our fear of mortality.

Its simplicity, directness, and poetic nature is truly remarkable for this period. I have read that the painter Joan Miró wanted to see only two paintings on his last visit to the Prado Museum. One was the Velázquez *Las Meninas*, and the other was *The Dog* by Goya.

This reverence for this work is due to the honesty of the painting and its deep emotional effect. The lack of color and bleak unadorned surface adds to the feeling

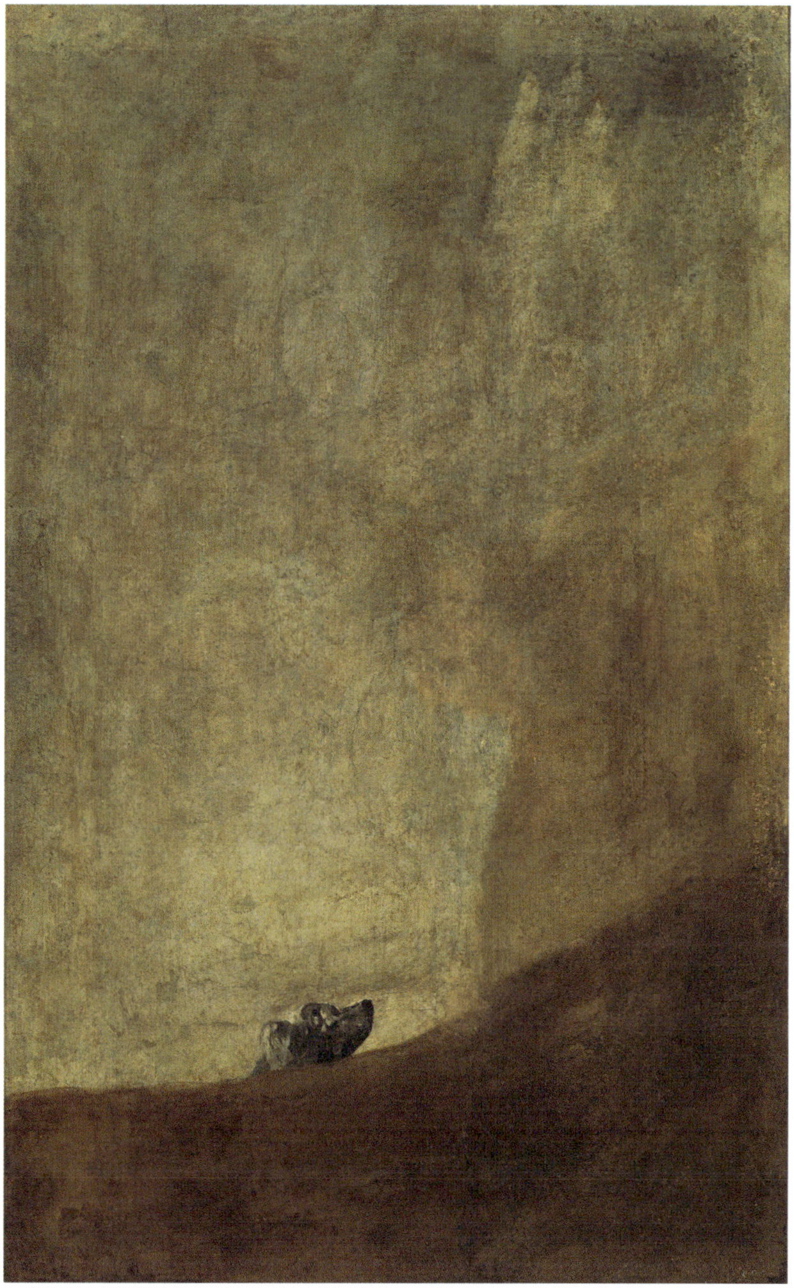

Fig. 125. Francisco Goya, THE DOG.

of loss. No description of pathos in words could better embody human loneliness and despair more accurately or poignantly than *The Dog*.

Transcending its time, Goya's inspirational painting lives on for all of us. It is also a lesson that what makes art meaningful is not that it is beautiful, but that it is expressive of our human condition and emotion. As only it can, it puts our psychology into visual form so we may experience and understand it.

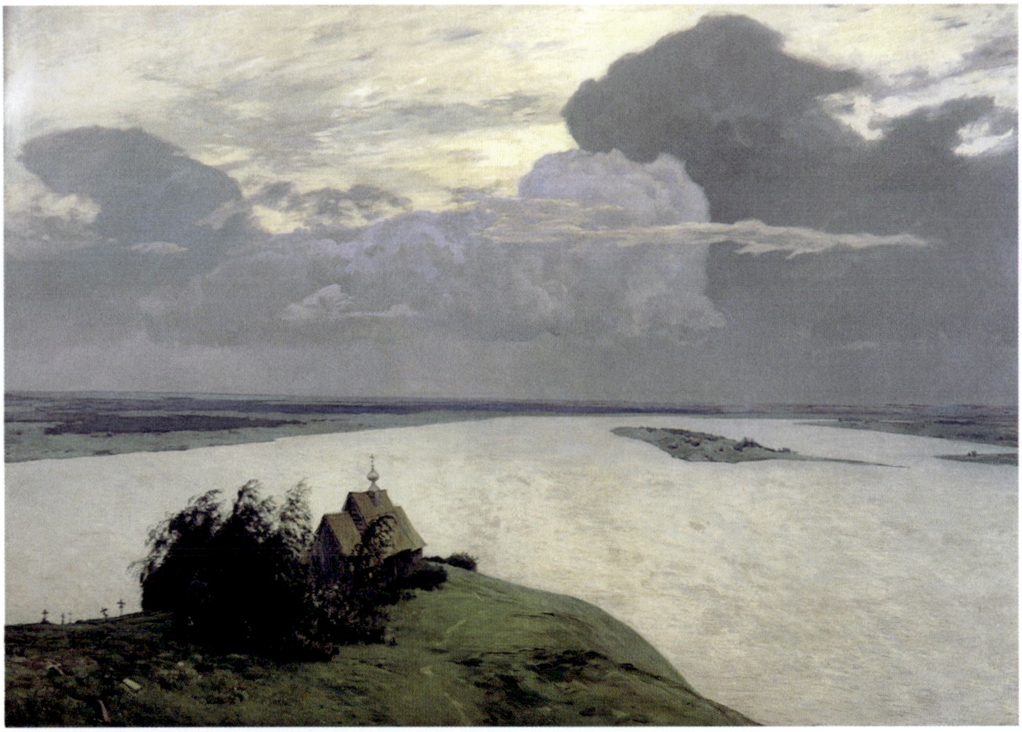

Fig. 126. Isaac Levitan, ABOVE THE ETERNAL PEACE.

The Russian Jewish painter Isaac Levitan said of this beautiful work, "This painting represents me completely, all my psychology, all my being" (Fig. 126). This is a rare statement and reveals so much about the artist. We know that Levitan, born in 1860, lived only forty years, during which he devoted himself to landscape painting. He was born into a shtetl in an area now known as Lithuania, and his family lived in abject poverty. Buoyed somewhat by his talent, Levitan was able to get a scholarship to study and was permitted to return to his hometown and later to Moscow even after Russian purges of Jews.

Levitan studied in the Moscow School of Painting, where he befriended the painter Nicolay Chekhov, brother of the playwright Anton Chekhov, who became Levitan's closest friend and with whom he subsequently lived.

Firstly, I selected this painting as an example because it conveys incredible emotion without including a single figure. This is an important message about art in general. Made by the human hand, brain, and feelings, every work of art delivers a message about the artist who created it, regardless of the subject. An apple can be as tenderly painted as a human cheek, a sky as exquisite as a breast.

This painting is a perfect example. *Above Eternal Peace* depicts a landscape of vast expanse with the upper third the sky. (Remember here the rule of thirds to which this work subscribes.) In the foreground we look down upon the small church and graveyard.

Consider the artist's point of view. To give us the incredible expanse of deep space, the eye view is taken from above. We look down and out into space as if we are looking at the view from a helicopter window, hovering over. Remember this is the imagination of the artist at work, and the composition is not accidental. It is the medium through which the artist delivers his message.

And what is that message? I think the painting tells us that the universe is a vast and boundless creation of God (the building depicted is a house of worship, not a residence) and that Nature, in its beauty and order, is a creation of that God. It is so magnificent that it astounds us with its majesty. The graveyard reminds us that we, as humans, are transitory occupants of this universe, and insignificant in the face of death.

With his glorious talent, subtle palette, and palpable textures of water and sky, Levitan elevates the message to tell us that we are blessed to live, see, and participate in the magnificence of Nature and God's gift. Knowing Levitan's difficult life, sickness, and early demise make his contribution even more poignant.

He was known as a "mood" painter of landscape, but I daresay this painting offers us much more than a mood. It is the work of a poetic man who translated his inner life onto canvas. This is lyricism, visual poetry, an elegy in paint. In savoring this work, pay attention to the atmospheric color—the cream-colored expanse of water and matching notes in that gorgeous sky, the somber deep color of the landmass that make that water and sky feel so vast.

I am excited to introduce you to the English painter and stained glass artist, Thomas Denny. I am a connoisseur of stained glass, being a glassmaker myself, and I discovered Mr. Denny's exceptional work in the course of my study of the medium.

Though stained glass, due to the fact that it has been employed and is associated with houses of worship, usually has a spiritual component, Denny's work has a particularly transfiguring beauty. Because light enters the glass and makes it glow, stained glass has a unique quality that imparts this feeling of glory or transcendence. In Denny's windows, where the pieces of glass are acid-etched and treated with silver stain and his figures are drawn in such compelling poses and painted so masterfully, the effects are mesmerizing. The light and color seem to vibrate and illuminate the subject as if it were struck with a beam of light from the heavens. This gives the work

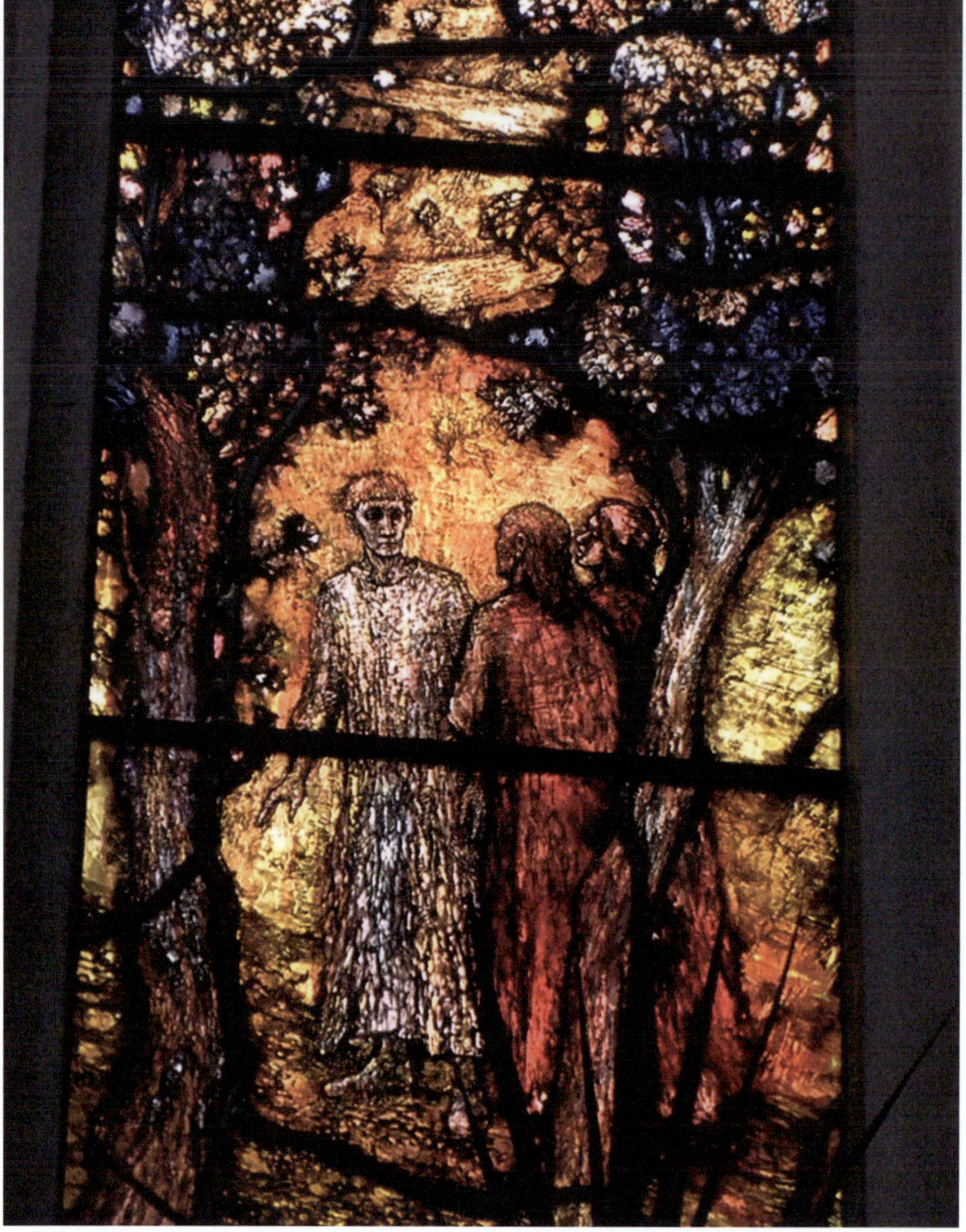

Fig. 127. Thomas Denny, RICHARD III WINDOW.

a quality that is really quite exalting and adds a particular beauty to the churches of which it is an essential part.

This is one of the windows in Leicester Cathedral made by Denny and derived from the life of Richard III (Fig. 127). Other Denny works can be found in cathedrals throughout England, and I encourage you to go and see them. These are windows that surpass other examples in the medium and take glass to a new level of excellence and beauty. I am enthralled by them and, hopefully, will get to see them in person along with you. They are truly special works of art.

QUESTIONS. Consider these:

- What do you think is the difference between religious painting and these examples, which are more spiritual in nature?
- Are you moved by these three examples?
- Can you think of another work with a spiritual dimension?
- Stained glass is a feature of churches. What is it about this medium that merits this application?

5. COLOR STORIES: LIMITED PALETTE

The use of color in painting is highly personal, just as it is in fashion. Some artists love robust primary colors; others muted or minor notes, and some eschew a palette of many colors, opting for a limited palette. The painter Andrew Wyeth was the latter, partial to browns and neutrals. Some viewers warm to the dustiness and sincerity of his palette; others find it dull and uninspired.

But Color with the capital *C* in art, despite common belief, is not a result of using many hues. It results from the sensitive juxtaposition of notes that together give a sensation of light and therefore, color.

Another artist who enjoyed a limited palette and the use of neutrals was Edgar Degas, painter of dancers, horses, and here in this wonderful little example, laundresses (Fig. 128). It illustrates what can be achieved with a paucity of colors, a few warms and a few colds, and a distribution of values.

The laundress, a warm dark—an orange and black mixture—is the center of attention, and she is framed by a powerful, warmish light. The light in the window is even stronger, a bit colder than the light on the table. The only other hue is the blue in the clothing hanging to dry.

So simple, really, and so very effective and beautiful. Created with white paint, some cerulean blue, sienna, orange, yellow, and a black. The values tell the story. A more blackened skirt, a slightly lighter value of the blouse, with a warmer tone. A slight glance of white to say apron, and voilà, a moment captured.

Also take note of the texture around the hands and iron. So little definition, yet with this fluffing of the paint, you can almost feel the heat of the iron and the feeling of pressure from the laundress.

We appreciate this work not in spite of but rather because of the limited palette, which does not distract from the commanding composition and long gamut. It just would not have worked with a whole bunch of colors.

With this example in mind, take note of the palette the artist has chosen and relate it to the subject and mood of the painting. Is there a match?

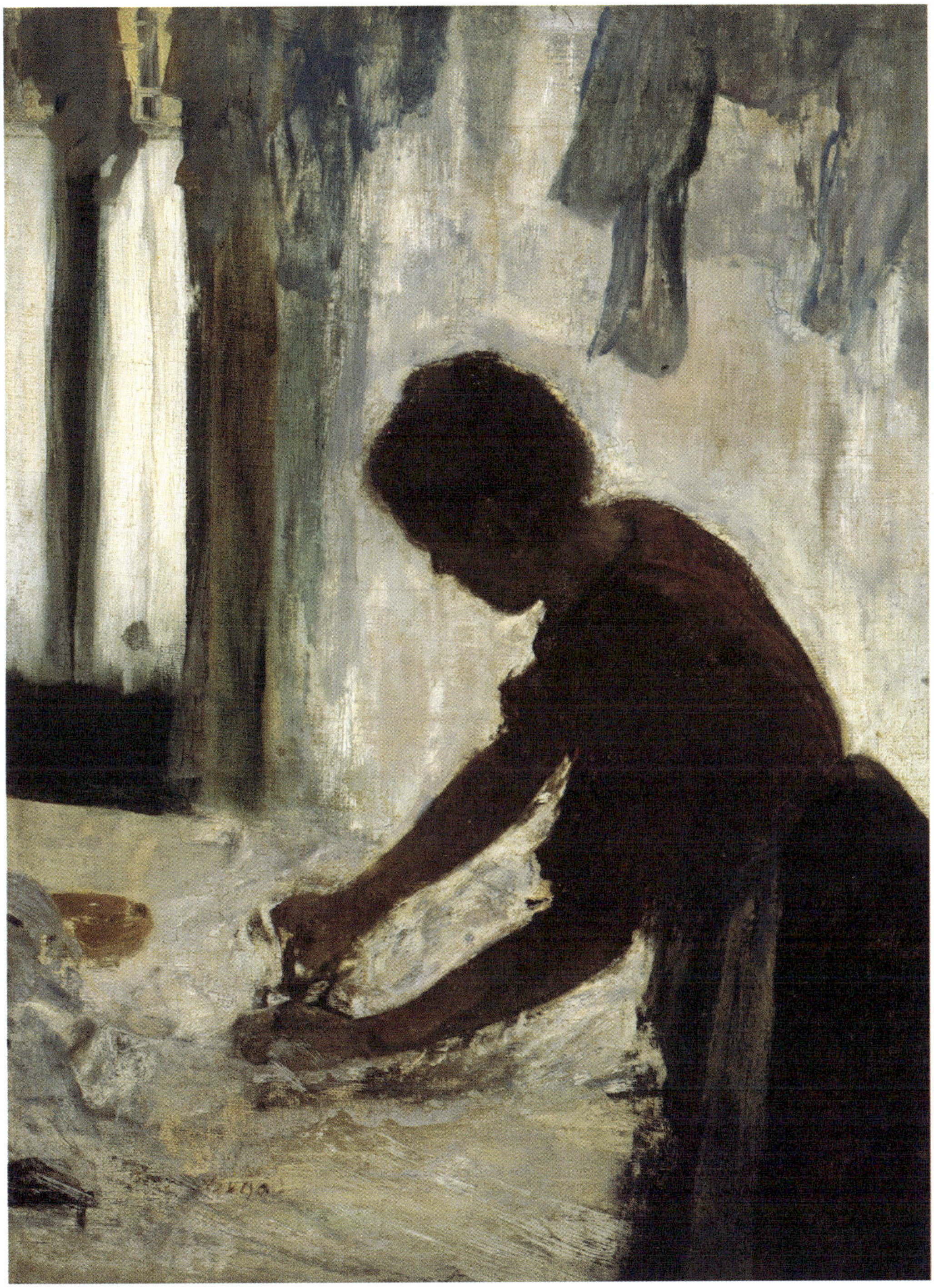

Fig.128. Edgar Degas, A WOMAN IRONING.

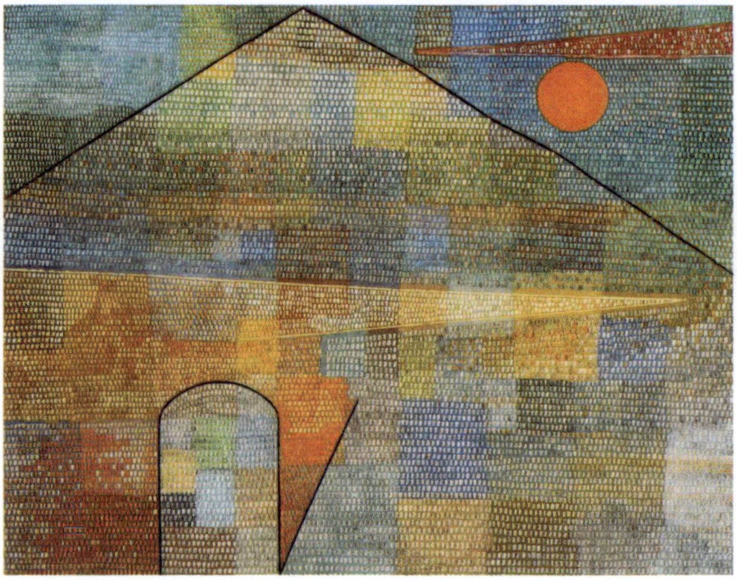

Fig. 129. Paul Klee, AD PARNASSUM.

Color Vibrations

Paul Klee, a Swiss artist, was a complex personality. He was a visual artist who also had a bent for music, having come from a musical family and having considered music as a career path before turning to visual art. He was also a bit of a scientist as well, and took a scientific interest in the way nature was constructed, offering theories on these and other matters, including the science of color. He was a writer who outlined his thinking in the book *Writings on Form and Design Theory* (a.k.a. *Paul Klee Notebooks*).

I give you this information as a prelude to discussing this impressive late work (Fig. 129). It was created in his last decade during a fervently prolific period. It is reported that he completed about five hundred works in the year 1933 alone—more than one a day! *Ad Parnassum* is a large work, especially for Klee, who made many small and intimate pieces.

Klee's work is both playful and ordered. Some of his works even have a childlike quality though they are very expertly executed. This is the signature of his work as an artist. Very imaginative works done in a very precise style. A contradiction, to be sure.

In this work, little spots of color are placed next to one another similarly to the Pointillists like Seurat, who preceded Klee. He called his method "Divisionism." If you look closely, you will see that the dots are surrounded by fine lines, differentiating the bits of color. These are the divisions he is referring to. A few bolder black lines define a triangle and a doorway, suggesting a house, but in the most minimal way.

In the upper right we see an orange circle, which you might assume symbolizes a sun, and another triangular shape giving us some kind of structure in the distance.

The name of the piece tells us he is depicting Mount Parnassus, home of Apollo and the Muses. Many see the piece as a pyramid. Klee viewed the Egyptian pyramids in 1928, so this might be a reference.

Klee referred to the dots of color within lines as "magic squares." Why magic? Presumably because of the total effect these geometric shapes make when they sit side by side. They reverberate, shimmer, and glow. As a musical person, Klee likened these reverberations to melodies, with each "note" of color working with its neighbors to make music.

Klee is telling us how to read this work. He is telling us what is important to him and how he sees the world. In doing so, he creates an imaginative vision we can enjoy. Here, color has a voice and, in a neat, buttoned-up manner, gives us music.

Fascinating, no?

Symbolic Color

It is interesting to look at this Mondrian work (Fig. 130) on the next page and compare it to the Klee, as each is composed of geometric shapes of color. *Broadway Boogie Woogie* was Mondrian's last painting, so perhaps we can see it as the culmination of his work and ultimate goal.

Mondrian is considered one of the seminal modernist artists who moved from semi-abstract into fully abstract work by the end of his life, as typified by this piece. He was a spiritual man who gradually dispensed with realist elements for the sake of his vision of universality. By shucking specific references, he believed he was transcending cultural divisions and nationalist biases, to create a new artistic vocabulary of abstract forms. The more abstract, the less specific and the more pure. He called his concept "neo-plasticism," a new way to represent truths by simple forms and colors arranged on the canvas.

This is very different from the Klee point of view, though the simplification of forms is something both artists have in common. Klee does not throw out the baby with the bathwater, so to speak—his work is semi-abstract. Mondrian's late work is

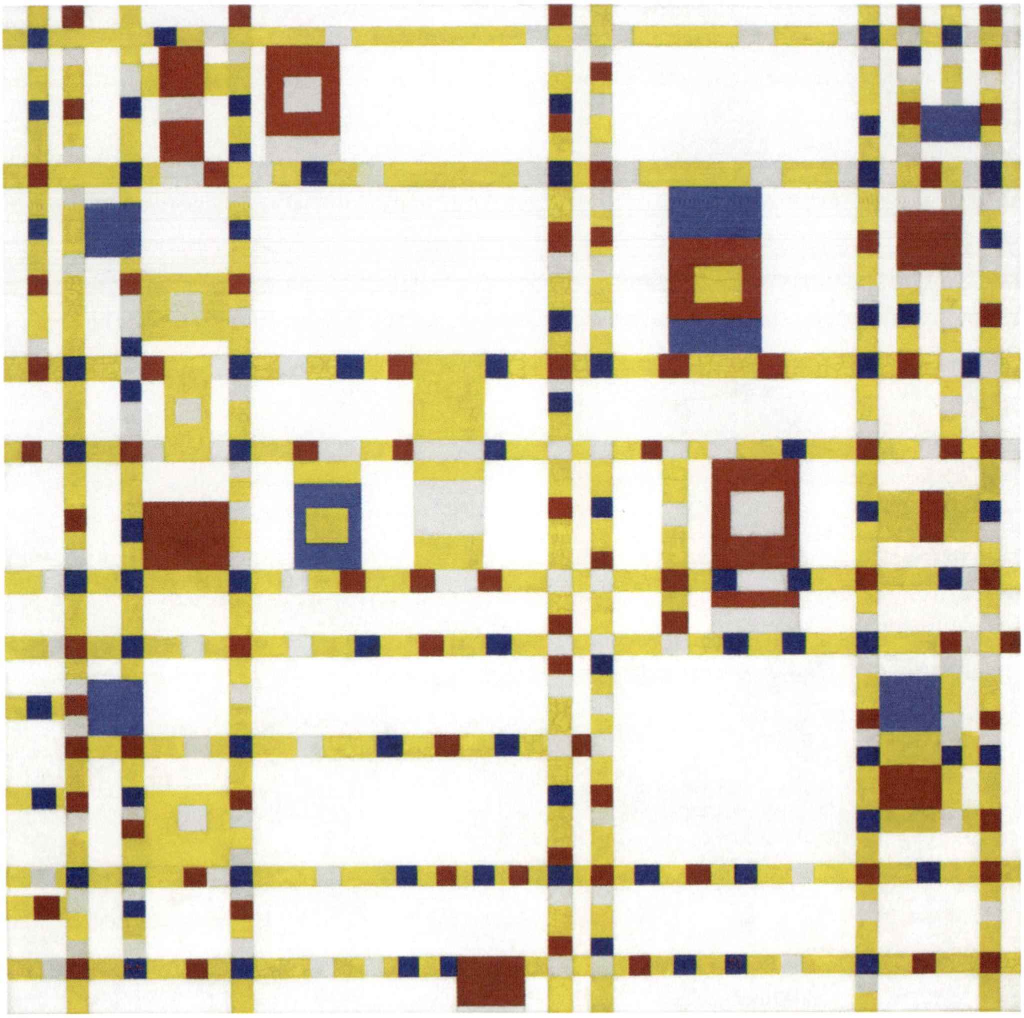

Fig. 130. Piet Mondrian, BROADWAY BOOGIE WOOGIE.

not—it is fully abstract—alas, no baby. There is no suggestion of objects or illusion of three-dimensional space. The simple colored shapes in Mondrian's world live on a flat plane.

Something the artists do share are their musical references. Mondrian's piece is named after a place and a style of music. Is he suggesting a certain kind of rhythm is depicted therein? Apparently, Mondrian was very interested in both music and dance—other pieces of his are named after dance forms, like *Fox Trot*—so I think we can assume that the squares and colors are organized to suggest a certain kind of movement. They may also suggest the flashing lights of Broadway. (Having lived in New York most of my life, I see a reference to the New York City subway map too, but this may be too far-fetched—Mondrian may never have seen it.)

Klee's squares of color have a sensuality that Mondrian lacks, this quite deliberately. Klee's color variations are sensitive as they vibrate one against the other. Mondrian's colors are primary, painted flat, and their overall effect is due more to their positioning in the grid he creates. Perhaps they suggest neon lights, where Klee's suggest daylight.

Klee is still connected to the real, to the senses. Mondrian's construction is more a visual created out of a concept.

QUESTIONS. Color conundrums:

- Why do you think an artist might prefer a limited palette over many colors?
- Do you enjoy black-and-white photographs as much as color ones?
- What are your favorite or preferred colors, and why?
- Do you respond emotionally to the Klcc and Mondrian works, and why?
- Could you enjoy art if you were color-blind?

6. FOUR SCULPTURES: FOUR INTENTIONS

The crouching figure has a long history in art. There is something about the human being assuming this posture that has interested artists through the ages. Perhaps it says something about humility to see the figure brought down on his knees. In any case, the posture is a much interpreted subject.

On the next few pages, let's look at some images and try to discern the artists' intentions (Figs. 131–134). Here we are looking at four sculptures of crouching figures, the first created in the ancient world, three to ten centuries before Christ; the second by the Renaissance master Michelangelo in the sixteenth century; the third a small crouching figure created by the sculptor Maillol in the twentieth century; and lastly a massive twenty-first-century piece called *Exposure* created by the sculptor Antony Gormley.

What they have in common is that they are all depictions of crouching figures. What is pertinent about them is how they arose, for what purpose, what they meant to the artist creating them, and how we view them. They spring from utterly different realms, times, cultures, artistic credos, and intents.

It is remarkable that the ancient stone sculpture has survived intact, and that the subtle etching on the face is still visible.

The figure is depicted with the arms covering the ears, perhaps in fear. The figure in crouch always suggests the human in somewhat humbled state, brought to its knees. Here we have no idea what the humbling factor might have been.

Stylistically the ancient sculpture is reminiscent of sculptures made millennia later by Derain, who made his own little crouching figure, and the better-known sculptor Brancusi, who created a work called *The Kiss*. In their works, the artists deliberately simplify their forms to give them a primitive look. This is not due to lack of observation or lack of knowledge, but rather to their desire to reduce the figure to a simple form. These figures arise out of Cubism, a movement whose aim was to see and describe nature as a series of planes, shapes, and layers without allegiance to their representational complexities. Look up the Derain and Brancusi sculptures for comparison.

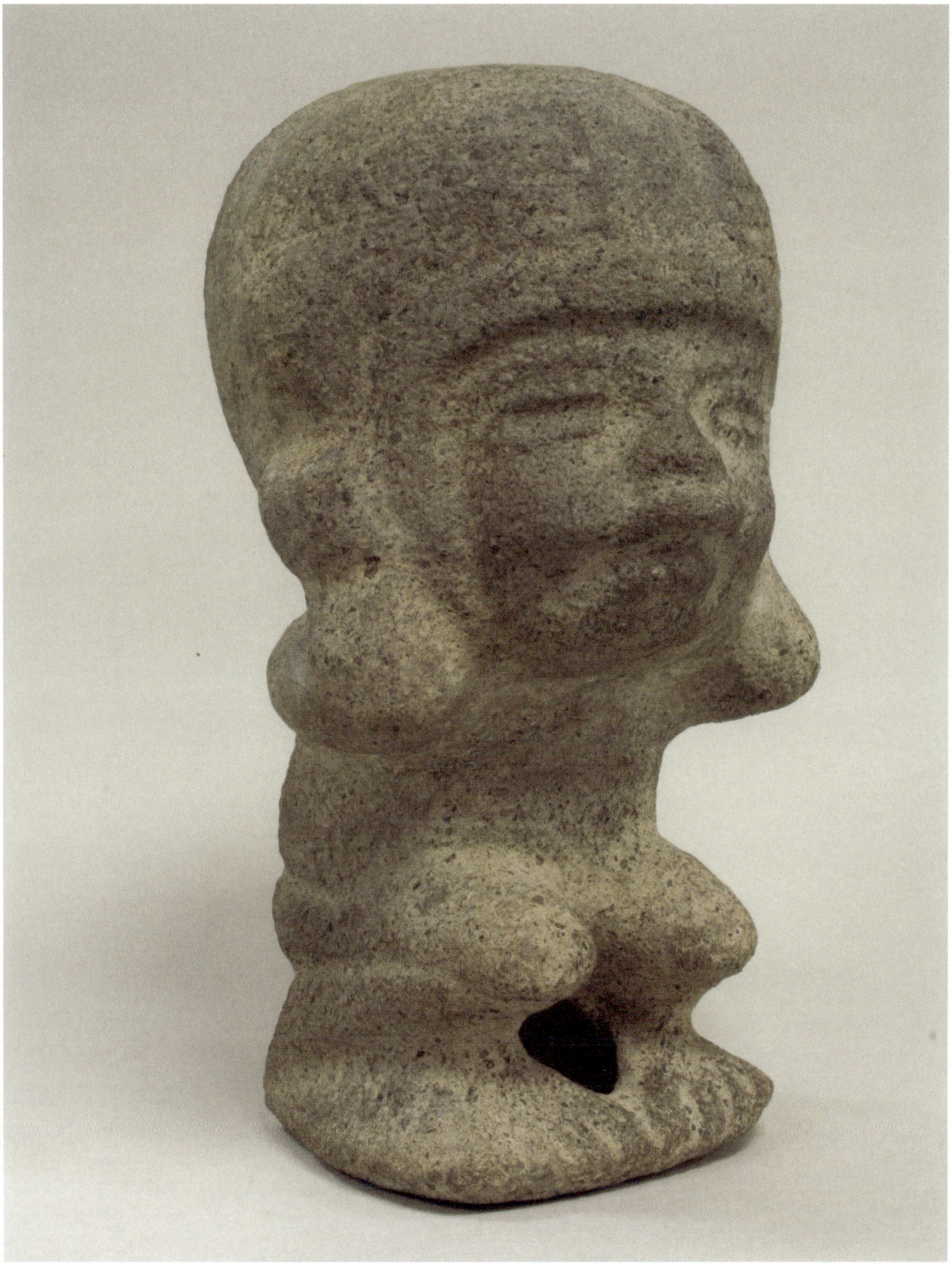

Fig. 131. Artist unknown, CROUCHING FIGURE.

Classical

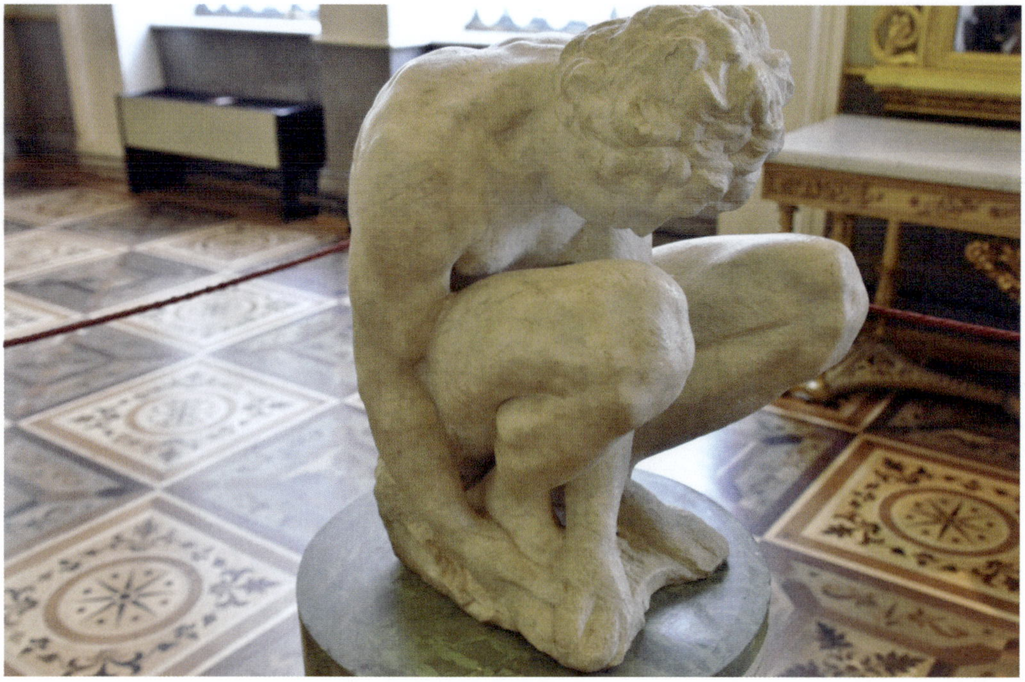

Fig. 132. Michelangelo, CROUCHING BOY.

Modern

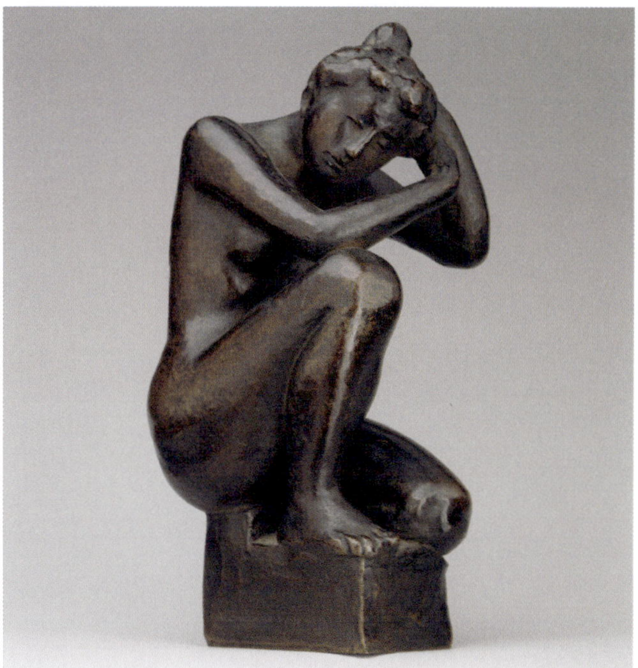

Fig. 133. Aristide Maillol, CROUCHING GIRL.

Contemporary

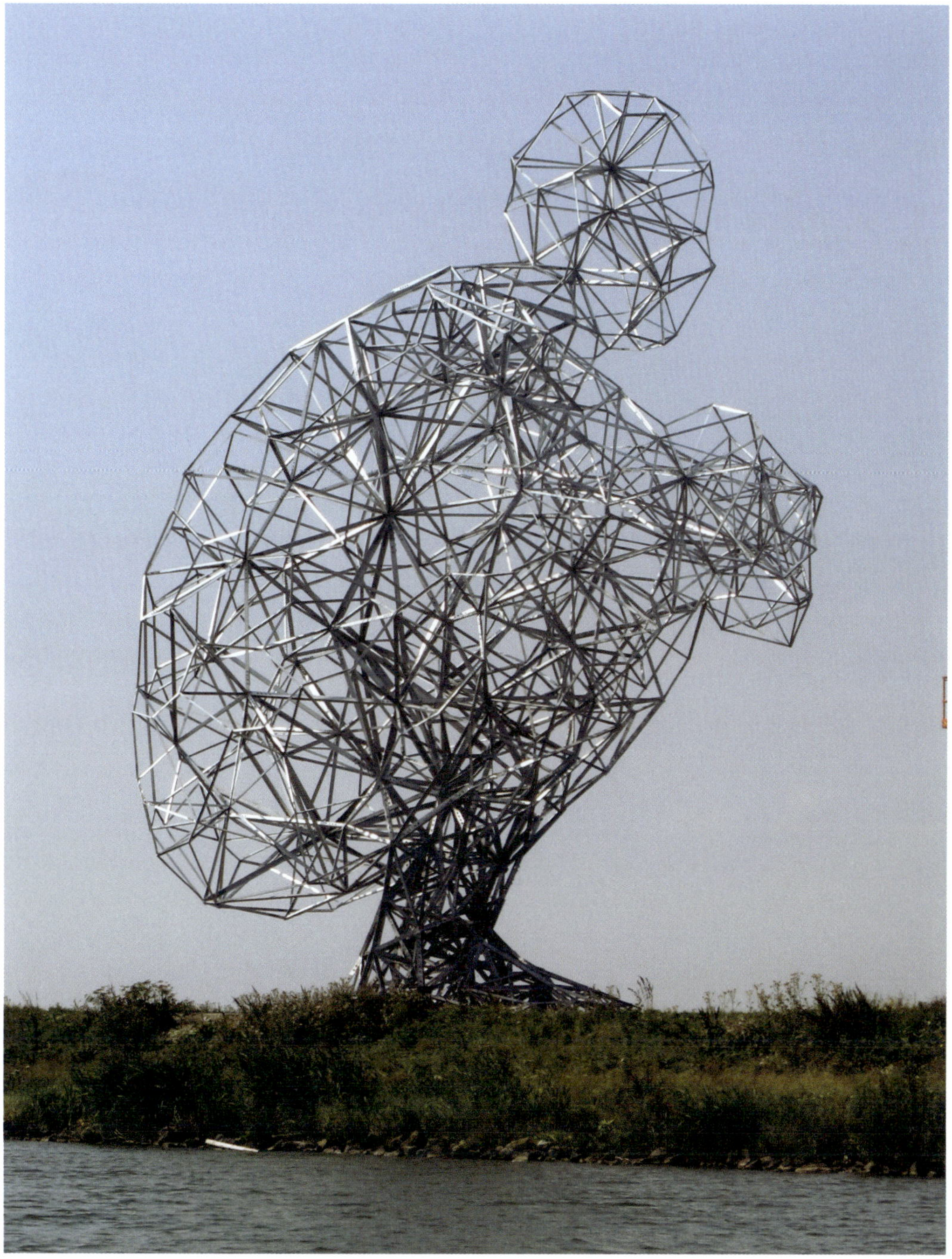

Fig. 134. Antony Gormley, EXPOSURE.

The Michelangelo sculpture was originally made for the Medici Chapel and ultimately found a home in the Hermitage. It is a small sculpture, a gangling collection of muscled limbs folded in on themselves. The boy is tending to his foot and is caught is an unselfconscious moment. The downcast pose has suggested to scholars that the boy is more than an ordinary boy and that the work represents an "unborn soul" or a "suffering soul." This seems like a stretch, perhaps an attempt to aggrandize the work.

It is a realistic work.

The Maillol, to the contrary, is a stylistic work, made for a decorative purpose as the artist made it to sit atop a fountain. It is a small, naturalistic, rather delicate work. Though the croucher seems uncomfortable, there is no particular gravitas to this work.

When we turn to the modern work, we have an entirely different purpose and intensity. This is a work of exceptional scale, a piece of earth art actually, designed to become part of an environment and define it. It is a conceptual work and created to carry a message.

At eighty-five feet tall and weighing sixty tons, the Gormley sculpture is a work of engineering that could not have been created by the artists of the past. It took six years to create, and this with the aid of a manufacturing company and engineering firm. The original form of the crouching figure is based on a plaster cast the artist made of himself in the desired position. The form was then translated into a geometrical system of metal rods with the aid of a computer program.

It was essential that the work be made of rods and not solid because the sculpture is made to become part of the environment, to define it, and to change as the environment changes. It is a sculpture that is connected to the environment and carries a message about climate change. As the climate changes and the sea rises, the sculpture will begin to disappear. This was anticipated by the artist and made for that purpose; the message is more important than the piece itself. The open spaces between the rods allow the viewer to look into and through the work out to the land and sky. The work becomes a living part of our time and a statement by the artist. Is this conceptual art?

There is no accident that all four artists chose the crouching figure as thematic material. A figure bent in this way shows his humanity, may suggest sorrow, a bowing to the reality of existence. It is a subject that interests artists who are attuned to the human condition and a very expressive way to express humility and, ultimately, mortality.

QUESTIONS. Comparing and contrasting:

- Which of these four works do you prefer, and why?
- Does a work which has a message, like the Gormley, impress you more?
- Do you think it is important for art to have a message?
- What message would you choose to deliver through art?

7. DRAWING AND PAINTING:

As we've mentioned, the distinction between drawing and painting is a fine one, as every two-dimensional work includes elements of both. (I am not neglecting other two-dimensional media like photography and collage as they also have equivalent emphases.) But every artist has a different orientation and passion. For some it is the line, and we call these exemplars draftsmen or draftswomen. For others it is the color and materiality of the paint, and we call these exemplars painters. There are many examples in each category, and nuances within those categories.

In many cases, the demarcation follows other categorizations—classicists tend to fall on the drawing side, and romantics on the painting. This is why: To draw requires strength of mind—clarity, organization, the ability to visualize space. Painting is more visceral and sensual and requires a certain exuberance.

The very greatest artists do both well, but even if they do, they are still stronger on one side or the other, and are generally thought of as great draftsmen or painters. In our games chapter, you'll have a chance to do your own analysis as far as this is concerned. It may help as we look at three works of art over the next few pages—one by a great draftsman, Ingres (Fig. 135); one by a consummate painter, Degas (Fig. 136); and one of my own on the same subject (Fig. 137). Eighty-plus years separate the execution of the Ingres and Degas works, and it is more than a century from the Degas to my effort. This is evidence that the evolution of art is slower than one might think and is characterized by small steps with occasional leaps.

If the subject interests you, I encourage you to study the magnificent bath paintings by Pierre Bonnard, who found the subject so resonant. They are symphonies of juicy, sparkling color. Note how he treated the bathroom tiles with as much gusto and attention as the woman in the tub.

Ingres is considered a neoclassicist, and this work was created while he was a student at the French Academy in Rome. It has been in residence at the Louvre since 1879, which is a testament to its merit.

Ingres made both drawings and paintings, and his draftsmanship is really exceptional. Here we have a beautifully rendered figure in an elegant pose, and everything about the work—the composition, color scheme, balance between darks and lights, the foreshortening of the legs, etc.—could not be more harmonious, pleasing, and correct. Ingres's point of view creates a lovely but non-sensual image, and there is nothing that is discordant or out of place.

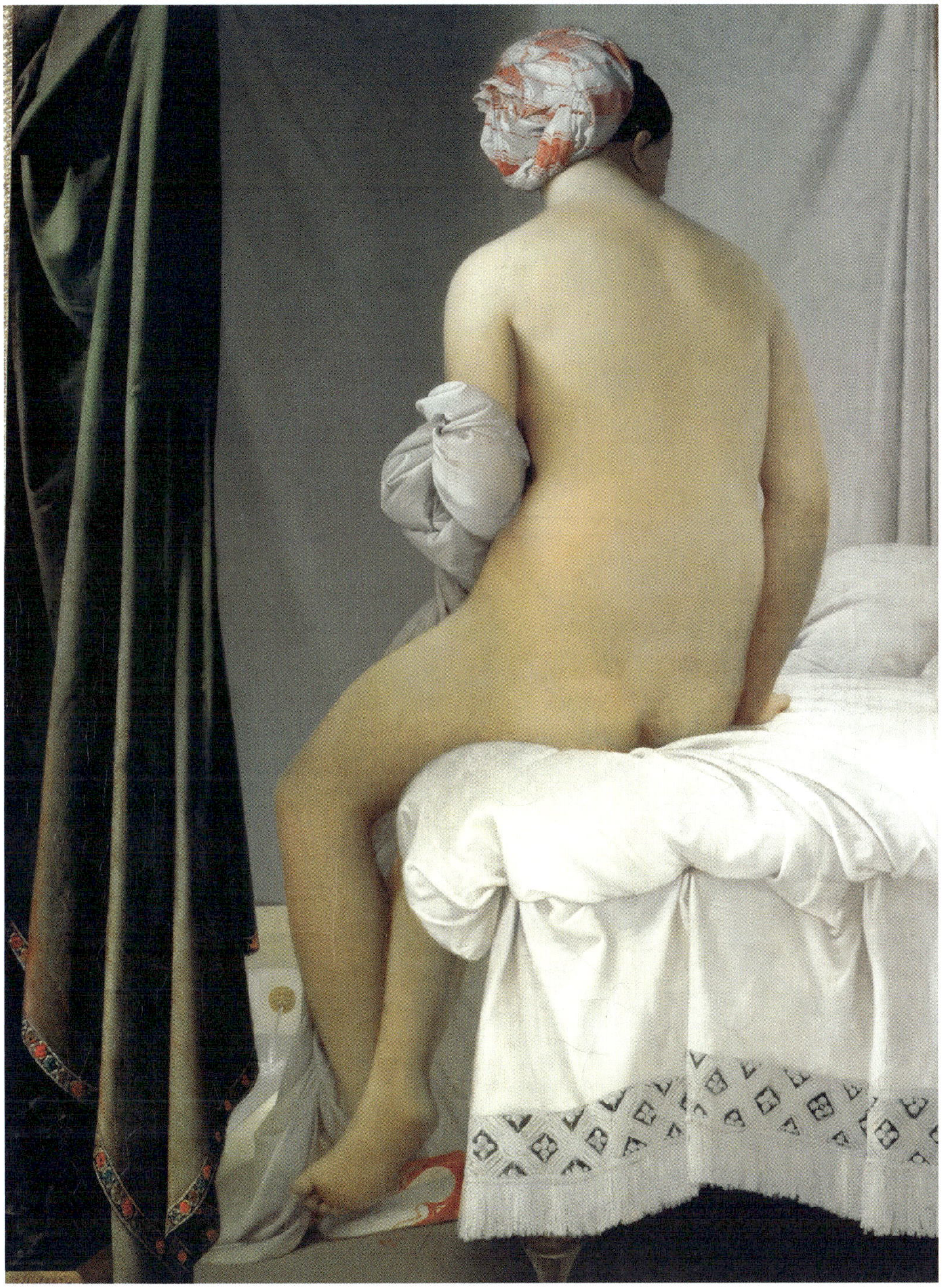

Fig. 135. Jean-Auguste-Dominique Ingres, LA GRANDE BAIGNEUSE.

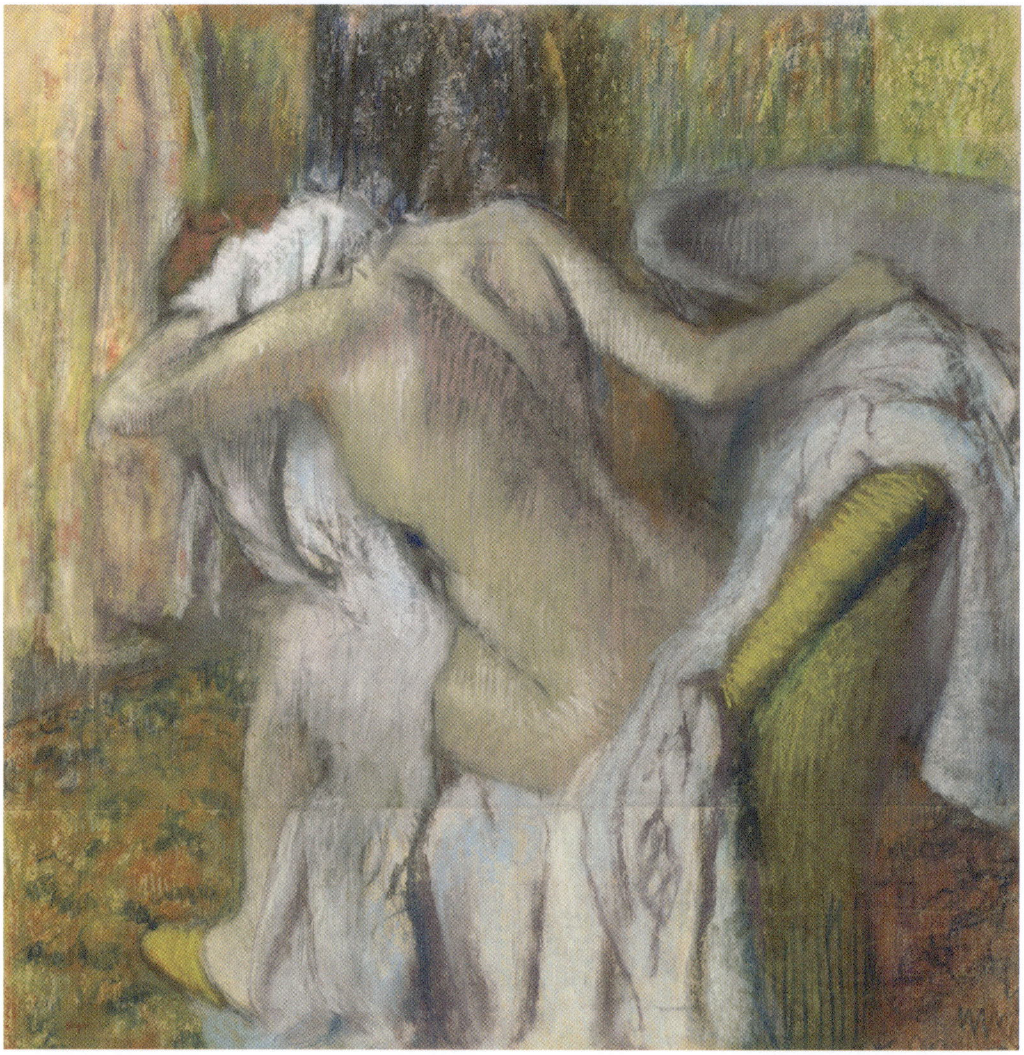

Fig. 136. Edgar Degas, AFTER THE BATH, WOMAN DRYING HERSELF.

Degas was a sensualist, and this lovely pastel is a superb example of his perceptual talents. As opposed to the classical Ingres with its clearly defined outlines and solid forms, Degas gives us a fog of resonating contiguous color mixtures, a virtual tapestry of notes.

Not only is the figure itself diffuse, the soft notes connect her to the chair and tub, the figure no more or less important than they. We see the picture as a whole, a weaving of texture and color.

Note also the expressive drawing, another characteristic of romanticized imagery. While the Ingres figure sits straight and tall, the Degas is oddly positioned, the better to emphasize the expressive quality of this work. Though his drawing is masterful, Degas is a painter par excellence.

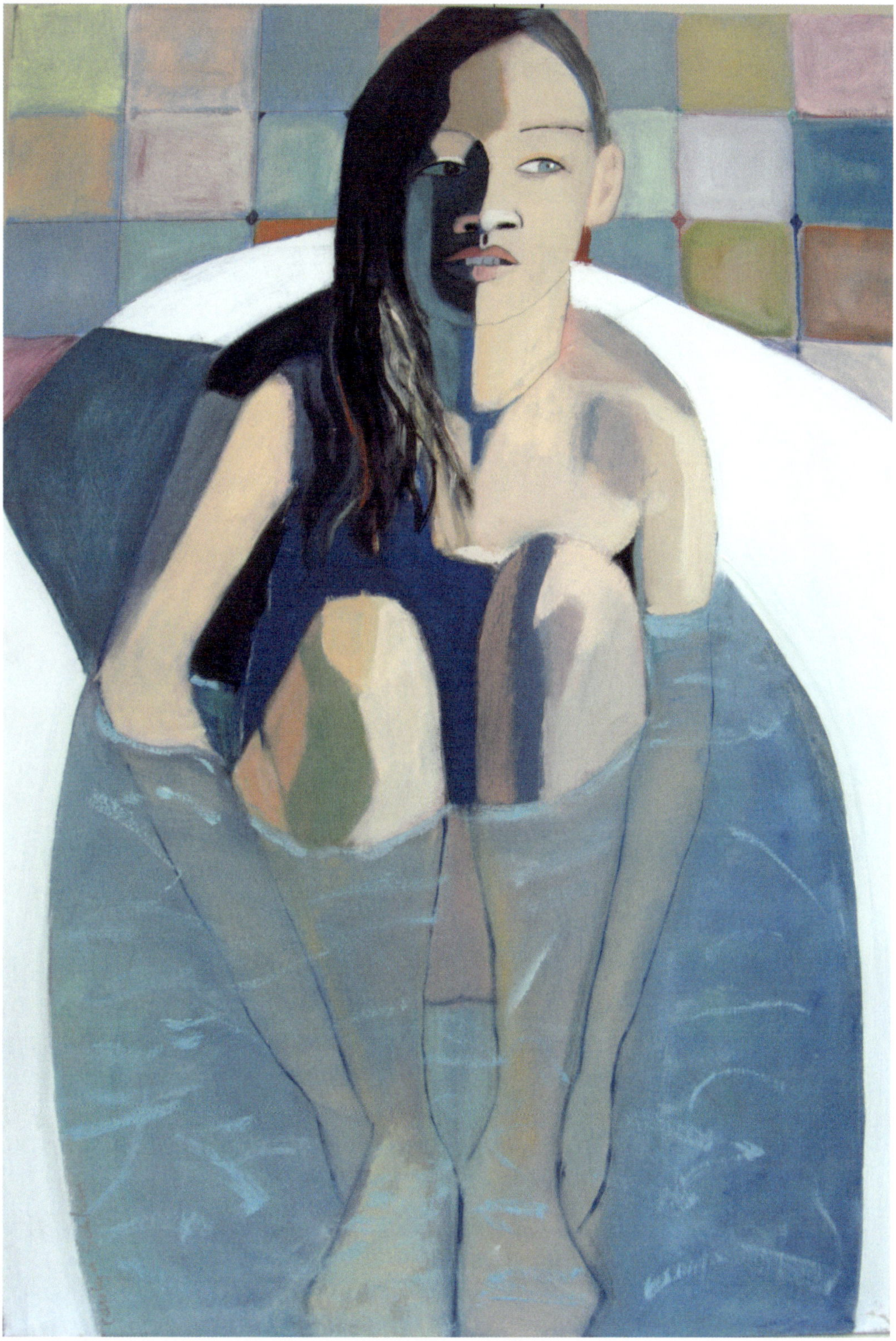

Fig. 137. Carolyn Schlam, BATH.

As every painter explores the drawing and painting proportions a little differently, my own work, *Bath*, lands somewhere in the middle of these two. It is neither as clearly demarked as the Ingres nor as fluid and painterly as the Degas.

I include it here not to compare my own work to that of these great painters, but simply to illustrate this point. When you look at art from any period, try to identify the artist's intention and focus, his preferences and special talents. This is another way to understand and appreciate what you are looking at.

With *Bath*, I was interested in the water's effect on the immersed portions of the figure and the way they contrasted with the sharper delineation of her body parts not affected by water. Describing these subtleties with paint was my intention.

QUESTIONS. Making it personal:

- What do you think would be your strong suit: drawing or painting?
- What would you choose as a subject?
- Would you be a realist or an abstract artist?
- What would be unique about your vision?

8. FLIGHTS OF FANTASY

All artworks are works of the imagination, but some have a more fanciful bent. Not every artist is content to study the light on an apple and render it with solemnity. Some are dreamers, and their bent is to conjure fantastic creatures or new worlds, or environments where gravity has no place and donkeys fly.

There are actually many more examples of artists attempting to imitate the real rather than inventing the surreal, or the unreal. Perhaps the world is fantastic enough to most artists. To a select contingent, though, the real will not suffice, and these artists inspire us.

Let's have a look at a few of these.

Seen on the next page and measuring roughly 7 × 9 inches, this tiny etching by the visionary English poet and artist William Blake is an example of the use of art to depict an imaginary scene or vision (Fig. 138). Here in this work, which was purported to be Blake's favorite, he shows the figure Urizen crouching on a cloud and measuring the dark void with a tool.

Blake was also a poet who viewed imagination as primary, an emanation of God, but in reality his depictions of gods and angels were not as fanciful as they might have seemed. He claimed to have visions of these throughout his life, so though hailed a visionary, perhaps he was just painting his own reality. Something to ponder. Interestingly, this work of art was chosen for the cover of another visionary's book—Stephen Hawking's *God Created the Integers*.

One of the greatest and most beloved practitioners of the fanciful in art was the Russian painter Marc Chagall, who studied in St. Petersburg and painted primarily in France. He was born Moishe Segal and spent his childhood in a town near Vitebsk in what was then Belarus. His family were Hasidic Jews. *Chagall* is a variant of *Segal*.

In spite of humble roots, Chagall was blessed with a wonderful childhood and the happiness of his early family life, as well as the cast of whimsical characters of his folk art environment. They continued to inform and embellish his work even as he became a master of the visual arts and expressed himself as a painter, illustrator, and in myriad media including stained glass, stage sets, ceramics, and the like.

His work is peopled by brides and grooms, musicians of all types, lovers and acrobats and donkeys and birds, all of them released from the mundane. Gravity was an irrelevance to this painter of visions as he often permits his animals and figures to float in the sky. Chagall's work is joy incarnate, and if he was as happy an individual as his canvases suggest, he was a lucky man indeed.

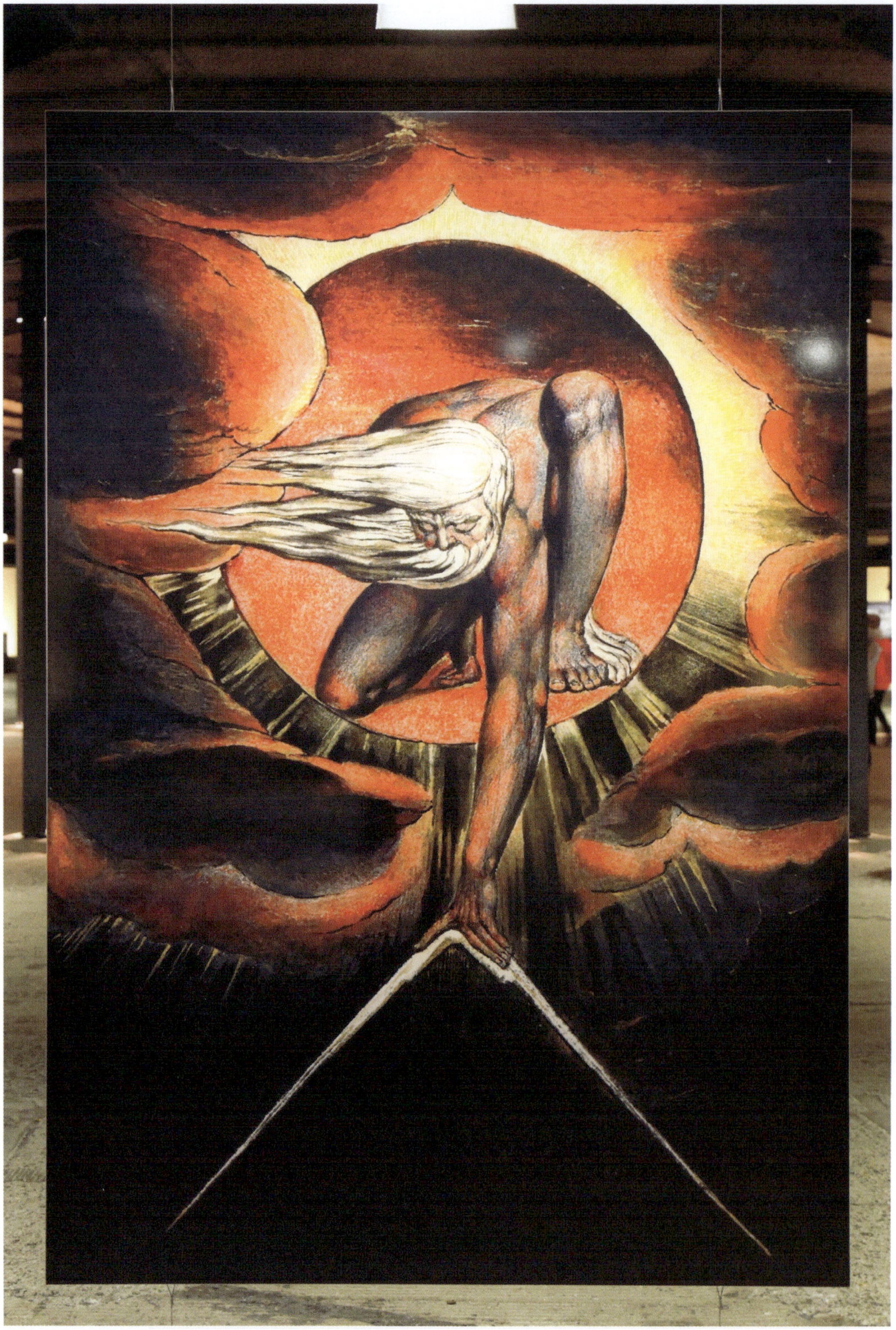

Fig. 138. William Blake, THE ANCIENT OF DAYS.

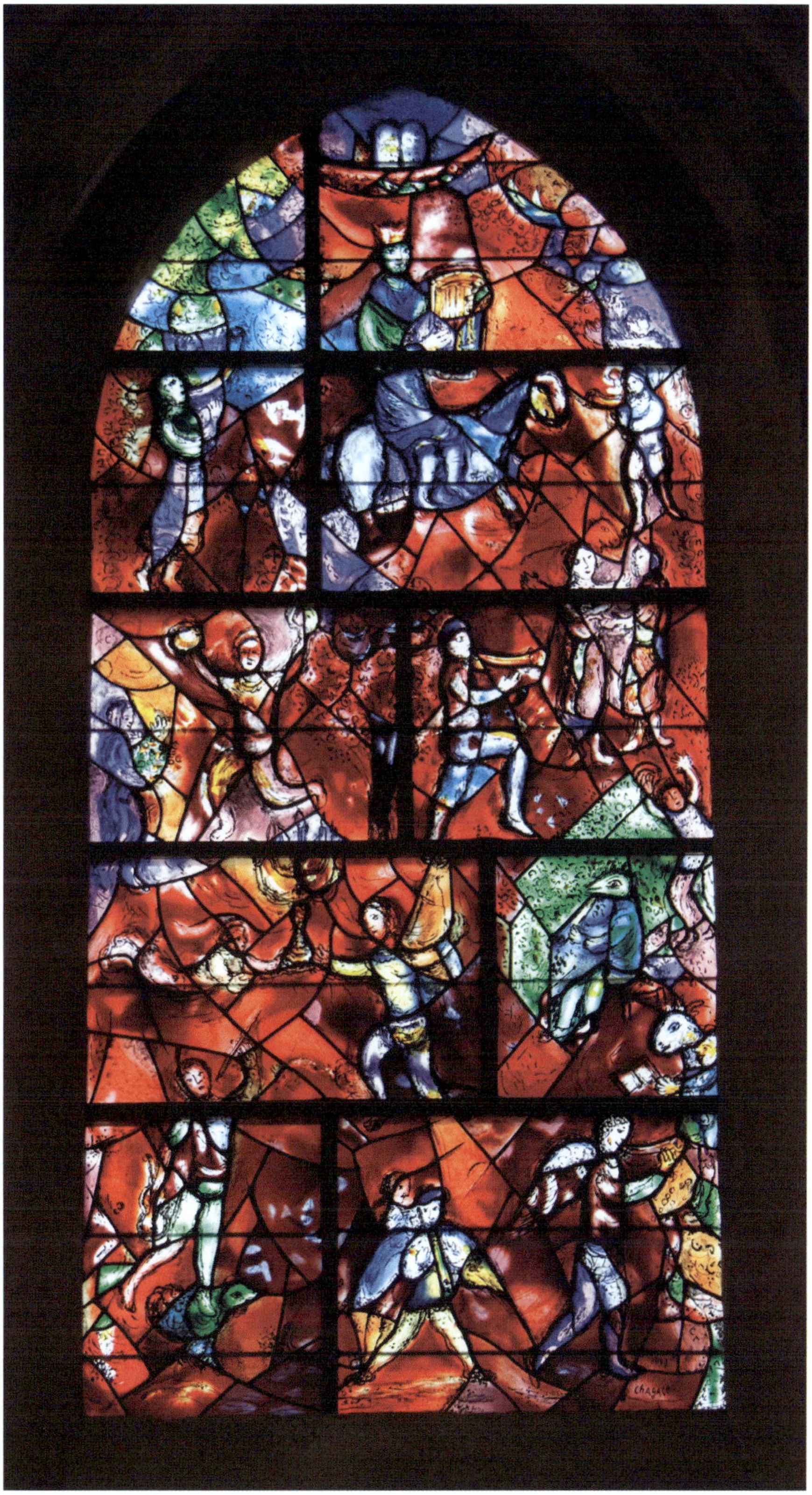

Fig. 139. Marc Chagall, WINDOW AT CHICESTER CATHEDRAL.

Chagall mostly drew from his imagination, which, as you might agree, is difficult. It requires that the artist have a pretty good visual memory and be able to imagine figures in different positions and relationships. Being willing to draw without dependence on actual models or photographs, though not a prerequisite to bring an artist, is certainly a gift.

Chagall's joyous world was delivered in primary colors. His love of color probably propelled him to work in glass, where the actual light is a participant in the art, and works in this medium have a special transcendent quality. His exquisite Jerusalem windows at Hebrew University depict the twelve tribes of Israel, and are something to see. On the previous page, we are looking at the last commissioned window Chagall executed at the age of ninety for Chichester Cathedral in the United Kingdom (Fig. 139).

It encompasses the vision of a happy man who elevated folklore to a kind of spiritual joy. His inspiration for this window is so telling—it is inspired by Psalm 50, "Let everything that hath breath praise the Lord."

Childlike? No child could communicate this way. It is the innocence and childlike qualities that only a master painter could realize. A true visionary, his life and work expressed the joy of art more than anyone else I can think of.

Now we leap to a painting by Rousseau, also a work of fantasy, and entirely different from the two we have discussed. Here we have a reclining nude—think of the traditional nudes we have analyzed here—on a couch in the jungle (Fig. 140). The figure is said to be that of his Polish mistress, Yadwigha, and the stylized jungle taken from studies at the Paris Museum of Natural History and the Jardin des Plantes.

So the work was created from observation, not imagination, but what is fantastical is the juxtaposition of the figure and the highly stylized jungle environment. It is the incongruity that establishes the dreamlike motif so effectively.

This is literally a painting of a dream. It is really quite wonderful, for several reasons.

First, its size. Here, it has been set at a small size for the purpose of reprinting it in a book, but when viewed in person, the work is so large that the viewer feels he can penetrate the environment. The flat paint and stylized drawing are beautiful and they totally fill the space. It is a tapestry without any holes or minor notes.

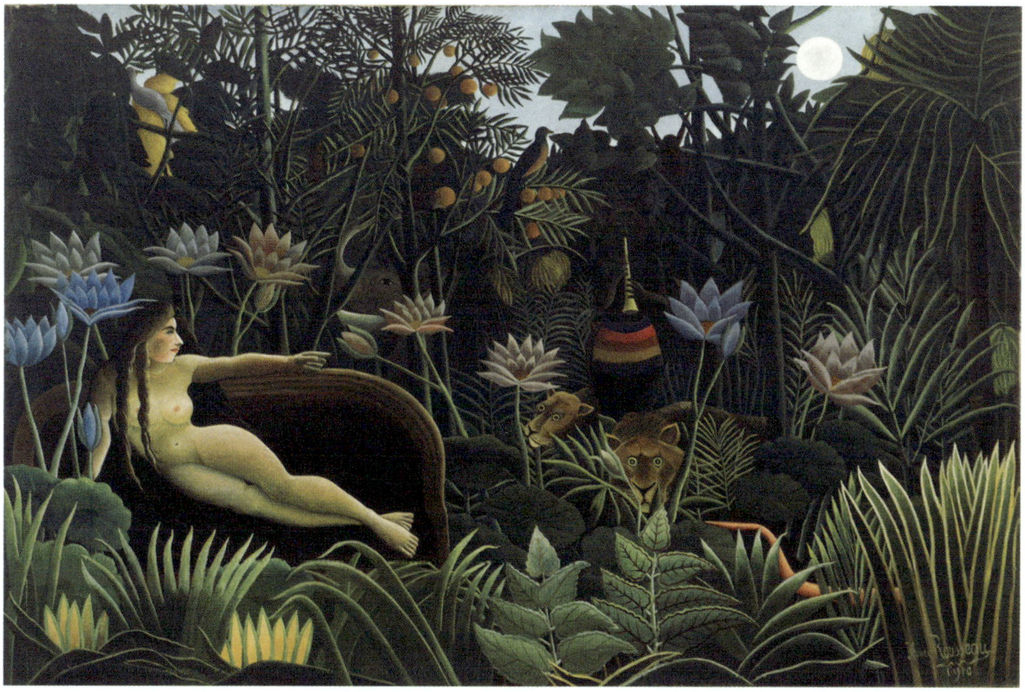

Fig. 140. Henri Rousseau, THE DREAM.

I remember seeing this painting in the Museum of Modern Art when I was quite young, before I went to art school. It made a tremendous impression on me for its harmony and complexity. I still like it very much after all these years. You too?

QUESTIONS. Think on these:

- How does the depiction of fantasy differ from surrealism?
- What do Chagall's flying figures signify, and how do they make you feel?
- How would you paint an angel?
- What is your favorite genre in literature, and how does it correspond to your favorite genre in art?

9. DOWN TO EARTH: THREE REALISTS: EAKINS, HENRI, HULINGS

To classify a painting as a realist work is only a first step in identifying it and does not begin to define the artist. In fact, there are myriad ways to depict what we think of as the "real," and each realist's signature is different. The painter is creating an illusion out of paint and we should keep this in mind as we study his often mesmerizingly and seemingly accurate creations. There are no actual figures or water or sky—what we see is a brilliant translation of an observation of three-dimensional space.

I've selected three realist artists for you to examine and consider here. The first, **Thomas Eakins** (1844–1916), is acknowledged as one of the most important and gifted American artists, and he was also an art educator. **Robert Henri** (1865–1929), who we will consider next, was also a prominent voice in arts education, and in fact, I studied painting with a student of his, Norman Raeben. **Clark Hulings** (1922–2011) was an American painter with a keen eye and deft hand.

Eakins was an exacting academician, and his goal was almost scientific accuracy. To this objective, he went so far as to take anatomy lessons and even observe surgeries. He worked from the live nude model, slightly scandalous at the time, and strove, above all, for clear and deliberate authenticity. No romantic flourishes for Eakins.

Eakins is probably best known for a painting he did of an actual surgery, entitled *The Gross Clinic*, one of his largest, and one he was exceedingly proud of. The surgical skill with which he depicted the event, blood and all, made this excellent work rather uncollectible, and in the end, he sold it to his college for a disappointing $200.

As you would expect, Eakins's work has a rather somber palette, naturalistic, to be sure, and reminiscent of an artist he much admired, Velázquez. For this book, I selected a painting of rowers, partly because the sketch he did for the painting was available for you to study (Figs. 141 and 142).

Superb execution and restraint are the Eakins signatures. Though he achieves a verisimilitude of water, sky, and stone, these are rendered in a tight manner, without evidence of brushstrokes. The work is very purposefully composed. Without doubt, he shows us what beauty can be found in this most stern and sober context.

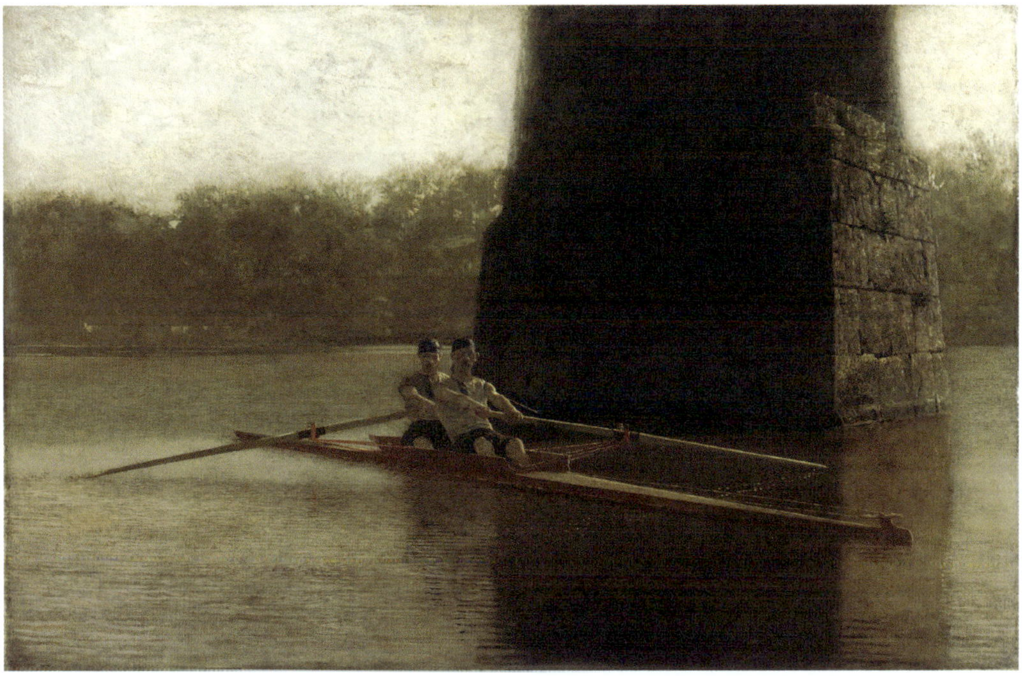

Fig. 141. Thomas Eakins, THE PAIR-OARED SHELL.

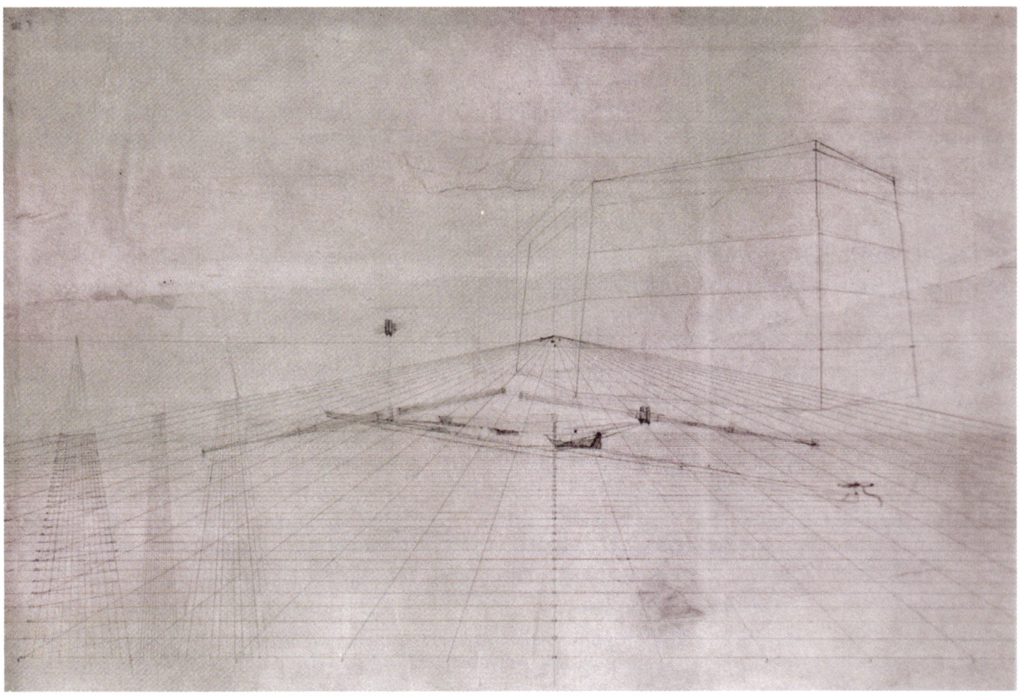

Fig. 142. Thomas Eakins, PERSPECTIVE DRAWING FOR "THE PAIR-OARED SHELL."

Eakins was a forerunner of another movement in American art called the Ashcan School. We've discussed here how new movements in art often arise in reaction to existing ones, and so too with this group. Several were students of realist teachers at the Pennsylvania Academy of the Fine Arts, and included Henri, Luks, Glackens, and Sloan. Other artists like Prendergast later joined this group. They worked primarily in New York, and sought out urban scenes of everyday life.

A departure from the carefully composed and rendered realism of Eakins, for instance, the Ashcan School painters went in for a more spontaneous, gestural, and animated painting style. They preferred the gritty streets to languid country landscapes, boxing matches to scenes of domestic life, prostitutes to grandes dames.

Robert Henri was one of these, and also a spokesperson for the group. With the help of one of his students, Margaret Ryerson, he put his thoughts into a book called *The Art Spirit*. My painting teacher, Norman Raeben, with whom I studied in the studios of Carnegie Hall, was a student of Henri's and passed his teaching down to his students.

I wrote a book called *The Creative Path: A View from the Studio on the Making of Art*, which encapsulates the kind of hands-on direct painting from life that Henri taught and Norman passed on to us. I encourage you to get a copy of my book if you would like to learn more about this worldview and approach to painting.

In any case, we have an example of a Henri work to look at and review (Fig. 143).

This painting of a snowy winter street is emblematic of the Ashcan approach. Neatness flies out the window. The artist's intention is to capture the feeling of the scene, the crunch of cold snow, the gray gloom of the winter day, the trudge of the horse-drawn carriage through the city streets.

Notice the scribbles to define the windows, the loose brushwork marking a human figure, the little patches of white to say snow. Nothing is defined because it all exists in an atmospheric soup. This was derived from the Impressionists, but the Ashcanners' atmosphere was not one of sunshine and iridescent color, rather the drear of a New York cloudy day.

Kind of a workingman's world, the reality not of high fashion and elite environments, but an urban grit and grime in paint. This is a realism based on impression, sensation, and affect, where description is not the intent. The specificity is in the emotion engendered by the scene, not the objects that it includes.

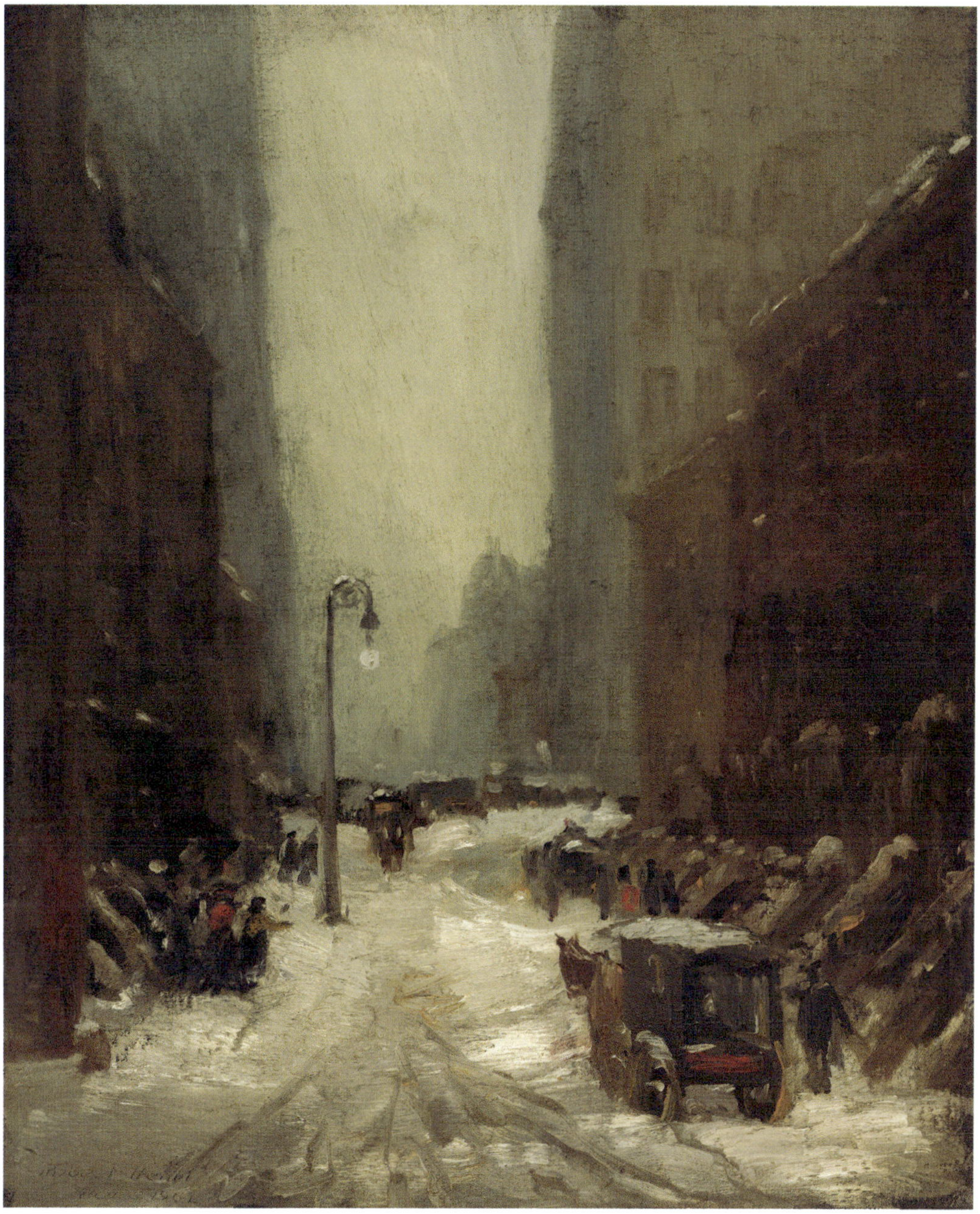

Fig. 143. Robert Henri, SNOW IN NEW YORK.

Many people connect modern art with abstraction, but realism is not a thing of the past. Modern and contemporary artists have found and continue to find the genre stimulating as they endeavor to make it personal and incorporate a modern world view. Clark Hulings (1922–2011) who lived into the twenty-first century, was considered a kind of modern documentarian, as he continued to represent a portrait of the people and places he encountered in a rich lifetime of art-making.

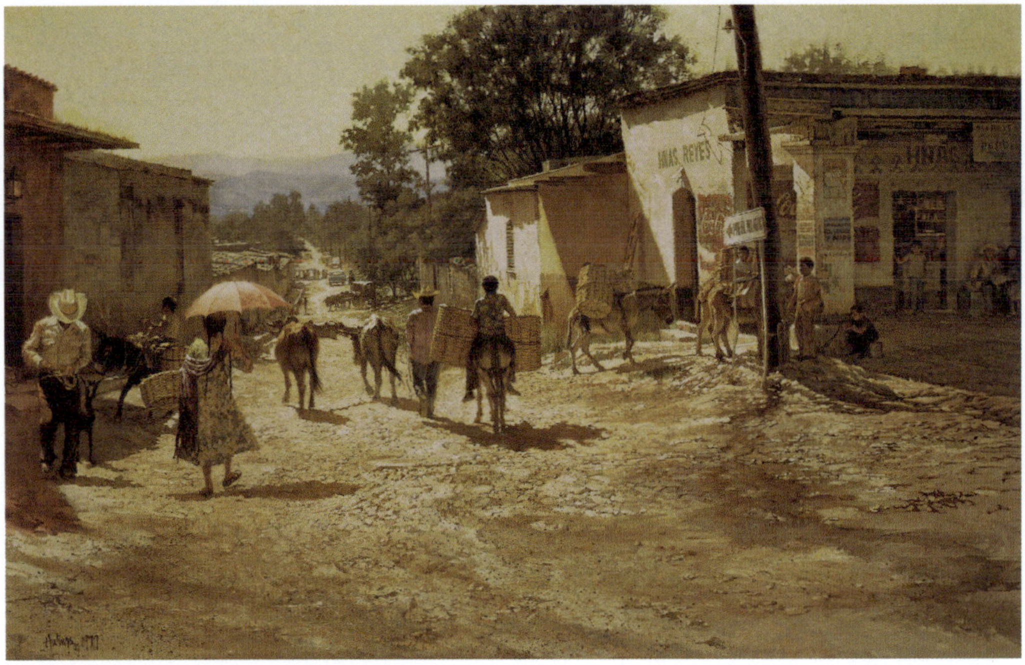

Fig. 144. Clark Hulings, THE PINK PARASOL.

We looked at two practitioners of realism—Eakins and Henri—who had a very different methodology, Eakins constructing and planning his works and Henri painting alla prima to capture the moment. Hulings's method was rather an amalgam of the two. He worked from life, but his pictures are not "of the moment." They are composites of multiple views and scenes, combined to achieve a very deliberate realism, with carefully selected elements. Not a slave to the camera's eye, he even went so far as to cut and paste figures onto the canvas, trying them out for placement and effect, and when pleased, to add these figures into the appropriate area. I was surprised to learn that he was not averse to using modern tools like Photoshop to manipulate and design his imagery.

With this information in mind, have a look at the painting of *The Pink Parasol* (Fig. 144). I am told that the lady in the *Parasol* was not present in the scene but introduced by Hulings from another source. This makes the painting even more impressive, as this figure seems perfectly in place, with appropriate shadows, correctly sized, and taking her place in a river of motion with the other figures in the painting.

Hulings's eye for light and texture is first-rate, and he manages to create a palpable light and temperature that makes the use of the parasol so believable in this context. The cracked earthen floor, bright sunlight on the side of the building, and coolness of shade and shadows, is so well rendered that you not only see it and believe it, but can feel its authenticity.

This is what good realism is all about, but know that the authenticity is not a function of copying or imitation. It is the result of considerable thought, experiments (as with the placement of objects), observation, and practice. I read that Hulings always included a bit of red in every painting. It was his way of calling attention to something important; using the red to attract the viewer's eye. Red is a power color (remember that red signature in the Courbet?). Be on the lookout for red notes as you hunt through the museum.

QUESTIONS. Some final ones:

- What are the features that make a painting look "real"?
- Do you prefer a hard-edged, linear realism or a soft-edged, painterly realism?
- What wows you the most?
- Has this book made you want to make some art yourself?

There is so much that goes into making a work of art—all that I have mentioned and then, on top of it, that soupçon of personal magic that each artist brings to his work. The spark of genius that makes a picture a work of art.

As you look at art more and more, try to compare works one to the other, as I have tried to do here. Finding connections, seeing patterns, echoes of one artist's work in another—all will contribute to your appreciation of art. Though we are all individuals, artists borrow ideas from one another and are inspired by work that is similar and also very different. They then go on to reinterpret it in their own ways. That's how we grow as individual artists and how we advance the art form.

Chapter 14

The Future of Art: Where We Go from Here

Every now and then someone declares that "Painting is dead." Tired. Exhausted. Yesterday. Is this true?

I think not. Painting and, in fact, all of the art forms and media continue to enthrall children, adults, and seniors both as viewers and as practitioners. Making art is an engaging activity and one that is very personalized. No two individuals do it in identical fashion, and many people want to try their hand at it. Whether or not they are interested enough to do the hard work to become professional artists is something else entirely.

But many people do. We all have a strong desire to individuate, to claim an identity and then to express it to others. Art as an advanced communication methodology fulfills that desire. Humans also have a strong desire to develop skill, to perfect an activity, and to become masters of it. Art-making fulfills that desire as well.

But times do change, tastes change, fashion creates new winners and losers, and new ideas and activities come to the fore. We can forecast trends based on what is just now appearing on the horizon and also what history teaches us about change in general.

As we conclude this short course in the big themes in Western art through the centuries, I can't resist making some speculations as to what I see as the future of visual art. It's all speculation, but here's what I predict:

1. FROM THE STATIC TO THE KINETIC

Art began as object-making, the creation of two- and three-dimensional works that the viewer stood and gazed upon. Art objects were enhancements, beautiful and thoughtful pieces we considered and admired. These objects morphed into all manner of irregular and unfamiliar creations, as the picture was broken and copying nature became just one activity in the artist's vocabulary.

Then, art got blown up and released from static bounds. Artists began to use materials that moved, and the object came alive, was energized and changed form. Pictures started to move and video and film animated the still images and brought art into the realm of time. Artists became integral parts of their creations, and performance art was born.

What now? Technology has entered the art world. Artists draw and paint images on computer screens and change the images with a flick and a click. Several of the people in my drawing group are working on computer screens as the rest of us still use our pencils and crayons to draw from the live model.

Many already design paintings on a computer screen and then print them on canvas, metal, fabric. They can magnify images to enormous sizes, make a billboard in an instant. A wonderful tool for the artist.

And yet . . .

What about the feeling of the paint, the hand that tenderly strokes the canvas as the artist strives to communicate the softness of a surface, the luminance of a patch of sunlight on an apple? What about that? Something about the directness, the intimate feel of the hand to brush to canvas, is difficult to replicate with a machine, even a smart one.

My guess is that despite the allure of these devices, artists will continue to use traditional materials and make artwork by hand. New technology may captivate artists, but after a while, they are called back to the simple, direct forms—paint to canvas, hands gripping and molding clay, all without intermediary, the only energy required that of the artist.

In essence, that's what we love about making art. Getting our hands dirty. It may start with finger painting but it lives on and continues to enthrall us throughout our working lives. I don't think that will change any time soon.

2. OFF THE CANVAS

Why paint on a canvas at all? Why use paint?

The art tent will continue to get larger as formerly distinct art disciplines blur. Architect, designer, painter, sculptor, all these definitions and professions will change.

Or maybe they will be subsumed by the one word: *artist*.

Painters may no longer just paint and sculptors sculpt. Painters will sculpt as they apply paint to surfaces they construct, and sculptors will paint as they use all kinds of chemicals and substances to surfaces they construct. They both can design structures that are so large they can be entered, which takes them into the realm of architecture.

I predict even more breaking of the structures and strictures of art.

3. NEW MEDIA AND MORE MIXING OF MEDIA

Why limit oneself to a medium when so many are readily available, and why use only one or two? Technology is a tool that all artists can learn to use to take their art to the next level.

One of the most exciting is 3-D printing, now in its infancy, but soon to radically transform art-making. For example, I understand we are now close to designing an actual house on a computer, and then pressing "print" on a 3-D printer.

As these marvelous tools become available, artists will be the first to utilize this device to conjure . . . well, we'll have to wait and see what exactly, won't we?

I predict these new tools will be sampled and incorporated into a repertoire, and will enhance art-making at the same time as the traditional methods live on.

4. MORE INTERACTIVITY

Just as the making of art has changed, so will the viewing of it. In fact, *viewing* will not be a relevant term and will be replaced by the more active *experiencing*, as museums and other showplaces for art adapt to a population that has gone way beyond just standing and looking, a population that has experienced virtual reality, and wants to participate, not just spectate.

And yet . . .

5. MORE OF THE FAMILIAR

"The more things change, the more they remain the same." A familiar phrase. What does it mean in this context?

Even though Rembrandt created the most astonishing self-portraits in the seventeenth century, people in the twenty-second century will still be looking into the mirror and desiring to reproduce what they see and feel. And even though they will have had the benefit of seeing all the clever ways artists made self-portraits in the eighteenth, nineteenth, twentieth, and twenty-first centuries, I think these people of the future will still want to try it for themselves. We've got that inbuilt competition; I still am competing with Rembrandt every time I step up to the easel to make a portrait.

Just because another artist accomplished a feat doesn't negate my desire to "do it my way." So, yes, I think artists of the future will still be interested in realism, semi-abstraction, abstraction, and all of the prior attempts to depict and express human feelings, thoughts, and experiences.

They will just have more tools to do it with. Better paint and myriad other substances. Does that mean they will surpass Rembrandt and Picasso?

No. That's because it isn't a contest, and since we are all individuals, there is no competition. You are the only being that can do you, and that's what matters. There won't be another Rembrandt or another Picasso, and that's a good thing. I just can't wait to see who's going to show up next—can you?

AND WHAT OF ART IN THE SCHEME OF THINGS?

This past winter I went on holiday to the Yucatán. I had visited the area twice before in the past decade. It is a tropical paradise, and the waters are known for their beautiful turquoise color and abundant sea life. However, this visit clearly illustrated the toll the area has suffered due to climate change and the impact of excessive tourism. I even attended a lecture on the resort's attempt to restore, revitalize, and somehow preserve the fragile ecosystem.

Swimming in a lagoon now designated as a national park, I was stunned by the diminution of tropical fish since my last visit, only a few years ago. Once teeming with fish of all varieties, the now cloudy water revealed a paucity of species. This park is notable not only for the beauty of the lagoon and marine life, but also for a collection of stunning bronze sculptures that are strategically placed beside the waters. Artists like Zuniga, Gonzales, Amaya, and others, some internationally known and others local, are represented. They are really quite beautiful, especially in this glorious setting.

It occurred to me that if and when the final death toll is sounded on the life in these waters, what would remain would be the rocks and, strangely, the art. How significant that when humans, through neglect and disrespect, manage to decimate and eventually destroy nature—the paradise that is earth—what might remain is art. Ironically, art that has been inspired by that very nature.

Something to think about: In the far future, will these sculptures stand as silent witnesses to the insensitivity and abject cruelty of the human race, to the beings who created them? How sad that they forgot and forsook the gift that is the natural world, without which all their endeavors to beautify and celebrate life through art would be for naught.

As we continue, as artists and art lovers to take pleasure in making and viewing art, we must remember this most urgent call so that, above all, we strive to protect and preserve nature in whatever way we can. Nothing is more urgent, as it overrides all else that we do and are.

IN CONCLUSION

I know as a working artist that I never tire of the process of making art, that each start feels like the creation of a new world. I meet it with expectation—and when the process has taken me to the end of the road and my work is complete, what do I want? To go again, of course.

Why? Because we can't step in the same river twice, and a new effort is just that, new. Every artist feels this way, and I predict that no matter how advanced or sophisticated society becomes, as long as there are humans, there will be art.

There will be art-makers and there will also be art lovers, people like you who enjoy engaging their minds and vision and feelings with visual art, whether it is static or kinetic, whether it is a small drawing on a wall or a huge sculpture that surrounds you.

Enjoy it all, the past and the future. You don't have to choose, you know. In fact, as we talked about here, you can love and respect it all, even as you recognize your specific preferences.

I hope I have helped to make art a wee bit more understandable and interesting, and that you will take your new looking and evaluating skills out for a walk. Take them to art centers and galleries and museums and let them roam. Get some books on particular artists that stir your imagination. Try your hand at a medium that appeals to you. Make art a part of your life.

I especially encourage you to seek out the many wonderful unsung living artists who are building their bodies of work and consider supporting them by buying one of their works that you like. By doing so, you are playing your part in keeping art alive.

In closing, let me share my joy in bringing you these ideas, and my joy in knowing that I have possibly enhanced your appreciation of art. It is truly one of the joys of life to express ourselves and to share ourselves with our peers.

May the joy of art buoy your spirits and add meaning to your life in whatever way you choose to experience it. Whether artist or student or appreciator, you are surely a card-carrying member of the Joy of Art Club. See you at the museum.

—Carolyn Schlam

Appendix A

Art Games: Sharpen Your New Skills

Dear Reader,

The following are some art exercises and games you may want to have a go at, now that you have collected all this information and, hopefully, a new framework to help you understand visual art. Some are subjective and have no right or wrong answers—only a chance to see where you stand and what you may have absorbed in reading this book. Others do have specific answers; for these, I have provided an answer key at the end of the appendix.

If you are not familiar with an artist mentioned and are curious, just type his or her name into Google Images and see what comes up. When you find artists that are of particular interest to you, dig deeper—get a book of their work or study them more deeply online.

So play along if you will, and I hope you enjoy.

EXERCISE #1: LATITUDES

(No answer key)

Am I a classicist or a romantic? Place me on the scale.

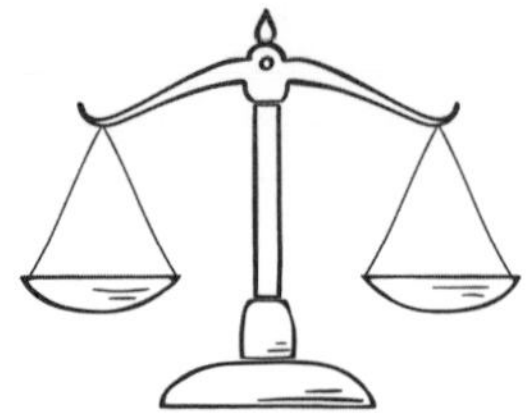

Classical ——————●—————— **Romantic**

PICASSO	**Classical** ______________________ **Romantic**
TITIAN	**Classical** ______________________ **Romantic**
SALVADOR DALÍ	**Classical** ______________________ **Romantic**
ÉDOUARD MANET	**Classical** ______________________ **Romantic**
JOHN CONSTABLE	**Classical** ______________________ **Romantic**
CHUCK CLOSE	**Classical** ______________________ **Romantic**
GEORGE BRAQUE	**Classical** ______________________ **Romantic**
PAUL GAUGUIN	**Classical** ______________________ **Romantic**
RUBENS	**Classical** ______________________ **Romantic**
CLAUDE MONET	**Classical** ______________________ **Romantic**
VINCENT VAN GOGH	**Classical** ______________________ **Romantic**
MARC CHAGALL	**Classical** ______________________ **Romantic**
FRANZ HALS	**Classical** ______________________ **Romantic**
GEORGES SEURAT	**Classical** ______________________ **Romantic**
JACKSON POLLOCK	**Classical** ______________________ **Romantic**
EDVARD MUNCH	**Classical** ______________________ **Romantic**
HENRY MOORE	**Classical** ______________________ **Romantic**
GEORGES ROUAULT	**Classical** ______________________ **Romantic**
JEAN ARP	**Classical** ______________________ **Romantic**
CHAIM SOUTINE	**Classical** ______________________ **Romantic**
VASILY KANDINSKY	**Classical** ______________________ **Romantic**
MARCEL DUCHAMP	**Classical** ______________________ **Romantic**
ROBERT MOTHERWELL	**Classical** ______________________ **Romantic**
SANDRO BOTTICELLI	**Classical** ______________________ **Romantic**
PAUL CÉZANNE	**Classical** ______________________ **Romantic**
EDGAR DEGAS	**Classical** ______________________ **Romantic**

EXERCISE #2: MATCH THE TERMS

(Answer key on page 312)

value	biomorphic
chiaroscuro	linear texture
vanishing point	environment
minimalism	contrast
formalism	No name
negative space	attachments
hue	criteria
cross-hatching	3-D
organic shape	feeling first
abstraction	of itself
illusion	outdoors
collage	lightness
aesthetics	essentials
tone	red
proportion	perspective
patterning	air
expressionism	relative size
plein air	repetition

EXERCISE #3: MATCH QUALITIES WITH ARTISTS

(No answer key)

Note: There may not be a match, or a quality can match with more than one artist.

QUALITIES	ARTISTS
free	Eakins
soft	Matisse
liquid	Ingres
sensual	Vermeer
bright	Modigliani
playful	Chagall
harsh	Rembrandt
faint	Picasso
emotional	Monet
robotic	Sargent
loud	Pollock
poetic	Van Gogh
neat	Klee
elegant	Cassatt
innovative	Bonnard
boring	Seurat
technical	Kandinsky

EXERCISE #4: FILL IN THE BLANK

(No answer key)

Here's your chance to use those parts of speech.

1. The ________________________________ of Picasso.
2. The ________________________________ of Warhol.
3. What I love about Rembrandt is ________________________
4. If I could be any artist, I'd like to be ____________________
5. When I think of expertise, this name comes to mind: ____________
6. Cubism is ________________________________
7. My favorite style is ____________________________
8. Van Gogh's texture is ____________________________
9. When I think color, I think __________________________
10. If I could use a sculptural medium, I would choose ______________
11. Abstraction is ________________________________
12. The ________________________________ of Vermeer.
13. Manet or Monet? Which do I prefer? ____________________
14. Figure or landscape? Which interests me? __________________
15. Who's hot? ________________________________
16. Who's cold? ________________________________
17. The most outrageous artist is __________________________
18. The least outrageous artist is __________________________
19. My favorite artist is ____________________________
20. The ________________________________ of Mondrian.
21. My favorite Picasso period was __________________________
22. I could do without ____________________________
23. I would like to make a collage using ______________________
24. ________________________________ makes me sad.

25. The ____ of Diebenkorn.

26. The ____ of Caravaggio.

27. Subtlety and ____

28. If I could mix two media, I would mix ________________________ and ________________________.

29. I want to paint ____

30. The sensuality of ____

31. The playfulness of ____

32. The exuberance of ____

33. The intelligence of ____

34. The heart of ____

35. I dislike ____

36. I used to dislike but now I like ____

37. The most interesting idea is ____

38. The joy of ____

EXERCISE #5: FUN WITH PUNS AND TRICKY QUESTIONS

(Answer key on page 313)

1. What painter made his point? ________________________________
2. He was Monet's precursor, not his cousin. ________________________
3. He was a storm chaser in his day. ____________________________
4. Who am I? I'm a homebody in my art, and I love mirrors too. __________
5. If you go for verisimilitude, you are ______________.

    a. very simple c. a realist
    b. itchy d. a Nabi

6. Which of these is a mixed media exercise?

    a. graffito c. action painting
    b. color field d. crayon resist

7. Alizarin is ______________.

    a. a value c. a hue
    b. a reptile d. a flavoring

8. When we are at the visual end of the road, we have met ______________.

    a. our fate c. the vanishing point
    b. the point of no return d. God

9. I'm a bowl . . . well, kind of. I think I am, but maybe not. I guess I must be ____.
10. I stick out, and I'm glad. What am I? ________________________.
11. I'm not an imposter, but I'm pretty heavy, for paint that is. ____________
12. I can be round or square, but I'm flat. ________________________
13. I'm a good model. I don't move. ____________________________
14. Glue is my thing. I'm a ________________________________.
15. If you add some white to paint, you will change its ______________.

    a. hue c. palette
    b. value d. consistency

EXERCISE #6: ARTIST SCRAMBLE

(Answer key on page 313)

1. VINICDA ____________________
2. MDRATBERN ____________________
3. CIAAAVGOGR ____________________
4. TINIAT ____________________
5. YAOG ____________________
6. IORREN ____________________
7. SGAED ____________________
8. HRDNAIC ____________________
9. LRRANIO ____________________
10. SOPCISA ____________________
11. GSIR ____________________
12. TESLITGIZ ____________________
13. NKAIKDNSY ____________________
14. ARNSUCHEEGRB ____________________
15. KINAES ____________________
16. GATRENS ____________________
17. ARP ____________________
18. UINBARCS ____________________
19. OLOPLCK ____________________
20. EMLOEIGHNCAL ____________________
21. RRLAEAEHNTNKF ____________________
22. ALSH ____________________
23. EKNHYOC ____________________
24. DANMRNIO ____________________
25. TAMSSIE ____________________

EXERCISE #7: USE FIVE TERMS TO DESCRIBE THESE WORKS AND WRITE A PARAGRAPH ABOUT THEM

(No answer key)

I have asked a few artists whom I know personally to contribute a work to this section, and I am adding one of my own as well. We may have all kinds of ideas about the well-known personalities in art history but have little familiarity with the many truly gifted contemporary artists at work today.

Now that you've gone through this book and have some new skills, you may have a greater respect for these talented people as well as the understanding to interpret their work.

Here's the challenge. Look at their works of art. You have no preconceived ideas about them, so you can see them with new eyes. Challenge yourself to use five terms to describe the work, and then write a paragraph or two about it.

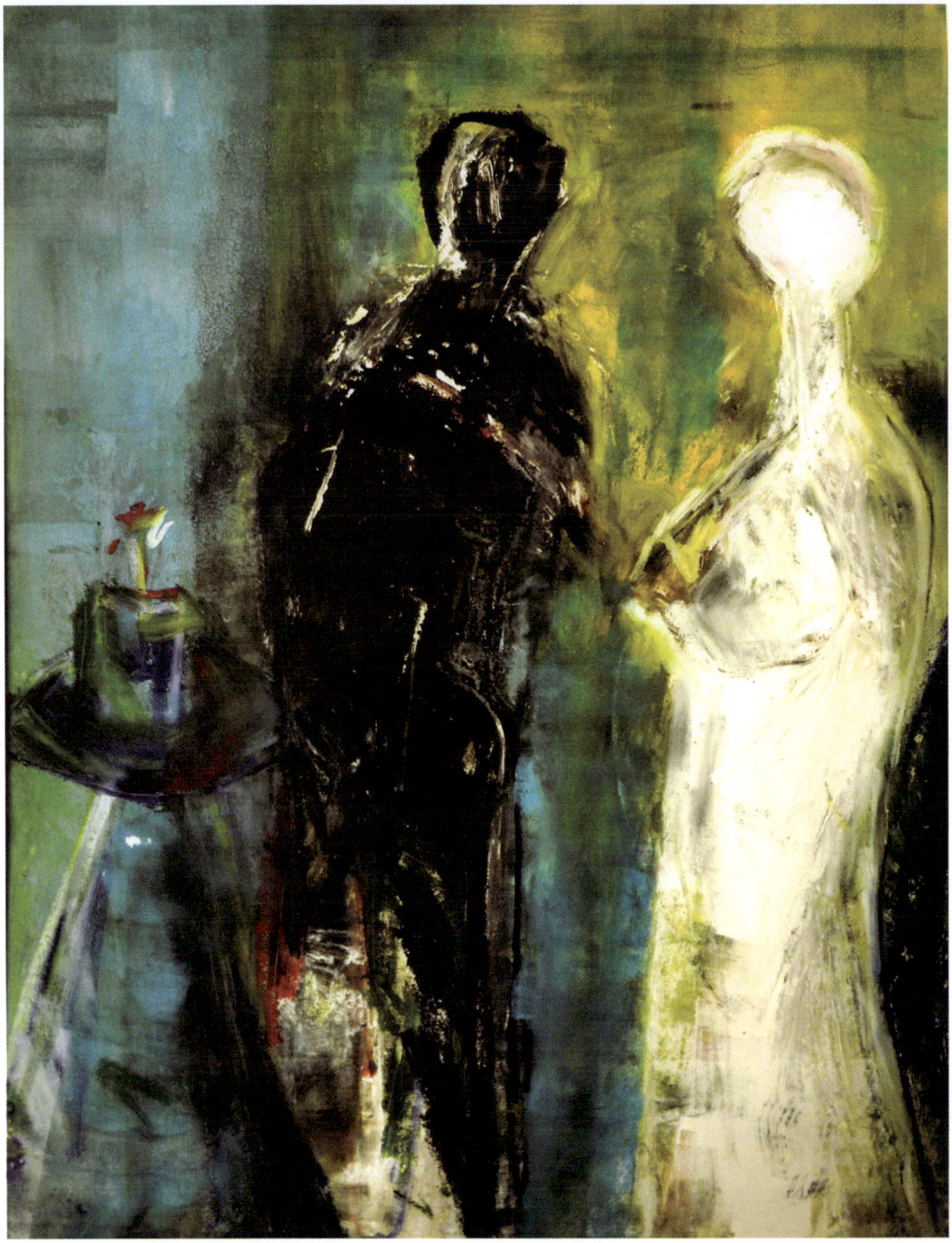

Fig. 145. Sirarpi Heghinian Walzer, BODY AND SOUL.

Sirarpi is a mixed-media artist. See her website at www.swalzer.com for more examples.

Five Terms to Describe This Work:

1. ______________________________
2. ______________________________
3. ______________________________
4. ______________________________
5. ______________________________

How I Would Describe *Body and Soul*:

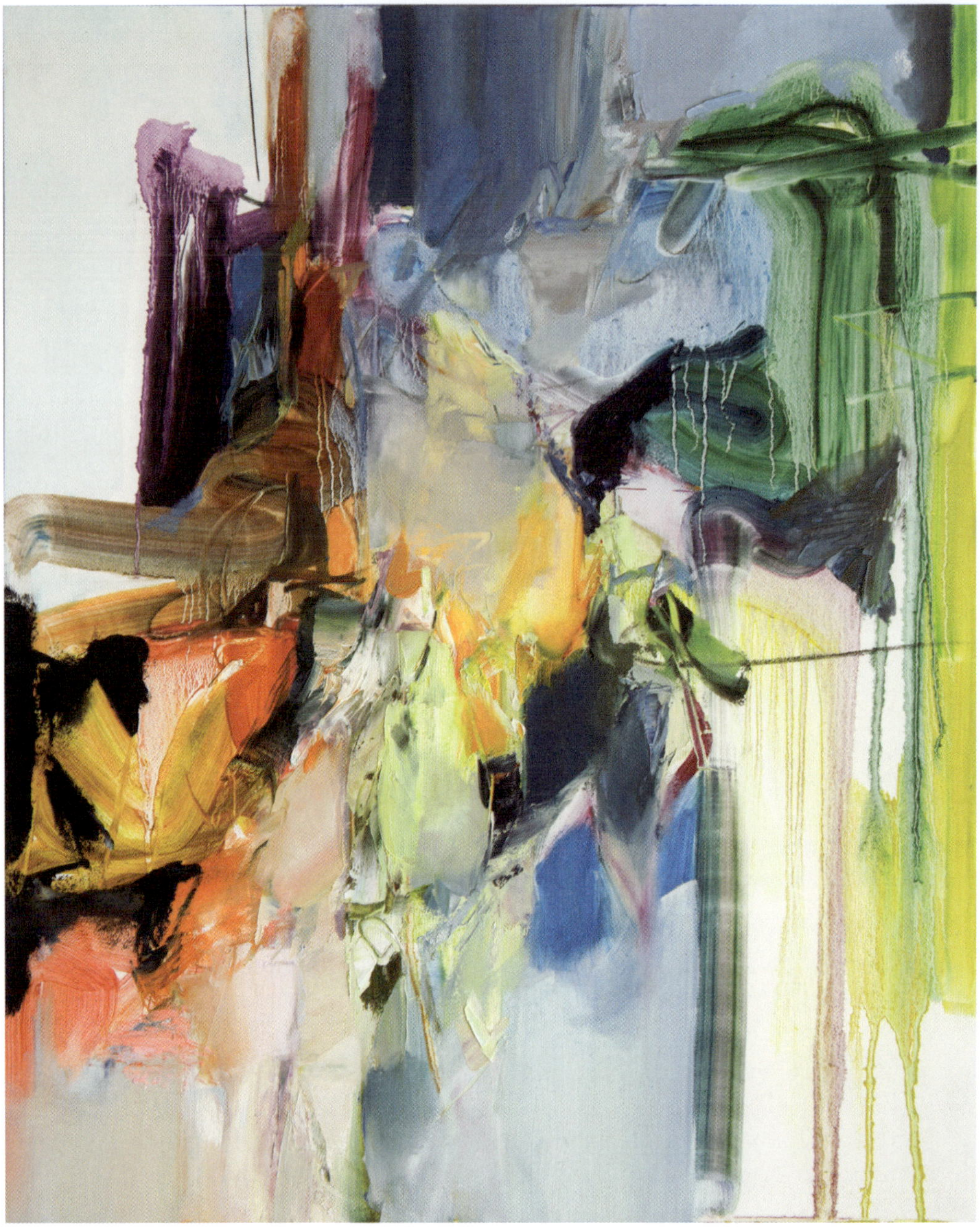

Fig. 146. Elana Kundell, I WANT YOU INEVITABLE.

Elana is a painter. See her website at www.elanakundell.com for more examples.

Five Terms to Describe This Work:

1. ______________________________
2. ______________________________
3. ______________________________
4. ______________________________
5. ______________________________

How I Would Describe *I Want You Inevitable*:

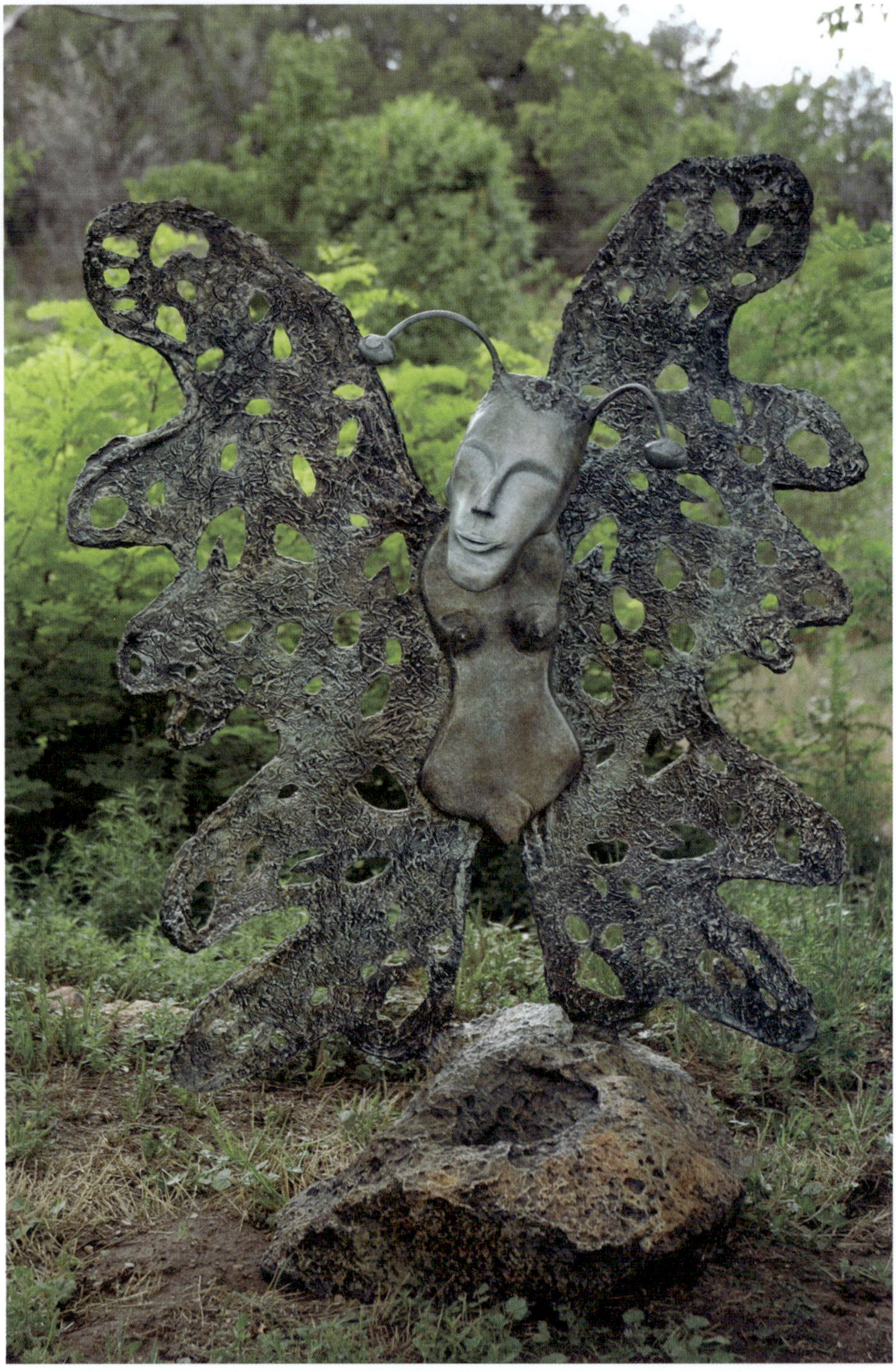

Fig. 147. Claire Haye, SEEKING TRUTH—BOTH SIDES.

Claire is a sculptor. See her website at www.claireworks.com for more examples..

Five Terms to Describe This Work:

1. ______________________________
2. ______________________________
3. ______________________________
4. ______________________________
5. ______________________________

How I Would Describe *Seeking Truth—Both Sides*:

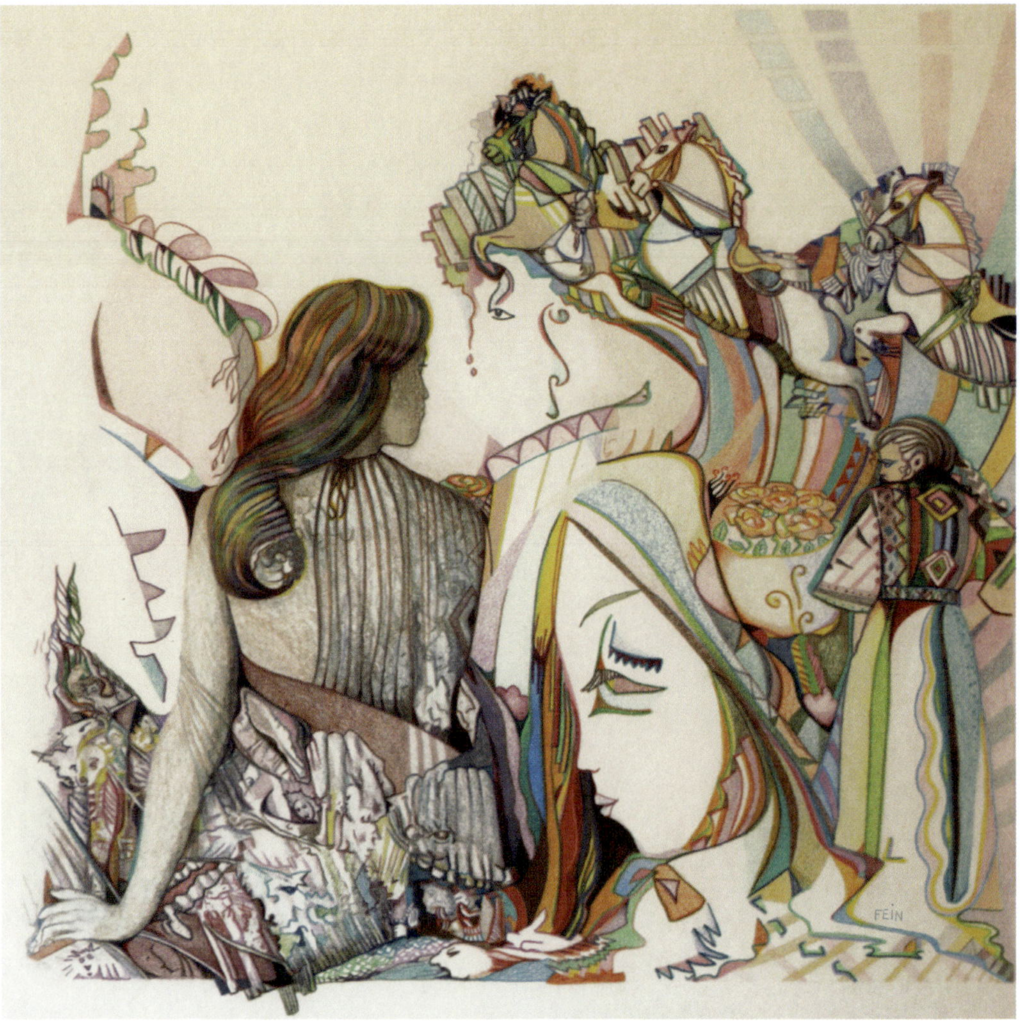

Fig. 148. Sheila Fein, COUNTING PONIES.

Sheila is a painter and illustrator. See her website at www.sheilafein.com for more examples.

Five Terms to Describe This Work:

1. ______________________________
2. ______________________________
3. ______________________________
4. ______________________________
5. ______________________________

How I Would Describe *Counting Ponies*:

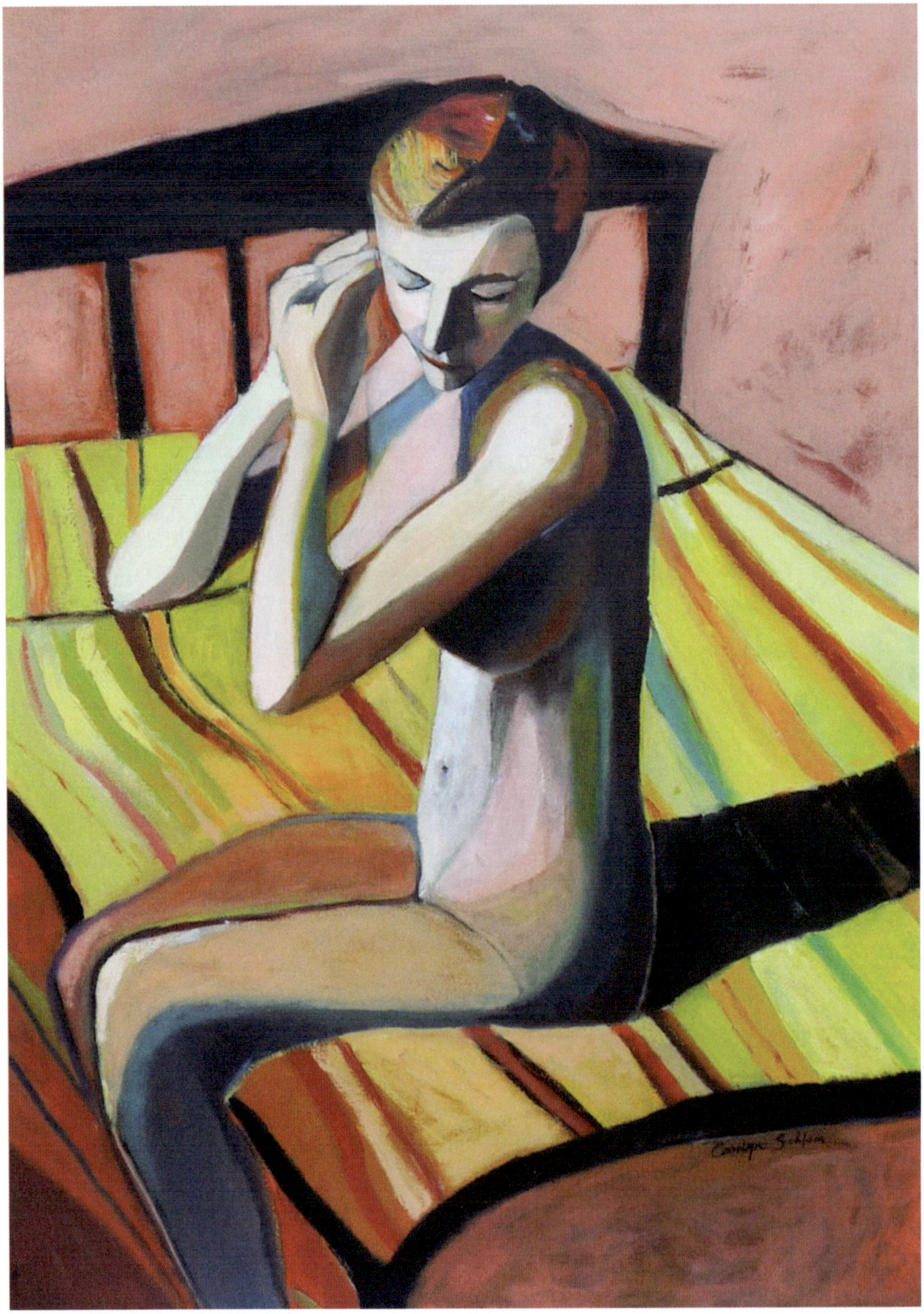

Fig. 149. Carolyn Schlam, THE BED.

Carolyn is a painter, glass artist, and author. See her website at www.carolynschlam.com for more examples.

Five Terms to Describe This Work:

1. ______________________________
2. ______________________________
3. ______________________________
4. ______________________________
5. ______________________________

How I Would Describe *The Bed*:

ANSWER KEY—EXERCISE #2: MATCH THE TERMS

value. . . . . lightness

chiaroscuro. . . . . contrast

vanishing point . . . . perspective

minimalism . . . . essentials

formalism. . . . . of itself

negative space. . . . . air

hue. . . . . red

cross hatching. . . . . linear texture

organic shape . . . . biomorphic

abstraction . . . . no name

illusion . . . . 3rd dimension

collage . . . . attachments

aesthetics . . . . criteria

tone . . . . environment

proportion . . . . relative size

patterning. . . . . repetition

expressionism . . . . feeling

plein air . . . . outside

ANSWER KEY—EXERCISE #5: FUN WITH PUNS AND TRICKY QUESTIONS

1. Seurat
2. Manet
3. Turner
4. Vermeer
5. c. realist
6. d. crayon resist
7. c. hue
8. c. vanishing point
9. semi-abstract
10. a relief
11. impasto
12. shape-making
13. still life
14. collage
15. b. value

ANSWER KEY—EXERCISE #6: ARTIST SCRAMBLE

1. DA VINCI
2. REMBRANDT
3. CARAVAGGIO
4. TITIAN
5. GOYA
6. RENOIR
7. DEGAS
8. CHARDIN
9. LORRAIN
10. PICASSO
11. GRIS
12. STIEGLITZ
13. KANDINSKY
14. RAUSCHENBERG
15. EAKINS
16. SARGENT
17. ARP
18. BRANCUSI
19. POLLOCK
20. MICHELANGELO
21. FRANKENTHALER
22. HALS
23. HOCKNEY
24. MONDRIAN
25. MATISSE

Appendix B
List of Images

Fig. 1. Juan Gris, CHECKERBOARD AND PLAYING CARDS, 1915, gouache, graphite, and resin on cream-colored wove paper, mounted to paperboard, 8.25 × 11.75 inches. Metropolitan Museum of Art, New York, New York, United States of America. Leonard A. Lauder Cubist Collection, Gift of Leonard A. Lauder, 2016. Photograph by Metropolitan Museum of Art. Wikimedia Commons. Available under the Creative Commons CC0 1.0 Universal Public Domain Dedication. https://commons.wikimedia.org/wiki/File:Checkerboard_and_Playing_Cards_MET_DP302916_ms.jpg

Fig. 2. Jean-Baptiste-Camille Corot, LE CHEMIN DE SÈVRES, 1855–1865, oil on canvas, 13.3 × 19.2 inches. Musée du Louvre, Paris, France. Photograph by the Yorck Project. Wikimedia Commons. Public domain. https://commons.wikimedia.org/wiki/Jean-Baptiste-Camille_Corot#/media/File:Jean-Baptiste-Camille_Corot_051.jpg

Fig. 3. Carolyn Schlam, Vanishing point (illustration).

Fig. 4. Carolyn Schlam, Box (illustration).

Fig. 5. Michelangelo, AWAKENING SLAVE, 1520–1523, marble, 8.8 feet. Galleria dell'Accademia, Florence, Italy. Photograph by Jörg Bittner Unna. Wikimedia Commons. Available under the Creative Commons Attribution-Share Alike 3.0 Unported license. https://commons.wikimedia.org/wiki/File:%27Awakening_Slave%27_by_Michelangelo_-_JBU_02.jpg

Fig. 6a. Claude Monet, HAYSTACKS (EFFECT OF SNOW AND SUN), 1891, oil on canvas, 25.75 × 36.25 inches. Metropolitan Museum of Art, New York, New York, United States of America. H. O. Havemeyer Collection, Bequest of Mrs. H. O. Havemeyer, 1929. Photograph by Google Cultural Institute. Wikimedia Commons. Public domain. https://commons.wikimedia.org/wiki/File:Claude_Monet_(French,_Paris_1840%E2%80%931926_Giverny)_-_Haystacks_(Effect_of_Snow_and_Sun)_-_Google_Art_Project.jpg

Fig. 6b. Claude Monet, HAYSTACKS (END OF SUMMER), 1891, oil on canvas, 23.62 × 39.37 inches. Musée d'Orsay, Paris, France. Photograph by Google Cultural Institute. Wikimedia Commons. Public domain. https://commons.wikimedia.org/wiki/File:Claude_Monet_-_Haystacks,_end_of_Summer_-_Google_Art_Project.jpg

Fig. 7. Amadeo Modigliani, GIRL IN A SAILOR'S BLOUSE, 1918, oil on canvas, 25.7 × 18.2 inches. Metropolitan Museum of Art, New York, New York, United States of America. Gift of Charles F. Iklé, 1960. Photograph by Metropolitan Museum of Art. Wikimedia Commons. Available under the Creative Commons CC0 1.0 Universal Public Domain Dedication. https://commons.wikimedia.org/wiki/File:Girl_in_a_Sailor%27s_Blouse_MET_CT_2860.jpg

Fig. 8. Claude Monet, MORNING ON THE SEINE NEAR GIVERNY, 1897, oil on canvas, 32.1 × 36.6 inches. Metropolitan Museum of Art, New York, New York, United States of America. Bequest of Julia W. Emmons, 1956. Photograph by Metropolitan Museum of Art. Wikimedia Commons. Available under the Creative Commons CC0 1.0 Universal Public Domain Dedication. https://commons.wikimedia.org/wiki/File:Morning_on_the_Seine_near_Giverny_MET_DT1903.jpg

Fig. 9. Carolyn Schlam, GIRL WITH GREEN EYES, 2017, oil on canvas, 24 × 30 inches. Private collection. Courtesy of the artist.

Fig. 10. Pierre Bonnard, GARDEN, 1935, oil on canvas, 35.5 × 35.625 inches. Metropolitan Museum of Art, New York, New York, United States of America. The Walter H. and Leonore Annenberg Collection, Bequest of Walter H. Annenberg, 2002. The Metropolitan Museum of Art. Public domain. https://www.metmuseum.org/art/collection/search/492745

Fig. 11. Henri de Toulouse-Lautrec, DANSEUSE ASSISE AUX BAS DE ROSES, 1890, pastel on board, 22.36 × 18.27 inches. Dickinson Gallery, London, England. Photograph by Dickinson Gallery. Wikimedia Commons. Public domain. https://commons.wikimedia.org/wiki/File:'Danseuse_assise_aux_Bas_de_roses'_by_Toulouse-Lautrec,_1890.jpg

Fig. 12. Juan Gris, STILL LIFE WITH A GUITAR, 1913, oil on canvas, 26 × 39.5 inches. Metropolitan Museum of Art, New York, New York, United States of America. Jacques and Natasha Gelman Collection, 1998. The Metropolitan Museum of Art. Public domain. https://www.metmuseum.org/art/collection/search/489983

Fig. 13. Paul Cézanne, MADAME CÉZANNE IN A RED ARMCHAIR, 1877, oil on canvas, 28.5 × 22 inches. Museum of Fine Arts, Boston, Massachusetts, United States of America. Photograph by Google Cultural Institute. Wikimedia Commons. Public domain. https://commons.wikimedia.org/wiki/File:Paul_C%C3%A9zanne_-_Madame_C%C3%A9zanne_in_a_Red_Armchair_-_Google_Art_Project.jpg

Fig. 14. Albert Bierstadt, THE ROCKY MOUNTAINS, LANDER'S PEAK, 1863, oil on canvas, 73.5 × 120.75 inches. Metropolitan Museum of Art, New York, New York, United States of America. Rogers Fund, 1907. The Metropolitan Museum of Art. Public domain. https://www.metmuseum.org/art/collection/search/10154

Fig. 15. Vincent van Gogh, SHOES, 1888, oil on canvas, 18 × 21.75 inches. Metropolitan Museum of Art, New York, New York, United States of America. Purchase, The Annenberg Foundation Gift, 1992. The Metropolitan Museum of Art. Public domain. https://www.metmuseum.org/art/collection/search/436533

Fig. 16. Edvard Munch, THE SCREAM, 1893, oil, tempera, and pastel on cardboard, 35.8 × 28.9 inches. National Gallery of Norway, Oslo, Norway. Photograph by National Gallery of Norway. Wikimedia Commons. Public domain. https://commons.wikimedia.org/wiki/File:Edvard_Munch,_1893,_The_Scream,_oil,_tempera_and_pastel_on_cardboard,_91_x_73_cm,_National_Gallery_of_Norway.jpg

Fig. 17. Phoebe Scott, TORSO, PRESSED, 2017, stoneware, 48 × 38 inches. Private collection. Courtesy of the artist.

Fig. 18. Henri de Toulouse-Lautrec, POSTER FOR ARISTIDE BRUANT, 1896. Photograph by Charles Hiatt. Wikimedia Commons. Public domain. https://commons.wikimedia.org/wiki/File:PP_D087_poster_by_toulouse-lautrec_for_aristide_bruant.jpg

Fig. 19. Jean-Auguste-Dominique Ingres, JOSÉPHINE-ÉLÉONORE-MARIE-PAULINE DE GALARD DE BRASSAC DE BÉARN (1825–1860), PRINCESSE DE BROGLIE, 1851–1853, oil on canvas, 47.75 × 35.75 inches. Metropolitan Museum of Art, New York, New York, United States of America. Robert Lehman Collection, 1975. The Metropolitan Museum of Art. Public domain. https://www.metmuseum.org/art/collection/search/459106

Fig. 20. Chaim Soutine, VIEW OF CAGNES, 1924–1925, oil on canvas, 23.75 × 28.875 inches. Metropolitan Museum of Art, New York, New York, United States of America. The Mr. and Mrs. Klaus G. Perls Collection, 1997. The Metropolitan Museum of Art. Public domain. https://www.metmuseum.org/art/collection/search/486840

Fig. 21. Vasily Kandinsky, KLEINE WELTEN III, 1922, lithograph, 14.0625 × 11 inches. Metropolitan Museum of Art, New York, New York, United States of America. Harris Brisbane Dick Fund, 1931. The Metropolitan Museum of Art. Public domain. https://www.metmuseum.org/art/collection/search/360146

Fig. 22. Edgar Degas, DANCERS, PINK AND GREEN, 1890, oil on canvas, 32.375 × 29.75 inches. Metropolitan Museum of Art, New York, New York, United States of America. H. O. Havemeyer Collection, Bequest of Mrs. H. O. Havemeyer, 1929. The Metropolitan Museum of Art. Public domain. https://www.metmuseum.org/art/collection/search/436140

Fig. 23. Paul Gauguin, IA ORANA MARIA, 1891, oil on canvas, 44.75 × 34.5 inches. Metropolitan Museum of Art, New York, New York, United States of America. Bequest of Sam A. Lewisohn, 1951. The Metropolitan Museum of Art. Public domain. https://www.metmuseum.org/art/collection/search/438821

Fig. 24. Egon Schiele, CROUCHING NUDE IN SHOES AND BLACK STOCKINGS, BACK VIEW, 1912, watercolor, gouache, and graphite on paper. Metropolitan Museum of Art, New York, New York, United States of America. Bequest of Scofield Thayer, 1982. The Metropolitan Museum of Art. Public Domain. https://www.metmuseum.org/art/collection/search/483437

Fig. 25. Jacques-Louis David, THE DEATH OF MARAT, 1793, oil on canvas, 64.9 × 50.3 inches. Royal Museum of Fine Arts of Belgium, Brussels, Belgium. Photograph by Google Cultural Institute. Wikimedia Commons. Public domain. https://commons.wikimedia.org/wiki/File:Jacques-Louis_David_-_Marat_assassinated_-_Google_Art_Project_2.jpg

Fig. 26. Edward Hopper, NIGHTHAWKS 1942, oil on canvas, 33.1 × 60 inches. Art Institute of Chicago, Chicago, Illinois, United States of America. Photograph by Art Institute of Chicago. Wikimedia Commons. Public domain. https://commons.wikimedia.org/wiki/File:Nighthawks_by_Edward_Hopper_1942.jpg (Note: This work is in the public domain because it was published in the United States between 1923 and 1963 and although there may or may not have been a copyright notice, the copyright was not renewed.)

Fig. 27. Mary Cassatt, ELLEN MARY CASSATT, 1899, pastel on laid paper, 12 × 14.5 inches. Metropolitan Museum of Art, New York, New York, United States of America. Gift of Mrs. Gardner Cassatt, 1959. Metropolitan Museum of Art. Public domain. https://www.metmuseum.org/art/collection/search/13532

Fig. 28. Paul Klee, DRAWING KNOTTED IN THE MANNER OF A NET, 1920, ink on paper mounted on cardboard, 12.25 × 7.5 inches. Metropolitan Museum of Art, New York, New York, United States of America. The Berggruen Klee Collection, 1984. Metropolitan Museum of Art. Public domain. https://www.metmuseum.org/art/collection/search/483137

Fig. 29. Jan Brueghel the Elder, BOUQUET OF FLOWERS, 1600–1625, oil on panel, 63.7 × 51.9 inches. National Museum of Art of Romania, Bucharest, Romania. Photograph by National Museum of Art of Romania. Wikimedia Commons. Public domain. https://commons.wikimedia.org/wiki/File:Jan_Brueghel_I_-_Bouquet_of_flowers.jpg

Fig. 30. Odilon Redon, ETRUSCAN VASE WITH FLOWERS, 1900–1910, tempera on canvas. The Metropolitan Museum of Art, New York, New York, United States of America. Maria DeWitt Jesup Fund, 1951; acquired from The Museum of Modern Art, Lillie P. Bliss Collection. The Metropolitan Museum of Art. Public domain. https://www.metmuseum.org/art/collection/search/437381

Fig. 31. Arthur Dove, MOUNTAIN AND SKY, c. 1925, oil on wood panel, 15.625 × 11.875 inches. Metropolitan Museum of Art, New York, New York, United States of America. Gift of Carl D. Lobell, 1994. The Metropolitan Museum of Art. Public domain. https://www.metmuseum.org/art/collection/search/486392

Fig. 32. Piet Mondrian, COMPOSITION, 1921, oil on canvas, 19.5 × 19.5 inches. Metropolitan Museum of Art, New York, New York, United States of America. Jacques and Natasha Gelman Collection, 1998. The Metropolitan Museum of Art. Public domain. https://www.metmuseum.org/art/collection/search/490012

Fig. 33. Antonín Procházka, LADY IN SWEATER, 1921, mixed media on cardboard. Photograph by Ablakok. Wikimedia Commons. Available under the Creative Commons Attribution-Share Alike 4.0 International license. https://commons.wikimedia.org/wiki/File:Anton%C3%ADn_Proch%C3%A1zka_-_Lady_in_Sweater.jpg

Fig. 34. Rembrandt van Rijn, SELF-PORTRAIT, 1628–1629, oil on oak panel, 8.8 × 18.7 inches. Rijksmuseum, Amsterdam, Netherlands. Photograph by Web Gallery of Art. Wikimedia Commons. Public domain. https://commons.wikimedia.org/wiki/File:Self-portrait_(1628-1629),_by_Rembrandt.jpg

Fig. 35. Johannes Vermeer, THE LOVE LETTER, c. 1669, oil on canvas, 17.3 × 5.1 inches. Rijksmuseum, Amsterdam, Netherlands. Photograph by Google Cultural Institute. Wikimedia Commons. Public domain. https://commons.wikimedia.org/wiki/File:Johannes_Vermeer_-_The_Love_Letter_-_WGA24693.jpg

Fig. 36. Juan Gris, PORTRAIT OF PABLO PICASSO, 1912, oil on canvas, 36.73 × 29.29 inches. Art Institute of Chicago, Chicago, Illinois, United States of America. Photograph by Google Cultural Institute. Wikimedia Commons. Public domain. https://commons.wikimedia.org/wiki/File:Juan_Gris_-_Portrait_of_Pablo_Picasso_-_Google_Art_Project.jpg

Fig. 37. Michelangelo Merisi da Caravaggio, THE CONVERSION ON THE WAY TO DAMASCUS, 1600, oil on canvas, 90.5 × 68.8 inches. Cerasi Chapel, Rome, Italy. Photograph by Web Gallery of Art. Wikimedia Commons. Public domain. https://commons.wikimedia.org/wiki/File:Caravaggio-The_Conversion_on_the_Way_to_Damascus.jpg

Fig. 38. Franz Stuck, THE SIN, 1893, oil on canvas, 37.2 × 23.4 inches. Neue Pinakothek, Munich, Germany. Photograph by the Yorck Project. Wikimedia Commons. Public domain. https://commons.wikimedia.org/wiki/File:Franz_von_Stuck_004.jpg

Fig. 39. J. M. W. Turner, RAIN, STEAM AND SPEED—THE GREAT WESTERN RAILWAY, 1844, oil on canvas, 35.8 × 47.9 inches. National Gallery, London, England. Photograph by National Gallery. Wikimedia Commons. Public domain. https://commons.wikimedia.org/wiki/File:Turner_-_Rain,_Steam_and_Speed_-_National_Gallery_file.jpg

Fig. 40. Claude Monet, THE HOUSES OF PARLIAMENT (EFFECT OF FOG), 1903–1904, oil on canvas, 32 × 36.375 inches. Metropolitan Museum of Art, New York, New York, United States of America. Bequest of Julia W. Emmons, 1956. The Metropolitan Museum of Art. Public domain. https://www.metmuseum.org/art/collection/search/437128

Fig. 41. Frederick Carl Frieseke, AFTERNOON—YELLOW ROOM, 1910, oil on canvas, 32 × 32 inches. Indianapolis Museum of Art, Indianapolis, Indiana, United States of America. Photograph by Google Cultural Institute. Wikimedia Commons. Public domain. https://commons.wikimedia.org/wiki/File:Frieseke,_Frederick_Carl_-_Afternoon_-_Yellow_Room_-_Google_Art_Project.jpg

Fig. 42. Paul Cézanne, GARDANNE, 1885–1886, oil on canvas, 31.5 × 25.25 inches. Metropolitan Museum of Art, New York, New York, United States of America. Gift of Dr. and Mrs. Franz H. Hirschland, 1957. The Metropolitan Museum of Art. Public domain. https://www.metmuseum.org/art/collection/search/435871

Fig. 43. Winslow Homer, THE BRIDLE PATH, WHITE MOUNTAINS, 1868, oil on canvas. Clark Art Institute, Williamstown, Massachusetts. Photograph by the Bridgeman Art Library. Wikimedia Commons. Public domain. https://commons.wikimedia.org/wiki/File:Winslow_Homer_The_Bridle_Path,_White_Mountains.jpg

Fig. 44. Vasily Kandinsky, SKETCH II FOR COMPOSITION VII, 1913, oil on canvas. Lenbachhaus, Maxvorstadt, Germany. Photograph by Ermell. Wikimedia Commons. Public domain. https://commons.wikimedia.org/wiki/File:Kandinsky_-_Entwurf_2_zu_Komposition_VII_PA291213.jpg

Fig. 45. Pierre Bonnard, THE BROTHERS BERNHEIM-JEUNE, 1920, oil on canvas, Musée d'Orsay, Paris, France. Photograph by Paul Hermans. Wikimedia Commons. Public domain. https://commons.wikimedia.org/wiki/File:Pierre_Bonnard_(1867-1947)_De_gebroeders_Bernheim-Jeune_-_Mus%C3%A9e_d%27Orsay_Parijs_22-8-2017_16-21-41.JPG

Fig. 46. Alfred Henry Maurer, LANDSCAPE WITH HOUSE, 1909–1912, oil and egg tempera on paperboard, 21.5 × 18 inches. The Barnes Collection, Philadelphia, Pennsylvania, United States of America. Public domain. https://collection.barnesfoundation.org/objects/3428/Landscape-with-House/

Fig. 47. James Fitton, SELF-PORTRAIT, 1981, oil on canvas. Private collection. Photograph by Leutha. Wikimedia Commons. Available under the GNU Free Documentation License and under the Creative Commons Attribution-Share Alike 3.0 Unported, 2.5 Generic, 2.0 Generic and 1.0 Generic licenses. https://commons.wikimedia.org/wiki/File:Looking_at_Les_Fauves_1981_(detail).jpg

Fig. 48. Johannes Vermeer, THE ART OF PAINTING, 1666–1668, oil on canvas, 47.24 × 39.37 inches. Kunsthistorisches Museum, Vienna, Austria. Photograph by Google Cultural Institute. Wikimedia Commons. Public domain. https://commons.wikimedia.org/wiki/File:Jan_Vermeer_-_The_Art_of_Painting_-_Google_Art_Project.jpg

Fig. 49. Édouard Vuillard, MADAME VUILLARD SEWING BY THE WINDOW, RUE TRUFFAUT, 1899, oil on cardboard on panel, 19.5 × 20.75 inches. Metropolitan Museum of Art, New York, New York, United States of America. Robert Lehman Collection, 1975. The Metroplitan Museum of Art. Public domain. https://www.metmuseum.org/art/collection/search/459174

Fig. 50. Leonardo da Vinci, SELF-PORTRAIT, c. 1512, red chalk on paper, 13.11 × 8.38 inches. Royal Library of Turin, Turin, Italy. Photograph by Web Gallery of Art. Wikimedia Commons. Public domain. https://commons.wikimedia.org/wiki/File:Leonardo_da_Vinci_-_presumed_self-portrait_-_lossless.png

Fig. 51. Michelangelo, DAVID (detail), 1501–1504, marble. Galleria dell'Accademia, Florence, Italy. Photograph by Jörg Bittner Unna. Wikimedia Commons. Available under the Creative Commons Attribution 3.0 Unported license. https://commons.wikimedia.org/wiki/File:%27David%27_by_Michelangelo_JBU14.JPG

Fig. 52. Titian, BACCHUS AND ARIADNE, 1520–1523, oil on canvas, 69.4 × 75.1 inches. National Gallery, London, England. Photograph by National Gallery. Wikimedia Commons. Public domain. https://commons.wikimedia.org/wiki/File:Titian_Bacchus_and_Ariadne.jpg

Fig. 53. El Greco, EL SALVADOR, 1608–1614, oil on canvas, 28.3 × 21.6 inches. Museo del Prado, Madrid, Spain. Photograph by Museo del Prado. Wikimedia Commons. Public domain. https://commons.wikimedia.org/wiki/File:El_Salvador_(El_Greco).jpg

Fig. 54. Michelangelo Merisi da Caravaggio, SAINT JOHN THE BAPTIST IN THE WILDERNESS, 1604–1605, oil on canvas, 68 × 52 inches. Nelson-Atkins Museum of Art, Kansas City, Missouri, United States of America. Photograph by Google Cultural Institute. Wikimedia Commons. Public domain. https://commons.wikimedia.org/wiki/File:Michelangelo_Merisi,_called_Caravaggio_-_Saint_John_the_Baptist_in_the_Wilderness_-_Google_Art_Project.jpg

Fig. 55. Johannes Vermeer, GIRL WITH A PEARL EARRING, 1665, oil on canvas, 17.5 × 15.3 inches. Mauritshuis, The Hague, Netherlands. Photograph by Mauritshuis, copied, sampled, and uploaded by Crisco 1492. Wikimedia Commons. Public domain. https://commons.wikimedia.org/wiki/File:Meisje_met_de_parel.jpg

Fig. 56. Rembrandt van Rijn, PORTRAIT OF SASKIA VAN UYLENBURGH (1612–1642), 1633, oil on oak panel, 18.8 inches wide. Rijksmuseum, Amsterdam, Netherlands. Photograph by Geheugen van Nederland. Wikimedia Commons. Public domain. https://commons.wikimedia.org/wiki/File:Rembrandt_Harmensz._van_Rijn_088.jpg

Fig. 57. Diego Velázquez, LAS MENINAS (detail), 1656–1657, oil on canvas, 10.4 × 9.05 feet. Museo del Prado, Madrid, Spain. Photograph by Web Galley of Art. Wikimedia Commons. Public domain. https://commons.wikimedia.org/wiki/File:Diego_Vel%C3%A1zquez_-_Las_Meninas_(detail)_-_WGA24451.jpg

Fig. 58. John Singer Sargent, MORNING WALK, 1888, oil on canvas, 19.7 × 26 inches. Private collection. Photograph by freeparking. Wikimedia Commons. Available under the Creative Commons Attribution 2.0 Generic license. https://commons.wikimedia.org/wiki/File:John_Singer_Sargent_-_Morning_Walk.jpg

Fig. 59. Édouard Manet, A BAR AT THE FOLIES-BERGÈRE, 1881–1882, oil on canvas, 37.7 × 51.1 inches. Courtauld Institute of Art, London, England. Photograph by Courtauld Institute of Art. Wikimedia Commons. Public domain. https://commons.wikimedia.org/wiki/File:Edouard_Manet,_A_Bar_at_the_Folies-Berg%C3%A8re.jpg

Fig. 60. James Abbott McNeill Whistler, SYMPHONY IN WHITE, NO. 1: THE WHITE GIRL, 1861, 83.8 × 42.4 inches. National Gallery of Art, Washington DC, United States of America. Photograph by National Gallery of Art. Wikimedia Commons. Public domain. https://commons.wikimedia.org/wiki/File:Whistler_James_Symphony_in_White_no_1_(The_White_Girl)_1862.jpg

Fig. 61. Gustav Klimt, THE KISS, 1907–1908, oil on canvas, 70.8 × 70.8 inches. Österreichische Galerie Belvedere, Vienna, Austria. Photograph by Google Art Project. Wikimedia Commons. Public domain. https://commons.wikimedia.org/wiki/File:The_Kiss_-_Gustav_Klimt_-_Google_Cultural_Institute.jpg

Fig. 62. Henri Matisse, ODALISQUE SEATED WITH ARMS RAISED, GREEN STRIPED CHAIR, 1923, oil on canvas, 25.625 × 19.75 inches. National Gallery of Art, Washington, DC, United States of America. Chester Dale Collection. Photograph by National Gallery of Art. National Gallery of Art. Public domain. https://www.nga.gov/collection/art-object-page.46642.html

Fig. 63. Pablo Picasso, PAULO ON A DONKEY, 1923, oil on canvas, 39 × 32 inches. Fundación Almine y Bernard Ruiz-Picasso para el Arte, Madrid, Spain. Photograph by Arthive user. Arthive. Public domain. https://arthive.com/pablopicasso/works/376296~Paul_on_a_donkey

Fig. 64. Richard Diebenkorn, WOMAN IN A WINDOW, 1957, oil on canvas, 59 × 56 inches. Albright-Knox Art Gallery, Buffalo, New York, United States of America. Gift of Symour H. Knox, Jr., 1958. Photograph by Richard Diebenkorn Foundation. Catalogue raisonné no. 2185. © Richard Diebenkorn Foundation. Reprinted here with permission. https://collection.diebenkorn.org/objects/225/woman-in-a-window?ctx=204461ad-b1d8-4c4e-b8a4-776c697f8be6&idx=0

Fig. 65. Norman Rockwell, FACT AND FICTION, 1917, color halftone reproduction of painting, used as cover illustration for *Leslie's Illustrated Weekly Newspaper*, vol. 124, no. 3201, 11 January 1917. US Library of Congress Prints and Photographs division. Wikimedia Commons. Public domain. https://commons.wikimedia.org/wiki/File:Fact_%26_Fiction_by_Norman_Rockwell_1917.jpg

Fig. 66. Pieter Bruegel the Elder, THE HUNTERS IN THE SNOW, 1565, oil on oak panel, 46 × 63.8 inches. Kunsthistorisches Museum, Vienna, Austria. Photograph by Google Cultural Institute. Wikimedia Commons. Public domain. https://commons.wikimedia.org/wiki/File:Pieter_Bruegel_the_Elder_-_Hunters_in_the_Snow_(Winter)_-_Google_Art_Project.jpg

Fig. 67. Claude Lorrain, PASTORAL LANDSCAPE: THE ROMAN CAMPAGNA, circa 1639, oil on canvas, 40 × 53.5 inches. Metropolitan Museum of Art, New York, New York, United States of America. Bequest of Adele L. Lehman, in memory of Arthur Lehman, 1965. Photograph by Metropolitan Museum of Art. Wikimedia Commons. Available under the Creative Commons CC0 1.0 Universal Public Domain Dedication. https://commons.wikimedia.org/wiki/File:Pastoral_Landscape-_The_Roman_Campagna_MET_DT218105.jpg

Fig. 68. Jacob van Ruisdael, WHEAT FIELDS, c. 1670, oil on canvas, 39.375 × 51.25 inches. Metropolitan Museum of Art, New York, New York, United States of America. Bequest of Benjamin Altman, 1913. Photograph by Mctropolitan Museum of Art. Wikimedia Commons. Available under the Creative Commons CC0 1.0 Universal Public Domain Dedication. https://commons.wikimedia.org/wiki/File:Wheat_Fields_MET_DP145911.jpg

Fig. 69. Caspar David Friedrich, THE WANDERER ABOVE THE SEA OF FOG, c. 1817, oil on canvas, 38.5 × 29.1 inches. Kunsthalle Hamburg, Hamburg, Germany. Photograph by Cybershot800i. Wikimedia Commons. Public domain. https://commons.wikimedia.org/wiki/File:Caspar_David_Friedrich_-_Wanderer_above_the_sea_of_fog.jpg

Fig. 70. John Constable, STONEHENGE, 1835, watercolor, 15.24 × 23.5 inches. Victoria and Albert Museum, London, England. Photograph by Google Cultural Institute. Wikimedia Commons. Public domain. https://commons.wikimedia.org/wiki/File:John_Constable_-_Stonehenge_-_Google_Art_Project.jpg

Fig. 71. J. M. W. Turner, THE LAKE OF ZUG, watercolor over graphite, 11.75 × 18.375 inches. Metropolitan Museum of Art, New York, New York, United States of America. Marquand Fund, 1959. Photograph by Metropolitan Museum of Art. Wikimedia Commons. Available under the Creative Commons CC0 1.0 Universal Public Domain Dedication. https://commons.wikimedia.org/wiki/File:The_Lake_of_Zug_MET_DP821057.jpg

Fig. 72. Jean-Baptiste-Camille Corot, THE HEIGHTS ABOVE SÈVRES, 1865–1870, oil on canvas, 20.8 × 39.5 inches. Royal Museum of Fine Arts of Belgium, Brussels, Belgium. Photograph by Rvalette. Wikimedia Commons. Available under the Creative Commons Attribution-Share Alike 4.0 International. https://commons.wikimedia.org/wiki/File:Corot-S%C3%A8vres-Mus%C3%A9e_de_Bruxelles.jpg#mw-jump-to-license

Fig. 73. Thomas Cole, VIEW FROM MOUNT HOLYOKE, NORTHAMPTON, MASSACHUSETTS, AFTER A THUNDERSTORM—THE OXBOW, 1836, oil on canvas, 51.4 × 75.9 inches. Metropolitan Museum of Art, New York, New York, United States of America. Photograph by Metropolitan Museum of Art. Wikimedia Commons. Public domain. https://commons.wikimedia.org/wiki/File:Cole_Thomas_The_Oxbow_(The_Connecticut_River_near_Northampton_1836).jpg

Fig. 74. Alfred Sisley, THE BRIDGE AT VILLENEUVE-LA-GARENNE, 1872, oil on canvas, 19.5 × 25.75 inches. Metropolitan Museum of Art, New York, New York, United States of America. Gift of Mr. and Mrs. Henry Ittleson Jr., 1964. Photograph by Metropolitan Museum of Art. Wikimedia Commons. Available under the Creative Commons CC0 1.0 Universal Public Domain Dedication. https://commons.wikimedia.org/wiki/File:The_Bridge_at_Villeneuve-la-Garenne_MET_DT1040.jpg

Fig. 75. Claude Monet, WATER LILIES, 1919, oil on canvas, 39.75 × 78.75 inches. Metropolitan Museum of Art, New York, New York, United States of America. The Walter H. and Leonore Annenberg Collection, Gift of Walter H. and Leonore Annenberg, 1998, Bequest of Walter H. Annenberg, 2002. The Metropolitan Museum of Art. Public domain. https://www.metmuseum.org/art/collection/search/438008

Fig. 76. Georges Seurat, STUDY FOR "A SUNDAY AFTERNOON ON THE ISLAND OF LA GRANDE JATTE," 1884, oil on canvas, 27.75 × 41 inches. Metropolitan Museum of Art, New York, New York, United States of America. Bequest of Sam A. Lewisohn, 1951. The Metropolitan Museum of Art. Public domain. https://www.metmuseum.org/art/collection/search/437658

Fig. 77. Paul Cézanne, VIEW OF THE DOMAINE SAINT-JOSEPH, late 1880s, oil on canvas, 25.625 × 32 inches. Metropolitan Museum of Art, New York, New York, United States of America. Catharine Lorillard Wolfe Collection, Wolfe Fund, 1913. The Metropolitan Museum of Art. Public domain. https://www.metmuseum.org/art/collection/search/435885

Fig. 78. Vincent van Gogh, IRISES, 1889, oil on canvas, 29.25 × 37.125 inches. The J. Paul Getty Museum, Los Angeles, California, United States of America. Getty Open Images. Public domain. http://www.getty.edu/art/collection/objects/826/vincent-van-gogh-irises-dutch-1889/

Fig. 79. Henri Matisse, WINDOW AT TANGIER, 1913, oil on canvas, 45.27 × 31.5 inches. The Pushkin State Museum of Fine Arts, Moscow, Russia. Public domain. https://arthive.com/henrimatisse/works/366710~Window_at_Tangier

Fig. 80. Carolyn Schlam, Simplified landscape (illustration).

Fig. 81. August Haake, FIELD WITH SHEAFS, 1911–1914, oil on cardboard, 19.7 × 28.1 inches. Private collection. Photograph by Michael Gäbler. Wikimedia Commons. Public domain. https://commons.wikimedia.org/wiki/File:Feld_mit_Kornhocken_von_August_Haake.jpg

Fig. 82. Richard Diebenkorn, OCEAN PARK #54, 1972, oil and charcoal on canvas, 100 × 81 inches. San Francisco Museum of Modern Art, San Francisco, California, United States of America. Gift of Friends of Gerald Nordland. Photograph by Richard Diebenkorn Foundation. Catalogue raisonné no. 4117. © Richard Diebenkorn Foundation. Reprinted here with permission. https://collection.diebenkorn.org/objects/473/ocean-park-54?ctx=9dccdc2d-38f7-42f7-b6c0-aadda5f97592&idx=6

Fig. 83. Jean-Baptiste-Siméon Chardin, STILL LIFE WITH FISH, VEGETABLES, GOUGÈRES, POTS, AND CRUETS ON A TABLE, 1769, oil on canvas, 27 × 22.9 inches. J. Paul Getty Museum, Los Angeles, California, United States of America. Photograph by J. Paul Getty Museum. Wikimedia Commons. Public domain.https://commons.wikimedia.org/wiki/File:Jean-Sim%C3%A9on_Chardin_-_Still_Life_with_Fish,_Vegetables,_Goug%C3%A8res,_Pots,_and_Cruets_on_a_Table_-_2003.13_-_J._Paul_Getty_Museum.jpg

Fig. 84. Henri Fantin-Latour, SUMMER FLOWERS, 1880, oil on canvas, 20 × 24.3 inches. Metropolitan Museum of Art, New York, New York, United States of America. Gift of Susan S. Dillon, 1997. Photograph by Metropolitan Museum of Art. Wikimedia Commons. Available under the Creative Commons cc0 1.0 Universal Public Domain Dedication. https://commons.wikimedia.org/wiki/File:Summer_Flowers_MET_DT4204.jpg

Fig. 85. Paul Cézanne, APPLES, 1878–1879, oil on canvas, 9 × 13 inches. Metropolitan Museum of Art, New York, New York, United States of America. Photograph by Metropolitan Museum of Art. Wikimedia Commons. Public domain. https://commons.wikimedia.org/wiki/File:Paul_C%C3%A9zanne_-_Apples.jpg

Fig.86. Camille Pissarro, STILL LIFE WITH APPLES AND PITCHER, 1872, oil on canvas, 18.25 × 22.25 inches. Metropolitan Museum of Art, New York, New York, United States of America. Purchase, Mr. and Mrs. Richard J. Bernhard Gift, by exchange, 1983. Photograph by Metropolitan Museum of Art. Wikimedia Commons. Public domain. https://commons.wikimedia.org/wiki/File:Pissarro_-_Still_Life_with_Apples_and_Pitcher.JPG

Fig. 87. Juan Gris, STILL LIFE BEFORE AN OPEN WINDOW, PLACE RAVIGNAN, 1915, oil on canvas, 45.65 × 35 inches. Philadelphia Museum of Art, Philadelphia, Pennsylvania, United States of America. Photograph by Google Cultural Institute. Wikimedia Commons. Public domain. https://commons.wikimedia.org/wiki/File:Juan_Gris_(Jos%C3%A9_Victoriano_Gonz%C3%A1lez_P%C3%A9rez),_Spanish_-_Still_Life_before_an_Open_Window,_Place_Ravignan_-_Google_Art_Project.jpg

Fig. 88. Vincent van Gogh, FOURTEEN SUNFLOWERS IN A VASE, 1889, oil on canvas, 37.4 × 28.7 inches. Van Gogh Museum, Amsterdam, Netherlands. Wikimedia Commons. Public domain. https://commons.wikimedia.org/wiki/File:Van_Gogh_-_Vierzehn_Sonnenblumen_in_einer_Vase2.jpeg

Fig. 89. Paolo Monti, MORANDI STUDIO, 1981, photograph of still-life setup in studio of Giorgio Morandi. Bibliotecha Europea di Informazione e Cultura, Milan, Italy. Photograph by Fondo Paolo Monti. Wikimedia Commons. Available under the Creative Commons Attribution Share-Alike 4.0 International license. https://commons.wikimedia.org/wiki/File:Paolo_Monti_-_Servizio_fotografico_(Bologna,_1981)_-_BEIC_6333212.jpg

Fig. 90. Robert Rauschenberg, TRACER, 1963, mixed media. San Francisco Museum of Modern Art, San Francisco, California, United States of America. Photograph by Sharon Mollerus. Wikimedia Commons. Available under the Creative Commons Attribution 2.0 license. https://commons.wikimedia.org/wiki/File:Robert_Rauschenberg,_Tracer,_1963_11_20_17_-sfmoma_(40482628341).jpg

Fig. 91. Edgar Degas, LITTLE FOURTEEN-YEAR-OLD DANCER, 1922, bronze, 38.5 × 17.25 × 14.375. Metropolitan Museum of Art, New York, New York, United States of America. Bequest of Mrs. H. O. Havemeyer, 1929. Photograph by AgnosticPreachersKid. Wikimedia Commons. Available under the Creative Commons Attribution-Share Alike 4.0 International license. https://commons.wikimedia.org/wiki/File:Degas_3x.jpg

Fig. 92. Jeylina Ever, ORLANDO, 2009, mixed media. Photograph by Jeylina Ever. Wikimedia Commons. Available under the Creative Commons Attribution-Share Alike 3.0 Unported license. https://commons.wikimedia.org/wiki/File:Orlando_by_jeylina_Ever.jpg

Fig. 93. Marcel Duchamp, FOUNTAIN, 1917. Photograph by Alfred Stieglitz. Wikimedia Commons. Public domain. https://commons.wikimedia.org/wiki/File:Duchamp_Fountaine.jpg (Note: This media file is in the public domain in the United States. This applies to US works where the copyright has expired, often because its first publication occurred prior to January 1, 1924, and if not then due to lack of notice or renewal.)

Fig. 94. Arshile Gorky, GARDEN OF WISH FULFILLMENT, 1944, oil on canvas. Museu Calouste Gulbenkian, Lisbon, Portugal. Photograph by Pedro Ribeiro Simoes. Wikimedia Commons. Available under Creative Commons Attribution 2.0 license. https://commons.wikimedia.org/wiki/File:Garden_of_wish_fulfilment_(1944)_-_Arshile_Gorki_(1904-1948)_(43954519964).jpg

Fig. 95. Willem de Kooning, WAVES #1, 1960, lithograph, 45.8125 × 31.75 inches. Fine Arts Museums of San Francisco, San Francisco, California, United States of America. Photograph by Theresa Papanikolas and Stephen Salel, *Abstract Expressionism: Looking East from the Far West* (Honolulu: Honolulu Museum of Art, 2017). Wikimedia Commons. Public domain. https://commons.wikimedia.org/wiki/File:Litho_-1_(Waves_-1)_by_Willem_de_Kooning,_1960.JPG (Note: This work is in the public domain in the United States because it was published in the United States between 1924 and 1977 without a copyright notice.)

Fig. 96. Art & Language, UNTITLED PAINTING, 1965, mirror mounted on canvas, 32.12 × 22.95 inches. Tate Modern, London, England. Photograph by Smuconlaw. Wikimedia Commons. Available under the Creative Commons Attribution-Share Alike 4.0 International license. https://commons.wikimedia.org/wiki/File:Art_%26_Language,_Untitled_Painting_(1965),_Tate_Modern,_London_-_20130627.jpg

Fig. 97. Frank James Graham, UNTITLED, early 1970s, acrylic on canvas. Photograph by Beergas. Wikimedia Commons. Available under Creative Commons Attribution Share Alike 4.0 International License. https://commons.wikimedia.org/wiki/File:LANE_72x90_ac_Frank Graham_1973.jpg

Fig. 98. Thutmose, BUST OF NEFERTITI, 1345 BC (ancient Egypt), limestone and stucco, 19 inches tall. Neues Museum, Berlin, Germany. Photograph by Philip Pikart. Wikimedia Commons. Available under the Creative Commons Attribution-Share Alike 3.0 Unported license. https://commons.wikimedia.org/wiki/File:Nofretete_Neues_Museum.jpg

Fig. 99. Michelangelo, DAVID, 1501–1504, marble, 17 feet tall. Galleria dell'Accademia, Florence, Italy. Photograph by Livioandronico2013. Wikimedia Commons. Available under Creative Commons Attribution Share Alike 4.0 International License. https://commons.wikimedia.org/wiki/File:Michelangelo%27s_David_2015.jpg

Fig. 100. Auguste Rodin, THE THINKER, 1903, bronze on patina, 70.8 × 38.1 × 55.1 inches. Museo Soumaya, Mexico City, Mexico. Photograph by ProtoplasmaKid. Wikimedia Commons. Available under Creative Commons Attribution Share Alike 4.0 International License. https://commons.wikimedia.org/wiki/File:Auguste_Rodin_The_thinker_02.JPG

Fig. 101. Paul Landowski, CHRIST THE REDEEMER, concrete and soapstone, 98 feet tall. Mount Corcovado, Rio de Janeiro, Brazil. Photograph by Arian Zwegers. Wikimedia Commons. Available under the Creative Commons Attribution 2.0 Generic license. https://commons.wikimedia.org/wiki/File:Rio_de_Janeiro,_Christ_the_Redeemer_(15744447380).jpg

Fig. 102. Daniel Chester French, LINCOLN MEMORIAL, 1920, marble, 19 feet tall. Washington, DC. Photograph by Erick Robert Joli Weber. Wikimedia Commons. Available under the Creative Commons Attribution-Share Alike 3.0 Unported license. https://commons.wikimedia.org/wiki/File:Lincoln_Memorial_(12).jpg

Fig. 103. Jean Arp, CLOUD SHEPHERD, 1953, bronze, 5 feet tall. Kröller-Müller Museum, Otterlo, Netherlands. Photograph by Gerardus. Wikimedia Commons. Public domain. https://commons.wikimedia.org/wiki/File:KMM_Arp_01.JPG

Fig. 104. Henry Moore, RECLINING FIGURE: ANGLES, 1980, bronze, 48.5 × 86.5 × 61.8 inches, Art Gallery of New South Wales, Sydney, Australia. Photograph by Paul Holloway. Wikimedia Commons. Available under the Creative Commons Attribution-Share Alike 2.0 Generic license. https://commons.wikimedia.org/wiki/Category:Reclining_Figure:_Angles_-_Henry_Moore_(LH_675,_Art_Gallery_of_New_South_Wales)

Fig. 105. Amedeo Modigliani, WOMAN'S HEAD, 1912, limestone, 26.875 × 6.25 × 9 .5 inches. Metropolitan Museum of Art, New York, New York, United States of America. The Mr. and Mrs. Klaus G. Perls Collection, 1997. Wikimedia Commons. Available under the Creative Commons CC0 1.0 Universal Public Domain Dedication. https://commons.wikimedia.org/wiki/File:Woman%27s_Head_MET_DT203050.jpg

Fig. 106. Umberto Boccioni, ANTIGRACEFUL, 1913 (cast 1950), bronze, 23 × 21 × 16.5 inches. Metropolitan Museum of Art, New York, New York, United States of America. Bequest of Lydia Winston Malbin, 1989. Wikimedia Commons. Available Creative Commons CC0 1.0 Universal Public Domain Dedication. https://commons.wikimedia.org/wiki/File:Antigraceful_MET_ma1990.38.R.jpg

Fig. 107. Deborah Butterfield, RORY, 1992, painted steel. Samuel P. Harn Museum of Art, Gainesville, Florida, United States of America. Photograph by Soulbust. Wikimedia Commons. Available under the Creative Commons Attribution-Share Alike 4.0 International license. https://commons.wikimedia.org/wiki/File:%22Rory%22_by_Deborah_Butterfield_at_the_Samuel_P._Harn_Museum_of_Art.jpg

Fig. 108. Anthony Caro, AURORA, 2000–2003, painted metal. Leeds Art Gallery, Leeds, England. Photograph by Tim Green. Wikimedia Commons. Available under the Creative Commons Attribution 2.0 Generic license. https://commons.wikimedia.org/wiki/File:Aurora_(Anthony_Caro),_Headrow,_Leeds_(21310776699).jpg

Fig. 109. Mark di Suvero, (sculptures left to right) OLD BUDDY (1993–1995), DREAMCATCHER (2005–2012), MOTHER PEACE (1970), and HURU (1984–1985), metal, varying sizes. San Francisco Museum of Modern Art at Crissy Field, San Francisco, California, United States of America. Photograph by Chedasaurus. Wikimedia Commons. Available under the Creative Commons Attribution-Share Alike 3.0 Unported license. https://commons.wikimedia.org/wiki/File:Mark_di_Suvero_sculptures.jpg

Fig. 110. Anish Kapoor, TALL TREE AND THE EYE, 2009, stainless steel and carbon steel, 4.4 × 4.4 × 13 meters. Guggenheim Museum, Bilbao, Spain. Photograph by Kamahele. Wikimeida Commons. Available under Creative Commons Attribution-Share Alike 3.0 Germany license. https://commons.wikimedia.org/wiki/File:Bilbao-Kapoor-11_318.jpg

Fig. 111. Alfred Stieglitz, A SNAPSHOT, PARIS, 1911, photogravure, 13.8 × 17.4 centimeters. Metropolitan Museum of Art, New York, New York, United States of America. Gift of J. B. Neumann, 1958. Photograph by Metropolitan Museum of Art. Wikimedia Commons. Available under the Creative Commons CC0 1.0 Universal Public Domain Dedication. https://commons.wikimedia.org/wiki/File:A_Snapshot,_Paris_MET_DP316963.jpg

Fig. 112. Carolyn Schlam, REFLECT/REFRACT, 2018, collage, 40 × 32 inches. Courtesy of the artist.

Fig. 113. Titian, VENUS OF URBINO, 1538, oil on canvas, 47 × 65 inches. Uffizi Gallery, Florence, Italy. Photograph by Uffizi. Wikimedia Commons. Public domain. https://commons.wikimedia.org/wiki/File:Venus_de_Urbino,_por_Tiziano.jpg

Fig. 114. Giorgione, SLEEPING VENUS, 1508, oil on canvas, 42.7 × 68.8 inches. Gemäldegalerie Alte Meister, Dresden, Germany. Photograph by Google Cultural Institute. Wikimedia Commons. Public domain. https://commons.wikimedia.org/wiki/File:Giorgione_-_Sleeping_Venus_-_Google_Art_Project.jpg

Fig. 115. Francisco Goya, THE NUDE MAJA, 1795–1800, oil on canvas, 38.5 × 75.1 inches. Museo del Prado, Madrid, Spain. Photograph by Museo Nacional del Prado. Wikimedia Commons. Public domain. https://commons.wikimedia.org/wiki/File:Goya_Maja_naga2.jpg

Fig. 116. Édouard Manet, OLYMPIA, 1863, oil on canvas, 51.1 × 74.8 inches. Musée d'Orsay, Paris, France. Photograph by Google Art Project. Wikimedia Commons. Public domain. https://commons.wikimedia.org/wiki/File:Edouard_Manet_-_Olympia_-_Google_Art_Project_4.jpg

Fig. 117. Diego Velázquez, LAS MENINAS, 1656–1657, oil on canvas, 10.4 × 9 feet. Museo del Prado, Madrid, Spain. Photograph by the Prado in Google Earth. Wikimedia Commons. Public domain. https://commons.wikimedia.org/wiki/File:Las_Meninas,_by_Diego_Vel%C3%A1zquez,_from_Prado_in_Google_Earth.jpg

Fig. 118. John Singer Sargent, THE DAUGHTERS OF EDWARD DARLEY BOIT, 1882, oil on canvas, 87.3 × 87.6 inches. Museum of Fine Arts, Boston, Massachusetts. Photograph by the Museum of Fine Arts. Wikimedia Commons. Public domain. https://en.wikipedia.org/wiki/Museum_of_Fine_Arts,_Boston

Fig. 119. Manolo Valdés, LAS MENINAS, 2006, bronze. Hofgarten, Düsseldorf, Germany. Photograph by Ralf Hüls. Wikimedia Commons. Available under the Creative Commons Attribution-Share Alike 3.0 Unported license. https://commons.wikimedia.org/wiki/File:Manolo_Vald%C3%A9s_Las_Meninas.jpg

Fig. 120. Jacqueline Roberts, A MENINAS DREAM, 2008, photograph. Courtesy of the artist. Flickr. https://www.flickr.com/photos/jacqueline_roberts/3147102911/in/photolist-5N6J42-9f7r9r-cAd3Qo-7WyAWr-bkxEiR-gbzMjK-7Ec8B3-2JLwwL-4bsT4P

Fig. 121. Jimmy Wright, SELF #4, 2002, pastel on paper, 25.5 × 19.5 inches. Private collection. Courtesy of the artist. http://www.jimmywrightartist.com/works/#lightbox[works-on-paper]/60/

Fig. 122. Rembrandt van Rijn, LARGE SELF-PORTRAIT, 1652, oil on canvas, 44 × 32 inches. Kunsthistorisches Museum, Vienna, Austria. Photograph by MyStudios. Wikimedia Commons. Public domain. https://commons.wikimedia.org/wiki/File:Rembrandt,_Large_Self_Portrait,_1652,_Kunsthistorisches_Museum_Wien.jpg

Fig. 123. Gustave Courbet, THE DESPERATE MAN (self-portrait), 1843, oil on canvas, 17.7 × 21.2 inches. Private collection. Wikimedia Commons. Public domain. https://commons.wikimedia.org/wiki/File:Gustave_Courbet_auto-retrato.jpg

Fig. 124. Vincent van Gogh, SELF-PORTRAIT, 1889, oil on canvas, 26 × 21 inches. Musée d'Orsay, Paris, France. Photograph by Google Cultural Institute. Wikimedia Commons. Public domain. https://commons.wikimedia.org/wiki/File:Vincent_van_Gogh_-_Self-Portrait_-_Google_Art_Project.jpg

Fig. 125. Francisco Goya, THE DOG, 1820–1823, oil on canvas, 51.5 × 31.1 inches. Museo del Prado, Madrid, Spain. Photograph by Museo del Prado. Wikimedia Commons. Public domain. https://commons.wikimedia.org/wiki/File:Goya_Dog.jpg

Fig. 126. Isaac Levitan, ABOVE THE ETERNAL PEACE, 1894, oil on canvas, 37.4 × 50 inches. State Tretyakov Gallery, Moscow, Russia. Photograph by Anagoria. Wikimedia Commons. Public domain. https://commons.wikimedia.org/wiki/File:1894_Levitan_Ewiger_Ort_anagoria.JPG

Fig. 127. Thomas Denny, RICHARD III WINDOW, 2016, stained glass, 8 × 3 feet. Leicester Cathedral, Leicester, England. Photograph by Amanda Slater. Wikimedia Commons. Available under the Creative Commons Attribution Share Alike 2.0 Generic license. https://commons.wikimedia.org/wiki/File:Richard_III_Windows._Leicester_Cathedral_(33860452352).jpg

Fig. 128. Edgar Degas, A WOMAN IRONING, 1873, oil on canvas, 21.375 × 15.5 inches. Metropolitan Museum of Art. H. O. Havemeyer Collection, Bequest of Mrs. H. O. Havemeyer, 1929. Photograph by Metropolitan Museum of Art. Wikimedia Commons. Available under the Creative Commons CC0 1.0 Universal Public Domain Dedication. https://commons.wikimedia.org/wiki/File:A_Woman_Ironing_MET_DT1910.jpg

Fig. 129. Paul Klee, AD PARNASSUM, 1932, tempera on linen, 26.1 × 41.7 inches. Kunstmuseum Basel, Basel, Switzerland. Wikimedia Commons. Public domain. https://commons.wikimedia.org/wiki/File:Polyphony2.jpg

Fig. 130. Piet Mondrian, BROADWAY BOOGIE WOOGIE, 1942–1943, oil on canvas, 50 × 50 inches. Museum of Modern Art. Wikimedia Commons. Public domain. https://commons.wikimedia.org/wiki/File:Piet_Mondrian,_1942_-_Broadway_Boogie_Woogie.jpg

Fig. 131. Artist unknown, CROUCHING FIGURE, 10th–4th century BC, Olmec (Mexico), andesite (stone), 10.375 × 5.25 × 6.125 inches. Metropolitan Museum of Art. The Michael C. Rockefeller Memorial Collection, Bequest of Nelson A. Rockefeller, 1979. Photograph by Metropolitan Museum of Art. Wikimedia Commons. Available under the Creative Commons CC0 1.0 Universal Public Domain Dedication. https://commons.wikimedia.org/wiki/File:Crouching_Figure_MET_1979.206.691.jpg

Fig. 132. Michelangelo, CROUCHING BOY, 1530–1534, marble, 21 inches. Hermitage Museum, St. Petersburg, Russia. Photograph by Richard Mortel. Wikimedia Commons. Available under the Creative Commons Attribution 2.0 Generic license. https://commons.wikimedia.org/wiki/File:Crouching_Boy_by_Michelangelo,_ca._1530-34,_Hermitage_Museum,_St._Petersburg_(8)_(36374833903).jpg

Fig. 133. Aristide Maillol, CROUCHING GIRL, 1900, bronze, 8.25 × 3.75 × 4.25 inches. Metropolitan Museum of Art, Bequest of Jane Costello Goldberg, 1987. Photograph by Metropolitan Museum of Art. Wikimedia Commons. Available under the Creative Commons CC0 1.0 Universal Public Domain Dedication. https://commons.wikimedia.org/wiki/File:Crouching_Girl_MET_DT5773.jpg

Fig. 134. Antony Gormley, EXPOSURE, 2010, metal pylons. Haven van Lelystad, Netherlands. Photograph by Herman Verheij. Wikimedia Commons. Available under Creative Commons Attribution-Share Alike 3.0 Unported. https://commons.wikimedia.org/wiki/File:Exposure_of_Antony_Gormley_by_Herman_Verheij_at_Lelystad.jpg

Fig. 135. Jean-Auguste-Dominique Ingres, LA GRANDE BAIGNEUSE, 1808, oil on canvas, 57.4 × 38.6 inches. Musée du Louvre, Paris, France. Photograph by Gallerix. Wikimedia Commons. Public domain. https://commons.wikimedia.org/wiki/File:Jean-Auguste-Dominique_Ingres_-_La_Baigneuse_Valpin%C3%A7on.jpg

Fig. 136. Edgar Degas, AFTER THE BATH, WOMAN DRYING HERSELF, 1890–1895, pastel on woven paper mounted on millboard, 40.7 × 38.7 inches. National Gallery, London, England. Photograph by National Gallery. Wikimedia Commons. Public domain. https://commons.wikimedia.org/wiki/File:Edgar_Degas_-_After_the_Bath,_Woman_drying_herself_(1890s).jpg

Fig. 137. Carolyn Schlam, BATH, 2017, oil on canvas, 40 × 30 inches. Private collection. Courtesy of the artist.

Fig. 138. William Blake, THE ANCIENT OF DAYS, 1794, etching, 9.125 × 6.875 inches. British Museum, London, England. Photograph by Frank Vincentz. Wikimedia Commons. Public domain. https://commons.wikimedia.org/wiki/File:Oberhausen_-_Gasometer_-_Der_sch%C3%B6ne_Schein_-_The_Ancient_of_Days_(William_Blake)_01_ies.jpg

Fig. 139. Marc Chagall, WINDOW AT CHICHESTER CATHEDRAL, 1978, stained glass. Chichester Cathedral, Chichester, England. Photograph by Tony Hisgett. Wikimedia Commons. Available under the Creative Commons Attribution 2.0 Generic license. https://commons.wikimedia.org/wiki/File:Chagall_Window_(5696736662).jpg

Fig. 140. Henri Rousseau, THE DREAM, 1910, oil on canvas, 80.5 × 117.5 inches. Museum of Modern Art, New York, New York, United States of America. Photograph by The Yorck Project. Wikimedia Commons. Public domain. https://commons.wikimedia.org/wiki/File:Henri_Rousseau_005.jpg

Fig. 141. Thomas Eakins, THE PAIR-OARED SHELL, 1872, oil on canvas, 24 × 35.9 inches. Philadelphia Museum of Art, Philadelphia, Pennsylvania, United States of America. Gift of Mrs. Thomas Eakins and Miss Mary Edline Williams, 1929. Photograph by Gallerix. Wikimedia Commons. Public domain. https://commons.wikimedia.org/wiki/File:The_pair-oared_shell_thomas_eakins.jpeg

Fig. 142. Thomas Eakins, PERSPECTIVE DRAWING FOR "THE PAIR-OARED SHELL," 1872, drawing. Philadelphia Museum of Art, Philadelphia, Pennsylvania, United States of America. Photograph by Raul654. Wikimedia Commons. Public domain. https://commons.wikimedia.org/wiki/File:Perspective_Drawing_for_The_Pair-Oared_Shell.png

Fig. 143. Robert Henri, SNOW IN NEW YORK, 1902, oil on canvas, 32 × 25.7 inches. National Gallery of Art, Washington DC, United States of America. Photograph by National Gallery of Art. Wikimedia Commons. Public domain. https://commons.wikimedia.org/wiki/File:Snow_in_New_York.jpg

Fig. 144. Clark Hulings, THE PINK PARASOL, 1979, oil on canvas, 32 × 46 inches. Private collection. Photo courtesy of The Clark Hulings Estate.

Fig. 145. Sirarpi Heghinian Walzer, BODY AND SOUL, 2018, mixed media, oil on paper, 24 × 32 inches. Private collection. Courtesy of the artist.

Fig. 146. Elana Kundell, I WANT YOU INEVITABLE, 2011, oil and charcoal on panel, 20 × 16 inches. Private collection. Courtesy of the artist.

Fig. 147. Claire Haye, SEEKING TRUTH—BOTH SIDES, 2008, bronze sculpture, 44 × 16 × 30 inches. Private collection. Courtesy of the artist.

Fig. 148. Sheila Fein, COUNTING PONIES, 2018, colored pencil with turpentine. Private collection. Courtesy of the artist. http://sheilafein.com/wp-content/gallery/color-pencil/fein_sheila_counting-ponies.JPG

Fig. 149. Carolyn Schlam, THE BED, 2011, oil on canvas, 50 × 36 inches. Private collection. Courtesy of the artist. http://carolynschlam.com/portfolio_page/oils/#!prettyPhoto[1]/ML/51

Acknowledgments

I would like to acknowledge and extend my thanks to the foundations and individuals who contributed photographs to *The Joy of Art*. Finding public domain photos was a challenge, and these contributions were a great help. My thanks to the Richard Diebenkorn Foundation and The Clark Hulings Estate and to artists Jacqueline Roberts, Claire Haye, Elana Kundell, Phoebe Scott, Jimmy Wright, Sheila Fein, and Sirarpi Heghinian Walzer.

I would also like to thank my tireless editor Chamois Holschuh, my literary agent Susan Schulman, and the team at Skyhorse Publishing who all contributed to bringing *The Joy of Art* to fruition. It was surely a group effort.

Index

Note: Bold numbers indicate an image on the page.